# REGIONAL
# SECURITY IN
# SOUTHEAST
# ASIA

# REGIONAL SECURITY IN SOUTHEAST ASIA

## Beyond the ASEAN Way

**Mely Caballero-Anthony**

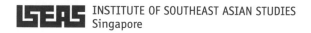 INSTITUTE OF SOUTHEAST ASIAN STUDIES
Singapore

First published in Singapore in 2005 by
ISEAS Publications
Institute of Southeast Asian Studies
30 Heng Mui Keng Terrace
Pasir Panjang
Singapore 119614

*E-mail*: publish@iseas.edu.sg
*Website*: http://bookshop.iseas.edu.sg

© 2005 Institute of Southeast Asian Studies, Singapore
First Reprint 2007

*The responsibility for facts and opinions in this publication rests exclusively with the author and her interpretations do not necessarily reflect the views or the policy of the publisher or its supporters.*

**ISEAS Library Cataloguing-in-Publication Data**

Anthony, Mely Caballero-
   Regional security in Southeast Asia : beyond the ASEAN way.
   1. ASEAN.
   2. Conflict management—Asia, Southeastern.
   3. National security—Asia, Southeastern.
   4. Asia, Southeastern—Politics and government.
   I. Title.
JX1979 A621                 2005

ISBN 981-230-260-3 (soft cover)
ISBN 981-230-261-1 (hard cover)

Typeset by Superskill Graphics Pte Ltd
Printed in Singapore by Utopia Press Pte Ltd

# Contents

# Acknowledgements

This is a book about ASEAN and its experience on managing regional security. It is also as much a chronicle of how ASEAN's mechanisms of managing conflicts have evolved over a span of more than three decades. This narrative of ASEAN is also about a journey of someone who has sojourned, lived, and worked in many of the capitals in the region and in the process benefited immensely from the guidance and insights of a number of teachers, colleagues and friends whose valuable help made this book possible. In my research and writing of this work, I owe a great many debts of gratitude along the way.

This book started out as doctoral dissertation and I am very grateful for the intellectual guidance of James Tang, Amitav Acharya, and Khong Yueng Foong, who have generously helped me in the process of producing this work. I have never been able to thank them properly, and I wish to do so here. My thanks also to Barry Desker, Director of the Institute of Defence and Strategic Studies (IDSS), Singapore who has always encouraged his staff to publish their work.

The following institutions have also made my research work possible. My thanks to the Institute of Southeast Asian Studies (ISEAS), Singapore, which welcomed me as a Research Fellow in 1997 and gave me the research grant to embark on this project. To the Institute of Strategic and International Studies (ISIS), Malaysia, which allowed me to do much of my earlier writings on ASEAN during my time with them as Senior Analyst from 1997–2001, and to its ASEAN-ISIS network members — the Centre for Strategic and International Studies (CSIS), Jakarta, the Institute of Strategic and Development Studies (ISDS), Philippines, and Institute of Strategic and International Studies (ISIS), Thailand — I am extremely grateful for their generosity in providing me the research facilities and the important introductions to a number of valuable resource persons and experts in the field of security and international relations in Southeast Asia.

My debt of gratitude to the following individuals for their unstinting support and patience to an itinerant scholar who had little much to offer except a keen interest in domestic and regional politics of the region. My thanks especially to Mohamed Jawhar Hassan, Noordin Sopiee, and Stephen Leong of ISIS Malaysia who were my patient mentors on ASEAN and track two diplomacy in Southeast Asia and the broader Asia-Pacific, and never failed to encourage a young colleague to learn more about Malaysia and the rest of region. My time at ISIS Malaysia also became more meaningful with the help and encouragement of my former colleagues, especially Patrick Pillai who always lent an ear and Susan Teoh who is a gem of a librarian and a great friend.

Let me once again express my sincerest thanks and deepest gratitude to a community of scholars and experts whose dedication to the ASEAN cause is not only inspiring but also humbling: Jusuf Wanandi, Hadi Soesastro, Clara Joewono, Suchit Bunbongkarn, Kusuma Snitwongse, and Kwa Chong Guan who in many ways broadened my understanding of track two diplomacy in Southeast Asia and beyond. And not the least, a heartfelt thanks to Carolina Hernandez, who continues to be an inspiration and role model for what it is to be a mother and a wife, an activist/advocate and an excellent scholar rolled into one.

In my journey with this community, I also have learnt so much from my interactions with Rizal Sukma, Pranee Thiparat, Herman Kraft, Grace Gorospe-Jamon and many others who not only became my sounding board on the various issues of Southeast Asian regionalism but whose friendship and unfailing encouragement I shall always value.

My sincere thanks and appreciation to a number of ASEAN officials and personalities who have unselfishly shared their time and provided me with valuable information on the nature of regionalism in this region. I am most grateful to Surin Pitsuwan, Rodolfo Severino, and Sukhumbhand Paribatra for their generous insights and advice. A special thanks also to Triena Ong and her publication team at ISEAS for their valuable help in the production of this book.

Finally, these expressions of gratitude would not be complete if I do not mention the people closest to me. To my mother, brothers, and sisters, whose constant love and support are blessings I shall always treasure. To my son, Jeremy Miguel, whose patience and tolerance of his mother's long hours and absence from home, I am forever grateful. And to my partner Denis — thank you for making it all worthwhile.

Mely Caballero-Anthony
November 2004

# Introduction

Until the late 1990s, the Association of Southeast Asian Nations (ASEAN) had been described as one of the most successful regional organizations in the world. Founded in 1967 in a region that was once characterized as conflict-ridden and akin to the "Balkans of the East", ASEAN's efforts in maintaining peaceful relations among its members and with states beyond Southeast Asia has made ASEAN an important actor in the bigger international arena of the Asia-Pacific. Moreover, at least until the Asian financial crisis in 1997, ASEAN was also one of the fastest developing economic regions in the world. This made ASEAN a pivotal actor in the much larger multilateral initiatives that emerged, which were geared towards closer political and security co-operation, as well as deeper economic co-operation. These multilateral initiatives include the Asia-Pacific Economic Co-operation (APEC, in 1989); the Asia Regional Forum (in 1994), Asia-Europe Meeting (ASEM, in 1995) and the ASEAN + 3 (in 1997).

This relatively impressive story of ASEAN experienced a drastic twist in fortune when the Southeast Asian region went through a series of crises, starting from the onset of the Asian financial crisis in 1997. Since then, the organization came under closer scrutiny from scholars, policy-makers, members of the media, and casual observers who wrote about the unravelling of the ASEAN success story. The dramatic turn in the way ASEAN was characterized from a story of success to one of growing irrelevance pointed to the inefficacy of the organization to deal with new challenges and its adherence of old principles and norms. The latter, in particular, was cited by many ASEAN observers as a major stumbling block to ASEAN becoming a more dynamic organization and responsive to the call of the times.

Since the series of crises that have hit the region, the ambiguity in portraying ASEAN as a story of success or failure only deepened. To be sure, amidst a period of crises and rapid global changes, the complex tasks of objectively assessing ASEAN do not only lie with those who are telling the story and analysing events. One would also expect that ASEAN as the object of scrutiny has found itself having to steer through rough waters. Given the significant changes to its organization brought on, among others, by its enlargement in membership, one would want to explore if there has been any recalibration of its modalities as it faces up to new dynamics and challenges as a consequence of these changes.

The modalities referred to in this study are the norms, principles, and practices that have defined ASEAN's approach to inter-state relations. These norms and principles have been popularly encapsulated in the term *the ASEAN Way*. The ASEAN way has been described by many scholars who have studied the organization, as a characteristic feature in the way ASEAN manages conflicts and maintains peace and security in Southeast Asia. But, against the ebb and flow of changes that have taken place in the region, questions have been raised about the ASEAN Way. As member states in ASEAN adjust to the new realities of a bigger organization and the new challenges that it brings, one would ask — whither the ASEAN way? Are there any significant trends in managing security in the region that point us beyond the ASEAN way? In a rapidly changing Southeast Asia, are we missing certain dynamics that are evolving in ASEAN, and between ASEAN and its people that are yet to be captured in the study of this organization?

This book is about ASEAN and its work on regional security. Within the context of the new regionalism that is taking shape in Southeast Asia, it examines the way ASEAN has dealt with new regional security challenges by examining its responses to crises and its mechanisms in dealing with them. A key question that this book seeks to address in the analyses of ASEAN's responses to challenges is whether ASEAN's mechanisms of conflict management have moved beyond the ASEAN way. Although several scholars have also written about ASEAN and examined the mechanisms used to respond to crises through the analyses of its institutions or lack thereof, as well as regional norms,[1] the main objective of this book is to uncover emerging developments that may have been overlooked by scholars in their analyses of ASEAN's modalities and institutions. The aim is to look beyond these challenges and examine what has happened as far as the development of ASEAN's mechanisms is concerned. In discussing what these developments are, this book argues that there is more beyond the ASEAN way that has yet to be captured when we talk about ASEAN.

In suggesting that there is more beyond the ASEAN way, the study calls attention to the changing dynamics in the region, particularly with regard to political developments that have occurred since the 1997 financial crisis. One notes that some members in the old ASEAN-5,[2] like Indonesia, the Philippines, Thailand and even Cambodia, have experienced democratic transitions that have significant impact on the nature of the domestic politics in these countries. To some, these democratic transitions were peaceful but quite dramatic in others. In Indonesia, for example, the country is still very much at the cusp of political transition after thirty-three years under the Soeharto New Order regime. The societal forces that have been unleashed after the downfall of Soeharto in 1998, and the chaos that ensued has been a major cause for concern for the stability of the region. It has been argued that a stable Indonesia is important for peace and security in Southeast Asia. Indonesia has carried the mantle of leadership in ASEAN since the organization was established in 1967 and the long-serving Soeharto regime was a constant feature in the region. The unexpected downfall of Soeharto therefore has resulted, among others, in a leadership vacuum that has yet to be filled with the current changes in political leadership in other countries in the region. Similarly, the processes of political transitions are ongoing in Malaysia and Singapore as long-serving leaders change guards. Malaysia's Mahathir Mohamad has stepped down after twenty-two years in power while Singapore's Goh Chok Tong has made way for Lee Hsien Loong after more than ten years at the helm of the People's Action Party (PAP)-led government.

The Philippines and Thailand have had their own share of "people-power" induced change in political leadership. In the case of the Philippines, the country has seen three "people-power" revolutions since the toppling of Ferdinand Marcos in 1986, the forced resignation of Joseph Estrada in 2001, and the attempted overthrow of the Arroyo administration in 2002. As the country prepares for presidential elections in 2004, the political uncertainties brought on by troubled political leaderships and the unending list of security challenges make the task of democratic consolidation an uphill battle. On the other hand, Thailand since its "people-power" revolution in 1992 seemed to enjoy better prospects than the Philippines. Yet the country too has to confront the major task of accommodating various interests as civil society groups actively seek to assert their role in the political arena that was once the monopoly of the military, bureaucracy, and business elites. ASEAN's new member, Cambodia, has also not been immune to the various pressures of democratic consolidation as its government struggles to provide order and coherence in a turbulent political environment brought on by competing political forces and unsettled popular mandates. While Vietnam and Laos appear to be rather less prone to political crises, the same could not be said of Myanmar, which continues to grapple with the problem of regime legitimacy both within and outside the country.

Thus, the changes in domestic politics — at least for the original ASEAN-5 and its impact on the dynamics of state-society relations would have had salient effects on the viability of the ASEAN way. In fact, one of the important questions that would have to be examined is the extent (if any) to which societal factors influence the practice and norms imbued in the ASEAN way. If the ASEAN way is quintessentially a process-oriented approach defined by norms and principles of non-interference, peaceful settlement of disputes, non-confrontational attitudes to conflicts, emphases on *musyawarah* (consensus) and *muafakat* (consultation), then when juxtaposed against the changes found in the domestic and regional environment, would it render the ASEAN way obsolete? Or would it in fact make the ASEAN way to be a dynamic process-oriented approach? But unless one looks beyond the state-centric approaches in ASEAN, the dynamism that could be emerging in the constitution and practice of the ASEAN way may yet go unnoticed.

In analysing the changes in the region on several fronts — be it in the political, economic, and security spheres — it is therefore suggested that research should now focus on the changing nature of domestic politics in member states, and examine how these may have a bearing on the modalities of ASEAN. If indeed there is a new regionalism that is taking place in Southeast Asia, we need to explore whether there are any social movements, organized by civil society organizations that are shaping the current discourse on the ASEAN way. We need to analyse the extent to which unofficial diplomacy through track two activities have in any way contributed to regional governance through their ideas on how conflict and security should be managed in the region. Moreover, we need to examine how these various tracks — starting from track three (that is, civil society organizations) to track two and track one — interact within ASEAN and understand, among others, the contestations that are taking place within these actors. In short, this work is but an attempt to understand the salience of these non-state dynamics in terms of the broader region-wide constitution of norms and principles in inter-state conduct and the impact these would have on the normative structure of the ASEAN way.

## IS NOTHING CONSTANT EXCEPT CHANGE?

The nature of these multifaceted changes taking place in ASEAN and in the region can be best understood as we track the distinct phases that the organization has been through since its establishment in 1967. If we were to divide these phases loosely into three periods of (1) consolidation, (2) expansion, and (3) reconsolidation, we would be better able to locate where ASEAN is now within the context of a rapidly changing regional and global environment. More importantly, we would be able to assess the extent to which ASEAN has recalibrated its principles, norms, and mechanisms in managing change and conflicts in Southeast Asia.

During the early stages of its consolidation as a fledgling regional organization, ASEAN had been through several periods of inter-state conflicts that threatened the stability and security of the region. These were the conflicts that occurred in non-ASEAN members at that time that would include the decades-long war in Vietnam and its eventual re-unification in 1976. The Vietnam War formed a large part of the regional leitmotif at the time of ASEAN's establishment. This was followed by the Vietnamese occupation of Cambodia until the resolution of this conflict in 1991 and the rebuilding of the "new" Cambodia following the elections in 1993. During these periods, ASEAN was an active player in the management of these conflicts, and its role in defining the norms and mechanisms to manage regional order became more discernable. To many observers of ASEAN, these mechanisms of managing conflict have been internalized among the old members of ASEAN while states that were outside the grouping were being socialized into imbibing these norms in the conduct of inter-state relations.

After a respite from the turmoils of internecine conflicts in states that were then outside the organization, ASEAN went through an enlargement phase with the expansion of its membership to include Vietnam in 1995, Laos and Myanmar in 1997, and Cambodia in 1999. Hence, three decades after its inception, ASEAN has grown from an original membership of five to ten. It was during these two phases of consolidation and enlargement that the so-called ASEAN way became largely debated and contested, largely because many scholars took notice of them and started to write about them in their characterization of ASEAN's development.

The third phase of reconsolidation could be traced to the time when ASEAN experienced the ravages of the Asian financial crisis until the present time when the capacity of ASEAN to manage a series of seemingly unending lists of regional challenges are being tested. To name just a few of these challenges were, the replay of economic uncertainties triggered by the regional health crisis that was caused by the infectious disease, Severe Acute Respiratory Syndrome (SARS) and the threats of terrorism. At this time of writing, ASEAN has also had to confront the current complex "war on terrorism" and its repercussions on regional security.

As we track the phases that ASEAN has been through, we examine the dynamics as to how the norms and processes of socialization have either weathered several challenges or have become irrelevant in the face of these challenges. If indeed the ASEAN way has become irrelevant, was it just a myth? If indeed it has stood the test of time, what accounts for these enduring characteristics? Finally, in responding to crises and challenges that confronted the association, is there something beyond the ASEAN way?

Against the backdrop of a sea change in the regional environment and the complex nature of the challenges that ASEAN has had to confront, ASEAN launched the idea of an ASEAN Community at the Ninth ASEAN Summit held in Indonesia in October 2003. In adopting the Bali Concord II, the ASEAN leaders called for the establishment of an ASEAN Community by the year 2020 comprising three pillars — ASEAN Security Community, ASEAN Economic Community, and ASEAN Socio-Cultural Community.[3] The Bali Concord II has come full circle to the time when ASEAN adopted the first ASEAN Concord (Bali Concord I) in 1976, soon after the end of the Vietnam War. The ASEAN Bali Concord I was the first attempt by the fledgling organization to outline its goals and aspirations founded on the shared vision of a region living in peace, stability, and prosperity. Three decades later, one observes that while similar goals have been re-articulated, the mechanisms and institutions that are being envisioned to attain these goals had changed substantially. For one thing, the word "community" has evidently become more pronounced in reference to the member states of ASEAN. In plotting the way forward for closer economic co-operation, notions of an ASEAN "economic community" have indicated some movements towards an integrated, common market in the region. It can be recalled that the idea of economic integration was something that had been avoided for several decades, and even considered taboo. Hence, the ASEAN Economic Community is certainly a *bold* initiative when compared with the current modalities of economic co-operation in the region. More significantly, usage of the phrase "security community" and the modalities that are currently being considered in advancing this idea are certainly indicative of moving beyond the norm-based framework of political and security co-operation to more institutionalized and rule-based structure of managing conflicts. The ideas being floated with regard to the modalities for an ASEAN Security Community are discussed in more detail in Chapter 8. Suffice it to say that these developments are certainly "new" and reflective of the current thinking in both the official and non-official levels in the region. In particular, these trends towards bolder mechanisms are now being heard in the official discourses as attempts are being done to make ASEAN more responsive amidst emerging realities and global uncertainties.

## WHY BEYOND THE ASEAN WAY?

There is also another reason to look beyond the ASEAN way. For a long time, the narrative on ASEAN has been mostly about the story of regional reconciliation. ASEAN was portrayed as a successful framework that brought together conflicting states such as Indonesia, Malaysia, and the Philippines to form a regional organization. Throughout its history one could also see how this goal of regional reconciliation eventually brought together other states in Southeast Asia that once posed as "threats" to the original ASEAN members as in the case of Vietnam, and those that were of different political orientations like Cambodia, Laos, and Myanmar. Hence we saw how ASEAN membership eventually expanded to include all the ten states in Southeast Asia.

But, as noted earlier, although ASEAN had gone through several phases, the examination of ASEAN's modalities in managing regional tensions and conflicts have been largely *seen through the prisms* of the ASEAN way. Hence, the depiction of ASEAN is all about its norms and principles in inter-state conduct; its informal mechanisms and lack of formal institutions in dealing with issues and problems; its preference for *musyawarah* (dialogue) and *muafakat* (consensus) in decision-making; and last but not least, its preference for avoiding conflicts rather than resolving them. ASEAN has therefore been portrayed as this organization that has stood still as time passed by — an unchanging entity, impervious to change.

Hence, it is not a surprise that in most of these writings, a point has been made for ASEAN to rethink many of its norms and mechanisms in addressing regional challenges. In fact, the common theme in many of these writing is for ASEAN to reinvent itself.[4]

Amitav Acharya's work on *Constructing a Security Community in Southeast Asia* offers a superb analysis on the norms developed by ASEAN in its management of regional order. In examining how ASEAN norms — also known as the ASEAN way — served their regulatory and constitutive functions towards building a security community in the region, Acharya concludes that after three decades of progress ASEAN is now in serious need to reinvent itself. He posed questions as to the effectiveness of these norms given the different crises ASEAN had to face and the attempts by some members in the grouping to revise ASEAN's norm such as the non-interference principle.

Other writers have been more direct in their criticisms of these norms. Shaun Narine, in *Explaining ASEAN: Regionalism in Southeast Asia*, wrote about the ineffectiveness of ASEAN and its institutions in addressing the problems brought on by the financial crisis. Narine argues that ASEAN must change to cope with the new regional environment. More specifically, ASEAN must institutionalize rather than continue to rely on its informal mechanisms in addressing problems.

Similarly, Jurgen Haacke in his book *ASEAN's Diplomatic and Security Culture* also ponders on the prospects of the ASEAN way in the light of the new dynamics in intramural relations brought on by the group's expanded membership, the political consequences of the Asian financial crisis and so on. Haacke's meticulous scholarship presents an excellent analysis of the diplomatic and security in ASEAN and how these inform the dynamics of foreign policies in the region. Yet he himself concedes that the ASEAN way would still be resilient though not necessarily "impervious to change".

It is not the intention of this book to dismiss the relevance or diminish the importance of the ASEAN way. Acharya and Haacke's excellent works have provided valuable contribution in the study of norms, values, and practices and the processes of socialization in defining and understanding international relations in Southeast Asia. Both works have eloquently provided the theoretical framework and sophisticated articulation of what have already been commonly accepted practices and dominant themes found in the works of many ASEAN scholars, experts, and policy-makers.[5] Nonetheless, in the light of the ever-changing security environment it would be remiss and an oversight in scholarship to ignore the current developments that are taking place in the region and how these have impact on ASEAN modalities. To be sure, the study of ASEAN can no longer be confined to the study of ASEAN as an inter-state organization participated mostly by its political elites. There is enough evidence to suggest that non-state actors are now taking an active interest in ASEAN and are actively advocating being part of the processes that are constitutive of the way the region should go with regard to managing regional security.

A major theme addressed in this book is the way non-state actors are actively moving to be a part of the ASEAN process. One needs only to survey the plethora of regional meetings that are being organized across different sections of ASEAN societies to see how these meetings are generating policy recommendations to feed into ASEAN policy-makers. In particular, the nature of track two (non-official) diplomacy that has been taking place has significantly altered the way discourses and arguably inter-state relations have been developing in the region. Moreover, one would also note that the policy interventions carried out by track two networks within the region and beyond have been duly recognized by ASEAN officials. This would lead us to examine whether non-state actors through their work on track two diplomacy have any influence on the development of regional norms and the extent to which their ideas have found their way in the formulation of foreign policies in ASEAN, particularly with regard to the mechanisms of managing conflicts and security in the region.

This book also argues that the quest of security in ASEAN is no longer the monopoly of state actors. If security, as defined by Barry Buzan, is about "the ability of states and societies to maintain their independent identity and their functional integrity", then the current literature on ASEAN's co-operative efforts that had focused mainly on state actors are no longer adequate. So far, the study of ASEAN in maintaining regional security has been about how this group of sovereign states have worked together while maintaining their independent identity to address regional problems. But the task of maintaining and working towards a secure environment, as noted by Buzan is no longer confined to just states but also societies. This is especially so since the conceptualization of security has also undergone a dramatic transformation for many years now.

Even before the end of the Cold War, the concept of security has shifted from a military-centred definition to include a wider range of threats to state security. Security is no longer just about threats to military affairs and the protection of state boundaries. Security threats have expanded to include non-military threats that would threaten and risk the core values of the state such as economic security and environmental security. As argued by Richard Ullman[6] and Jessica Matthews,[7] the concept of security should go beyond military threats to include a wider range of issues from environmental degradation, economic insecurity brought on by threats to unemployment and poverty, ethnic conflicts and so on. The expansion of security threats also led to the reconsideration and inadvertent expansion of security approaches beyond the conventional geopolitical approaches of deterrence, power balancing and military strategy to comprehensive and co-operative security.

More significantly, the expansion of security agenda has also shifted the focus on states as the main unit of analysis to include individuals and societies. Hence the security lexicon has also expanded from the conventional binaries of traditional and non-traditional security issues to the highly contested notion of human security.[8] International relations scholars like Ken Booth, Simon Dalby, and Barry Buzan have argued that the referent of security should move beyond the state to people or human collectivities.[9] Security must be seen as encompassing all issues — both at the domestic and international level — that affect the emancipation or interests of the people. Therefore, security issues should no longer be confined to deliberate threats to the state, but more importantly on the threats against humanity. These would include issues such as human rights abuses, large scale displacement of civilian population, illegal migration, trafficking of illegal drugs and small arms, extreme poverty, infectious diseases like the AIDS pandemic and food scarcity.

It is not the place here to deal comprehensively with the conceptual discussion on security but suffice it to say that these new contestations on "new" security agenda and focus on individuals and societies are all part of the new landscape that is emerging which has redefined how states, as well as societies, should deal with security issues. The discourses and contestation on security, and the expansion of the units of analysis, that is, security referents, resonate in this part of the world. Hence, the call for the expansion of the security agenda and the need to promote human security would have significant impact on the way ASEAN deals with security challenges in the region. Following this point, another theme that this book addresses is how civil society groups either at track two or track three relate to state actors in ASEAN and the processes that are emerging in the reconceptualization of security in the region. Are alternative ideas being promoted in the processes of redefining security? Is there political space created for these non-state actors to add their voices on how regional governance should take shape and how regional security ought to be achieved? Where do we place/locate the emerging processes taking place in both track two and track three in setting the security agenda of ASEAN and the modalities that would have to be adjusted or rejected in managing security issues in the region?

As the narrative of explaining the ASEAN story continues, this book therefore aims to probe further into areas which have been largely ignored in the study of ASEAN norms. Taking off from Haacke's study of ASEAN's diplomatic and security culture, this book therefore proceeds to look at ASEAN and the study of regional security beyond the prisms of the ASEAN way.

## ORGANIZATION OF THE BOOK

This book is essentially divided into two parts. Chapters 1 to 4, which make up the first half of this study, provides a historical narrative of the way ASEAN has evolved in its many roles as manager of regional security in Southeast Asia. Chapter 1 begins with locating ASEAN in the experience of regional organizations and their role in managing regional security. It then proceeds to explore the various types of mechanisms that regional organizations that manage conflicts have by drawing the linkages between regional security approaches with the types of mechanisms that regional organizations have. The constructivist approach in international relations have been adopted in this study to identify the kinds of mechanisms that regional organization have in order to analyse how and why distinct mechanisms, particularly in the case of ASEAN, are constructed.

Chapter 2 traces the evolution of ASEAN's mechanisms of managing conflict by providing a historical narrative of ASEAN's development as a regional organization. It was during this formative period of ASEAN when the ASEAN way was constructed and became the defining approach in the way the association had managed regional conflicts and crises.

While ASEAN was generally successful in establishing a framework to manage regional security, Chapter 3 discusses how this success was tested when the region was caught in the Cambodian conflict. ASEAN's involvement in the Cambodian conflict has offered interesting insights on the extent to which its mechanisms had been useful and/or irrelevant in the search for the political settlement to what was then considered as an extramural conflict. Chapter 3 analyses how ASEAN's diplomacy in Cambodia had tested the limits of the ASEAN way.

The qualified success of ASEAN on Cambodia paved the way for an application of the ASEAN way in the wider Asia-Pacific region. Chapter 4, therefore, discusses the extent to which the ASEAN way had been extended into a wider region with the establishment of the ASEAN Regional Forum. It is in this chapter on the ARF that we begin to track some perceptible trends in the evolving changes of the ASEAN way.

Chapters 5 to 8 make up the other half of the study that describes what is beyond the ASEAN way. Taking off from the developments brought on ASEAN's role in establishing the ARF, Chapter 5 turns our attention to the role of ideas and agents in reconstructing ASEAN's mechanism beyond the ASEAN way. It describes the role of non-state actors who have been actively involved in the ASEAN process and analyses the kinds of interaction and influence that these actors, i.e. the ASEAN Institutes for Strategic and International Studies (ASEAN-ISIS) and the Council for Security Co-operation in the Asia Pacific (CSCAP) have had on the development of mechanisms in ASEAN and the ARF.

In response to the periods of crises that hit ASEAN, as highlighted in Chapter 6, Chapter 7 extends our discussion of non-state actors that have had an impact on the way new mechanisms have evolved in ASEAN. In this chapter, we study the emergence of civil society organizations under the umbrella of the ASEAN People's Assembly (APA) that had joined the track two networks in engaging ASEAN to be a more proactive organization. It is suggested in this chapter that the convening of the APA can be regarded as another embryonic mechanism that ASEAN, through its engagement with the latter, has developed and is indicative of emerging trends that point us to regional mechanisms beyond the ASEAN way. Finally, Chapter 8 concludes by summing up all these developments and reflects on the implications of the new actors and emerging processes on ASEAN's way of managing security, its goal in setting up the ASEAN Community, and on Southeast Asian regionalism in general.

## Notes

1.  See, for example, Shaun Narine, *Explaining ASEAN: Regionalism in Southeast Asia* (Boulder, CO: Lynne Rienner Publishers, Inc., 2002); Amitav Acharya, *Constructing a Security Community in Southeast Asia: ASEAN and the Problem of Regional Order* (London and New York: Routledge, 2001); and Jurgen Haacke, *ASEAN's Diplomatic and Security Culture: Origins, Development and Prospects* (London and New York: RoutledgeCurzon, 2003).

2. ASEAN-5 usually refers to the original members of ASEAN when it was founded in 1967. These are Indonesia, Malaysia, the Philippines, Singapore, and Thailand.
3. See the *Declaration of ASEAN Concord II (Bali Concord II)*, at <http://www.aseansec.org/15160.htm>.
4. Several authors have been sceptical about the prospects of ASEAN and have shared the idea of ASEAN needing to reinvent itself. See for example, Acharya, *Constructing a Security Community*; Narine, *Explaining ASEAN*; Jurgen Ruland, "ASEAN and the Asian Crisis: Theoretical Implications and Practical Consequences for Southeast Asian Regionalism", *Pacific Review* 13, no. 3: 421–51; Jeannie Henderson, *Reassessing ASEAN*, Adelphi Paper 323 (London: Oxford University Press for IISS, 1999); and Michael Wesley, "The Asian Crisis and the Adequacy of Regional Institutions", *Contemporary Southeast Asia* 21, no. 1 (1999): 54–73.
5. See, for example, Hoang Anh Tuan, "ASEAN Dispute Management: Implications for Vietnam and an Expanded Vietnam", *Contemporary Southeast Asia* 18, no. 1 (1996): 61–80; Kamarulzaman Askandar, "ASEAN as a Process of Conflict Management: ASEAN and Regional Security in Southeast Asia: 1967–1994" (Unpublished Ph.D. thesis, University of Bradford, Department of Peace Studies, 1996); Mely Caballero-Anthony, "Mechanisms of Dispute Settlement: The ASEAN Experience", *Contemporary Southeast Asia* 20, no. 1 (1998): 38–66.
6. Richard Ullman, "Redefining Security", *International Security* 8, no. 1 (1983): 129–53.
7. Jessica T. Matthews, "Redefining Security", *Foreign Affairs* LXVIII, no. 3 (1989): 162–77.
8. See *Human Security Now: Protection and Empowering People* (New York: Commission on Human Security, 2003), and Astri Suhrke, "Human Security and the Interests of States: Reviving the Oslo-Ottawa Axis", *Security Dialogue* 30, no. 3 (1999).
9. See Barry, Ole Waever and Jaap de Wilde, eds. *Security: A New Framework of Analysis* (Boulder, CO: Lynne Rienner, 1998).

# 1

## REGIONALISM AND REGIONAL SECURITY
## Locating ASEAN

### INTRODUCTION

This chapter sets out the framework in examining ASEAN's mechanisms in managing conflicts and relates its experience in the broader study of regionalism and regional security. The first part begins with a brief discussion of regional organizations and their role in managing regional security. This section highlights the experiences of regional organizations, particularly in the developing world in responding to regional crises. It then proceeds to argue that in spite of its chequered history, regional organizations play a significant role in managing and resolving regional conflicts, particularly if one looks at their specific experiences.

The second part of this chapter identifies the kinds of mechanisms that regional organizations develop and deploy in responding to conflicts. In exploring what these mechanisms are, regional security approaches are also examined to establish their linkages with the kind of mechanisms that regional organizations generate. In drawing the linkages between these two elements, the study demonstrates that one informs the other — that is, security approaches influence the nature of mechanisms regional organizations develop.

The third part then proceeds to locate these mechanisms of conflict management within the constructivist school of international relations theory in order to analyse why distinct mechanisms are constructed. Through the prism of social constructivism, this section examines how mechanisms of conflict management have evolved and identifies the kinds of influences that would have informed the choice of certain types of mechanisms that would be applied under given circumstances. A key question that is being asked here is whether norms and identity matter.

The purpose of adopting a three-step approach in this first chapter is to present ASEAN as a regional organization that has actively been engaged in managing the security of Southeast Asia. As the other chapters of this book will show, ASEAN has dealt with regional conflicts in a rather distinctive manner, characterized by the observance of informal mechanisms in managing inter-state disputes. This three-step approach is, therefore, characteristically deductive as a prelude to the overall thrust of this book that seeks to explore how ASEAN may have changed its modalities in dealing with conflicts and, more importantly, to argue the point that there is more beyond the ASEAN way in its approach in working towards regional security.

## I. REGIONAL ORGANIZATIONS AND REGIONAL SECURITY

By their very nature, regional organizations have been ascribed the role of managing regional conflicts. This is not really an entirely new phenomenon. Regional organizations were established with the primary aim of maintaining peace and resolving conflicts or containing conflicts to avoid further escalation. In fact in the late 1960s and early 1970s, regional organizations were already regarded as possible building blocks of peace and for regions to become "islands of peace".[1]

Prior to this period, the potential role of regional organizations for settlement of disputes was also recognized by the United Nations at the end of the Second World War. At the 1945 San Francisco Conference for the drafting of the United Nation's Charter, a vigorous debate over the merits of universalism versus regionalism took place. While the debate ensured the superiority and seniority of global organization over any regional organizations, Chapter VIII nevertheless envisaged "regional arrangements or agencies" which would deal with such matters relating to the maintenance of international peace and security as are appropriate for regional action.[2]

Although the basic idea was to enable and empower regional organizations to settle local disputes before referring them to the United Nations, the record of this role was unimpressive. As one scholar noted, forty-five years hence, the UN found "only limited use for regional organizations".[3] The failure of such relationship was attributed to superpower conflict. The Cold War *politik* prevented the development of what could have been a potentially close relationship when the major antagonists — the United States and the former Soviet Union — excluded the Security Council from being involved in the regional conflicts in which they were respectively involved. For example: when the cases of Guatemala of 1954, the Cuban complaint against the United States in 1962, and that of Panama in 1965 were brought up in the Security Council, the United States insisted successfully that these matters belonged under the purview of the Organization of American States (OAS) and not in the Security Council. Similarly, the former USSR denied the Security Council's competence in dealing with the suppression of the Hungarian uprising in 1956 and the Soviet intervention in Czechoslovakia in 1968. The former Soviet Union insisted that these matters were the concern of the socialist community bound by the Warsaw Pact.[4] In these cases, regional organizations were used by each superpower as instruments for hegemonic supremacy in a region and not as agencies for broader collective security and conflict resolution.[5] The "original" role of regional organizations as "first stop" base in local conflicts was therefore overwhelmed by the geopolitics of the Cold War. Rather than stepping stones to the United Nations' action, regional organization became more like "stooges" of superpower rivalries.

The perceived emasculation of the UN also frustrated many Third World countries which sought regional actions as a means of preventing external meddling in local affairs. Against the trends at that time, it was no surprise then that there was almost disillusionment in many Third World states on the efficacy of regionalism as a means of resolving regional conflicts. Lucian Pye's earlier description of regions becoming "islands of peace" became more like "pawns of superpower rivalries". It became increasingly clear at that time that regional organizations were "frequently little more than bystanders to unfolding international events".[6]

However, other than the Cold War politics that prevailed at that time, there was the issue of competence in dealing with regional conflicts, influenced largely by the very nature of the conflicts as well. It did not take long for some regional organizations to realize that regional conflicts, some of them inter-state, were far too complex for them to resolve among themselves. In some cases, it became even more complex when non-members were involved. Furthermore, it was soon realized that certain types of regional conflicts were simply beyond the capabilities of their respective institutions to resolve on their own. This was illustrated in the cases of the Arab League when faced with the problem of Israel, and the Organization of African Unity (OAU) with South Africa and the OAS with Cuba.[7] Certain limitations also came to the fore, leading one noted scholar to conclude that certain types of regional organizations suffered from problems of "credibility, relevance, and compatibility".[8]

In spite of this unimpressive past, the structural changes brought about by the end of the Cold War has renewed attention on regionalism and a reconsideration of the role of regional security organizations. The collapse of the bipolar post-World War II security architecture has left the United States as the only remaining superpower in the world, given the break-up of its rival, the former USSR. In spite of its supremacy however, the United States had been perceived — at least in the early post-Cold War period — as having neither the political will nor the resources to become the world's policeman.[9]

Similarly, while the security role of the UN had increased after being involved in the major conflicts in the Gulf War, Cambodia, Mozambique, El Salvador, and others, its resources have been severely stretched. This had been made more acute with the ever-growing number of peacekeeping operations undertaken by the UN. According to one study, since the UN's intense mediation of Soviet withdrawal from Afghanistan in 1989 and the end of the Iran-Iraq War, the UN had undertaken thirteen new operations, the same number in the previous forty years. And, while the unpaid arrears of the UN in 1992 reached one billion dollars, its operations for that year alone were estimated to cost thrice the given arrears. With member nations cutting back on financial contribution and support, the UN's capacity to undertake additional responsibilities has become problematic while the will of its dominant members to do was often weak.[10]

Given the above factors, it has been realized that a task-sharing arrangement between the United Nations and regional organizations could be undertaken to advance international order. To quote the words of the former UN Secretary-General Boutros Boutros-Ghali in his work, *An Agenda for Peace*:

> ...Under the Charter, the Security Council has and will continue to have primary responsibility for maintaining international peace and security, but regional action as a matter of decentralisation, delegation and cooperation with United Nations efforts could contribute to a deeper sense of participation, consensus and democratization in international affairs. Regional arrangements and agencies have not in recent decades been considered in this light...Today a new sense exists that they have contributions to make.[11]

Aside from the call from the United Nations for more regional involvement, there were also other factors that provided the new impetus for regional organizations to have a hand in managing regional conflicts. One of these factors was the renewed desire on the part of medium and small powers for greater control over their strategic environment.[12] This desire for regional autonomy became a characteristic feature of Third World regional organizations like the OAU, which had as their slogans statements like "African solutions for African problems" and "Asian solutions to Asian problems". Moreover, regional actors felt that they were best suited to mediate in local conflicts as they understood the dynamics of strife and cultures more intimately than outsiders. Related to this was also the fact that the issues that were related to local conflicts would most likely be given more attention in regional fora than in the global one, since the latter have had a much broader agenda.[13]

Finally, the other significant factor stems from the effects of economic regionalism mirrored in the emergence of regional economic groupings like the North American Free Trade Agreement (NAFTA) and the ASEAN Free Trade Area (AFTA). These groups had displayed the potential to enhance self-confidence among regional states and encourage them to put greater reliance in matters of security.[14]

Thus, given the above considerations on why regional organizations were more suitable to handle regional conflict, one could argue that in spite of the ambiguous experience that regional organizations had in the past, they have in fact the potential to play a significant role in managing regional security. One could further add that the success of regional organizations would also be predicated on the extent to which they have been able to maintain regional peace and stability by either managing, containing, or resolving regional conflicts.

To briefly summarize the chequered experience of regional organizations, one could safely conclude that while certain factors like the intervention of major powers in regional conflicts and lack of competence in dealing with conflicts had been major obstacles in preventing some regional organizations to effectively carry out their functions in managing conflicts, particularly during the Cold War, there is nevertheless enough evidence to show that some regional organizations have been reasonably successful in their particular experience. One of these organizations is ASEAN.[15] In analysing ASEAN's own history of managing regional conflicts, it is notable that the association had been able to carefully navigate through turbulence and crises even during the Cold War. Therefore, of major interest in examining its relative success would be the way ASEAN had handled crises at various points in its history as a regional organization in Southeast Asia.

The crucial test of a regional organization is in the way it has handled conflicts so as to avoid its disintegration or demise. Thus, the very survival of an organization is telling of the way it has successfully managed or resolved regional conflicts. This success could be explained by the manner in which members have worked in defining regional affairs, as well as the nature of the political space created for its respective members to play a part in securing their interests. More importantly, its success in managing and/or resolving regional conflicts is also instructive of the types of mechanisms it has deployed to address various challenges to regional security. In this regard, one can therefore locate the study of the ASEAN way within the framework of mechanisms of conflict management that regional organizations generate to resolve or manage problems in order to achieve regional peace and security. Before proceeding any further, I shall first explain why ASEAN was chosen as a case study.

## Locating ASEAN

Since its establishment in 1967, ASEAN has made its mark in the international community as a successful regional grouping. Its success can be said to lie in its ability to cope reasonably well with the numerous challenges that had confronted the organization, as well as its relations with other states in the international arena. As this study intends to show, ASEAN appeared not only to have weathered both internal and external pressures that may have threatened its very existence as a regional body but more importantly, it has earned for itself a significant role as a key player in regional and international affairs. Even against the rapid changes and uncertainties that have occurred in the global environment, for example the recent financial crisis that have rocked the region in the middle of 1997, the civil war in Indonesia's East Timor in 1999, and the current global "war on terrorism", ASEAN has proven to be resilient.

Looking back over thirty-five years since its inception, ASEAN's political achievements have been remarkable by any standard. Although security did not formally enter its agenda until ASEAN's Fourth Summit in 1992, the success of ASEAN is primarily in the political-security realm. This has been the paradox of ASEAN. If one were to examine the ASEAN Bangkok Declaration, which explained what ASEAN was all about, one would get the impression that it was created as an economic grouping. After all, the Bangkok Declaration stated that the objectives of

ASEAN are to promote regional economic growth, social progress and cultural development through active collaboration and mutual assistance on matters of common interests in the economic, social, cultural, technical, scientific, and administrative fields.[16]

For more than three decades, and in spite of a highly decentralized and loosely organized ASEAN Secretariat, the member states of ASEAN have indeed established a framework for close regional co-operation that would give credence and substantive effect to the very broad objectives of regionalism as articulated in the Bangkok Declaration. Yet, if one were to really zero in on what these achievements have been, perhaps it is its ability to maintain peace in what was once a trouble-ridden region that stands out the most.[17] ASEAN was considered in the early 1960s as the Balkans of the East. However, it is quite inconceivable nowadays for any member state to go to war with each other. Although ASEAN has moved beyond its initial security role of managing intramural disputes among its members, it has also paradoxically shied away from addressing the role of force in enforcing regional order, thus rejecting the traditional approach of building alliances. Instead, ASEAN has achieved its security objective through informal mechanisms of conflict management. More specifically, ASEAN has set an example of how a regional security organization can, over the years, develop a "tangible set of informal but effective procedures ... in policy behaviour by the leaders of its respective member-states and has built up on shared visions and expectations related to regional security".[18]

In this regard, the development of a set of informal procedures or mechanisms to manage conflict is indeed notable, given the tendency to regard solutions to conflicts within the framework of the realist perspective of international politics. In this framework, it is the *diktak* of realpolitik that really matters and where more often than not in international affairs, regional actors have had to act or at least, are constrained to act in accordance with the interests of major powers. As mentioned in the earlier section of this chapter, the smaller regional states are more likely to be mere bystanders in the unfolding of international events. More significantly, the power and status of states in the international arena are determined hierarchically. In a realist world, a hegemonic state determines the structure of international relations.

But in a changed international environment, especially when the hegemon declines in power, questions as to what would happen certainly arise. The realists would say that there would be a re-emergence of anarchy as a number of states manoeuvre to be in control. However, in contrast to the realists, the more optimistic view of the neo-liberals would argue that the hegemon's co-ordinating role which had laid out this balance could be assumed by a "regime" of states that would maintain "on a collaborative basis, many of the rules and regulations that had originally been imposed unilaterally by the hegemon".[19] An interesting question to ask as we study the ASEAN experience is where to place these competing paradigms. Or is it the case that a more appropriate approach can be applied to look at the experience of ASEAN and its mechanisms of conflict management?

While the main objective of this book is to examine what is beyond the ASEAN way, a necessary step to start the process of exploring these other factors is to first address the task of describing and explaining what is the ASEAN way. More importantly, one has to also relate the ASEAN way to the general study of mechanisms of conflict management and explain the linkages between the two. Moreover, in identifying what these mechanisms of conflict management are as they relate to the ASEAN way, one would also be mindful of the fact that these mechanisms could be closely linked to ASEAN's approach to maintaining regional security.

In order to incorporate the dynamics of these two intertwined factors into the theme of this book, that is, the ASEAN way and beyond, these two factors would then have to be teased out separately in order to: (1) understand their linkages, and (2) to provide a more coherent approach in the study of changing modalities in ASEAN. Once again, this deductive approach is necessary to comprehensibly track the processes by which the ASEAN states have developed mechanisms of conflict management from the time of ASEAN's inception in 1967 up to the present. Thus, as we follow the trends and evolution of the ASEAN way and beyond, a number of key issues would be addressed.

- Firstly, what explains the emergence and evolution of these mechanisms?
- Secondly, have these mechanisms changed over time? If so, what are these changes?
- Thirdly, what are the factors that account for these changes?

Before proceeding further, it is important at this point to define what is meant by mechanisms of conflict management and identify what they are in the context of regional organizations.

## II. MECHANISMS OF CONFLICT MANAGEMENT AND SECURITY APPROACHES: ESTABLISHING LINKAGES

### What Are Mechanisms of Conflict Management?

Broadly, the mechanisms for managing conflicts refer to the processes, methods, devices, techniques, and strategies employed to resolve or manage a conflict.[20] The next chapter will deal with this more comprehensively as we examine the mechanisms found in ASEAN. Suffice it to say at this point that there are several types of mechanisms that regional organizations can use in managing conflict. Muthiah Alagappa provides a useful analytical framework on how regional organizations manage conflict. Alagappa identified several mechanisms which he referred to as "strategies" that regional organizations could adopt, depending on the nature of the conflict — whether domestic, inter-state and involving external actors — and at which stage the conflict management is at — prevention, containment, and termination.[21] Alagappa's framework is used in this study since most of the strategies that he identified relate closely to the kind of mechanisms peculiar to ASEAN. Since most of the mechanisms predominantly employed by ASEAN are informal in nature, these mechanisms do not necessarily find their way in the available literature on conflict.[22] Thus for the purposes of understanding ASEAN, I shall rely heavily on the strategies identified by Alagappa. A brief description of these strategies is provided below.

The strategies for managing conflict which are available to regional organizations are: norm setting, assurance, community-building, deterrence, non-intervention, isolation, intermediation, enforcement and internationalization.[23] Norm-setting defines identities of states as well as regulates behaviour. Through this strategy, regional institutions can be expected to influence "the collective expectations and the internal and international behaviour of member states in the political, economic, and security arenas".[24] The strategies of assurance, community-building, and deterrence are primarily concerned with preventing conflicts. Assurance strategies, for example, help to increase transparency, reduce uncertainty and help to build confidence. Its purpose is to mitigate the security dilemma and minimize the use of force but not eliminate them.[25] A step further would be community-building strategies which seek to eliminate the use of force and culminates in the creation of a security community where members of the community will not fight each other but will instead settle disputes in other ways. This is similar to Karl Deutsch's idea of a security community.[26] Deterrence strategies which include collective security, and collective defence seek to deter aggressive behaviour on both member states as well as non-member states.[27]

Strategies which are applied to contain conflicts are non-intervention, isolation, and intervention. Non-intervention is when regional organization avoids being involved in a particular conflict. Isolation, on the other hand, serves the purpose of preventing geographical spillovers or widening of the conflict through involvement of others. Intervention refers to direct and active involvement in a conflict by using the available collective resources of the regional organization like collective defence to contain and terminate the conflict.[28]

Lastly are the strategies of intermediation and internationalization that are applied to terminate conflict. Intermediation refers to a non-partisan and non-coercive approach to dispute settlement wherein conflicting parties are urged to use regional or global mechanisms for pacific settlement of disputes. The strategy of internationalization refers to instances when regional organizations mobilize the resources of external actors and organizations in support of their strategies while denying the same to adversaries.[29]

Table 1.1 provides a summary of the above-mentioned strategies at each stage of conflict management (that is, managing, containing, and terminating) together with the types of conflicts involved. While many of these strategies are not necessarily found in ASEAN nor are they consistent in usage, these strategies nevertheless provide us with a good point of reference and even a benchmark in analysing the regional organization's success in managing conflict. In this regard, Alagappa's framework is indeed useful since this study will argue that the uniqueness of ASEAN's way in managing a conflict lies in the manner it selects, combines, and uses the strategies that Alagappa listed in managing conflicts. The specific applications and examination of these strategies in this case study will be dealt with in more detail in Chapter 2.

## Identifying Regional Security Approaches

Regional security approaches refer to the orientations and predispositions of member states towards the means of achieving regional security. A region's approach to security is often reflected in how member states structure their relations among other states within and outside the grouping in pursuing the goal of regional security. Factors such as shared value systems, mutual flow of ideas, and level of social communication

## TABLE 1.1

## Regional Institution and Security: A Framework for Analyses

*Domestic conflicts*
**Issues of contention: identity, legitimacy, socio-economic grievances**

| | Tasks | Measures/strategies |
|---|---|---|
| Conflict prevention | 1. Protection of individual and minority rights<br>2. Support for socio-political development<br>3. Support for economic development<br>4. Early warning | 1. Norm-setting<br>2. Redress by regional institutions<br>3. Encourage and facilitate dialogue<br>4. Preventive deployment<br>5. Collective inducement and sanctions<br>6. Regional economic co-operation<br>7. Maintain a stable and conducive regional environment |
| Conflict containment | 1. Prevent escalation<br>2. Preventive torture, killing and genocide<br>3. Humanitarian relief | 1. Preventive deployment<br>2. Enforce sanctions<br>3. Isolate conflict<br>4. Peacekeeping<br>5. Internationalize conflict<br>6. Humanitarian assistance |
| Conflict termination | 1. End violence<br>2. Negotiate and guarantee settlement<br>3. Election monitoring<br>4. Address underlying issues | 1. Encourage dialogue<br>2. Intermediation<br>3. Enforcement action<br>4. Encourage and support long range strategies for nation- and state-building<br>5. Internationalization |

*Conflicts among member states*
**Issues of concern: identity, legitimacy, autonomy, territorial disputes**

| | Tasks | Measures/strategies |
|---|---|---|
| Conflict prevention | 1. Ameliorate security dilemma<br>2. Deter aggressive behaviour<br>3. Build a society leading eventually to a community of nations | 1. Foster development of normative context that rejects threat and use of force as an instrument of state policy |

**TABLE 1.1 — *continued***

|  |  |  |
|---|---|---|
|  | 4. Encourage dispute resolution | 2. Built regimes — assurance and regulatory<br>3. Regional dispute resolution mechanisms<br>4. Collective security arrangements<br>5. Regional integration measures |
| Conflict containment | 1. Deny victory to aggressor<br>2. Prevention escalation<br>3. Humanitarian relief | 1. Enforce collective security arrangements<br>2. Isolate conflict<br>3. Peacekeeping<br>4. Internationalization<br>5. Humanitarian assistance |
| Conflict termination | 1. Stop armed conflict<br>2. Negotiate and guarantee settlement<br>3. Resolve dispute | 1. Encourage dialogue among parties to conflict<br>2. Intermediation<br>3. Enforcement action<br>4. Internationalization |

*Conflicts with external actors*
**Issues of concern: security dilemma, specific issues in dispute, aggressive behaviour by external actors**

|  | **Tasks** | **Measures/strategies** |
|---|---|---|
| Conflict prevention | 1. Ameliorate security dilemma<br>2. Deter aggressive behaviour<br>3. Encourage dispute resolution | 1. Dialogue and negotiations<br>2. Security regimes — assurance and regulatory<br>3. Collective self-defence |
| Conflict containment | 1. Deny victory to aggressor<br>2. Prevent escalation<br>3. Humanitarian relief | 1. Implement collective self-defence<br>2. Internationalization<br>3. Humanitarian assistance |
| Conflict termination | 1. Defeat aggressor<br>2. Negotiate settlement<br>3. Resolve dispute | 1. Implement collective self-defence<br>2. Internationalization<br>3. Intermediation |

**Source:** Adapted from Muthiah Alagappa, "Regional Insitutions, The UN and Regional Security", *Third World Quarterly* 18, no. 3 (1997): 421–41.

all become important in shaping security policy orientations of states. In fact, it was in this context that the term *security community* emerged and was most systematically developed by Karl Deutsch.[30]

So far, we can identify three major types of security approaches in the Third World, which more or less approximate the types of regional organizations that have also emerged in the Third World.[31] These are:

1.  *Alliance-building* reflects the preferred security approach chosen by organizations such as the OAS and the North Atlantic Treaty Organization (NATO), which are allied to a superpower like the United States. This means that OAS members, for example, were within the ambit of the U.S. "sphere of influence" which consequently prevented them from forming other alliances with any extra-regional power. This type of regional approach to security was referred to as hegemonic regionalism.[32]

2.  *Co-operative approach* emphasizes the habit of co-operation as a means of settling local disputes. This approach is similar to what is referred to as "regionalism as conflict control", a type of security approach aimed at and adopted by regional groupings in the 1960s and 70s, including ASEAN, which reflected the aspirations of regional states to have greater latitude and gain more control over their immediate strategic environment.[33]

3.  *Market-integrative approach* is a functional approach to security couched in economic language and anchored on the thinking that economic co-operation would lead to political co-operation. This approach is predicated on the assumption that incremental change would then spill over into other areas leading to the creation of political community. This kind of regional security framework is also based on the assumption that if functional regional groups could succeed in promoting economic integration, the states as well as its actors will eventually learn to resolve their conflicts peacefully and co-operate in the establishment of common security community.[34]

### Drawing Linkages between Mechanisms of Conflict Management and Regional Security Approaches: The Case of ASEAN

Given the types of mechanisms of conflict management identified earlier and the kinds of security approaches that regional organizations take, one can then proceed with establishing the linkages between these two factors. The step-by-step process in teasing what each of these factors mean is necessary to understand their dynamics, particularly in relation to how they inform ASEAN's modalities in addressing regional conflicts. If ASEAN's experience in managing regional security is a qualified success, then one could argue at this point that ASEAN's success had been largely due to the nature of its regional approach to security, and — as informed by its security approach — the kind mechanisms it has employed to manage conflicts.

The relationship between these two factors can be regarded as the dynamics between the "idea" and the "action" in explaining the behaviour of states. In the broader security discourse, one could assume in this instance that the region's security approach is the abstract and ideational element that informs the nature of the region's mechanisms — referring to the action-oriented tools that states act upon to achieve security goals. To illustrate the dynamics of this relationship further, I will now turn to the constructivist framework of international relations to explain ASEAN's security approach and then link this to its tools and techniques, that is, mechanisms in managing conflict. The main objective of using the constructivist approach is to guide us in better understanding why ASEAN prefers certain mechanisms to others and how the security approaches of each member states may have influenced the choice of mechanisms. More significantly, constructivism also helps us to better appreciate the paradoxes that define ASEAN and the way it has managed regional security over the years.

## III. CONSTRUCTIVISM AND MECHANISMS OF CONFLICT MANAGEMENT: NORMS, IDENTITY, AND INTEREST OF REGIONAL MECHANISMS

The neo-realist and neo-liberal perspectives of international relations have largely influenced the discourse on regionalism, particularly in understanding the motivations why states join regional organizations. According to the realist theory, in an international environment characterized by anarchy and with no overarching authority in the international system, states are preoccupied with their very survival.[35] Driven by self-interest, states act to seek and maximize benefits. As states seek relative gains, co-operative behaviour is therefore only possible as long as the relative powers of the state remain the same.[36]

In studying regionalism among states, this preoccupation about survival is analogous with the common denominator referred to in some work as the "security orientation" of states.[37] This means that unless some measure of insecurity are perceived by national actors, there will be little, if no cause at all for states to organize. Thus by becoming members of a regional organization, the security dilemma of states would be minimized.

In applying this theory to regional security approaches and mechanisms of conflict management, one would proceed to expect regional states to enter into regional security arrangements which would guarantee the logic of balance of power politics such as defence ties and alliances with major powers. By doing so, states help themselves by arming and increasing their defence expenditures or create alliances in order to maintain a stable balance of power.[38] Thus in the earlier patterns of regionalism over the past decades, states did in fact form alliances like the OAS and the now defunct South East Asian Treaty Organization (SEATO), which were allied with a superpower like the United States. This type of regional approach to security was termed as hegemonic regionalism and also referred to as "pactomania".[39] Consequently, resolution or management of conflicts was approached through collective defence, having more elaborate peacekeeping machinery, or having an organization that is structured to present a common military and diplomatic front against an outside factor. By maintaining the balance and distribution of power, security is thus assured.

However, the experience of Asia-Pacific security in general and Southeast Asian security in particular do not adequately reflect the approaches to security as informed by the realist or neo-realist perspective of international relations. The need for regional states to form formal alliances as a natural regional security response to their security dilemma has not really taken off in the region. Although one might argue that many of the states in Southeast Asia have defence links with outside powers, the most obvious of which are the U.S. alliances with Thailand and the Philippines, the nature of Indonesia's security agreement with Australia, and the Five Powers Defence Arrangements (FPDA) among Malaysia, Singapore, Great Britain, Australia, and New Zealand are very different from traditional notions of alliances. Most of these ties are remnants of the decolonization process when these newly independent states were too weak to provide for their own defence.[40] In fact, the old arrangements like the FPDA have now more or less become an exercise of confidence-building measures among the states involved, where mostly training and exchange of information and technology take place. These arrangements do not in any way guarantee military joint action against third parties and are not based on political commitments required for effective deterrence. The U.S.-Philippine Defense Arrangement, for example, does not guarantee that the United States will come to the aid and defence of the Philippines in case of possible Chinese aggression over the South China Sea dispute. Thus, while these formal alliance type of security arrangements are ideally tools of balancing power and provide as a mechanism for deterrence, such features are not found in Southeast Asian security.[41]

It is equally important to note that to date, the ASEAN states have shied away from any regional defence military arrangements, in spite of the fact that there had been proposals for some kind of a defence agreement from among its member states in the past. For example as early as 1976, Indonesia was reported to have secretly proposed some kind of a joint defence council along with other forms of military co-operation.[42] Malaysia, in 1989, had also expressed the possible creation of a "defence community" that would "take [ASEAN states] to new heights of political and military co-operation".[43] This was announced at the time when the Cambodian conflict was showing greater promise of settlement. None of these proposals, however, ever commanded broad support from the leaders of ASEAN. At best, an ASEAN military was deemed unnecessary and at worst, it was regarded as counter-productive as it would only set off negative reaction from Vietnam (who was then an adversary) and possibly the former Soviet Union.[44] This is an important factor in understanding approaches to security in the region in case one gets caught up in the influence of mainstream realist perspective of analysing regional relations.

Against this regional experience, it seemed that power and material considerations, which neo-realist perspective posit as the main driving forces determining a state's actions, were not the only overriding factors that led states to join regional organizations. This appeared to be true even if one were to understand regionalism from the neo-liberal perspective of international relations.

The neo-liberal approach differed from the realists in that it believed that through co-operation among states, the effects of anarchy could be mitigated through institutions and regimes. According to the neo-liberals, states will co-operate as long as each state reaps absolute gain from the interaction, and it does not really matter which state gains more. The incentives and mechanisms for co-operation in this context are mostly through trade and international commercial activities. At the simplest, this approach carries the notion that peace gradually occurs with commerce in a natural process. This point is summed up by Keohane and Nye as follows: "free trade increases the 'vulnerability of states' and therefore reduces their incentives to resort to force."[45] The most sophisticated expression of this type of perspective on international and regional relations is the functional type of regional organizations, sometimes referred to as micro-regional economic organizations, which had the former European Economic Community — now the European Union — as its model. It was envisioned that by emphasizing co-operation on the "low" politics of economics, the "high" politics of political and security co-operation could eventually be promoted. In doing so, a supra-national body would have to be created as states amalgamate and this would require the member states to surrender some of their sovereignty to the former.[46] As noted in the previous section on regional security approaches, this type of approach is similar to the regional integrative approach to security.

However, even this regional integrative approach to security as informed by the liberal perspective and which initially held more promise in the Third World was not successful in the Asia-Pacific region. Even outside the Third World, there was a decline in the enthusiasm about integration as new patterns of international interdependence emerged, rendering one scholar to bemoan the "obsolescence of regional integration theory".[47] According to one scholar, the micro-regional integration groups which mushroomed in Africa and Latin America in the 1960s and 70s "foundered on the reefs of distrust, non-co-operation and parochial nationalism", which raised the questions regarding the applicability of functionalist approach to the Third Word security.[48] Thus while the arguments for increased economic co-operation was supposed to have increased interdependence, this did not necessarily provide guarantee against conflict.

Nevertheless, compared with the neo-realist perspective, the emphases of the neo-liberal approach on institutions and regimes do offer a more positive approach to security as it explains the politics of co-operation. International institutions can help maintain regional order and in effect, the supremacy of the balance and distribution of power need not be the only determinants in maintaining world order. This is particularly relevant when viewed in the context of increased interdependence among states. Furthermore, it also cannot be denied that certain regions of the world are characterized by a high degree of economic and other forms of interdependence and are already in the process of moving towards a situation of complex interdependence or a pluralistic security community.

However, this development, which is mainly focused on political-economic co-operation, is mostly found in the advanced industrial world. Thus the relevance of commercial liberalism is limited to relatively few states.[49]

More importantly also, the neo-liberal approach tend to downplay the potentially costly effects of interdependence by simply assuming that the incentives for co-operation, that is, economic and political, will induce more co-operation and less conflict. The fact is that states can and do engage in conflict and co-operation at the same time, and in both cases, interdependence is possible. Finally, the arguments of neo-liberalism that focuses mainly on economic ties and interest tend to ignore political feelings and aspirations.

It is argued in this study that the mainstream theories of international relations do not adequately explain the nature and the dramatic changes that have occurred in the world system since the end of the Cold War, particularly in the Asia-Pacific region. This is largely because both theories place great emphasis on the state's material interest. More importantly, the focus on the states alone as the main actors do not take into consideration the influence of non-state and individual level political or ideological factors in the shaping of these interests. Going back to the neo-realist perspective for example, at the heart of its approach is the importance of power in maintaining the state's interest. Thus a state's behaviour can be predicted on its relative position in the international system, which is determined by the distribution of power. Since states are regarded as the main actors who are rational, states' actions are then predicated mainly on the rationalist approach of preserving its basic interests, that is, the physical survival of the state, power, and wealth.

The main limitation of such school of thought is that it fails to explain the types of co-operative behaviour among states that are observable during this post-Cold War era. If states were only concerned about relative gains, how would one explain the emergence of multilateral types of negotiations on issues like trade liberalization and the environment, where relative gains become extremely difficult to calculate?[50] While this limitation of the realist thinking has been addressed by the neo-liberal approach, on the other hand this theory also has been criticized for being overwhelmingly materialistic in that it still projected states as pursuing their "national interests", which are shaped mostly by geopolitical and economic realities. It does not take into account other important variables such as the influence of ideas, values, and identities in explaining states' behaviour.

The other limitation of these theories, particularly from the neo-realist perspective, is that it does not give more attention to the role of non-state actors in analysing why certain decisions were made. The focus on state-centricity fails to recognize the equally important contribution made by certain actors or "agents" in influencing policy decisions. Furthermore, by being state-centric it does not fully explain the dynamics between domestic and international systems and how the events in one influence the other.

Finally, there is also the salient point that in a dynamically changing international environment, there is the element of choice. Thus by focusing only on the material constraints faced by states, the neo-realist and neo-liberal approaches have been silent on the question on why states or certain groups of states chose particular paths or specifically, why certain regional approaches to security were taken despite the given availability of alternatives. It can, therefore, be said that the traditional perspectives are limited in their explanations of states' actions and in this regard, project a wrong sense of inevitability in states' behaviours because these approaches neglect choice and could not consider alternative outcomes.

## The Constructivist Approach

The limitations of the realist and neo-liberalist approaches, which have been highlighted above regarding the centrality of state, the stress on the frontiers between the domestic and international, and the inability to account for change, have been addressed by the constructivist perspective on international relations.

A simplified way of grasping the constructivist approach is to understand the idea that much of the world we live in is of our own making. This means that our world is a social reconstruction of reality where what people believe shapes what they do. In short, it is all about human consciousness and how it is applied to international relations.

The constructivist approach in international relations views state as social actors rather than merely rational actors. By being social actors, states thus operate within the context of their social structures which are driven by rules, norms, institutions, and identities. It follows that a state does not act independently outside these structures, oftentimes referred to as institutions. Instead, these structures help define the behaviour of states and its interactions with other states.

To elaborate further, a more detailed discussion of the elements of the constructivist approach is given below:

- *Actors and structures are mutually constituted:* One of the main tenets of constructivist thinking is that there is no *a priori* in international relations. Structures are not exogenously given. The international environment, hereinafter referred to as international structure, is a social structure comprising shared knowledge, material resources, and practices. In turn, these three factors help shape and define structures.[51]

This line of thinking is starkly different from the neo-realist approach which is based on the premise that only material resources — that is, power — define international structure and because of that, the nature of the international structure is anarchic. In the neo-realist construct, the anarchic condition of the international environment is the *a priori* condition which defines the behaviour of states and explains why the international structure is characterized as inherently a self-help system. The stability of the international environment can, therefore, be secured only through a balance of power.

The neo-liberal approach to international relations also follows basically the same premise. Where it differs (as mentioned in the earlier section of this chapter) is in the fact that while it does not challenge the fundamental realist claim that states behave in a self-interested manner, certain rules or regimes generated through economic co-operation constrain the behaviour of states. Through increased co-operation, it is presumed that the likelihood of war is significantly reduced. Thus, increasing issue linkages other than economics can, therefore, increase interdependence among states.

For constructivists, however, the material factors are not the only decisive factors in explaining states' behaviour. This is because material capabilities as such explain nothing and are nothing unless meanings are attached to them. This is where shared knowledge or the idea of intersubjective understanding comes in. Constructivism argues that material resources will only have meaning for human action through the structure of shared knowledge in which they are embedded.[52] One of the classic example cited to illustrate this idea is how the United States could possibly react to two parties if they had nuclear weapons. For the United States, 500 British nuclear weapons can be perceived as less threatening than five North Korean nuclear weapons, since for the Americans, the

British are friends while the North Koreans are not. The dynamics of amity or enmity in this instance is a function of shared understanding.[53] Hence, since states, as the main actors, are also social actors who operate within a social structure which are defined, in part, by shared understanding, expectations, or knowledge, their behaviour will be predicated not only from given or *a priori* circumstance but on their intersubjective understanding of the world or structures around it. Furthermore, determining the outcome or behaviour will require knowing more about the situation than the distribution of material power or the structure of authority. In knowing more about the situation, "one needs to know about the culture, norms, institutions, procedures, rules, and social practices that constitute the actors and the structures alike."[54]

As Alexander Wendt forcefully argued, "material capabilities as such explain nothing; their effects presuppose structures of shared knowledge, *which vary and which are not reducible to capabilities.*"[55] The international structure is such that it is a social structure, and this structure is intersubjectively constituted. To quote Wendt's famous line, "anarchy is what states make of it", which means that if the international structure is anarchic, it is quite possible for anarchy to have multiple meanings for different actors, based on their own communities of intersubjective understanding and practices.[56] And if multiple understanding of anarchy is possible, it is then quite possible also to have "anarchy of friends as well as anarchy of enemies". Thus from a constructivist view, an environment that is conflict-prone and which makes co-operation difficult is a reflection not of a given (exogenous) reality but a product of socially constructed institutions of the world.[57]

- *Shared knowledge*, comprising principles and norms — which can be either constitutive or regulatory — shape state identities and interests as well as inter-state normative structures.[58]

An important element in constructivist thinking is the concept of identity defined as "a relatively stable, role-specific understanding and expectation of self".[59] Identities are important in that they serve as the basis to what is referred to as "state interest". In turn, state identities and interests are constructed by social structures which are endogenous within the system rather than given exogenously by the world system.

Identities perform three functions: (1) they tell you and others who you are; (2) they tell you who others are; and (3) by doing so, tell you a particular set of interests or preferences with respect to choices of action in particular domain and with respect to particular actions.[60] The crucial observation here is that the producer of identity is not in control of what it means to others — but it is the intersubjective structure which is the final arbiter of meaning. In constructivist thinking, the selves or identities of states are treated as variables which depend largely on historical, cultural, political, and social context. By focusing on the cultural-institutional context, it also highlights the hows and whys of incentives for behaviour of states aside from how they shape identities. Note that identities and interests are again socially contingent and not intrinsic to states. Identities also do not only come from within the state alone but are also shaped by the kind of interactions that happens between states.

## Norms: Constitutive and Regulatory

The process involved in the shaping of states' interests and identities cannot be fully understood unless one analyses the role of norms. Norms can be loosely defined as accepted standards of behaviour or a way of behaving or doing things that most people agree with. They could also be referred to as rules. International norms are thought of as sources of actions in three ways: they define what counts as certain activity; they may enjoin an actor from behaving in a particular way; or they may allow specific actions.[61]

In constructivist thinking, norms can be either constitutive or regulatory. Constitutive norms "define the set of practices that *make up* a particular class of consciously organized social activity — that is to say, they specify what counts as that activity."[62] An understanding of how norms are constituted enriches one's understanding of the structures and interest and identities of states because it goes down to the roots of how they come about. Constitutive rules, therefore, are the very foundations of all social life. As Ruggie clearly explained,

> No consciously organized realm of human activity is imaginable without them, including international politics ... and lacking a conception of constitutive rules makes it impossible to provide endogenously the non-causal explanations that constitutive rules embody and that are logically prior to the domain in which causal explanations take effect.[63]

An understanding of how norms are constituted is essential before one can proceed to understand how these norms can become regulatory. Norms become regulatory after they are constituted. They are regulatory because they are intended to have causal effect, for example, the rule of driving either on the left or right side of the road to prevent cars from bumping into each other and to avoid traffic jams. Therefore, the constitutive norms are the non-causal (what is) rules while regulatory norms are the causal rules (that is, they regulate a specific activity). An example to illustrate this difference between constitutive and regulatory rules is the game of American football. The constitutive rules in this game give meaning to action on the field by defining what counts as a touchdown and a goal. Regulatory norms, on the other hand, are those that guide the play, such as no clipping or holding.

In the arena of international relations, the concept of modern state system became conceivable only when the constitutive rule of reciprocal sovereignty took hold. Regulative rules that came about such as non-interference and non-use of force came and had meaning only after this constitutive rule of sovereignty. States behave according to the norms that constitute international systems and their inter-state conduct or behaviour is regulated by these norms. Examples of these regulatory norms would include the Montevideo Convention of 1933 on the Rights and Duties of States, the 1982 Law of the Sea and various international conventions. In short, international norms influence behaviour that shapes state identities and by providing "inference warrants" from which states can draw conclusions about "whether a class of actions is required, forbidden or allowed".[64]

Linking this to the idea of states' interest and identity, it follows that the two are constructed by the constitutive system that is endogenous to them. States define their identities and interests in terms of the international community. Therefore, in the treatment of interests and identities, states are expected to have "a far wider array of potential choices of actions before them". This is something that is not assumed by neo-realist thinking and that "these choices will be constrained by social structures that are mutually created by states and structures via social practice".[65]

The subject of states' choice(s) of actions and the dynamics behind it are elaborated further by John Ruggie when he stated that states actually "make" circumstances, rather than find them. Reinforcing the idea that there are no *a priori* in international relations, Ruggie teases out the concept of making choices to mean: (1) what people make of their circumstances in the sense of *understanding* them, and (2) what they make of them in the sense of *acting* on whatever understanding they hold. According to Ruggie, "actors (states) engage in an active process of interpretation or construction of a reality."[66]

The constructive approach lends particular relevance to the politics of identity. It explains "how nationalism, ethnicity, race, gender, religion and other intersubjectively understood communities, are each involved in an [explanation] of global politics".[67] The politics of identities brings significance to how identities are constructed, what norms and practices accompany their reproduction and how they construct each other. By focusing on the identities of states, it enriches the understanding that the same state can become many different actors in world politics, and that different states behave differently towards other states, based on the identities of each. More importantly, focusing on identities offer each state an understanding of other states — its nature, motives, interests, probable actions, attitudes, and role in any given context.[68]

- *State's practice* matter in that they inform and are informed by structure, which is both the "medium and outcome" and can be transformed by actions of capable and knowledgeable agents.

Constructivists believe in the power of practice which is brought about by the reproduction of the intersubjective meanings that constitute social structures and actors alike. The meaning of actions of members of a community, as well as the action of others, becomes fixed through practice and thus the boundaries of understanding become well known. The importance of practice is its capacity to reduce uncertainty among actors within a socially constructed community, thereby increasing predictability. Thus the ultimate power of practice lies in its ability to "reproduce and police" an intersubjective reality. According to Hopf, social practices, "to the extent that they authorize, discipline and police, have the power to reproduce entire communities, including the international community, as well as the many communities of identity found therein".[69]

In the arena of foreign policy, the actions of states are either constrained (regulated) or empowered by prevailing social practices at both domestic and international level. Richard Ashley, for example, writes that a foreign policy choice reflect the kind of social practice that at once constitute and empowers the state and defines its socially recognized competence. But importantly, he argues that foreign policy depends on the existence of intersubjective "precedents and shared symbolic material — in order to impose interpretations upon events, silence alternative interpretations, structure practices, and orchestrate the collective making of history".[70]

This is where institutions come in as a reflection of state practices. Institutions are defined as "relatively stable collection of practices and rules defining appropriate behaviour for specific groups of actors in specific situations". Institutions become the locus of socialization and reinforce states' practices. Socialization in turn becomes the "dominant mechanisms" through which states are taught and persuaded to adhere to norms. Moreover, it is the mechanism through which new states are induced to *change* their behaviour by adopting those norms preferred by an international society of states.[71]

## On Change, Transformation, and the Role of Ideas

Although states' practices do in fact reproduce and police an intersubjective reality, the process is far from static. Note that the key point in the constructivist approach is that (state) relationships are social constructions, shaped by shared identities and interests. These are reproduced through constant interaction within international institutions. These institutions, which are products of an interplay of identities and interests, are dynamic in nature and "in process during interaction" which are then subject to the possibility of change. As Wendt had pointed out, states that interact constantly among each other will develop over time a more inclusive sense of identity and collective interest. But, they may also come to alter their interest and identities to and with one another over time and through institutional interactions.[72] This is where change and transformation can take place.

According to Koslowski and Kratochwil, the fundamental change of the international system occurs when actors, through their practices, change the rules and norms which are constitutive of international interaction. They also argued that the reproduction of the practice of international actors (that is, states) depends on the reproduction of practices of domestic actors (that is, individuals and groups). Therefore, "fundamental changes in international politics occur when beliefs and identities are altered thereby also altering the rules and norms that are constitutive of their political practices."[73]

Furthermore, alternative actors with alternative identities, practices, and sufficient material resources can effect change. In constructivism, since the politics of identity is conceived as a continual contest for control over the power necessary to produce meaning in a social group, this makes the potential of change to be always there for as long as there is difference.[74] In fact change, though difficult, is always possible under the constructivist construct because it allows for an unlimited number of discourses, that is, knowledge, ideas, and language.

The influence of ideas is crucial on the behaviour of states, particularly as they impact on identity formation, interest, and policy learning in international relations.[75] To quote Keohane and Goldstein on the role of ideas:

> Ideas influence policy when the principled and causal beliefs they embody provide road maps and increase the actor's clarity about goals and ends-mean relationship ... and when they become embedded in political institutions.[76]

The role of ideas in effecting change is an important element in constructivism because it argues that behaviour, attitudes, institutions, and structures are not just products of inanimate material forces but also of ideas. Writing on the role of ideas, Risse-Kappen stated that ideas intervene between material power-related factors on the one hand and state interests and preferences on the other.[77] Ideas do not exist only in individuals' head but translate into a social force and are socially causative. Ideas in short can be the driving force of history.

Ideas do not emerge in a vacuum but come with preceptors. This is where the key role of intellectual elites and experts come into play as they transform the language and discourse about international relations and help shape the flow of ideas about world politics. It is of particular relevance if these experts comprise individuals from different states since they become the transnational elites who form the "epistemic communities" which formulate and spread communitarian ideas.[78] Understanding the dynamics of the process involved between these ideas and the knowledge-holders in effecting change has been a subject of intense debate between constructivists and non-constructivists.

### Limitations

The causative effects of ideas have been targets of criticism by non-constructivist. Mearsheimer, for example, cited three reasons why constructivism does not offer a convincing argument to replace neo-realism as the dominant framework in analysing international relations. Firstly, he argued that the constructivist's ideas on change in states' behaviour taking place when the discourse changes have not been fully explained. He added that this lack of explanation leads to further questions, notably the fact that constructivism has not been able to offer strong arguments to explain why realism has been the dominant discourse over the past 700 years. Secondly, Mearsheimer argued that while constructivists talk about change, they are also unable to predict change. Linking this with his first point, he argued that critical theory (which to him includes all the different strands of constructivism) "cannot serve as the basis for predicting which discourse will replace realism because the theory says little about the direction change takes.[79] Finally, Mearsheimer pointed to the lack of empirical support for their theory.[80]

Mearsheimer's criticisms of constructivist thinking were responded to by Alexander Wendt in the latter's article published in the same journal in the summer 1995 edition.[81] Basically, Wendt's response countered Mearsheimer's criticisms by pointing to the latter's lack of understanding of the constructivist's arguments and his "lumping together" of all "theories" including constructivism under the one single "critical IR theory". Wendt counter-argued Mearsheimer's criticisms on constructivism's lack of explanatory power in accounting for change by stating that in fact it does. Reinforcing the constructivist's arguments that social structures have three elements — shared knowledge, material resources, and practices — Wendt insisted that these structures are real and objective. However, objectivity depends on shared knowledge making social life "ideas all the way down". It follows then that "ideas do matter and they do effect change since power and interest do not have effects apart from the shared knowledge that constitutes them as such.[82] The lacunae in explaining international relations, as argued by Wendt, can be addressed by understanding social and not solely material factors.

On the subject of change, Wendt pointed out that the constructivist's focus on structures as socially constructed in fact does not automatically guarantee change, but rather that structural change depends very much on changing a system of expectations that may be mutually reinforcing. He added that analysing the social construction of international politics brings one to analyse how processes of interaction produce and reproduce the social structures — co-operative or conflictual — that shape actors' identities and interests and the significance of their material contexts.[83]

Constructivism then focuses a lot on processes. As Ted Hopf has pointed out, constructivism is an approach, not a theory, and if it is a theory, it is a theory of process, not substantive outcome.[84] The problem of its non-specificity of change as cited by Mearsheimer is because constructivism, as a theory of process, does not "specify the existence, let alone the precise nature or value of its main causal/constitutive elements: identities, norms, practices and social structures. Instead, constructivism specifies how these elements are theoretically situated vis-à-vis each other, *providing an understanding of a process and an outcome, but not* a priori *prediction per se.*"[85] Thus while Mearsheimer highlights the non-specifity of the direction of change, constructivism's empirical mission is to surface the background that makes uncertainty a variable to understand, rather than a constant to assume.

Finally, on the point of lack of empirical data, Ruggie argued otherwise. According to him, there has been growing empirical evidence that change can occur and how ideas and norms effect changes in behaviour of states.[86] According to him, there has been empirical research to show how, for example, the roles of "epistemic communities" has had an impact on resolving particular policy problems like ozone depletion, helping redefine states' interests including the case of the antiballistic missile treaty and pollution control regimes. And, as reinforced by Hopf, the burden on constructivist research in studying processes, lies in the gathering of evidence which is necessarily vast and varied.

## Back to Ideas

The emphasis on ideas in the constructive approach to international relations in general and in the understanding the regional mechanisms of conflict management in particular is indeed important in that it puts into proper perspective the processes that take place in the development of "intersubjective structures" at the regional level. These structures, which are "the shared understandings, expectations ... international institutions", in turn help us to understand how and why new policies and mechanisms are initiated in the region. More importantly also, these structures help us to understand the nature of co-operation and policy co-ordination that takes place in the Asia-Pacific region, particularly among ASEAN states. Crucial to this is the role of policy community comprising governmental and non-governmental members of a policy network which facilitate policy-making and co-ordination. The role of this community will be examined in greater detail in the course of this study. Suffice it to say that members of the policy community are the agents who are crucial in helping to bring about change. These agents are part of the process of shaping and generating "ideas" about what states are and what roles they can best perform.

To summarize, constructivism has three basic claims.[87] Firstly, that the structure of the international system is social and includes not only the material resources but also shared knowledge and state practices. Material capabilities have no meaning in themselves but their significance is derived from shared understanding and practices. Secondly, the cultural-institutional context affects not only the incentives for behaviour, as argued by neo-liberalism, but also identities. And thirdly, that state practices matter in that "they inform and are informed by structure", which is both "medium and outcome" and *can be transformed by actions of capable and knowledgeable agents.*[88]

## IV. CONCLUSION

After having discussed the features of constructivism, the question now is how this theory provides a better understanding of ASEAN's approach to security and its choice of mechanisms of conflict management? The other questions are, how does constructivism explain the changes that are evolving in the ASEAN way and what accounts for these changes?

One of the advantages that the constructive approach provides in the study of states is its focus on ideational factors, including norms and ideas. In the context of examining ASEAN's mechanisms of conflict management, that is, the ASEAN way, and exploring what is beyond this approach, the emphases on the ideational factors help us understand how and why "distinct" mechanisms have emerged and were shaped. The constructivist's attention to these elements is instructive in that it allows for the identification of certain mechanisms or strategies which are not necessarily found in standard tools and techniques identified in the existing literature on conflict management.

Specifically, the focus on norms also provides students of international relations a better understanding of how the norms encapsulated in the ASEAN way actually works in managing conflict. As described by many, the ASEAN way had been translated into several norms or principles such as, the principles of: seeking agreement and harmony, sensitivity and politeness; the principles of non-confrontation and of quiet, private and elitist diplomacy versus the principle of being non-Cartesian.[89] These principles are the underlying bases on the kinds of formal and informal mechanisms of conflict management, which have been identified in this study, and will be discussed in full in Chapter 2.

Morever, the constructivist approach is also useful in understanding how the region's security approaches inform the development of certain mechanisms in ASEAN. For example, an understanding of ASEAN's concept of co-operative security as an approach to regional security that emerged in the late 1970s would explain why a legal instrument for managing conflicts, that is, ASEAN's Treaty of Amity and Co-operation (TAC), was introduced. Later on in 1994, this same approach of co-operative security which emphasizes inclusiveness of parties, both partners and adversaries, would help inform ASEAN's rationale for spearheading the establishment of the ASEAN Regional Forum (ARF) which is the first multilateral security forum in the region. The linkages between security approaches and mechanisms will be discussed in more detail in Chapters 3 and 4. Nevertheless, the point being made here is that locating these two elements within the constructivist framework allows for a better understanding of ASEAN, its *raison d'être* and how this could be significantly changing in response to the current developments in the regional and global environment. The usefulness of the constructivist framework in understanding ASEAN — its mechanisms and beyond — is best encapsulated in the words of one scholar who noted that:

> ...structural factors play only a limited role in determining the extent and nature of both multilateral activity and multilateralism in a given regional security complex. It is the cognitive features of the environment — the attitudes of the players toward each other, the rule and norms governing international interaction, the scope and nature of the security dilemmas that the actors perpetuate among themselves — that effectively determine the particular form of regional order that results.[90]

Nonetheless, the preference to use the constructivist approach in this study does not invalidate the usefulness of the neo-realist and neo-liberal approaches. These theories are not necessarily incompatible. The neo-realist's perspective of power and the neo-liberal's emphases on the politics of co-operation are representations of the features of the international environment. However, they are not fully conclusive. The same could be said of the constructivist approach: it does not provide a general theory of action. But, in as far as this study revisits the ASEAN way and explores what is beyond it, what the constructivist approach offers is a broader understanding of ASEAN as a dynamic and changing organization, something which the two other approaches are not fully able to do.

Thus, guided by the framework of the constructivist approach, we begin our study of ASEAN by: first, understanding the dynamics of the intersubjective understanding found in ASEAN among actors, which includes both state and non-state actors; second, we explore how these actors construct mechanisms to address regional challenges and effect changes to mechanisms that are deemed ineffective against new realities; and finally, we try to capture the changing dynamics in the region by paying more attention to developments beyond state actors. Thus, as we extend our analysis beyond the states of ASEAN and turn our attention to other actors/voices bearing ideas that provide the impetus for this organization to adjust and recalibrate its mechanisms of managing crises, we hope to better able to understand ASEAN beyond the prism of the ASEAN way.

## Notes

1. Joseph Nye, *Peace in Parts* (Boston: Little, Brown and Company, 1971), Chapter 5.
2. Michael Barnett, "Partners in Peace? The UN, Regional Organisations and Peacekeeping", in *Review of International Studies* 21 (1995): 411-33.
3. Ibid., p. 411.
4. For more in-depth discussion on this, see Benjamin Rivlin, "Regional Arrangements and the UN System for Collective Security and Conflict Resolution: A New Road Ahead?", *International Relations* XI, no. 2 (1992): 95-110.
5. Ibid., p. 96.
6. Barnett, "Partners in Peace?", p. 412.
7. Francis W. Wilcox, "Regionalism and the United Nations", *International Organization* 19 (Summer 1965): 789-811.
8. Amitav Acharya, "Regional Approaches to Security in the Third World: Lessons and Prospects", in *The South at the End of the Twentieth Century*, edited by Larry A. Swatuk and Timothy M. Shaw (London: Macmillan, 1994), pp. 79-94.
9. See Muthiah Alagappa, "Regionalism and Conflict Management: A Framework of Analysis", *Review of International Studies* 21 (1995): 359-97.
10. S. Neil MacFarlane and Thomas G. Weiss, "Regional Organizations and Regional Security", *Security Studies* 2 (Autumn 1992): 6-37.
11. See Boutros Boutros-Ghali, *An Agenda for Peace: Preventive Diplomacy, Peacemaking and Peacekeeping* (New York: United Nations, 1992).
12. Alagappa, "Regionalism and Conflict Management", p. 360. See also Paul Taylor, "Regionalism: The Thought and the Deed", in *Framework for International Relations*, edited by A.J.R. Groom and Paul Taylor (New York, 1990), pp. 151-71.
13. MacFarlane and Weiss, "Regional Organizations and Regional Security", p. 11.
14. Alagappa, "Regionalism and Conflict Management", p. 361.
15. Established in 1967, the original members of the Association of Southeast Asian Nations (ASEAN) were Indonesia, Malaysia, the Philippines, Singapore, and Thailand. Brunei Darussalam joined in 1984 and Vietnam in 1995. In December 1998, the ASEAN members included the other Southeast Asian

states of Laos and Myanmar, while Cambodia was admitted in 1999, making ASEAN a ten-member association of Southeast Asia.

16. See the ASEAN Declaration (also known as the Bangkok Declaration, 8 August 1967) in *Handbook on ASEAN Political Documents* (Jakarta: ASEAN Secretariat, 1998).

17. Most ASEAN experts even scholars outside the region agree with this view. See, for example, Michael Leifer, *ASEAN and the Security of Southeast Asia* (London: Routledge, 1989).

18. William T. Tow, *Subregional Security Cooperation in the Third World* (Boulder, CO: Lynne Rienner Publishers, 1990), p. 14.

19. For more current discussion of both realism and neo-liberalism in international relations, see Sheldon W. Simon, "Realisms and Neoliberalism: International Relations Theory and Southeast Asian Security", *Pacific Review* 18, no. 1 (1995): 5–24.

20. Scholars dealing with conflict usually draw the distinction between the terms "conflict resolution" and "conflict management". Conflict resolution would involve the elimination and termination of conflict, involving the fundamental differences and grievances underlying the conflict, whereas conflict management involves elimination of violence or a de-escalation of hostilities without really eliminating the root cause(s) of conflict. See C.R. Mitchell, *The Structure of International Conflict* (New York: St. Martin's Press, 1981), Parts 1 and 4.

21. See Alagappa, "Regionalism and Conflict Management". The framework has been updated also in his most recent article on "Regional Institutions, The UN and International Security", *Third Word Quarterly* 18, no. 3 (1997): 421–41.

22. See, for example, Mitchell, *Structure of International Conflict* and Peter Wallersteen, "Understanding Conflict Resolution: A Framework", in *Peace Research: Achievements and Challenges*, edited by Peter Wallensteen, pp. 119–43. See also Volker Tirrberger, "International Regimes and Peaceful Conflict Regulation", in ibid., pp. 144–65.

23. This section relies heavily on Alagappa's more recent article on "Regional Institutions, The UN and International Security".

24. Ibid., p. 427.

25. Ibid., p. 427. For a related discussion on this particular strategy and also on the strategy of deterrence, see also Janice Gross Stein, "Reassurance in International Conflict Management", *Political Science Quarterly* 106, no. 3 (1991): 431–51.

26. See Karl Deutsch, *Political Community and the North Atlantic Area* (Princeton, NJ: Princeton University Press), 1957.

27. Ibid.

28. Ibid.

29. Ibid.

30. Deutsch, *Political Community*.
31. This classification is taken from Acharya's work, "Regional Approaches to Security", pp. 79–94.
32. Ibid.
33. Ibid.
34. Ibid.
35. A classic on the realist perspective of international relations theory is Hans J. Morgenthau, *Politics Among Nations: The Struggle for Power and Peace* (New York: Alfred A. Knopf, 1938).
36. This has more or less been the crux of the neorealists perspective of international relations which takes into account the rationalist approach of state to seek co-operation for as long as relative gains are achieved.
37. Lynn Miller, "The Subordinate System: Types of Regional Organizations", in *The International Politics of Regions: A Comparative Approach*, edited by Louis J. Cantori and Steven L. Spiegel (Englewood Cliffs, New Jersey: Prentice Hall, Inc., 1970), Chapter 1.
38. Stephen Walt, *The Origin of Alliances* (Ithaca and London: Cornell University Press), 1987.
39. Ibid.
40. For more on this argument, see Nikolas Busse, "Constructivism and the Southeast Asian Security", *Pacific Review* 12, no. 1 (1999): 39–60.
41. Ibid., p. 43.
42. Frank Frost, "The Origins and Evolution of ASEAN", *World Review* 19, no. 3 (1980).
43. *New Straits Times*, 5 May 1989.
44. See Amitav Acharya, "The Association of Southeast Asian Nations: 'Security Community or Defence Community'?", *Pacific Affairs* 64, no. 2 (1991): 159–78.
45. Robert Keohane and Joseph S. Nye, *Power and Interdependence*, 2nd ed. (Glenville, IL: Scott Foresman, 1989), pp. 28–29.
46. There are a number of studies on the theory of regional integration. See, for example, Philip E. Jacob and James V. Toscano, eds., *The Integration of Political Communities* (Philadelphia: Lippencott, 1964), Ernst B. Haas, *Beyond the Nation-State* (Stanford: Stanford University Press, 1964), and Leon Lindberg and Stuart A. Scheingold, eds., *Regional Integration: Theory and Research* (Cambridge, MA: Harvard University Press, 1971).
47. See Ernst B. Haas, *The Obsolescence of Regional Integration Theory* (Berkeley: University of California Press, 1975).
48. Charles A. Duffy and Werner J. Feld, "Wither Regional Integration Theory", in *Comparative Regional Systems*, edited by Gavin Boyd and Werner Feld (New York: Pergamon Press, 1980), p. 497.
49. See Muthiah Alagappa, ed., *Asian Security Practice: Material and Ideational Influences* (Stanford, California: Stanford University Press, 1998), pp. 53–62.

50. As pointed out by Robert O. Keohane, "International Institutions: Can Interdependence Work?", *Foreign Policy* (Spring 1998), p. 88.
51. See Alexander Wendt, "Constructing International Politics", *International Security* 20, no. 1 (1995).
52. Ibid., p. 73.
53. Ibid.
54. Ted Hopf, "The Promise of Constructivism in International Relations Theory", *International Security* 23, no. 1 (1998): 173.
55. Wendt, "Constructing International Politics" (emphasis added).
56. Alexander Wendt, "Anarchy is What States Make of It: The Social Construction of Power Politics", *International Organization* 46, no. 2 (1992): 391–425.
57. Shaun Narine, "ASEAN and the International Relations Theory", in *CANCAPS Bulletin*, No. 11 (November 1996), pp. 8–10.
58. See Ron Jepperson, Alexander Wendt, and Peter Kazenstein, "Norms, Identities and Culture in National Security", in *The Culture of National Security: Norms and Identity in World Politics*, edited by Peter Kazenstein (New York: Columbia University Press), 1996.
59. Wendt, "Anarchy is What States Make of It".
60. Henri Tajfel, *Human Groups and Social Categories: Studies in Social Psychology* (Cambrige, UK: Cambridge University Press, 1981), p. 255, as cited in Hopf, "The Promise of Constructivism", p. 175.
61. Gregory A. Raymond, "Problems and Prospects in the Study of International Norms", *International Studies Review*, No. 1 (1997), pp. 205–45. For this specific point, see p. 214. See also Martha Finnemore and Kathryn Sikkink, "International Norm Dynamics and Political Change", *International Organization* 52, no. 4 (1998).
62. John Gerard Ruggie, "What Makes the World Hang Together? Neo-utiliarianism and the Social Constructivist Challenge", *International Organization* 52, no. 4 (1998): 855–85 (emphasis added).
63. Ibid., p. 871.
64. Raymond, "Problems and Prospects", p. 214.
65. Hopf, "The Promise of Constructivism", p. 177.
66. Ruggie, "What Makes the World Hang Together?" (emphasis added).
67. Hopf, "The Promise of Constructivism", p. 193.
68. Ibid.
69. Ibid., p. 179.
70. Richard K. Ashley, "Foreign Policy as Political Performance," *International Studies Notes* (1988), p. 53.
71. Finnermore and Sikkink, "International Norm Dynamics", p. 902.
72. Alexander Wendt, "Collective Identity Formation and the International State", *American Political Science Review* 88 (June 1994): 386.
73. Rey Koslowski and Friedrich V. Kratochwil, "Understanding Change in International Politics: The Soviet Empire's Demise and the International

System", *International Organization* 48, no. 2 (1994): 215–47. See particularly pp. 216 and 222–27.

74. Hopf, "The Promise of Constructivism", p. 180.
75. Richard Higgott, "Ideas, Identity and Policy Coordination in the Asia-Pacific", *Pacific Review* 7, no. 4 (1994): 367–78.
76. Judith Goldstein and Robert O. Keohane, eds., *Ideas and Foreign Policy: Beliefs, Institutions and Political Change* (Ithaca: Cornell University Press, 1993), p. 3.
77. Thomas Risse-Kappen, "Ideas Do Not Float Freely: Transnational Coalitions, Domestic Structures, and the End of the Cold War", *International Organizations* 48, no. 2 (1994): 186.
78. See Peter M. Haas, ed., "Knowledge, Power and International Policy Coordination", Special Issue of *International Organization* 46, no. 1 (1992).
79. See John Mearsheimer, "The False Promise of International Relations", *International Security* 19, no. 3 (1994/1995): 5–49.
80. Ibid., p. 44.
81. See Wendt, "Constructing International Politics".
82. Ibid., p. 74.
83. Ibid., p. 81.
84. Hopf, "The Promise of Constructivism", p. 196.
85. Ibid., p. 197 (emphasis added).
86. John Ruggie, "What Makes the World Hang Together...".
87. This summary is found in Alagappa, ed., *Asian Security Practice*, p. 60. Alagappa's summary draws heavily on the work of Alexander Wendt whose various work include those that have been separately cited above.
88. Ibid. (emphasis added).
89. These principles were identified by Noordin Sopiee of the Institute of Strategic and International Studies (ISIS-Malaysia) and are reproduced in Hadi Soesastro, ed., *ASEAN in a Changed Regional and International Political Economy* (Jakarta: Centre for Strategic and International Studies, 1995), pp. iii–ix.
90. Brian Job, "Matters of Multilateralism: Implications for Regional Conflict Management", in *Regional Orders: Building Security in a New World*, edited by David A. Lake and Patrick M. Morgan (Pennsylvania: Pennsylvania State University Press, 1997), p. 176.

# 2

## ASEAN'S MECHANISMS OF CONFLICT MANAGEMENT
## Revisiting the ASEAN way

### INTRODUCTION

This chapter will discuss the evolution of ASEAN's mechanisms of conflict management (CM) by providing a historical narrative of ASEAN's development as a regional organization. In revisiting these mechanisms, it is useful to bear in mind the various kinds of techniques and strategies that regional organizations use to manage or resolve conflict as discussed in the previous chapter. To reiterate, these mechanisms range from: norm-building, assurance, community-building, deterrence, non-intervention, isolation, intervention, and internationalization.

Before we begin, it is helpful to highlight a number of significant points to consider in examining the way mechanisms are developed and how these mechanisms are used to manage conflicts. The first point to note is the classification of these various types of mechanisms. These mechanisms of CM can either be formally based on institutionalized methods or adopted informally with co-operation being tacit among member parties. A combination of both formal and informal methods can also be used. The next point to consider is that regardless of whether the mechanisms are formal or informal in nature, what is significant in assessing these mechanisms is the choice of which mechanism to deploy in certain times of crises. In this regard, the choice would also very much depend on the nature of the conflict itself and the kind of outcome desired.

The third point to note is the feasibility of these mechanisms in practice and their relevance in managing conflicts at both domestic and regional levels. Muthiah Alagappa, whose classification of the types of mechanisms of CM formed the basis of this study, noted that while there is a range of mechanisms that should be easily available to regional organizations — given the kind of communication and socialization that takes place among them — one needs to focus on the more important questions of whether these mechanisms are feasible in practice and whether these mechanisms are relevant in the context wherein they are used.[1] In this regard, one might realize that for most regional organizations, choosing and determining which mechanisms are feasible and relevant would often be dependent on their respective institutional capacity. Indeed, unless regional organizations have the resources and capacities to undertake such tasks, the decision to choose from a range of mechanisms available would make the exercise moot and academic.

There are also salient factors that would determine the feasibility and relevance of any chosen mechanism. These would include the degree to which member states abide or comply with regime norms and rules, and more significantly, the extent to which these norms have been institutionalized.[2] This brings us to the other point of examining the objectives of an organization to enable us to understand its norms and institutions. This would help inform our analysis of the types of mechanisms available, the choice of which mechanism to use, and then proceed to assess its feasibility and relevance in managing conflicts at regional and domestic levels.

Thus, if one were to weigh all these preliminary considerations in assessing the management or resolution of a particular conflict, it would not be surprising to discover that there are no clear guidelines or definitive framework from which a regional organization could work with. What is most often the case is that regional organizations eventually develop their own peculiar type of mechanisms for CM that are deemed appropriate to their own setting.

This seems to be the case when applied to ASEAN. Since the situational context is no doubt a salient factor in any discussion of conflict mechanisms, it is only fitting to start this discussion by revisiting the historical leitmotif that has shaped the nature of these mechanisms. Hence, we begin this chapter with a brief overview of ASEAN's history to provide the historical backdrop that had influenced and shaped its embryonic mechanisms of conflict management.

## I. ASEAN AND THE NEED FOR A REGIONAL MECHANISM OF CONFLICT MANAGEMENT

As noted in Chapter 1, one of the core reasons why regional security organizations are established is to ameliorate the insecurity complex of member states as well as to resolve disputes peacefully. ASEAN was formed with that reason in mind, although this was not explicitly mentioned in any of the documents that have been produced when it was established in 1967.

The political milieu of the 1960s very much explains the impetus why states in Southeast Asia decided to form ASEAN. It was a very significant decade for the new states in the region as most of them have just come out of the throes of colonialism. Each state in the region had to grapple with their new experiences of being independent, including the vital task of nation-building. To these states, the task of building a nation was in itself formidable. The founding members of ASEAN — Indonesia, Malaysia, the Philippines, Singapore, and Thailand — had to confront their domestic problems that ranged from rebuilding a ravaged economy, reconciling contending political forces in their respective societies, legitimizing political leadership, and consolidating their political regimes. More importantly also was the preoccupation of achieving and maintaining national peace and security.

Yet, while most states in the region were focusing their efforts on the primacy of nation-building, striking a stark contrast were the Indochinese states of Vietnam, Laos, and Cambodia that were still very much engaged in civil war. These wars spilled over their respective national boundaries. It was not until the momentous year of 1975 when South Vietnam fell to the communist North, leading to the establishment of the Socialist Republic of Vietnam, and followed by the fall of Laos and Cambodia to the communist forces when that part of the region had achieved some semblance of peace, albeit temporarily. Still, it was a region that was ideologically divided among the non-communist states of Indonesia, Malaysia, the Philippines, Singapore, and Thailand on the one side and their communist Indochinese neighbours on the other.[3] Myanmar (then Burma) on the other hand found itself isolated from this ideological divide and insulated itself from the contending forces of communism and anti-communism having adopted an isolationist stance since its independence from the British in 1948.

In the region, it was only Thailand that was not colonized. Nevertheless, it was not immune to the problems experienced by its newly independent neighbours, which not only found themselves beset by mammoth domestic troubles but also having had to similarly contend with the seriousness of the communist insurgency problems at home. Suffice it to say, however, that this troubled environment extended beyond the national border of these states. In fact, the regional conditions at that time were characterized by intramural tensions and mistrust, whilst the pattern of relations among these states was interfused with that of amity and enmity.

Beyond the region, the decade of the 1960s was also one that was marked by sudden shifts in the foreign policy of the United States, the former Soviet Union, and Great Britain. These were the major powers, which at some point in history held great stakes in the emerging new states in the region. Basically, that shift meant a gradual disengagement of their forces from the region, leaving the states with the perception that their own security guarantees were not only weakening but may in fact be diminishing. There was also the perceived re-emergence of China that further heightened the insecurity felt by these non-communist states particularly as seen against the light of their insurgency problems and China's support of the communist parties within their respective states. Thus, the perception about the possible threats emanating from their communist neighbours and the overarching concern over the possibility that the "domino theory" — the belief that when one non-communist state falls to communism, the rest will follow — were to become a reality further buttressed the argument for the need for these non-communist states to join forces and find a way to address their common problems. Underpinning this concern was also the realization by the national leaders of Indonesia, Malaysia, the Philippines, Singapore, and Thailand that in the midst of these conflicts something more had to be done to improve their deteriorating relations.

This was the political mood at that time in history. But this was not the first time these states decided to work together. Prior to the establishment of ASEAN, there had already been several attempts by certain states in the region to resolve regional problems. In 1961, there was the Association of Southeast Asia (ASA) formed in Bangkok on 31 July, comprising Malaysia (then known as Malaya), the Philippines, and Thailand. ASA's objectives emphasized regional co-operation in the economic, social, cultural, scientific, and administrative fields. ASA was significant because its principles and objectives were very much the same as those of ASEAN. While ASA was very much a low-profile organization, its success however was short-lived given the steady deterioration of relations between Malaysia and the Philippines when the latter staked its claim to North Borneo (now known as Sabah) in 1962, and when it became a part of the Malayan federation in September 1963.[4] The Philippines' claim to Sabah in fact later became a serious problem that threatened the future of a fledgling ASEAN and shall be dealt with separately in the later part of the chapter. ASA was also short-lived because it did not include Indonesia. At the time of ASA's inception, Indonesia apparently did not share the sentiments of the other states of the need to establish a regional organization. Furthermore, ASA was seen as too anti-communist, thus further deepening the ideological schism that already plagued the region.

The Philippine–Malaysian dispute gave rise to another, even short-lived, regional association called Maphilindo, which was an acronym for Malaya, the Philippines, and Indonesia. Formed in 1962, Maphilindo was supposed to be a diplomatic device "ostensibly intended to reconcile the contending interests over the legitimacy and territorial bounds of Malaysia".[5] However, like its predecessor, it could not be sustained since Indonesia had protested against the formation of the Malayan Federation on 16 September 1963. Soon after this protest, Indonesia launched the policy of *Konfrontasi. Konfrontasi* was a reflection of Indonesia's objections to the inclusion of the Borneo states of Sabah and Sarawak into the Malayan Federation. The formation of the new federation was perceived by Indonesia to be a neo-colonialist plot that ignored the wishes of the people of Borneo. The *Konfrontasi* episode lasted until August 1966 when Sukarno fell from power.[6]

It is indeed ironic that while the formation of Maphilindo, which was a Philippine initiative, was supposed to appeal to the three nations of Malay origin and thus deepen co-operation among them underpinned by their primordial affinities, on the contrary it actually exposed the mutual suspicions that these three states had of one another. In fact, it was their suspicions that led them to join the Association. For Malaysia, joining Maphilindo was intended to make it easier to expand the Malayan Federation that would have comprised the Peninsular Malaya, North Borneo (Sabah and Sarawak), Singapore, and even Brunei. For the Philippines, the motivation was to claim back Sabah, while for Indonesia, Maphilindo was an institution that provided the opportunity to exert its influence in the affairs of Malaya by appealing to the organization's spirit. Given these motivations, it was not surprising that Maphilindo could not get off the ground. Furthermore, as one scholar aptly described, "the acts of aggression during *Konfrontasi* ... basically destroyed the credibility of both Indonesia and Maphilindo."[7]

In spite of the earlier failed attempts and the acrimonious relations notably between the Philippines and Malaysia and that of Malaysia and Indonesia, these setbacks did not stand in the way for these states to restart their efforts in embarking on another venture of regional co-operation. On 8 August 1967, ASEAN was formed in Bangkok, Thailand with the Foreign Ministers of the five founding member states signing the first ASEAN document, known as the ASEAN Declaration. The ASEAN or Bangkok Declaration laid down the foundations for regional co-operation in Southeast Asia with the goals of regional peace and stability, and the commitment of member states to pursue the objectives of:

1. "active collaboration on matters of common interest in the economic, social, cultural, technical, scientific and administrative fields;
2. mutual assistance in training and research in the educational, professional, technical and administrative spheres;
3. collaboration for greater utilization of their agriculture and industries, expansion of trade (including study of the problems of the international commodity trade), improvement of transportation and communication facilities, and raising the living standard of their people; and
4. maintenance of close and beneficial co-operation with existing international and regional organization with similar aims and purposes."[8]

Thus, the formation of ASEAN in 1967 was an affirmation of the commitment of the founding members to relentlessly pursue co-operative efforts in building peace and stability despite of the initial setbacks.

On hindsight, the collapse of ASA and Maphilindo could be attributed to a significant factor that was not found in the earlier efforts to start a regional organization. Although it was obvious at the time that there was hardly any mutuality of interests and goals, and while the region was beset with intra-state disputes, there was also *no mechanism* in place to solve the regional problems that the states in the region were confronted with. Therefore, the formation of ASEAN could be considered as the first serious attempt by regional states to institutionalize a mechanism for managing regional conflicts. ASEAN's establishment had provided the overall framework where member states could manage their conflicting relations. Specifically, with the formation of ASEAN, the member states provided themselves "a stable structure of relations for managing and containing tensions among governments of corresponding political disposition".[9] In other words, ASEAN had, for all intents and purposes, become a "diplomatic device" for subregional reconciliation.[10]

Against this historical experience, we now turn to examine ASEAN's record in conflict management in Southeast Asia within the context of two inter-related domains, namely: (1) intramural domain, which refers to the affairs among the subregional members, and (2) extramural domain, which refers to the affairs extending within and beyond the Southeast Asian region. The following discussion will, therefore, be divided into these two domains to enable us to better identify the kinds of mechanisms that ASEAN has developed over a period of time, starting from its inception, its formative years, its consolidation and expansion, and at this current phase of reconsolidation. This will also help us better assess the effectiveness or limitations of such mechanisms as seen against the dynamics of both domestic and regional politics, as well as track the changes, if any, to the existing mechanisms.

The next section will now proceed to identify the mechanisms of conflict management that are relevant to the intramural or interstate conflict within ASEAN, while the extramural domain will be dealt separately in the subsequent chapters of this book.

## II. FORMAL MECHANISMS FOR MANAGING CONFLICT IN ASEAN

As observed earlier, the very formation of ASEAN institutionalized a framework for member states to manage their disputes. The institutionalization of ASEAN has subsequently generated a number of important mechanisms which can be classified into two types: (1) formal mechanisms and (2) informal or normative mechanisms. This distinction follows Alagappa's classification of mechanisms of conflict management as discussed earlier.

Formal mechanisms can be sub-divided into: (1) the institutionalized framework of discussions and consultations on matters of mutual interest, (2) the institutionalized bilateral mechanisms and processes, and (3) the legal instruments that are meant to prevent and manage disputes.

### Institutionalized Framework of Consultative Mechanisms

At the organizational level, this framework is reflected in the institutionalization of different meetings that are held regularly among ASEAN officials. These are divided into the following:

1.  The *ASEAN Summits* have been one of the most visible institutionalized mechanisms in promoting political co-operation among member states in ASEAN. It is during the summit meetings that the highest level of

decision-making takes place. The first summit was held in Bali in 1976, nine years after the establishment of ASEAN and was followed the next year in Kuala Lumpur. It took another ten years before the ASEAN Heads met again in 1987, and another five years before they met in Singapore in 1992. The reason for these long gaps in between will be explained in more detail in the latter part of this chapter. Nonetheless, these gaps were indicative of the kinds of tensions experienced among ASEAN members during these periods that prevented the holding of these meetings. These summits, however, became more frequent as relations improved and other mechanisms were set in place to address certain bilateral frictions.

At their Fourth Summit in Singapore, the ASEAN leaders decided to meet formally every three years — hence the Fifth Summit in Bangkok in 1995. But during the Bangkok Summit, they subsequently decided to meet informally every year in between their formal summits. The purpose was to improve ASEAN's capacity to set policy directions and to address regional issues more effectively and in a timely manner. Since then, the ASEAN leaders have been meeting formally or informally every year.

2.  The *ASEAN Ministers Meetings (AMM)*, the next level of decision-making in ASEAN, are held annually and are sometimes convened on an *ad hoc* basis. In the formative years of ASEAN until 1977, these ministerial meetings were initially held only among ASEAN Foreign Ministers. Since then, ASEAN ministers in charge of various sectors such as health, education, labour, and environment also began to meet regularly. The ASEAN Economic Ministers Meeting, for example, was established in 1977 and has been held annually. More recently, the ASEAN Finance Ministers have been meeting regularly since 1997 to discuss pertinent issues such as financial co-operation in the region.

3.  The *ASEAN Post-Ministerial Conference (PMC)* usually follows the annual ASEAN Ministerial Meetings among ASEAN Foreign Ministers. These meetings provide ASEAN Foreign Ministers the opportunity to meet their counterparts from dialogue partner countries.[11] During the early 1990s, the PMCs provided the venue for ASEAN states to discuss security concerns until the establishment of the ASEAN Regional Forum (ARF) in 1994, which was launched precisely for consultations on security matters.

4.  Initially, the *ASEAN Senior Official Meeting (SOM)* was established during the Manila Summit of 1987 to assist the ASEAN Foreign Ministers in matters pertaining to political co-operation. The ASEAN Senior Economic Officials Meeting (SEOM) was also established at the same Summit to assist in areas of economic co-operation. Subsequently, SOMs in certain issue areas that fall within the general ambit of intra-ASEAN co-operation were created and meetings held on a regular basis to provide inputs to AMMs and other ASEAN agencies. Since 1994, special SOMs were also held to bring together ASEAN's political and defence officials to enhance political and security co-operation.[12]

    The SOMS are complemented by numerous meetings of other *ad hoc* and permanent committees whose work dovetail with the work of the ASEAN Standing Committee that monitors and co-ordinates most the meetings taking place in ASEAN.[13]

In sum, these meetings have been a prominent feature of ASEAN's process of cementing regional ties and maintaining a convivial regional environment. With a total number of meeting averaging about 300 held within one year, the time and effort invested in such a venture need no further elaboration. Firstly, the functions of these institutional meetings serve more than just instilling the habits of dialogue and consultation among ASEAN members. Secondly, these meetings significantly make up more than the procedural elements of the types of mechanisms that are meant to build trust and assurance among members for closer political co-operation. Finally, these numerous functional meetings, which have been categorized as institutionalized mechanisms, also deepen the process of socialization of ASEAN political leaders and officials, hence inducting them into the overall ASEAN mechanisms of co-operation.

The foundations of this type of institutionalized consultative mechanisms were formulated in the Bangkok Declaration of 1967. The areas for consultative meetings were re-emphasized a decade later in the ASEAN Concord, a document that was adopted at the historic first ASEAN Summit in Bali, Indonesia in February 1976. Specifically, the ASEAN Concord strengthened the foundations of closer political co-operation and outlined three specific areas of action under the sub-section on political co-operation which are of particular interest in this chapter since these relate to the subject on conflict management. These areas are:

1.   "settlement of intra-regional disputes by peaceful means as soon as possible";
2.   "immediate consideration of initial steps towards recognition of and respect for the Zone of Peace, Freedom and Neutrality wherever possible," and
3.   "strengthening of political solidarity by promoting the harmonization of views, co-ordinating position and, where possible and desirable, taking common actions."

It can clearly be seen from the three areas cited above that political co-operation and peaceful settlement of dispute were already the dominant themes. In fact, it was only when ASEAN adopted the ASEAN Concord I and held its first summit that political co-operation was finally "accorded its obvious place in the practice of regionalism".[14]

Over time, the institutionalized framework of frequent consultations and regular meetings as provided in the ASEAN Concord I had been used increasingly to discuss regional and international issues, particularly those pertaining to political and security matters. During these meetings, contentious issues are ironed out to the extent possible and differences harmonized which consequently enabled ASEAN to adopt common positions in regional affairs. These institutionalized meetings enabled ASEAN to play a more effective role on regional and international matters and even exert some influence in regional affairs. The best example of this was ASEAN's role in the political settlement of the Cambodian conflict since its start in 1978 up to the culmination of the internationally supervised national elections held in 1993. This will be dealt with separately in Chapter 3. At this point, suffice it to say that the overarching framework of meetings and consultations not only complements but also further strengthens the bilateral avenues for co-operation and conflict management that already exist between member states.

## Institutionalized Bilateral Mechanisms and Processes

Before moving on to the legal instruments, it should be added that outside the formal ASEAN institutional framework of consultations are *bilateral mechanisms and processes* that have been in place. These bilateral mechanisms had been set up to address matters of security interests between member states. One of these is the *ad hoc* political and diplomatic dialogues which begin at the level of the Heads of

Governments to discuss matters of mutual interests, aside from security issues. Among these include the meeting between the Philippine President and the Malaysian Prime Minister in January 1993, which was held to foster better understanding between these two states still locked horns over the Sabah claim. This meeting did not only provide a psychological boost to what was once a lukewarm relationship but served to improve relations between these two states. More recently, were the meetings between former Singapore Prime Minister Goh Chok Tong and Malaysian Prime Minister Mahathir Mohamad held in Kuala Lumpur in November 1998, a period when Malaysia–Singapore relations were very strained due to the bilateral problems relating to Singapore Government's demands that Malaysia move its customs and immigration facilities from Tanjong Pagar in downtown Singapore to Woodlands near the border; Singapore's refusal to allow people from Peninsular Malaysia to withdraw their savings from Singapore's Central Provident Fund; and the negative comments in Singapore Senior Minister Lee Kuan Yew's memoirs regarding some former Malaysian leaders. The meeting agreed that outstanding bilateral issues like Airspace and Water Supply Agreements would not be compromised by these problems.[15] This series of bi-summits have almost become a regular feature in the Malaysia–Singapore relations as a way of clarifying certain positions with regard to bilateral disputes and paving the way for political settlements on some of them.

The other institutionalized bilateral mechanisms are the long-established joint committees and commissions that usually deal with border issues. These would include:

1.  Joint Border Commission between Malaysia and Indonesia
2.  Joint Border Commission between Malaysia and Thailand
3.  Joint Border Commission between Malaysia and the Philippines
4.  Joint Border Commission between Thailand and Myanmar

The Malaysia/Thailand and Malaysia/Indonesia General Border Committees were constituted specifically to combat insurgency problems along the two common borders.[16] The Malaysia–Philippines Joint Commission for Bilateral Co-operation was established in the mid-1990s to help, among others, patrol the illegal immigrants from Southern Philippines to East Malaysia and also enhance protection for Filipino workers. There are also the defence co-operation, joint military exercises, and intelligence exchanges which represent another important form of bilateral mechanisms for enhancing security in the region. The bilateral joint military exercises among Indonesia, Malaysia, and Singapore are the most common examples. While this mechanism has not been adopted region-wide, the importance of such mechanisms to building confidence, increasing transparency, and forging close personal ties among security personnel at the highest levels in nurturing a security community cannot be underestimated. In ASEAN, this has been of substantial value.[17]

## Legal Instruments

### The Treaty of Amity and Co-operation (TAC)

The TAC is the only attempt by ASEAN to provide the arrangement and the legal instrument for member states to order their relations according to explicitly prescribed, universally accepted principles and provide for peaceful settlement of disputes. These basic principles are:

1.  mutual respect for the independence, sovereignty, equality, territorial integrity, and national identity of all nations;
2.  the right of every state to lead its national existence free from external interference, subversion, and coercion;
3.  non-interference in the internal affairs of one another;
4.  settlement of differences or disputes by peaceful means;
5.  renunciation of threat or use of forces; and
6.  effective co-operation among members.

Although the Treaty can be regarded as a mere reiteration of ASEAN's vision, its significance is in its introduction of a specific mechanism for peaceful settlement of disputes among ASEAN members. Article 14 of the Treaty provides for a High Council comprising representatives at ministerial level from each of the contracting parties to take cognizance of the disputes. In Article 15, this entity is empowered "to recommend to the parties in dispute appropriate means of settlement such as good offices, mediation, inquiry or conciliation. If the disputing parties so agree, it may constitute into a committee of mediation, inquiry or conciliation."[18]

Ironically, while the Treaty finally provided ASEAN with a specific and formal mechanism for the pacific settlement of disputes, this High Council has not been constituted at all and to date no member state has sought recourse to any of the given provisions. It is important, therefore, to examine why this has been the case and note the caveats to this mechanism.

The first limitation to this Treaty is in the loose manner in which this Council may be allowed to act in instances of disputes. Secondly, and perhaps even more salient, is that parties to a dispute are not strictly bound to accept the mediation of the other members of the High Council. As one legal scholar acutely observed, the Treaty has many caveats, in effect making it ineffective. Examples of the caveats are:

"1. There is no specific provisions that the representatives in the High Council must be lawyers. If they were politicians, [the reservations would be that] the approach would tend to be political rather than legal.
2. The role of the High Council only comes into play 'in the event that no solution is resolved through direct negotiations'. If the disputing parties have not negotiated with each other directly, and failed to reach a solution, the High Council is not empowered to take the initiative in disputes settlement.
3. There is no compulsion for the parties to utilize the High Council, nor is there a means of imposing sanctions on the parties. The voluntary nature of the mechanism is thus based upon compromise rather than binding decisions. Moreover, the ASEAN mechanism is not exclusive in that the disputing parties may use other modes of peaceful settlement contained in Article 33(1) of the United Nations Charter."[19]

It appears from the given observations that the major limitations of the TAC lie in its emphases on voluntarism and the exercise of choice as provided for in the Treaty's provisions. But one can argue that it is precisely because of this flexible procedure — allowing for freedom to choose which course of action to take — that appears to work in ASEAN's advantage. Flexibility was a deliberate choice over rigid, well-defined procedures, and in its experience this has made the exercise of conflict management a more manageable task for ASEAN.

The significance of flexibility can be appreciated if one considers the issue of impartiality, particularly with reference to settling territorial disputes among member states. This has been a major concern for member states of ASEAN. If territorial disputes were referred to the High Council, convening it may be problematic considering that in Southeast Asia, other than Cambodia and Laos, almost all states have outstanding border or territorial dispute with Malaysia. This in effect already limits the parties eligible to comprise the members of the High Council.[20]

In the context of ASEAN's relations with the rest of the states within and outside the region, it is also important to note that the Treaty has been made open for accession by other countries in the region. During the Manila Summit in 1987, the Treaty was amended to allow non-Southeast Asian states "contiguous" to the region to accede to the Treaty by "the consent of all states in Southeast Asia which are signatories to this treaty and Brunei Darussalam". This amendment, dubbed the Manila Protocol, was met with caution by certain members within the association, particularly Indonesia which felt that this amendment will allow interference from external powers in certain domestic and regional problems and may abuse the Treaty's provision relating to pacific settlement of disputes.

Nevertheless, whatever limitations there are to the Treaty, it had at least laid down the principle that disputes between and among ASEAN states were to be settled bilaterally and/or preferably within the region to the extent possible and without outside interference. This approach yet again underscores the determination of ASEAN, at least at that time, to ensure that whatever and whenever disputes arise, these should be solved internally. This zealousness over keeping matters internally has been part of the broader principle, that is, of having "Asian solutions to Asian problems". It can be recalled that this phrase was made popular in the 1920s by Japan and was also a tenet of Thai foreign policy in the 1960s. This reflected the preference of Asians to solve their problems in their own way rather than "inviting" outsiders (in this case, usually the Western countries) to offer advice about policies concerning national development and international conflict. The phrase "Asia for the Asians" by the late president of the Philippines, Claro M. Recto, conveys a similar view that outsiders "have too marginal an interest or understanding of Asian problems to be in a position to make a genuine contribution to Asia, except under very limited and temporary circumstances".[21] This principle dovetails with Indonesia's recommended regional policy on "regional resilience" emanating from "national resilience". The extent that this principle has been practised is debatable but this theme has again resurfaced quite recently in the discourses of increasing ASEAN political and security co-operation. In fact this has been a favourite theme also echoed by ASEAN leaders, particularly the former Malaysian Prime Minister Mahathir Mohamad who has called for the ASEAN way to peace.[22] It is also interesting that many in the region share the same sentiment which therefore brings to the fore the inevitable question of whether there is in fact an ASEAN way to manage disputes.

## Zone of Peace, Freedom and Neutrality (ZOPFAN)

Complementing the TAC as a mechanism for CM is the Declaration of the Zone of Peace, Freedom and Neutrality (ZOPFAN). Although not a legal instrument, ZOPFAN is also an important document that was intended to guide and define ASEAN's relations vis-à-vis extra-regional states. ZOPFAN was the first clear indication of the association's idea of what the code of conduct of states, both within and outside the region, should be. While the theme of regional resilience would find itself echoed so often within the context of ASEAN's continuing efforts in defining regional security, ZOPFAN reflected the growing concern at that time of the political and security uncertainties confronting the region. With the communists having just consolidated their powers in Indochina, juxtaposed against the cutting down of the United States' presence in the region, the entente between China and the United States, and the Soviet Union's call for a collective security among the states of Asia and Pacific, ZOPFAN then seemed to be ASEAN's ideal response to what was perceived as an imminent communist threat.

The ZOPFAN document was not and is still not an ASEAN declaration of neutrality but rather a declaration of intent which does not (once again) impose legal obligations to its signatories.[23] However, drawn mainly from the preambles of the Bangkok Declaration, the ZOPFAN document actually reiterated the fundamental ideals and aspirations of ASEAN, which in essence has been the freedom from external interference. This was most clearly articulated in the statement "the right of every state, large or small, to lead its national existence free from outside inteference in its internal affairs."[24] According to one analysis, when applied in the regional context, neutrality in ZOPFAN is essentially about: "1) the non-participation and impartiality of the Southeast Asian states in conflict between other, especially extra-regional states, and 2) the non-interference of external powers in the domestic and regional affairs of the neutral states."[25]

In a way, the concern at that time for ASEAN members to be perceived as neutral in the midst of superpower rivalry fitted well with the region's sentiment for the observance and sanctity of the non-interference principle. This "rule of the game" has found its way ever so often in the statements of ASEAN leaders and officials.

At this juncture, one would ask that since the TAC and, to a lesser extent, the ZOPFAN Declaration have never been fully utilized, what had been ASEAN's *modus operandi* of settling disputes? As can be observed from the foregoing discussion, no dispute has been brought for ASEAN as a corporate entity to resolve. Bilateral disputes are left to the parties concerned to be resolved or managed bilaterally. ASEAN, through its formal mechanism, has so far provided only a framework for member states to structure their relationship with each other. However, some ASEAN states have also offered to act as facilitator in bilateral disputes. An example of this type of *ad hoc* arrangement at that time was Indonesia's role as some kind of an interlocutor in the Malaysia–Philippine conflict over Sabah. This "informal" third-party mediation is discussed in the next part of this chapter.

Following these formal and legal instruments of TAC and the Declaration of ZOPFAN were the Declaration on the South China Sea adopted in Manila on 22 July 1992, and the Treaty on the Southeast Asia Nuclear Weapons-Free Zone that was concluded in Bangkok on 15 December 1995. This will not be discussed in full detail but are mentioned here to highlight the point that legal instruments are now being developed by the association.

## III. INFORMAL MECHANISMS OF CONFLICT MANAGEMENT

Since the only legal mechanism of dispute management that can be found in ASEAN has not only allowed for so much flexibility but has *not* been used at all, this perhaps provides the best indication that the preferred ASEAN way of managing disputes is clearly outside the parameters of formal structures and institutions of conflict resolution. Nevertheless, the reluctance to use formal mechanisms is not only due to the inadequacy of formal structures but also in the preference of ASEAN states to limit its role in managing conflict to conflict prevention. Thus, whatever identifiable elements that one can discern which relate to the ASEAN's informal mechanisms of CM are limited within the framework of avoiding conflict or containing it to prevent it from disrupting interstate relations. In the literature on conflict management discussed in Chapter 1, conflict avoidance is the first stage of managing conflict in the whole gamut of processes for resolving conflicts.

The elements of conflict avoidance do not, however, preclude the use of other means of problem-solving mechanisms. In the case of ASEAN, not confronting certain problems head-on allows for time to focus on other important issues that promote closer regional co-operation. Moreover, by allowing time to pass, the expectation is that the intensity of a problem is reduced and the cost of solving the problem is also considerably lowered. Hence, the preference for conflict avoidance in ASEAN is an informed choice given the situational dynamics in the region. The rationale for a "limited" role will become clearer as we track the evolution of these informal mechanisms as they are applied in selected cases of conflict. Nevertheless, carrying out the task of avoiding conflict is not really as easy as it may appear. This has certainly necessitated an ASEAN member having to imbibe or internalize certain regular patterns of behaviour or habits over a period a time to meet the objectives of avoiding conflicts in the region. These discernable patterns of behaviour or norms and informal processes have been encapsulated in the so-called ASEAN way of doing things.

Indeed, much has already been written about the ASEAN way, but as a mechanism or set of mechanisms of managing conflict, it is useful for this study to draw out its elements. In their respective but similar works, Hoang and Caballero-Anthony have highlighted the elements of the ASEAN way of managing conflicts as: adherence to ground rules enshrined in ASEAN's diverse declaration and communiqués; emphasis on self-restraint, acceptance of the practices of *musyawarah* and *muafakat* (consultation and consensus), using third-party mediation to settle disputes, and agreeing to disagree while shelving the settlement of conflicts.[26] Moreover, as a mechanism for guiding behaviour and in mediating disputes, Acharya has conceived of the ASEAN way as a "process of identity building which relies upon the conventional modern principles of inter-state relations as well as traditional and culture-specific modes of socialization and decision-making that is prevalent in Southeast Asia".[27] Finally, as viewed within the broader context of examining the diplomatic and security of Southeast Asia, Haacke sums the ASEAN way as "this normative framework ... in mediating disputes, guiding interaction and underpinning a process of identity construction".[28]

Regardless of the differences in the way the ASEAN way has been conceptualized, a common feature is its usefulness as a mechanism to manage conflict. In the following discussion, the elements of these ASEAN informal mechanisms are revisited once again to examine how these had been applied to certain conflicts. These elements are grouped in a thematic way as outlined below for better illustration.

## Diplomacy of Accommodation

Adherence to ground rules and self-restraint are distinctive features of an ASEAN practice, which one scholar succinctly summed up as the "diplomacy of accommodation".[29] The diplomacy of accommodation in managing disputes entails a pattern of give and take among certain members and would encompass the three principles of the 3Rs — restraint, respect and responsibility. Restraint in this context means a general attitude of tolerance. It also means non-interference in other states, either by war, aid to insurgents, challenges to legitimacy, and comments about personalities. With restraint follows respect, which refers to "the willingness to forgo individualism by seeking other's advice and opinion". Respect is displayed when member states abide by the customary approaches to decision-making which is done through consultation and consensus. And finally, there is responsibility which is the consideration of other member's interest and sensitivities and the consciousness of the impact of one's domestic policy on their neighbours.[30]

The practice of this diplomacy of accommodation — or for our purpose as mechanism of dispute management — was clearly demonstrated in the formative stages of ASEAN, particularly when examined against the major crises that confronted the regional body in its embryonic years. Two major disputes will be briefly discussed below, namely the Malaysia–Philippine dispute over Sabah and the Indonesia–Singapore crisis.

### Territorial Dispute over Sabah (1968 – present)

As early as 1962, when the Malaysian Federation was being formed to include the North Borneo state of Sabah, the Philippines staked its claim on the territory on the historical basis that all the land on the northeastern part of Borneo were once subject to the Sultanate of Sulu, which is part of the Philippine Republic. Since then, the issue has cropped up several times in the course of ASEAN history and at certain periods, tested the limits of the association. In March 1968, barely a year after ASEAN was established, a Philippine newspaper reported the presence of a secret camp in Corregidor Island where a special force of Muslim recruits were supposed to be trained to infiltrate Sabah. No one knew exactly what happened as this account was "based" on one of the recruits who was supposed to have escaped after a mutiny occurred at the base. None the less, the Malaysian Government lodged a formal protest, providing other evidence to corroborate the fact that a plan to infiltrate Sabah was attempted. This happened at about the same time when senior officials from both countries were in the midst of conducting further talks on the Sabah claim. As discussions were getting nowhere, the Foreign Ministers of both countries agreed on a "cooling-off period" without reaching consensus on what the term "cooling-off" really meant.[31] Relations hit a low when a few months later, the Philippine Congress passed a resolution in September 1968 delineating the Philippine territorial boundaries to include Sabah. Matters got worse when the Philippines further sent a directive to its diplomats attending international conferences to "record a reservation concerning Malaysia's competence to represent Sabah". The reservation was made at a meeting of the ASEAN Permanent Committee on Commerce and Industry held on 30 September to 5 October 1968. In response, the Malaysian delegation remarked that until such reservation was retracted, it was not going to attend any further ASEAN meetings. The two countries then withdrew their diplomatic representatives from each other's capitals in November 1968. This led to a "hiatus" in ASEAN meetings until 1969.[32]

Whether influenced by the troubles at home brought about by the racial riots in Malaysia in May 1969 and the impending presidential elections in the Philippines in November of the same year, or even by the growing concern over the prospect of a political vacuum in the region brought about by U.S. President Nixon's announcement of the Guam Doctrine in July signalling the gradual disengagement of American forces in Asia, the two acrimonious neighbours decided to set aside their differences for the sake of regional co-operation. The Philippines finally agreed to revoke its reservation of the Malaysian representation of Sabah and the region saw the Third ASEAN Ministerial Meeting held in December 1969. In that meeting, the normalization of relations between the two countries was announced.

If one examines how the three principles of restraint, respect, and responsibility were applied in this case, it is interesting to note the way the dynamics of this crisis. First, in spite of the sabre-rattling that went on between the two states, restraint prevailed. At the height of the crisis, Malaysia did in fact display some semblance of military show of force. It had six RAF hunter jet fighters deliberately fly over Sabah's capital en route to Hong Kong to their base in Singapore and through its British alliance partner, a flotilla of British warships sailed through Philippine waters close to Sabah, although giving prior notice of their passage.[33] This could have triggered some military response from the Philippines, yet this did not occur. And when one considers the seriousness of the repercussions of the Corregidor affair, it is remarkable that Malaysia did not do more but settle for a formal diplomatic protest. While it would indeed be too much to expect an all-out military confrontation between these two acrimonious neighbours, the fact that no one considered anything more than diplomatic protest is in itself a manifestation of restraint exercised to the fullest.

The principle of respect was also illustrated in the Philippines' decision to drop its earlier diplomatic directive to question the competence of Malaysia to represent Sabah in its ministerial and other meetings. Respect was also shown when both Malaysia and the Philippines deferred to Indonesia's intervention to agree to a "cooling-off" period. In fact, it was also through Indonesia's intervention that the first ASEAN Summit was made possible in 1976 when it was able to seek an agreement from the Philippines that the Sabah issue was not going to be raised. As one scholar observed, the "attendance [of Indonesia, Malaysia, and the Philippines] to public consultation and ASEAN meetings ... demonstrate both awareness of interdependence with neighbours and willingness to forgo individualism by seeking others' advice and concerns".[34]

Finally, the principle of responsibility is perhaps best illustrated in the sensitivity displayed by both states of the possible repercussions of the domestic crises that were happening in their respective countries, which occurred around the same time when the bilateral dispute of Sabah was at its peak. The May racial riots in Malaysia could have been perceived by the Philippines as the ripe time to capitalize on the latter's vulnerability and push further its Sabah claim; or even a political chance to officially comment on the instability of the country due to its racial problems, but prudence prevailed at that time. Philippine officials refrained from commenting on its neighbour's problems. Malaysia displayed the same sensitivity when it did not push for the Philippine administration to drop the Sabah claim at the time when President Marcos was seeking re-election for another term.[35]

It has been over thirty years now since the Malaysia–Philippine dispute over Sabah began. While bilateral relations between both countries were restored in 1969, the Philippines has yet to drop its claim to Sabah. Since 1969, the Sabah dispute has continued to be an irritant in the relations between these two countries. However, there has been a conscious attempts by both governments not to let this issue stand in the way of improving and enhancing their bilateral relations. After a series of "start-and-stop" initiatives from the Philippines to drop the Sabah claim, the present Philippine administration has yet to announce its official renunciation.[36] In the meantime, the relations between the two governments have improved tremendously since the Sabah episode in the 1968, especially during former President Fidel Ramos' administration

(1992–98). During this period, bilateral relations were further strengthened by the development of closer economic ties. It is expected that economic linkages will be widened given the establishment of the East ASEAN Growth Area (BIMP-EAGA) that covers the Philippine province of Mindanao and its neighbouring localities in Brunei Darussalam, Indonesia, and Malaysia.

Interviews conducted with diplomats of these countries have also confirmed that bilateral relations have been enhanced since the Ramos administration. Even with the changes in leaderships in these two states, it is expected that the claim on the Sabah issue would remain dormant. Perhaps, with the increasing inter-linkages of people and economies across national boundaries, it will be much easier for the Philippines to shelve its claim indefinitely.[37]

## The Indonesia–Singapore Crisis (1968)

Another example that can demonstrate how this mechanism of diplomacy of accommodation has worked in the past is the Singapore–Indonesia tiff over the hanging of the two Indonesian marines in Singapore. This event was part of the legacy of the *Konfrontasi* period. Two Indonesian marines who had been found guilty of committing acts of sabotage in Singapore during the *Konfrontasi* period were sentenced to death and then hanged in Singapore on 17 October 1968, despite a call for clemency from former Indonesian President Soeharto. There was, in fact, also intervention from the Malaysian side when its former Prime Minister Tunku Abdul Rahman echoed calls for clemency. These calls fell on deaf ears as Singapore's position was that to have done so would have suggested that it succumbed to external pressure. The execution caused an uproar in Jakarta. The Singapore embassy in the capital was attacked while the local Chinese community in Indonesia were mobbed, indirectly becoming scapegoats for the wrath that followed.

How Singapore could have ignored the intervention of her "bigger" neighbour in the context of regional politics and good neighbourliness was quite puzzling, to say the least. This, however, was regarded as symptomatic of the insecurity of a small state caught in the middle of big neighbours. Michael Leifer offers a revealing observation as to why such a small island state like Singapore could not have had the discretion to defer to a big neighbour like Indonesia over this episode. Leifer calls this the "poison shrimp" policy adopted by Singapore to command respect from Malaysia and Indonesia, in particular.[38] According to him, Singapore being too conscious of its innate limitation "decided to adopt an abrasive, international posture in order to convince potential predators of [its] indigestible qualities".[39]

The Indonesia–Singapore crisis is perhaps an instructive example where the dynamics of accommodation is clearly demonstrated. In retrospect, perhaps Indonesia could have easily interpreted Singapore's action as highly insensitive (maybe, even disrespectful) to the wishes and sensitivities of her big neighbour. Instead, it was Indonesia's perceptive understanding of Singapore's insecurities and its sensitivity to the domestic limitations of the latter that had restrained the possibility of this crisis escalating to negative proportions. The Indonesian Government resisted popular pressure to take retaliatory actions against Singapore, and a formal commitment to suspend trade relations never went beyond nominal gestures. In fact, it is interesting to note that it was the Indonesian Foreign Minister at that time, Adam Malik, with the support of former President Soeharto, who took the initiative in trying to diffuse the conflict and engage in dispute management. And, whatever personal slight that former President Soeharto may have felt was concealed.[40]

The restraint displayed by Indonesia in adopting a magnanimous attitude to this episode, in spite of the domestic uproar did not go unnoticed by the Singapore leadership. This further convinced the other members in ASEAN and Singapore in particular of the seriousness of the Soeharto's personal commitment to ASEAN and regional co-operation. Although Indonesia–Singapore relations remained strained until the first official visit of Singapore's Lee Kuan Yew to Jakarta, Lee's gesture during this visit reciprocated Soeharto's accommodative stance. During his visit, Lee visited the Kalibata Heroes cemetery and personally scattered flower petals on the graves of the two executed marines at the national heroes' cemetery. The significance of the gesture was not lost on Soeharto and the Indonesian public. It was perceived both as an act of atonement and reconcialition and has led to a fresh start in bilateral relations. Since the visit, and at least during Lee Kuan Yew's premiership, great efforts have been taken to establish a close personal relationship with Indonesia's Soeharto.

## Singapore–Philippine Relations: A Replay?

Almost two decades later, this episode seemed to have been replayed — this time between the Philippines and Singapore over the hanging of a

Filipino maid in Singapore. Flor Contemplacion was convicted for the murder of another Filipino maid in 1995 and was hanged in spite of pleas for clemency from former Philippine President Fidel Ramos. Prior to Contemplacion's execution, the Philippine Government acting on domestic pressure insisted that the evidence pointing to the crime was questionable and that this matter be referred to a third party before the execution was to be carried out. The hanging of Contemplacion triggered an unexpected outcry in the Philippines to cut relations with Singapore. Philippine newspapers were filled with headlines of the domestic uproar, calling for the government to stop sending maids to Singapore. These public demands led to official attempts to recall back maids already in Singapore by putting on stand-by a Hercules cargo plane to bring them back to Manila. There were also reports of Singapore flags being set aflame in certain parts of the Philippines, leading Singapore to lodge an official protest with the Philippine Government. The crisis led to the resignation of the Philippine Foreign Minister Robert Romulo who was perceived by the Filipino public as having failed to carry out his job in protecting Filipino nationals overseas.

While the execution of Contemplacion touched on the bigger issue of the lack of protection for Filipino migrant workers around the world and was also exploited by the Filipino opposition during the congressional election campaign in the country, the backlash of the event nevertheless caught both administrations by surprise.[41] In spite of tremendous pressures on each side, both governments managed to exercise restraint in the months that followed, until the matter was finally referred to a third-party examination to review the evidence. The findings of the third party concurred with Singapore's claim that Contemplacion was indeed guilty of murder. The Philippines abided by the results and put the matter to rest.

In assessing the management of these crises, one would note that the Sabah dispute and the problems between Singapore and Indonesia as well as that of Singapore and the Philippines could have jeopardized bilateral ties between ASEAN member states and would have led to the disintegration of the association. While these problems may have had created diplomatic chills as in the dispute over Sabah and had in fact threatened bilateral ties as in the case of the Contemplacion case, the skilful and delicate balancing act displayed by all parties concerned in managing the problems through the adherence of certain subtle practices cannot be discounted. The process of internalizing these values of restraint, respect, and responsibility certainly took time to be achieved. Even in recent times, ASEAN has not been free from these problems. Occasional bilateral spats have surfaced from time to time. While some have gone without further ado, there were others that had caused disquiet in the domestic fronts. This would include the periodic spats between Singapore and Malaysia over a number of issues that would lead to public protests and calls by certain sections of the United Malays National Organization (UMNO), Malaysia's dominant political party, to cut ties with Singapore. Some of these events will be discussed in Chapter 6. Suffice it say at this point that in spite of these challenges that come periodically, the diplomacy of accommodation has been the informal mechanism that has allowed ASEAN to manage these bilateral frictions.

## The Practice of *Musyawarah* and *Muafakat* (Consultation and Consensus)

*Musyawarah* (consultation) and *muafakat* (consensus) are the trademarks of ASEAN in managing relations among each other. One of the major problems when a group of sovereign states come together is decision-making. It is often in this area where disputes are bound to arise, and managing competing interests requires delicate bargaining skills.

ASEAN leaders have often declared that the decision-making process within the association is guided by the practice of *musyawarah* and *muafakat*. *Musyawarah* refers to the process of discussion and consultation; and *muafakat* is decision by consensus reached through the process of *musyawarah*. These two processes are said to be adapted from the traditional village politics in certain parts of Indonesia and to some extent in Malaysia and the Philippines. Decision-making though *musyawarah* and *muafakat* have been practised by ASEAN particularly in coming out with common stance on regional affairs. For political issues, *muafakat* is strictly adhered to while a modification of this consensus through a 10-x formula (formerly 6-x) is adopted in economic matters.

In one insightful study on ASEAN negotiating styles, Thambipillai and Saravanamuttu described this pattern of decision-making as a slow, step-by-step, incremental process where decisions are arrived at only after several rounds of behind-the-scene bargaining. As explained by one scholar, cited in Thambipillai and Saravanamuttu's article:

> The concept involves the processes that develop general agreement and consensus in village assemblies which emerge as the unanimous decision or *muafakat*. This unanimous decision can be reached by a process in

which the majority and the minorities approach each other by making the necessary adjustments in their respective viewpoints or by an integration of the contrasting standpoints into a new conceptual synthesis.[42]

As a result, the process of decision-making naturally tends to be a long-drawn affair as it can involve a myriad of new positions, proposals, and initiatives, even just on a single issue, being floated for extensive consultations in several informal meetings to ensure that consensus can be reached. Note, however, that disagreements are not totally eliminated. If such occasions do arise and a consensus cannot be reached, a decision is then taken to put off decision or to decide to "agree to disagree". Disagreements, however, are rarely stated openly. As the former Malaysian Foreign Minister Tan Sri Ghazali Shafie has stated, whatever disagreements occur in any of these meetings are played down and matters are discussed behind closed doors "without the blare and glare of publicity". More importantly, this has served "to save face and maintain good relations between parties", particularly when contentious issues have to be addressed.[43]

The importance of this process cannot be ignored. One of its value as a dispute management mechanism is that it provides a way for a minority state to affirm its position without having to be dominated by the views of the majority. It is also valuable when one recognizes the fact that each member state has an equal voice, regardless of its size and economic power. According to the view of one Indonesian academic, "it is of great psychological value to have the biggest state in the group, Indonesia, to play ball with the rest of the group and for the smallest state, Brunei to have its own voice heard."[44]

While this process may appear tedious and long-drawn, it has its own advantages. As explained to me by one Filipino diplomat, before an issue is brought up for consideration by any ASEAN members, a lot of groundwork, that is, consulation, would have already been put in place by the initiating state. Since ASEAN's overall framework has allowed for extensive meeting among these ASEAN bureaucrats, there is the added advantage of officials knowing each other very well, up to the point that one could almost predict the reactions of their counterparts to a certain proposal. So, even before a proposal is introduced by the sponsoring state, it would have already been "polished" — having taken into consideration the possible reactions of other ASEAN officials.[45] These extensive meetings and more importantly the kind of socialization that takes place after that serve a strategic purpose. ASEAN officials do not only get to know each other well, but also develop the awareness of the kinds of sensitivities that involve certain political, economic, and security issues. It has been often said that to be part of the association, one must be able to play golf, sing in karaoke sessions, and eat durians. It is during these ASEAN "events" and meetings that informal negotiations do take place and, hence, for "corridor diplomacy" to work itself out.

A salient factor that also explains why the tedious practices of *muafakat* and *musyawarah* have prevailed in ASEAN, at least during its formative years to early 1990s, had been the fact that in most ASEAN states, decision-making was highly centralized and almost always limited to a small number of political elites. The political system of most of its members did not really require political leaders to explain to their respective populace why certain decisions have been reached.[46] The other factor is that the Foreign Ministers in ASEAN have been given the authorities by their Heads of Governments to speak on behalf of their leaders. It thus makes it easier for common positions to be reached among them behind closed doors, and this explains the lack of transparency in ASEAN decisions.

It is also worth noting that ASEAN until the mid-1990s was a relatively small organization with five original members and then six in 1995, until it grew to ten members in 1999. Moreover, compared to other regional groupings, ASEAN bureaucrats are very small in number, making it easier for a more comfortable camaraderie to exist. This type of camaraderie brings us to the other element of the ASEAN way of dispute management, that is, networking.

### Networking

It is easier to manage disputes when the group is small and when parties to the dispute have intimate knowledge of each other's culture, values, and norms. Arguably, being small and closely networked through a number of official's meetings held regularly also provide the benefit of making ASEAN officials and leaders aware of each other's domestic problems. This could foster better understanding of other's reactions to certain policy initiatives. Thus, the benefits of closing ranks on certain issues would be better appreciated and valued, given that the alternative could result in the possibility of issues escalating into problems which become costly to member states in ASEAN. The point, therefore, of networking among ASEAN officials and leaders is not only to speed up decision-making but also to promote trust and confidence.

In ASEAN's experience, this network can be seen at the highest levels of governments. Until the mid-1990s, to a large extent there was a continuity of ASEAN leaders who had known each other quite well over the years and had seen through each other's difficult periods. It had been easier, therefore, for ASEAN leaders to empathize with each other's predicament.

It is quite well known how ASEAN leaders resort to telephone diplomacy at crucial periods in their bilateral relations. A good example of this was the turn of events prior to the holding of the Third ASEAN Summit in Manila in 1987. At that time, the administration of former Philippine President Corazon Aquino was facing difficult challenges in the domestic front. In spite of the perceived security problems in the Philippines, Indonesian President Soeharto urged the rest of his ASEAN counterparts to attend the Summit as a show of support and solidarity to their ASEAN neighbour, and more specifically to support Corazon Aquino.[47] It did not matter at that time that Aquino was only in office for over a year and was still new in the ASEAN circle of Heads of Government. To Soeharto and the rest of the ASEAN leaders, pushing ahead with the Summit was important to let Aquino feel that she belonged to the ASEAN family — and to the ASEAN network — although for a long time, the ASEAN leaders only had to deal with the country's long-serving leader, Ferdinand Marcos, until his ouster in 1986.

The gesture had made a great impact on the Philippine leadership and since then a lot of effort was taken by the subsequent administrations to deepen the country's ties with its ASEAN neighbours. For a long time, Philippines' relations with the rest of her ASEAN neighbours suffered from neglect due to its preoccupation with domestic problems and its long dependence on the United States. Hence, it was during Corazon Aquino's presidency that this trend was reversed. A clear shift in its foreign policy orientation towards the region could be seen, and Filipino diplomats actively sought to enhance its relations with the rest of their ASEAN counterparts. The kind of closeness developed among ASEAN leaders and reinforced by the numerous meetings and other networking events have indeed facilitated better interaction among ASEAN officials. This has also made it easier for the practice of "agreeing to disagree" to be adopted as another informal mechanisms for CM.

## Agreeing to Disagree

The practice of agreeing to disagree is basically "shelving disagreement for later settlement".[48] This mechanism has proved to be useful particularly when discussions and negotiations among members have reached an impasse. Rather than resorting to confrontation, agreeing to disagree enables parties to buy time and avoid being bogged down by contentious issues. This mechanism also allows for "acceptance time" wherein states will be able, perhaps over a longer timeframe, to adjust their positions and eventually come to an agreement.

This mechanism has been employed by members in ASEAN in dealing with highly contentious issues. It can be recalled that in the first decade after its formation, the group's experience of formulating an ASEAN position of neutrality, that is, ZOPFAN, was problematic. When Malaysia originally proposed the idea of neutrality, it did not get the full support of other ASEAN members, particularly the Philippines and Thailand who had alliance commitments with the United States. Indonesia, on the one hand, was not in favour of the idea of neutrality that was predicated on the guarantees provided by major powers, and since it had campaigned for regional resilience, this made the proposal even more difficult. What came out after several rounds of negotiations over a protracted period was a watered down version of ZOPFAN.[49]

The other example of "agreeing to disagree" being practised was when ASEAN was crafting the idea of a security forum. Until the early 1990s, the idea of putting security in the agenda during the Annual ASEAN Foreign Minister's meeting and the setting up of a multilateral forum on security remained "swept under the carpet" for some time as it was deemed to be highly sensitive. However, this did not stop certain ASEAN members from broaching the idea, in spite of the fact that the other members were still uncomfortable with including security issues in the agenda and discussing it openly.

The importance of adopting the mechanism of "agreeing to disagree" yet again underpinned ASEAN's basic approach. Until members can get really comfortable with each other, and until elements of distrust can be substantially reduced enough to establish a level of comfort among members, then the slow, incremental and low-risk style, yet flexible, is still the effective way to go.

## Third-party Mediation

Until quite recently, the use of third-party mediation was not really officially adopted by ASEAN as a form of dispute management. As mentioned earlier, although TAC did provide for a High Council as the body that mediates and adjudicates in disputes, this has yet to be constituted. Yet there are some modification, if not indigenous adaptation, to this mechanism of bringing in a third-party to mediate in times of disputes.

In ASEAN's experience, it can be recalled that at the height of the Malaysia–Philippine dispute over Sabah, Indonesian President Soeharto was instrumental in getting both the parties to agree to a "cooling-off" period that was useful in the normalization of relations between the two countries. Prior to that, Thanat Khoman, who served as Thailand's Foreign Minister between 1959 and 1971, was instrumental in improving relations between Indonesia and Malaysia during the *Konfrontasi* period. His personal intervention and mediation led to a series of meetings between Indonesian and Malaysian officials until the end of the *Konfrontasi* with the change of Indonesian leadership.

During this period in ASEAN's history, tracking informal third-party mediation with key ASEAN personalities assuming this function was rather difficult since most of these mediations were done quietly and the details of the mediation often go unreported. Noting the sensitivity of ASEAN members in not being perceived as interfering in domestic or bilateral disputes, most accounts had been limited to general statements officially issued from ASEAN capitals that call on concerned parties engaged in bilateral disputes to exercise restraint. An example of these official pronouncements was the reported press statements that came from ASEAN leaders during the height of the Flor Contemplacion case. The official statements called on the authorities of the Philippines and Singapore to find a political solution to the crisis.

However, in recent years, this mechanism of engaging official third-party mediation has become more acceptable to some ASEAN members to settle long, drawn-out disputes particularly those that pertain to territorial problems. The disputes over the island of Pulau Batu Putih (Pedra Branca) between Malaysia and Singapore and the islands of Ligitan and Sipadan between Malaysia and Indonesia had been referred to the International Court of Justice (ICJ) for resolution. At this time of writing, the ICJ has already ruled in favour of Indonesia in the case of Ligitan and Sipadan while the Pedra Branca case is still pending. In both cases, the disputing states have agreed to abide by the court's judgement.

While one could argue that this mechanism is outside the ASEAN ambit, the use of such legal recourse is indeed a significant development for an organization that had long been uncomfortable with resorting to legal structures and institutions in resolving disputes. Yet it can also be argued that because it is outside the ASEAN framework, it ensures that the dispute can be resolved objectively without members having to lose face. Since settlement of territorial disputes are most often a zero-sum game, agreeing to use this mechanism has been a big step in ASEAN's way of managing or resolving disputes.

## IV. CONCLUSION

In Chapter 1, we concluded that in spite of the chequered experiences of regional organizations around the world, it has been established that they have a role to play in managing security in their respective regions. In looking at the case of ASEAN, we proposed that one of the ways to assess its role in managing security in Southeast Asia is to examine ASEAN's mechanisms of managing conflict. It has been argued in that chapter that the constructivist approach to international relations offers the best way to study ASEAN's mechanisms, since the approach goes beyond the consideration of power and material interest and draws attention to ideational factors, to actors and agents beyond the state and the possibilities for change. These ideational elements are, therefore, critical in the understanding of the nature of mechanisms of CM in ASEAN in so far as these factor inform the way certain mechanisms have evolved, explain why some mechanisms are preferred as a product of intersubjective understanding among actors, and in the way these factors help in determining whether and why these mechanisms may have changed over time.

Against this perspective, this chapter has identified the various mechanisms that ASEAN has generated over the years since its establishment in 1967. In the discussions that followed, we examined how certain types of mechanisms have been preferred by ASEAN in dealing with certain crises and analysed the motivations behind the choice of such mechanisms. We note that the major considerations for the preference of informal mechanisms over the legalistic, albeit extremely limited, alternatives were not only due to the lack of institutional capacity within ASEAN. It was also because of the overriding objectives to instil trust and build confidence among members that were getting to know each other during the formative years of ASEAN. Hence, the informal types of mechanisms of CM such as norm-building, assurance, community building through socialization and networking, and informal third-party mediations were the more distinctive types of mechanisms that were prevalent during those periods.

As the next chapter will show, these embryonic mechanisms of CM faced serious challenges as ASEAN came to face other cases of conflict. As ASEAN assumed a role in the settlement of the Cambodian problem throughout the duration of the conflict, it soon realized that this role was to be limited given its lack of institutional capacity and the very nature of the conflict itself. The next chapter will focus on ASEAN's role in the Cambodian saga and will examine the extent to which ASEAN's mechanisms of CM were found useful in the settlement of the conflict.

## Notes

1. See Muthiah Alagappa, "Regionalism and Conflict Management: A Framework for Analysis", *Review of International Studies* (1995), p. 371.
2. Fen Osler and Brian Mandell, "Managing Regional Conflict: Security Cooperation and Third Party Mediators", *International Journal* XLV (1990): 191–201.
3. Brunei Darussalam was the last state in Southeast Asia to gain its independence and only got it from the British in 1984. It joined ASEAN immediately after its independence.
4. Roger Irvine, "The Formative Years of ASEAN: 1967–1975", in *Understanding ASEAN*, edited by Alison Broinowski (London: Macmillan Press, 1982), Chapter 2. There are many works that has discussed the earlier attempts to form subregional organization in Southeast Asia under the context of ASEAN. See, for example, Estrella Solidum, *Towards A Southeast Asian Community* (Quezon City: University of the Philippines, 1974); Arfinn Jorgensen-Dahl, *Regional Organisation and Order in Southeast Asia* (New York: St. Martin's Press, 1982); Michael Leifer, *ASEAN and the Security of Southeast Asia* (London: Routledge, 1989); Michael Antolik, *ASEAN and the Diplomacy of Accommodation* (Armonk, NY: M.E. Sharpe, Inc., 1990).
5. Leifer, *ASEAN and the Security of Southeast Asia*, p. 19.
6. For a more detailed account of the *Konfrontasi* period, see J.A.C. Mackie, *Konfrontasi: The Indonesian–Malaysian Dispute 1963–1966* (Kuala Lumpur: Oxford, 1974).
7. Antolik, *ASEAN and the Diplomacy of Accommodation*, p. 14.

8. See the ASEAN Declaration or otherwise known as the Bangkok Declaration, 8 August 1987 in *ASEAN Documents* (Jakarta: ASEAN Secretariat, 1994).
9. Leifer, *ASEAN and the Security of Southeast Asia*, p. 150.
10. Ibid.
11. Current ASEAN's dialogue partners are Australia, Canada, China, the European Union, India, Japan, the Republic of Korea, New Zealand, Russia and the United States. The United Nations Development Programme (UNDP) is also considered a dialogue partner but does not take part in the PMC. See ASEAN Secretariat at < http://www.aseansec.org >.
12. For a more detailed description of ASEAN organizational meetings, see Jamil Maidan Flores, *ASEAN: How it Works* (Jakarta: ASEAN Secretariat, 2000).
13. See Mohamed Jawhar Hassan, "Managing Security in Southeast Asia: Existing Mechanisms and Processes to Address Regional Conflicts", *Australian Journal of International Affairs* 47 (1993): 210–20. See also Hoang Anh Tuan, "ASEAN Dispute Management: Implications for Vietnam and an Expanded ASEAN", *Contemporary Southeast Asia* 18, no. 1 (1996): 61–80.
14. David Irvine, "Making Haste Less Slowly: ASEAN from 1975," in *Understanding ASEAN*, edited by Broinowski, p. 50.
15. For more details of this meeting and its implications see Mely C. Anthony's chapter on Malaysia in *Asia Pacific Security Outlook 1999*, edited by Charles E. Morrison (Tokyo: Japan Center for International Exchange, 1999), pp. 112–20.
16. Mohamed Jawhar Hassan, "Managing Security in Southeast Asia", p. 211.
17. Ibid.
18. See the ASEAN's 1976 Treaty of Amity and Cooperation in *ASEAN Documents* (Jakarta: ASEAN Secretariat, 1994).
19. Vitit Muntarbhorn, *The Challenge of Law: Legal Cooperation among ASEAN Countries* (Bangkok: Institute of Security and International Studies, 1986), p. 19.
20. This point was stressed to me by a Malaysian academic in an interview in Kuala Lumpur, August 1997.
21. See Michael Haas, *The Asian Way to Peace: A Story of Regional Co-operation* (New York: Praeger Publishers, 1989), p. 5. He has elaborated on this Asian way to peace in Chapter 1.
22. See Dr Mahathir Mohamad's address at the 30th ASEAN Foreign Ministers' Meeting, "The ASEAN Way to Prosperity and Neighbourliness, in *New Straits Times*, 25 July 1997.
23. For a more intensive discussion of this concept, see Heiner Hanggi, *ASEAN and the ZOPFAN Concept* (Singapore: Institute of Southeast Asian Studies, 1991), particularly p. 51.
24. See the *Kuala Lumpur Document on the Zone of Peace, Freedom and Neutrality,* 27 November 1971.
25. Hanggi, *ASEAN and the ZOPFAN Concept*, p. 24.

26. See Hoang, "ASEAN Dispute Management", p. 63, and Mely Caballero-Anthony, "Mechanisms of Dispute Settlement: The ASEAN Experience", *Contemporary Southeast Asia* 20, no. 1 (1998): 38–66.

27. See Amitav Acharya, *Constructing a Security Community in Southeast Asia: ASEAN and the Problem of Regional Order* (London and New York: Routledge, 2001), p. 28.

28. See Jurgen Haacke, *ASEAN's Diplomatic and Security Culture* (London and New York: Routledge, 2003), p. 4.

29. Antolik, *ASEAN and the Policy of Accommodation*.

30. Ibid., pp. 156–57.

31. For more detailed account of the Philippines' claim on Sabah and the dynamics between Malaysia and the Philippine during this period, see Lela Garner Noble, "The National Interest and the National Image: Philippine Policy in Asia", *Asian Survey* 13, no. 6 (1973). On this "cooling-off" incident, see pp. 567–69. See also Lau Teik Soon, "Conflict Resolution in ASEAN: The Sabah Issue" (Department of Political Science, University of Singapore, undated).

32. Ibid., p. 20.

33. Chin Kin Wah, *The Defense of Malaysia and Singapore* (Cambridge: Cambridge University Press, 1983), pp. 256–59 as cited in Leifer, *ASEAN and the Security of Southeast Asia*, p. 34.

34. Antolik, *ASEAN and the Policy of Accommodation*, p. 156.

35. Ibid., p. 71.

36. There has already been several attempts by the Philippine administration to drop its claim but domestic politics has somehow hindered the official renunciation. As early as 1977, former President Marcos announced that the country was going to take steps to drop the claim, pending bilateral negotiations. Malaysia stood firm in its position not to negotiate and not settle for anything less than a formal renunciation. When the next President, Corazon Aquino, took over in 1986, steps were once again taken to drop the Sabah claim but the Philippine Congress stood in the way, insisting that Malaysia should meet certain conditions before the claim could be officially dropped. So far, after three administrations post-Aquino, the issue is yet to be resolved.

37. Separate interviews conducted with Malaysian and Philippine foreign ministry officials, August 1997.

38. Leifer, *ASEAN and the Security of Southeast Asia*, pp. 38–39.

39. Ibid.

40. Ibid.

41. In an interview with the Filipino diplomat who was based in Singapore at that time, he said that none of the Philippine embassy staff in Singapore nor the officials at the Ministry of Foreign Affairs in Singapore had expected the strong reactions from the Filipino public. The negative reactions pushed the

Philippine Government to a corner, forcing it to act decisively to diffuse the situation. (Interview with Philippine diplomat, Singapore, September 1997.)

42. Koentjaraningrat, "The Village in Indonesia Today", in *Villages in Indonesia*, edited by Koentjaraningrat (Ithaca: Cornell University Press, 1967), p. 397, as quoted in Pushpa Thambipillai and J. Saravanamuttu, *ASEAN Negotiations: Two Insights* (Singapore: Institute of Southeast Asian Studies, 1985), p. 11.

43. Interview with former Malaysian Foreign Minister, Tan Sri Ghazali Shafie, August 1997.

44. Interview with Indonesian scholar, Dr Dewi Fortuna Anwar, Jakarta, August 1997.

45. As told by a Malaysian diplomat and reaffirmed by a Philippine diplomat in the author's interviews with both. Kuala Lumpur and Manila, August–September 1997.

46. Interview with Philippine diplomat, Manila, September 1997.

47. This was narrated by former Singapore Prime Minister, Lee Kuan Yew, when he delivered his speech at the Third ASEAN Summit in Manila in December 1987.

48. Hoang, "ASEAN Dispute Management", p. 63.

49. For more detailed account on the workings behind the scene of ZOPFAN, see Hanggi, *ASEAN and the ZOPFAN Concept*.

# 3

## : ASEAN AND THE
## : CAMBODIAN CONFLICT
## : Testing the Limits of the ASEAN Way

### INTRODUCTION

The previous chapter discussed ASEAN's embryonic mechanisms of conflict management, which the organization had developed over the years since its inception. While it can be said that these mechanisms have proved successful in dealing with certain inter-state conflicts, assessing the effectiveness of these mechanisms in other types of conflicts, particularly if they are extramural and external to the grouping have to be qualified. As emphasized in the earlier chapter, the effectiveness of certain mechanisms would depend largely on the nature of the conflict and the kind of objectives set out to resolve the conflict. In this regard, ASEAN's role in the resolution of the Cambodian conflict best exemplified the limitations of its mechanisms as it attempted to manage an external conflict involving neighbours, Cambodia and Vietnam, that at that time were not yet part of the ASEAN grouping.

In describing ASEAN as a conflict manager in the region, Muthiah Alagappa had noted that ASEAN did not actually envisage conflict prevention, containment, and termination roles with regard to external conflicts. Instead, what it had hoped to achieve was for its proposals for peace and security to cover all of Southeast Asia. Hence, ASEAN's conflict prevention measures specifically had not applied to non-ASEAN Southeast Asia.[1] In this regard, ASEAN's involvement in the Cambodian conflict offers interesting insights on examining the extent to which its mechanisms had been useful or inadequate in the search for the political settlement to the conflict. To appreciate the extent and limits of ASEAN's modalities, one must be able to track the various initiatives that member states of the grouping undertook throughout the duration of the Cambodian conflict. This chapter will, therefore, begin with a somewhat discursive, chronological account of the development of the Cambodian conflict and ASEAN's involvement in the resolution of the conflict.

## I. THE NATURE OF THE CAMBODIAN CONFLICT IN BRIEF

Vietnam invaded Kampuchea[2] in December 1978 and occupied its capital, Phnom Penh, in January 1979. The Cambodian Government then headed by Pol Pot was ousted and was replaced by Vietnam with a puppet government headed by Heng Samrin. To ASEAN, the implications of the Vietnamese occupation of Cambodia were manifold. For a start, it had dashed the "dream" of the original founders of ASEAN of having one Southeast Asia, which would have eventually included Vietnam, Laos, and Cambodia. More significantly was the fact that Vietnam's invasion of Cambodia was a blatant violation of its norms of peaceful co-existence and non-use of force. The invasion also threatened the security of ASEAN's front-line state Thailand that shared a common border with Cambodia.

Understanding the nature of the Cambodian problem requires examining the geopolitical context at the time the conflict broke out since the role of the external actors, other than ASEAN, have proved to be extremely crucial in the way the conflict was eventually resolved. It also requires understanding the historical factors that had led to the conflict and examining how these had influenced the turn of events in Cambodia.

By various accounts, the origin of the Vietnamese–Kampuchean conflict go as far back as the seventeenth century. Three major factors can be identified as having a great bearing on the conflict.[3] One was the need to overcome Vietnam's rice shortage. Vietnam was unable to grow enough rice for its growing population. The Cambodian Mekong Delta had very fertile land, and the area had as much land for rice cultivation as Annam and Tonkin put together. Cambodia also was sparsely populated in contrast to Vietnam whose population was seven times larger. It was this need for rice and cultivable land that led the Vietnamese to expand into Cambodia.[4] The first territory to be annexed was Kampuchea Krom, later known as the French colony of Cochinchina. This took place in the seventeenth and eighteenth centuries. The Kampucheans had tried to fight off the Vietnamese without success. Through history, Vietnam had maintained that its people and those of Laos and Cambodia have been geographically connected. After the fall of Cambodia in 1979, Vietnam had systematically introduced a resettlement programme which resettled about ten million Vietnamese along the border areas of these three countries and in the territory of Cambodia and Laos. Vietnam's historical subjugation of the Cambodian people instilled a deep hatred and distrust for the Vietnamese.[5]

Another significant factor was the French colonial policy. In 1863, Cambodia became a French protectorate. In 1887, it was merged into the "Union of Indochinoise" with the French protectorates of Annam and Laos. This helped check further Vietnamese expansion into Cambodia but did not resolve the enmity between the two peoples. The French supported the settlement of Vietnamese in Cambodia, and up to half a million people did so. They dominated some sectors of the economy, such as fishing in the Tonle Sap, labour on the rubber plantations, and petty artisantry in the towns. The French colonial administration was also staffed largely by Vietnamese. This only worsened Cambodian–Vietnamese antagonism.[6]

The third major factor was the territorial disputes. Between 1869 and 1942, the French added large areas of Cambodian territory to their Cochinchina colony and their protectorate of Annam. After the French rule ended, these areas were not returned to Cambodia but remained with Vietnam. Thus, when Cambodia became independent, it inherited colonial borders, and these were not clearly demarcated. As a result, numerous border conflicts have occurred between Vietnam and Cambodia since 1954.[7] These conflicts increased after the Khmer Rouge victory in Cambodia and the fall of South Vietnam. In fact, Vietnam was said to have never completely withdrawn from the areas it occupied even when it launched its first major attack on Cambodia in December 1978.[8]

Apart from the territorial claims, Vietnam had wanted to forge "special relations" with Laos and Cambodia. These so-called special relations were designed to eventually lead up to a communist federation of the three Indochina countries. But when the Vietnamese were unable to realize this plan, they shifted their attention to the reunification of Vietnam which was achieved on 2 July 1976.[9] With reunification, the Vietnamese renewed their interest in the special relations plan. In July 1977, the Socialist Republic of Vietnam (SRV) and Laos signed a Treaty of Friendship and Co-operation. Cambodia, which was then under the Pol Pot regime, rejected the special relationship concept. Unable to exert influence on the Pol Pot regime, Vietnam decided to invade Cambodia and install a pro-Vietnamese regime. After Phnom Penh fell in January 1979, Cambodia entered into a twenty-five-year Treaty of Peace, Friendship and Co-operation with Vietnam.[10]

The Cambodian conflict was not only confined to the animosity between Vietnam and Cambodia. It took on an expanded dimension with the involvement of the former Soviet Union and China. However, it could be said that the Soviets got involved not by design. Up until the 1950s and early 60s, their geopolitical concerns were primarily centred on the developments in Europe. They expanded their focus to include Indochina only in later years to check China's influence in the region. China, on the other hand, had been actively involved in the region, having been Vietnam's main source of aid during the Vietnam War.[11] But since the end of the war, their relations had sharply deteriorated. China, while having supported the Vietnamese against the United States, did not want Vietnam to control all of Indochina. Hence, it backed the Pol Pot regime in Cambodia. The worsening of relations was marked by Sino-Vietnamese border incidents between 1977 and 1979. According to Vietnam, it was the escalating Sino-Vietnamese hostilities that forced it to establish a close bond with the Soviet Union.

The discussion above sketched very briefly the series of significant events that surrounded the Cambodian problem. These are significant in that it would put the analyses of ASEAN's role in the resolution of this conflict in the proper perspective. More importantly, it helps in evaluating the limits of ASEAN's attempt to resolve the conflict and the mechanisms ASEAN has employed in managing the problem.

## II. ASEAN'S VIEW OF THE CAMBODIAN ISSUE

From the start, ASEAN had rejected Vietnam's occupation of Cambodia, insisting that the government of the People's Republic of Kampuchea (PRK), which Vietnam had installed and was headed by Heng Samrin was illegitimate and illegal. ASEAN's position was that the Vietnamese had violated Cambodia's sovereignty and self-determination. In January 1979 at the Special ASEAN Foreign Ministers Meeting in Bangkok, ASEAN called for the withdrawal of all foreign forces from Cambodia. This was followed by the tabling of an ASEAN draft resolution on the Cambodian conflict in the UN Security Council in March 1979 which the UN General Assembly adopted in November 1979. The call for Vietnamese withdrawal from Cambodia became a constant issue that appeared in the several Joint Communiques, which ASEAN had issued since its fourteenth ASEAN Minister Meeting in 1981 in Manila.

The occupation of Cambodia also brought to the fore a number of security-related concerns to ASEAN. As an expression of its solidarity,

ASEAN gave primary consideration to the security of Thailand that was its front-line state in the conflict, having shared borders with Cambodia and Laos extending to a total of more than 2,000 kilometres. Thailand was also geographically proximate to Vietnam. The historical rivalry between Thailand and Vietnam also served to exacerbate Thailand's concern over the latter's invasion of Cambodia.

However, viewed from the longer perspective, ASEAN believed, at least at that time, that the occupation of Cambodia by a Soviet-backed Vietnam would only strengthen Moscow's foothold in the region and would increase the potential threat posed by the superpower rivalry in Southeast Asia.[12]

Given these concerns, ASEAN's Cambodian policy was more or less founded on three pillars. The first was to support the Cambodian nationalist in order to maintain the military pressure on the ground. The second was to isolate Vietnam and thereby exert political, diplomatic, and economic pressure on her to negotiate, and the third was to offer Vietnam an honourable political settlement which will restore Cambodia as a sovereign and independent state which will both safeguard the legitimate security interests of Cambodia's neighbours, including Vietnam.[13] ASEAN's involvement in the Cambodian conflict, which spanned more than a decade, and the nature of its diplomacy on Cambodia are discussed in more detail below.

## III. ASEAN'S DIPLOMACY ON CAMBODIA

At the start of the conflict, ASEAN's political response to Vietnam's occupation of Cambodia was swift and uncompromising. It issued a statement on 9 January 1979 deploring the armed conflict between the two Indochinese states. The statement issued during a special Foreign Ministers' Meeting in Bangkok in 12 January 1979 called on the UN Security Council to take immediate steps to end the conflict.[14] As Vietnam continued its military occupation of Cambodia, ASEAN stepped up the pressure with probably the strongest and most decisive stance on an issue since the grouping's formation in 1967. In several joint statements that followed, ASEAN affirmed the Cambodian people's right to self-determination, free from external interference, and demanded the immediate withdrawal of all foreign Vietnamese troops from Cambodian territory. This call for withdrawal was followed by the tabling of an ASEAN draft resolution on Cambodia in the UN Security Council in March 1979, which the UN General Assembly adopted in November

1979. In October 1980, ASEAN sponsored the UN General Assembly resolution on Cambodia calling for an international conference which was adopted with ninety-seven in favour and twenty-three against.[15]

## Internationalizing the Issue

ASEAN was, however, conscious of its limitation as a regional body in resolving the conflict. Given its limitation, ASEAN could only take up its cause in the international arena and employ collective diplomacy. Nevertheless, during the period 1979–89, ASEAN had been generally successful and effective in mobilizing sustained support from the international community. Its position as articulated in the July 1981 declaration of the UN International Conference on Kampuchea (ICK) received overwhelming endorsements in the UN General Assembly annual resolutions. These resolutions called for negotiations on:

"1. A ceasefire by all parties and withdrawal of all foreign forces in the shortest time possible;
2. An appropriate arrangement to ensure that armed Kampuchean factions cannot disrupt or control election outcomes;
3. A UN peacekeeping force to ensure law and order; and
4. The holding of free elections under UN supervision, which will allow the Kampuchean people to exercise their right to self-determination and elect a government of their own choice."[16]

ASEAN had also lobbied for diplomatic support from its official dialogue partners like Australia, Canada, the European Community, Japan, and the United States. It urged these partners to use economic sanctions against the SRV. This call was first made by former Singapore Prime Minister Lee Kuan Yew on 23 November 1979.[17]

To persuade Vietnam to accept a political settlement of the conflict, a part of ASEAN's strategy had been to sponsor the continuing presence of anti-Vietnamese Khmer liberation forces along the Thai–Kampuchean border. These forces were Pol Pot's Khmer Rouge, former Prime Minister Son Sann's Khmer People's National Liberation Front (KPNLF), and Prince Norodom Sihanouk's National United Front for an Independent, Neutral, Peaceful and Cooperative Cambodia (FUNCINPEC). In June 1982, ASEAN was able to bring together the three forces under the political framework of the Coalition Government of Democratic Kampuchea (CGDK). Although these three forces were operating independently, the coalition served the purpose of projecting a legitimate government against the Heng Samrin regime which was installed by Vietnam. In supporting the CGDK, it made it possible for ASEAN to project Prince Sihanouk and the anti-communist Son Sann as the legitimate spokesmen for an independent Kampuchea freed from Vietnamese occupation.[18] This also made it easier for ASEAN to defend the credentials of the CGDK in becoming the legitimate representative of the Cambodian people and for the latter to maintain its seat in the UN.[19]

While ASEAN stood united in its diplomatic stance, the question of indirect military assistance was left as a matter for members to address separately. Some ASEAN states were reportedly providing training for combat instructors of the non-communist factions of the CGDK.[20] Singapore, for instance, was reportedly supplying weapons to the KPNLF, while Malaysia was also reported to have provided jungle warfare training to the KPNLF troops.[21] Moreover, whatever military aid provided to the Khmer forces was allegedly facilitated by Thailand. In contrast, Indonesia had differed in view, particularly opposing direct arms link between ASEAN and the anti-communist forces, because it feared the possibility of a militarized ASEAN–Vietnam confrontation.[22]

## Dealing with the Differing Threat Perceptions and the Politics of Ambiguity

As the Cambodian crisis deepened, ASEAN's political stance towards the resolution of the conflict underwent a series of "changes", from one of an uncompromising position of Vietnam's immediate withdrawal from Cambodia to finding a political settlement to the problem. These changes, partly influenced by the turn of events in the international arena, reflected the difficulties faced by ASEAN during that period in maintaining a common position on the Cambodian conflict while trying to accommodate the various interests of its respective members. Accommodating these conflicting interests were also made more difficult since these interests were largely shaped by the differing perceptions of threats faced by the member states on the nature and impact of the conflict on regional security.

While the occupation was generally regarded by ASEAN as threatening the peace and stability in Southeast Asia, each member state had its own different perceptions of the kind of threats posed by the Cambodian problem. What were these different threat perceptions? For Thailand, it was primarily the geopolitical dimension of the threat. Thailand shared a common border with Cambodia and as the front-line state, it had to contend with the presence of Vietnamese troops right at its border. This had led to heightened tensions between the two countries. The incidents of border incursions had strengthened Thailand's claim that Vietnam intended to expand, leading the former to identify Vietnam as posing the immediate threat to its national security.[23] Moreover, the occupation had caused a host of problems for Thailand such as the presence of hundreds of refugees from Cambodia. In mid-1979, Thailand was already host to about 600,000 refugees taking shelter in camps set up along the Thai border.[24]

In stark contrast was the Philippines, which unlike Thailand, was geographically separated and not confronted with foreign troops at its borders. Nevertheless, to the Philippines, Vietnam's occupation of Cambodia was a violation of international norms, and within the regional context violated the principles enshrined specifically in ASEAN's Zone of Peace, Freedom and Neutrality (ZOPFAN) and its Treaty of Amity and Co-operation (TAC). The smaller states like Singapore and Brunei, while not sharing borders with Vietnam, shared the same indignation but also considered themselves vulnerable against foreign invasion and aggression. To these countries, an atmosphere of peace and stability in the region was essential to their survival, hence the Vietnamese invasion was indeed a bad precedent.

Thailand and Singapore became the staunchest critics of Vietnam and were seen as the hardliners in ASEAN in the group's diplomacy on Cambodia. Brunei, which only joined ASEAN officially in 1984, was seen to be following the position of its two immediate neighbours. In contrast was the Philippines which at that time was more reserved in its condemnation largely due to its preoccupation with its own domestic problems.

Malaysia and Indonesia's threat perceptions were rather different. For Malaysia, the geopolitical dimension of the conflict was also relevant. After all, Malaysia shared a land border with Thailand and was also a host to thousands of refugees. Around the same time that the Cambodian conflict broke out, Malaysia was already sheltering some 75,000 refugees.[25]

However, Malaysia's perception of the threat posed by the Cambodian problem was seen within the context of the involvement of major powers, specifically China and the former USSR. To Malaysia, these major powers' extended influence in the conflict had brought the rivalry of the two communist giants to the region. As the chief architect of ASEAN's ZOPFAN, Malaysia had wanted the USSR and China to have minimal role in the region. Therefore, the Cambodian problem as far as

Malaysia was concerned was also a major power confrontation. Accordingly, Malaysia believed that a viable solution to the conflict had had to involve the major powers.[26]

Like Malaysia, Indonesia's threat perceptions were also more nuanced. The country's historical affinity with Vietnam had helped shaped its threat perception of the latter's occupation of Cambodia. Both countries had similar historical experiences of having fought gallantly against their colonial masters — the Dutch for Indonesia and the French for Vietnam. Both countries also proclaimed their independence in 1945, and Indonesia was the first country to recognize Vietnam.[27] This similarity had the effect of bringing them closer together to support one another. For example in 1960, Indonesia gave its support to South Vietnam's anti-government revolutionaries who were fighting the Americans. Since Jakarta and Hanoi had had close bilateral relations, Vietnam was not considered by Indonesia as a threat to its national security and even to the region.

Indonesia, therefore, shared Malaysia's perception that the real threat of the Cambodian conflict could emanate from China and the Soviet Union. Indonesia feared that both could exploit the situation for their own advantage without considering the interest of ASEAN. This perception was articulated officially by former Indonesian Foreign Minister Mochtar Kusumaatmadja at his address during a seminar on "Southeast Asia as a Nuclear Arms Free Zone of Peace, Freedom and Neutrality" held in Jakarta in January 1985. At the seminar, Kusumaatmadja aired his fears of the possibility of Indonesia getting caught in between the superpower rivalry.[28] Within the context of the Cambodian conflict, this rivalry was reflected by the support that both China and the USSR had given to the warring Khmer parties which included military aid. During this period, Indonesia and Malaysia were also concerned that the impact of the consequences of the conflict on Thailand's security concern had brought Thailand too close to China. Both countries feared that as a consequence of this, China had become too involved in the affairs of the region — something that they had been trying to avoid.

Since Malaysia and Indonesia had similar perceptions of the complexity of the Cambodian conflict and given the involvement of China and the USSR, both countries had always been perceived as the soft-liners in ASEAN. This impression had been reinforced by the two countries' policy initiatives with regard to the resolution of the Cambodian conflict that will be elaborated in the next section of this chapter. Thus, it is against the dynamics of these differing threat perceptions within member states that we now proceed to track ASEAN's diplomacy on Cambodia during the duration of the conflict.

## The Problem of Accommodating Vietnam

When it appeared that the Cambodian conflict was reaching an impasse, ASEAN began to shift tack and work towards a political settlement to the conflict. This impasse was largely due to Vietnam's rigid position. Vietnam had consistently insisted that its occupation of Cambodia was to liberate the Cambodians from the oppressive and cruel Pol Pot regime. In defending their occupation, the SRV had stressed to ASEAN and to the rest of the international community that the Pol Pot government started the conflict as it repeatedly rebuffed Vietnam.[29] Vietnam also insisted that the Cambodians were the ones who started the border war that eventually led to Vietnam occupying Cambodia. Vietnam further asserted that the Cambodian situation was irreversible.[30]

Vietnam also maintained that the root of the problem lay with China's policy to realize its big-nation expansionist and hegemonic designs on Southeast Asia. At the UN Security Council Meeting in January 1979, Vietnam's Ambassador Ha Van Lau declared that it was China's policy to put the three Indochinese countries against each other, and to stir up the Hoa people (ethnic Chinese residents in Vietnam) to "cause disturbances" inside the SRV. To Vietnam, this was the real cause of the fighting in Indochina.[31] Moreover, Vietnam had consistently warned ASEAN of dangerously exposing Southeast Asia to China's expansionist ambitions, thus justifying that its occupation in Cambodia was part of its own as well as the PRK's security measures against Chinese aggression.[32]

However, in spite of its rejections of the ASEAN proposals and the resolutions of the UN-ICK, Vietnam made numerous efforts to relax local tensions. In July 1980, Vietnam proposed the dimilitarization of the Thai–Cambodian border area. In 1982, Vietnam announced a partial withdrawal of Vietnamese forces as a token of good faith. It also guaranteed safety zones along the Thai–Kampuchean border and proposed a non-aggression pact with Thailand to ensure that the presence of Vietnamese troops along its borders would not threaten Thai security. Furthermore, Vietnam formally recognized the United Nation's role in the settlement of the conflict on the condition that there was to be also withdrawal of recognition for Pol Pot's Khmer Rouge and that the

Cambodian seat at the United Nations was left vacant. And then in 1983, the Vietnamese announced schedules of more withdrawals from Cambodia at a pace that were to be determined by the security situation in Cambodia. In working towards a regional framework to resolve the conflict, Hanoi had proposed non-aggression pacts with ASEAN. It also proposed the holding of limited international conferences and an ASEAN-Indochina dialogue to discuss problems concerning peace and stability in Southeast Asia.

At first, the proposals from Vietnam were turned down by ASEAN and were perceived by the grouping as deliberate evasions and cover-up of the reality of the Vietnamese presence in Kampuchea. Vietnam's partial withdrawals were also dismissed by ASEAN as unverifiable and were instead only routine replacements and reassignments of troops. As far as ASEAN was concerned, Vietnam's refusal to invite an international body to observe troop withdrawals instead of some selected observers (for example, foreign journalists and guests) did support the claim that the withdrawals were doubtful. More importantly, ASEAN maintained its position that the SRV had flagrantly disregarded the principles of peaceful co-existence which it had offered for normal relations with ASEAN. To ASEAN at least, the SRV's repeated declarations of its benevolent missions to rid Cambodia of Pol Pot's atrocities could not justify Vietnam's prolonged occupation of Cambodia.[33]

Faced with the fact that Vietnam's occupation seemed irreversible, ASEAN decided to increase the pressure on Vietnam. However, against the hardening of ASEAN's position, there had always been the shared realization among members in ASEAN that in spite of the turn of events, a more accommodating stance and willingness to dialogue with Vietnam rather than being confrontational was still the better option in order to pave the way for a solution to an almost intractable conflict. Hence, as ASEAN had continued to strongly urge Vietnam to withdraw from Cambodia, certain ASEAN member states meanwhile started to introduce a number of policy initiatives to open doors to resolve the conflict.

## IV. THE PROBLEM OF MAINTAINING A COMMON RESPONSE AGAINST THE EXPEDIENCIES OF ACCOMMODATION

A major challenge to ASEAN throughout its efforts at managing the Cambodian conflict was to sustain a common diplomatic position, in spite of differing threat perceptions among its members on the nature of the conflict, and approaches to resolve the problem while avoiding the prospects of members breaking ranks. But the differences in approaches started to emerge as early as 1980 when Indonesia and Malaysia jointly issued the Kuantan Declaration after former Indonesian President Soeharto and former Malaysian Prime Minister Hussein Onn met in Kuantan, Malaysia on 26–28 March 1980. The Kuantan Declaration, which enunciated the Kuantan Principle, recognized among others, Vietnam's legitimate interests in Cambodia and its security interest with regard to China. But it also called for an end to Soviet's influence on Vietnam. The Kuantan Principle, interestingly, expressed Malaysia's and Indonesia's readiness to "accept" Vietnam's position on Cambodia in exchange for peaceful conditions along the Thai–Kampuchean border. More importantly, the Principle identified big power interference in Southeast Asia as the major cause of the Cambodian problem and not the Vietnamese occupation of Cambodia. It is important to note here that Malaysia and Indonesia had been the two ASEAN members that were most willing at that time to accommodate Vietnam in the search for a peaceful solution to the conflict.

The Kuantan Principle, however, was aborted because of strong opposition from Thailand. Thailand refused to accept that Vietnam had any legitimate rights on Cambodia. At that time, Thai's opposition appeared to threaten ASEAN's cohesion, resulting in Malaysia and Indonesia dropping the idea quietly. The Kuantan "episode" revealed the divergences among ASEAN members and began to seemingly split the group into two camps: the so-called hardliners and the moderates.

These differences in approaches appeared again in March 1983 when Malaysia proposed the "five-plus-two" talks at the Non-Aligned Ministerial Meeting in New Delhi. The "five-plus-two" talks envisaged the bringing together of the five ASEAN countries (at that time these were Indonesia, Malaysia, the Philippines, Singapore, and Thailand) with Vietnam and Laos. It became obvious at that time that Malaysia was one of the ASEAN members that advocated finding a *modus vivendi* with Vietnam. Kuala Lumpur believed that the strategy of "bleeding Vietnam white" which China had preferred would only be self-defeating since this would only increase Vietnam's dependence on the Soviet Union. This time, Indonesia and Singapore supported the idea. However, it faltered once again because of stiff opposition from Thailand and China that argued that while the proposed talks recognized Vietnam as one of the main parties in the negotiations, it completely excluded the

CGDK. Although the proposed talks would have also excluded the Heng Samrin regime, Thailand and China regarded the acceptance of the proposal as tantamount to ASEAN's approval in principle of post-invasion regional talks. Thus, the stiff opposition from Thailand and China doomed any prospects of the proposal ever taking off.

Nevertheless, while the "five-plus-two" initiative may have been a flop, it sent the clearest signal of the changes taking place in the diplomatic approach of some ASEAN states to the Cambodian problem. To be sure, some states no longer supported the China-sponsored policy of "bleeding Vietnam white". Signs of this flexibility of approach were evident when ASEAN issued the "Appeal on Kampuchean Independence" in September 1983. The significance of the "appeal" was that while ASEAN continued to call for Vietnamese withdrawal, it suggested that this be carried out gradually on a territorial basis, starting from the Thai-Kampuchean border. This appeal was a follow-up to Thailand's earlier efforts on extending an olive branch to Vietnam when it proposed a withdrawal of its troops 30 kilometres from the Thai border as an initial step towards total withdrawal. Hanoi has earlier rejected it on the grounds that such withdrawal would permit unchecked infiltration by the Khmer Rouges.

The appeal also demonstrated significant concessions by ASEAN when it offered a settlement of the Cambodian problem outside the UN framework — something which the group had insisted on earlier. Thus there was no mention of the ICK or the United Nations in the document. More importantly, instead of the previous call for an immediate withdrawal of Vietnamese troops from Cambodia, the appeal proposed a phased withdrawal. There was also recognition of the PRK's role in association with the CGDK that implied a future role of the PRK in post-settlement Cambodia.[34]

The conciliatory stance by ASEAN became even more evident between 1984 and 1985. This also coincided with Indonesia assuming the leadership on the Cambodian issue. In February 1984, former Indonesian Foreign Minister Mochtar Kusumaatmadja announced that ASEAN was prepared "to meet Vietnam halfway" in an attempt to break the deadlock in efforts to solve the conflict. The Indonesian move was further reinforced by the former Armed Forces Commander-in-Chief General Benny Murdani's visit to Vietnam. The purpose of Murdani's visit was to try to find evidence that Vietnam had come to accept the necessity of compromising with ASEAN on Cambodia. However, Murdani's visit was perceived more as a signal that Indonesia was willing to provide Vietnam with a sympathetic ear within ASEAN.[35] During this visit, Murdani officially declared that Vietnam did *not* pose a threat to the region. But while Murdani's statement was reassuring to Vietnam, it also served to reinforce the different perspectives that were coming out from Jakarta and Bangkok on the developments on the Cambodian conflict.[36]

The year 1984 also saw a number of exchange visits and secret discussions between Indonesian and Vietnamese officials and semi-officials. One of the more significant forums was the seminar jointly organized by the Indonesian Centre for Strategic and International Studies (CSIS) and the Vietnamese Research Institute for International Relations (IIR) on 23–25 February 1984, which facilitated a frank exchange of views between the two countries on the security situation in the region.

In the meanwhile, Indonesian Foreign Minister Mochtar Kusumaatmadja became very actively engaged in exploring further ways for an early settlement of the conflict. He became the ASEAN interlocutor and, until his retirement in 1989 initiated various meetings and consultations between ASEAN and Vietnamese officials, in particular his Vietnamese counterpart, Nguyen Co Thach. Kusumaatmadja also worked closely with his ASEAN counterparts in many of the ASEAN initiatives that followed. During his tenure as the ASEAN interlocutor, Kusumaatmadja had consistently given the impression that coming from an ASEAN state that was closest to Vietnam, he (on behalf of the Indonesian Government) was ready to act as a mediator between Vietnam and the hardliners in ASEAN like Thailand. And because of Kusumaatmadja's prominent visibility in most of the meetings and consultations on Cambodia, it gave the impression that resolving the Cambodian conflict was an Indonesian mission.[37]

## V. TESTING THE LIMITS OF ASEAN'S DIPLOMACY

### Striking a Balance while Managing Differences

In spite of the new initiatives coming from ASEAN, it seemed at that time that the obstacles to the resolution of the Cambodian problem continued to grow. Vietnam's launching of "dry season" military offensive along the Thai–Kampuchean border, the fiercest ever since the Vietnamese invasion of Cambodia in 1978, drew swift and severe condemnation from ASEAN members which rallied behind Thailand. ASEAN's next diplomatic move was to appeal to the former Soviet Union to play a constructive role in the Cambodian dispute by specifically cutting its aid to Vietnam if the latter persisted in seeking a military solution to the conflict.[38] This move was significant in that it was the first time that ASEAN had officially recognized the role of the former Soviet Union in the conflict.

Less than a week after the call to the Soviets, ASEAN delivered its strongest ever statement on the conflict in February 1985. Apart from its usual expressions of support for Thailand and condemnation of Vietnamese incursions, ASEAN called on the international community to increase support for the Cambodian people "in their military and political struggle". This was perhaps the first and the last time that ASEAN as a group openly called on other countries to provide military support to the resistance.

Despite the strong condemnations, efforts were however made to ensure that dialogue with Vietnam was not cut off. Indonesia quickly moved to correct the situation. During a visit by the Vietnamese Defence Minister to Jakarta in April 1985, Indonesia agreed on a programme of military co-operation with Vietnam. Moreover, during the visit, General Murdani reiterated that Vietnam did not pose a threat to the region and personally declared that he believed Vietnam had started to withdraw its troops from Cambodia.

Malaysia followed suit in ensuring that ASEAN had not locked itself into a hardline position. Malaysia floated the idea of "Proximity Talks" at the ASEAN Foreign Ministers Meeting in Kuala Lumpur in May 1985. The objectives of the talks were to bring together for the first time the UN-recognized CGDK and the Hanoi-backed Heng Samrin regime in an effort to make the Kampucheans resolve the conflict by themselves. More significantly, the meeting would have been a step towards a political settlement rather than a military solution. While Malaysia got the other countries to agree in principle to the proposed talks, Thailand however objected, pointing to the fact that the formula implied that the conflict was a civil war, unless Vietnam were included. So, the proposal was modified to include the PRK's participation as part of the Vietnamese delegation. This proposal was eventually endorsed in the ASEAN Foreign Minister's meeting in July 1985.[39] However, despite the success of forging a common ASEAN position, the group could not get Vietnam to agree. In fact, the proposal was quickly rejected by Vietnam since it objected to the other recommendations that were part of the proposal that highlighted the role of the UN. Specifically, the proposal called for UN control and supervision in elections and the establishment of a UN supervisory commission during the settlement. To Vietnam, bringing back the United Nations as part of the solution was significantly different from ASEAN's earlier position when it issued the Appeal.[40]

Notwithstanding its earlier setbacks, ASEAN continued to pursue a similar track. In December 1985, Indonesia, which has been rather lukewarm to Malaysia's proposal suggested that the "Proximity Talks" be modified or replaced by a "Cocktail Meeting". This idea was actually first floated by Prince Norodom Sihanouk in July when he proposed an informal meeting of all major parties in the Cambodian dispute, including Vietnam, China, and the USSR. However, Indonesia's proposal for a "Cocktail Meeting" was restricted only to the Cambodian factions. Once again, under Thailand's prompting, the format of the meeting was modified to become a two-staged one where the Khmers would meet first, followed by negotiations between the CGDK and Vietnam. However, the proposal was shelved momentarily to attend to the promotion of the CGDK.

In March 1986, ASEAN in consultation with the members of the CGDK put forward an eight-point proposal for resolving the Kampuchean conflict. The proposal called for the following conditions:

- two-phase Vietnamese withdrawal;
- UN supervision of the withdrawal and a ceasefire;
- negotiations on a quadripartite coalition after the first phase of withdrawal;
- UN-supervised free elections;
- establishment of a liberal democratic regime with a neutral and a non-aligned foreign policy;
- acceptance of reconstruction aid from all countries; and
- signing of a non-aggression and peaceful co-existence treaty with Vietnam.

Vietnam immediately dismissed the proposal partly, complaining that the proposal was allegedly authored by China. ASEAN, however, went ahead to endorse the proposal at their Annual Foreign Ministers meeting in June, together with the proximity proposal.[41]

During the latter half of 1986 until the first half of 1987, ASEAN's diplomacy on Cambodia had slackened, mainly also because during this period Vietnam was preparing for elections and the formation of a new government. The "Cocktail" proposal was revived during Mochtar

Kusumaatmadja's visit to Hanoi in late July 1987. In a Joint Communique on 29 July, Vietnam agreed to a proposal for an informal meeting without preconditions between the members of the CGDK and the PRK in Jakarta, which would also see Vietnam joining in the meeting at a later stage. When Indonesia presented this proposal to other ASEAN members at the Foreign Ministers meeting in Bangkok on 16 August, Thailand, with the support of Singapore, again wanted it revised.

They called for the Vietnamese to join in the talks immediately after the Khmers have met, making it a one-meeting, two-session arrangement. Thailand had argued that if the Vietnamese were to join in only at a later stage, it would give the appearance that the Cambodian conflict was a civil war.[42] The modified proposal also stipulated that the CGDK's "Eight-Point Proposal" should be the basis of discussion. This provision contravened the Mochtar-Thach understanding that the gathering be held without pre-conditions. It was, therefore, not a surprise that Vietnam once again rejected the proposal.[43] Thus negotiations on some form of a "Cocktail Meeting" continued into 1988 with both sides endorsing the idea in principle but not agreeing on the conditions or the time when the meeting might take place.

It is interesting to note that even before the ASEAN members met to discuss the Indonesian proposal, it was reported that Thailand was particularly unhappy over the way Indonesia had handled the proposal. Apparently, after Indonesia's Kusumaatmadja reached an agreement with his Vietnamese counterpart, he went ahead to publicize the proposal without first "running it past" the Thai Foreign Minister Siddhi Savetsila who was at that time ASEAN's Standing Committee chairman. In the meanwhile, Hanoi's rejection of the plan also disappointed the Indonesian Minister who reportedly had began to show his frustration over his inability to influence his ASEAN partners.[44]

Despite the setbacks, the proposal for the "Cocktail Meeting" eventually came into fruition when the Bogor peace talks, officially dubbed the Jakarta Informal Meeting (JIM I) kicked off on 25 July 1988. JIM I brought together for the first time the four Cambodian factions to discuss the political solution to the Cambodian problem. The meeting indeed became a two-staged meeting — the first stage involving only the four Khmer factions, represented by Prince Ranariddh (FUNCINPEC), Son Sann (KPLF), and Khieu Samphan (Khmer Rouge), who were the three representatives of the CGDK, and Hun Sen who was representing the PRK. At the second stage, Cambodia, Laos, and Vietnam as the concerned parties of the conflict were brought in. Indonesia's new Foreign Minister, Ali Alatas hosted the meeting. There were no preconditions allowed from any of the Cambodian factions although ASEAN complained that representatives from Vietnam and the PRK had come with prepared statements, evident by PRK's Seven-Point Proposal which was presented during the first day of the talks.[45] The plan essentially dwelt on excluding the Khmer Rouge and offering Prince Norodom Sihanouk the role as head of the proposed national reconciliation council.[46]

Vietnam's participation in JIM I was highly significant. The fact that it participated was perceived by ASEAN as an acknowledgement that Vietnam has failed in its attempts to subjugate the Khmers and that the only way out was a political solution under the terms that could accommodate its interests. However, during the meeting, Vietnam was still inflexible, linking its withdrawal from Kampuchea with the elimination of threats from China, Pol Pot, Thailand, and other reactionaries. This inflexibility, however, did not diminish the importance of the JIM I as a significant starting point for the Khmers and provided the groundwork for them to explore further negotiations. Notwithstanding the divergence of views on questions of implementing a solution, JIM I arrived at key elements for a comprehensive settlement of the conflict which the parties had agreed on. These were:

- the withdrawal of Vietnamese troops;
- the cessation of external aid to the opposing Khmer forces;
- the need for international supervision to monitor the withdrawal;
- the need for free elections and an interim government in post-withdrawal Cambodia; and
- the need for a sovereign, independent, and neutral Cambodia.

There was also understanding among the Khmers on two new fundamentals, namely: the "non-return" of the policies and practices of the Khmer Rouge and the linkage between the withdrawal of Vietnamese troops and the cessation of external aid to both sides of the Khmer divide.[47]

The Bogor peace talks or JIM I finally capped ASEAN's long-drawn effort to break the Cambodian stalemate, representing a very significant diplomatic achievement for ASEAN. More importantly, JIM I reflected the dynamics of ASEAN's politics of accommodation as seen in the shifts in its policies on Vietnam and the resolution of the Cambodian conflict. Considering that ASEAN had initially refused to endorse any direct and indirect meeting with Vietnam or its Cambodian proxy unless Vietnam withdrew its troops totally and unconditionally, the adjustments in its policies to meet Vietnam halfway reflected its desire to open channels of communication in order to continue with its established patterns of consultation.

The same could be said for Vietnam. When Cambodia fell, Vietnam had declared that its occupation was irreversible. Vietnam even refused to deal directly with the resistance groups. As events turned out, Hanoi actually did what ASEAN had been pressuring it to do, which was to pull out its troops from Cambodia. But the JIM success was short-lived as major obstacles prevailed.

## The Long Way Ahead: Pushing Further

JIM I was followed by JIM II which was held in February 1989. The meeting was supposed to follow up on the points agreed in principle at the first meeting.[48] However, the process once again hit a snag when discussions moved to the modalities of implementing them. This was because while the Khmer factions knew what they wanted, they could not agree on how to get there. At JIM II, Prince Norodom Sihanouk presented a five-point proposal which ASEAN had endorsed at JIM I. The proposal called for: a definite timetable for the Vietnamese withdrawal with no linkage to continued aid for the Khmer resistance; the dismantling of the PRK and the CGDK and the setting up of a quadripartite provisional government; the formation of a National Army of Cambodia comprising all armies of the four Cambodian factions; the holding of an International Conference on Cambodia (ICC) to supervise elections; and finally the changing of the country's name to "State of Cambodia" and adopting a new flag and a new national anthem.[49]

From the start of JIM II, Vietnam and the PRK became adamant in their position and refused to agree to Sihanouk's peace plan, particularly on the modalities of power-sharing. ASEAN, on the other hand, supported Sihanouk's proposal. It was not unexpected that JIM II turned out to be a disappointment and the meeting ended with the parties agreeing that as a continuation of JIM II, an international conference on Cambodia had to be held. The agreement consequently paved the way for the convening of the Paris Conference on Cambodia which was held on 30 July–30 August 1989.

At the time the Paris conference was being convened, several preparatory talks were held between Sihanouk and Hun Sen. However, the talks failed to break new grounds. Such was the atmosphere when the Paris Conference brought together a total of nineteen countries: the parties involved and the parties concerned namely, China, USSR, the United States, France, Britain, Canada, Japan, Australia, and India. Indonesia, by virtue of its visible involvement in the conflict became ASEAN's main representative and Co-Chair of the Paris Conference together with France.

The aim of the Conference was to lay the groundwork for a possible international body that would monitor the withdrawal of Vietnamese troops from Cambodia in September 1989, as declared by Vietnam, and also to monitor the proposed truce among the Cambodian warring factions.[50] Unfortunately, the Conference failed to achieve its aims. The two issues which divided the participants were, firstly, whether the UN should oversee the International Control Mechanism (ICM) that would supervise a settlement in Cambodia, and secondly, on how to bring about national reconciliation among all the Cambodian parties. The latter was the main stumbling block in the talks since the issue of a compromise power-sharing could not be resolved. Sihanouk wanted the Khmer Rouge representative to be included in the interim government while Hun Sen firmly opposed it.[51] The failure of the peace talks was further accentuated by the reluctance of the foreign ministers from the United States, USSR, and China to attend the closing ministerial session which reflected a fundamental lack of strategic interest. The reluctance was perceived as the major power's lack of urgency for a speedy and comprehensive settlement of the Cambodian conflict. In spite of ASEAN's prodding, it also appeared that during the Conference the United States had no overriding interest in breaking the deadlock on Cambodia.[52] The Conference was, therefore, adjourned indefinitely.

During that period, ASEAN's momentum on Cambodia received another blow when Thailand, suddenly and unilaterally decided to ease the pressure on Vietnam to push its national commercial interest. Thailand's newly elected Prime Minister General Chatichai Choonhavan announced the country's new policy in "turning the battlefields into marketplaces" around the same time that ASEAN was trying to break the deadlock on Cambodia. The rest of ASEAN members were caught by surprise, to say the least. When asked by his Malaysian and Singaporean counterparts, General Chatichai was reported to have explained that while Thailand's official policy remained unchanged, his government was pursuing a two-track policy on Cambodia. This meant that while diplomatic pressure would be maintained, private sector dealings would not only be permitted but also encouraged.[53]

## Shifts in the Peace Process

With all these developments, it is noteworthy that efforts at finding acceptable mechanisms to resolve the Cambodian conflict did not end. In spite of the fact that the Paris Peace Conference failed to produce any agreement, it marked an important shift in the peace process. The shift occurred when deliberations in the United Nations began in early 1990, specifically among the five permanent members (P5) of the UN Security Council. The P5 decided that instead of deferring to ASEAN's leadership role in the process, the United Nations was a more convenient and appropriate framework for seeking a comprehensive solution which could promote national reconciliation among the Khmer factions. The P5 deliberations aimed to create a neutral political environment in Cambodia that would enable every Khmer faction to have an equal chance to compete peacefully for office, thus providing the incentive for them to accept a negotiated political settlement.[54]

After a series of consultations among the P5 and the Khmer factions, the Agreements on a Comprehensive Political Settlement of the Cambodia Conflict were signed on 23 October 1991 at the end of the second sitting of the Paris Conference. The Agreements essentially gave the United Nations through the UN Transitional Authority in Cambodia (UNTAC) the mandate to bring about a comprehensive settlement of the conflict. Although ASEAN member countries, specifically Indonesia, Malaysia, Singapore, Thailand, and the Philippines, contributed troops to the UN peacekeeping forces, ASEAN's role which it assumed for more than a decade was significantly reduced because Cambodia was ultimately placed under the UNTAC.

## VI. SUMMARY

For many years since the Cambodian conflict began, ASEAN was labelled as a one-issue organization. This label stemmed from the nature of the unprecedented diplomatic efforts that ASEAN undertook to address the Cambodian problem. Cambodia was the issue that jelled ASEAN together and enhanced its image internationally. Yet, behind the united front, the conflict also exposed the differences among ASEAN members which became more pronounced in the later stages of its diplomatic efforts. Among the major reasons for these diverges were the different threat perceptions held by each ASEAN members of the implications of the conflict, the nature of their own bilateral relations with Vietnam and, of course, the need to balance their own national interest. One could, therefore, argue that ASEAN's diplomacy in Cambodia was remarkable considering the complexities involved in the nature of the conflict and the power equation that prevailed at that time among the many parties concerned including the major powers.

Despite the differences that appeared within ASEAN, one could still discern an underlying consistency in ASEAN's policy. These were reflected in the three aspects of its diplomacy, namely: (1) its consistent call for Vietnamese withdrawal from Cambodia, (2) the call for self-determination for the Cambodians, and (3) since the ICK was started — the establishment of a neutral and non-aligned Cambodia. But in trying to work out a formula acceptable to all the parties concerned, ASEAN was seen to have vacillated from taking on a hard stance on Vietnam to a more moderate, accommodating position. This was further complicated by the need for ASEAN to compete with Vietnam in the international arena but at the same time demonstrate that any obstacles to a settlement were not the result of its inflexibility. Thus while ASEAN basically insisted that proposals for a political settlement in Cambodia be worked out under the UN framework, some of its previous proposals were in fact outside the UN framework. Nevertheless these seeming contradictions were part and parcel of ASEAN's unceasing efforts in finding a political settlement to the Cambodian conflict. Moreover, these shifts in policies need not necessarily be viewed as weaknesses since these were part of the whole process of trying to resolve, what was at that time, an almost intractable conflict.

The essence of ASEAN's diplomatic approach to the Cambodian problem is well captured in this quotation from a Thai foreign ministry official when he said:

> There are many doors and some of them are open and others are closed. But one should not misjudge things. Open doors don't necessarily mean smooth passage while closed doors may not mean there is no light at the other end of the tunnel... If more doors are open, there could be room for accommodation. But when one can accommodate more, it could also harden the positions of some parties concerned. So don't think that a compromise would make every party soften its stand...[55]

From the above, one could discern why the policy of accommodation became the dominant mechanism of conflict management that ASEAN used in its diplomacy on Cambodia. It was not that the other mechanisms of isolation and mediation were irrelevant, but given the complexities of the conflict and ASEAN's limited capabilities, using both instruments would have been counter-productive to the resolution of the conflict. For instance, while most ASEAN members were exposed to the risks of the Cambodian conflict, particularly Thailand, which was the front-line state, the reality was that they did not have the material capabilities nor capacity to isolate Vietnam. ASEAN may have had a regional voice but this was truly insufficient. For one thing, ASEAN could not even put up any joint ASEAN military or peacekeeping force to help Cambodian forces or even to impose a *condon sanitaire* to keep the Cambodian refuges from flocking into the Thai borders. ASEAN's initial policy of "bleeding Vietnam white" was nothing more than an attempt to exert peer pressure on other states to avoid having any dealings with Vietnam in all fields of diplomatic, political, or economic activities. The reality was that beyond the hope of exerting pressure on others, their influence was limited and complicated by the other fact that ASEAN members themselves were not fully united in their approach in isolating Vietnam.

This was where the other conflict management mechanisms of consultation and consensus were significant in mitigating the effects of the conflict among ASEAN members. This was well illustrated in the numerous inter-ASEAN meetings that took place at various levels throughout the duration of the conflict. This process was also well reflected in Indonesia's unceasing efforts at consulting with her ASEAN counterparts on how best to proceed with regard to Cambodia. Indonesia's diplomatic activities were best depicted in Mochtar Kusumaatmadja's "shuttle diplomacy", named after the high-profile trips the former foreign minister had taken, actively criss-crossing the region and visiting ASEAN capitals, as well as Vietnam and Cambodia and even outside the region to the United States and the former USSR. Indonesia's Kusumaatmadja was, after all, ASEAN's designated interlocutor in the conflict.

Accommodation, consultation, and consensus could also be observed in ASEAN's deference to Thailand in recognition of its status as the front-line state. In spite of several attempts by Indonesia and Malaysia to change ASEAN's policy away from that which Thailand had sought, the latter was successful in having practically all of the proposals set aside, or amended in a manner which it found acceptable and satisfactory. Singapore's sentiments that were similar to that of Thailand's were also equally respected. These efforts to accommodate the interests of its other members could be seen in the way some of the initiatives proposed by Malaysia and Indonesia had to be changed or dropped. To recapitulate, these initiatives included: The Kuantan Principle of 1980, Malaysia's "five-plus-two" formula; and Indonesia's "Cocktail" proposals, as originally advanced by Malaysia in late 1985 and again in July 1987. In return, Thailand had displayed sensitivity and accommodated the position of her ASEAN colleagues. Thailand, for example, conceded on a number of issues like the proposals contained in the "Appeal on Kampuchean Independence" to seek a resolution of the conflict outside the UN framework, and her willingness to deal with Hun Sen's PRK in terms of their proposals for national reconciliation — it had once been considered as not opposed to the fundamental objectives of finding a comprehensive political settlement for Cambodia. The challenge for Thailand then was not only to manage her relations with her ASEAN neighbours while confronting the risks brought on by Cambodia, but also to ensure that her national security was not compromised when agreeing to a united position of ASEAN.

The search for a comprehensive political settlement of the Cambodian conflict ended with the 1993 UN-supervised elections in Cambodia. Five years later, Cambodia had had its second election, it had formed a coalition government and joined the rest of her Southeast Asian neighbours to become ASEAN's tenth member.

## VII. CONCLUSION

### Assessing ASEAN's role in the Cambodian Conflict

ASEAN did not resolve the Cambodian conflict. It had to take the P5 of the Security Council and UNTAC to come in before any comprehensive political settlement could be achieved. How should we then define ASEAN's role in the conflict? What ASEAN did throughout the duration of the Cambodian problem was to take the lead in the search for a comprehensive political settlement. From the start of the conflict, it was ASEAN that initiated, and, to the extent possible explored and exhausted, whatever practical means available to come up with mechanisms to resolve the conflict. What ASEAN lacked in terms of regional authority to influence the behaviour of the Khmer factions and the major power dynamics was made up for through its intense lobbying in the international arena and unceasing efforts at opening and maintaining channels of communications with the different Cambodian factions. It also never stopped consultations among all parties concerned.

Before one could dismiss the efforts of ASEAN, one must note that the Cambodia problem was basically considered an internal conflict within Cambodia (among the Khmer groups) for which ASEAN, the outsider, had no *locus standi* to intervene. Nor did it have the capacity to do so. As mentioned in the previous chapter, ASEAN started out as an exercise in regional reconciliation confined mainly to its original member states, which had a history of inter-state conflicts. Moreover, ASEAN's mechanisms for dispute settlement did not go beyond observance of regional norms and informal modalities of consultation and consensus. Hence, ASEAN was never prepared to manage nor resolve a conflict of this nature.

In getting involved in the Cambodian problem, ASEAN therefore stuck closely to its own modalities — defined largely by the practice of the ASEAN way. From the very start, ASEAN's involvement had been predicated on its protests and vocal rejection of Vietnam's violation of the international norms of respect for a country's sovereignty and the right of self-determination — principles which had been held reverently in the Southeast Asian region.

Denying recognition of Vietnam's legitimacy in Cambodia served a number of ends. Firstly, it sent a message to Vietnam that ASEAN would not tolerate its use of force in international relations. Its occupation of Cambodia violated the code of conduct in the region. Such act also ran counter to the core of which ASEAN's mechanisms of conflict management are founded, that is, respect and restraint in inter-state conflict and pacific settlement of disputes. Secondly, it forced the international community to take up Cambodia's cause and sustain the interest for as long as it could. Thirdly, it reassured Thailand, the front-line state of ASEAN, that its counterparts in the grouping were not only sympathetic to its security concerns but were also more than willing to extend help in protecting its national security from external aggression. Finally, this extension of support given to Thailand jelled ASEAN member states and gave the grouping a focus on its respective external relations.

The complications brought about by the international dimension of the conflict as reflected in the rivalry between China and the former USSR was beyond the regional grouping's scope and capability to resolve. This factor must be taken into consideration especially when smaller regional security organizations like ASEAN try to protect and project its interest, while working within the constraints of the international system characterized by Cold War politics. In the Cambodian conflict therefore ASEAN could only, at best, make its opinions heard in the international arena as actively and aggressively as possible. This accounts for the faithful sponsorship of ASEAN of UN resolutions year after year. ASEAN persistently put pressure on Vietnam, the PRK, and the former Soviet Union by effectively lobbying against them at the United Nations Assembly while supporting the Cambodian resistance forces. In doing so, pressure was constantly placed on the aggressor, Vietnam, and for a long time this pressure led to the further isolation of the country.

At the same time, isolating Vietnam did not mean that ASEAN did not recognize its security interest. This was why ASEAN was seen to vacillate between taking on almost simultaneously both a hard and soft, accommodating stance — the politics of ambiguity. ASEAN's choice for taking the path of accommodation was already discussed in the earlier section of this chapter but has to be reiterated here. Against all the other mechanisms available in the book, this was the only pragmatic way of going ahead considering the complex realities of the Cambodian conflict and ASEAN's own limitations.

Nevertheless, by promoting conciliation among the warring Khmers and between them and the Vietnamese, ASEAN as also a mediator. ASEAN's diplomacy on Cambodia reflected the skilful yet thoughtful skills of ASEAN as a conflict manager in the region. Furthermore, ASEAN's approach to the management and eventually the resolution of the Cambodian conflict, as well as types of mechanisms deployed reflected the group's inter-subjective understanding of the nature of the Cambodian conflict and the dynamics of the politics in the region.

In conclusion, what is instructive about ASEAN's experience in managing the Cambodian conflict has been the fact that, when viewed within the context of the constructivist approach, ASEAN's role in the conflict was not only an exercise of conflict management but also an exercise of identity and community-building in ASEAN. Through the unceasing efforts placed on consultations and towards consensus, the ASEAN member states were constantly involved in the process of defining and redefining their interest with one another throughout the duration of the Cambodian conflict. It was no doubt a tall order, considering the need to constantly balance national interests vis-à-vis the region's or ASEAN's communal interest. Nevertheless, the commitment displayed by its members throughout the crisis period provided the foundation for ASEAN to start building the community that its leaders envisioned.

The Cambodian experience, therefore, provided a point of reference as to where and what ASEAN stood for. The experience helped members define their identity as a regional organization constituted by its norms and diplomatic practices. While ASEAN's diplomacy on Cambodia was far from perfect, it nevertheless instilled the idea among its members that for ASEAN to succeed and for the region to achieve peace, its mechanisms and processes must be geared towards engendering a sense of community and regional identity — regardless of whether the results were incremental. In fact, it has been this same inter-subjective understanding of regional processes that underpinned ASEAN's rationale in developing a new conflict management mechanism. This mechanism comes in the form of a multilateral security forum — the ASEAN Regional Forum (ARF), which we will turn to in the next chapter.

## Notes

1. See Muthiah Alagappa, "Regionalism and the Quest for Security: ASEAN and the Cambodian Conflict", *Journal of International Affairs* 46, no. 2 (1993): 439–68.
2. Until the 1993 elections in Cambodia which eventually saw the legitimate formation of the Government of the State of Cambodia, the country was often referred to as Kampuchea. However, the formal change of name was announced earlier in May 1989 by Hun Sen, who at that time was the Prime Minister of the People's Republic of Kampuchea. In this chapter, the terms will be used interchangeably, especially in the historical section of this narrative.
3. These factors were identified by Warner Draguhn in "The Indochina Conflict and the Positions of the Countries Involved", *Contemporary Southeast Asia* 5, no. 1 (1983): 93–116.
4. For more historical discussion on Kampuchean–Vietnamese animosity, see, for example D.G.E. Hall, *A History of Southeast Asia* (Hong Kong: Macmillan Educational Limited, 1982), pp. 459–75. A more succinct summary is provided in Nayan Chanda's *Brother Enemy* (New York: Hardcourt, Brace, Javanovich, 1986), Chapter 2.
5. Draguhn, "The Indochina Conflict", p. 96.
6. Hall, *A History of Southeast Asia*, pp. 459–75. See also John Cady, *Southeast Asia: A Historical Development* (New York: McGraw-Hill, 1996).
7. Ibid.
8. Draguhn, "The Indochina Conflict", p. 98. Similar discussions can also be read in Gou Yan and Dong Nan, "The Kampuchean Issues: Its Origins and Major Aspects", in *Beijing Review*, No. 37 (September 1983), pp. 3–27.
9. David Chandler, "Strategies for Survival in Kampuchea", *Current History* (April 1985), pp. 141–53.
10. Ibid.
11. For more detailed discussion, see David Chandler, "Cambodia in 1984:

Historical Patterns Re-asserted", *Southeast Asian Affairs 1985* (Singapore: Institute of Southeast Asian Studies, 1985), pp. 177–86.

12. At the height of the Cambodian crisis, there have been many articles that discussed ASEAN's concern over this superpower rivalry that was being played out in the Cambodian imbroglio. See, for example, Donald Weatherbee's "The View from ASEAN's Southern Flank", *Strategic Review* (Spring 1983), p. 59.

13. Tommy Koh, *The Quest for World Order* (Singapore: Times Academic Press, 1998), p. 24.

14. See Joint Statement, Special Meeting of ASEAN Foreign Ministers on the Current Political Development in the Southeast Asian Region, Bangkok, 12 January 1979, *ASEAN Documents* (Bangkok, Ministry of Foreign Affairs, 1983), p. 179.

15. For a detailed chronology of ASEAN diplomacy in the Indochina crisis from 1979 to 1984, see Donald E. Weatherbee, ed., *Southeast Asia Divided: The ASEAN-Indochina Crisis* (Boulder, CO: Westview Press, 1985), pp. 131–45.

16. See Joint Communique, 16th ASEAN Foreign Ministers, 25 January 1983, Bangkok, Foreign Broadcast Information Service-AIA (hereinafter referred to FBIS-AIA), 22 June 1983.

17. Weatherbee, ed., *Southeast East Asia Divided*, p. 132.

18. Justus van der Kroef, "The Kampuchean Problem: Diplomatic Deadlock and Initiative", *Contemporary Southeast Asia* 5, no. 3 (1983): 263–72.

19. For more on the CGDK, see Lao Mong Hay, "Kampuchea: A Stalemate?", *Southeast Asian Affairs 1984* (Singapore: Institute of Southeast Asian Studies, 1984) pp. 153–61.

20. Wire News, Agency France Press, 14 March 1985.

21. "Malaysian FM: Khmer factions need beef and teeth", *The Nation*, 26 November 1981.

22. Ibid.

23. For more extensive discussion on Thai's threat perceptions, see "Thailand's Policy Towards the Vietnam–Kampuchean Conflict: Issues on Thai National Interest, Policy and Alternatives on the Kampuchean Problem as seen by the Thai Foreign Ministry Officials and Academics", *Asian Studies Monograph No. 132* (Bangkok: Institute of Policy Studies, 1985).

24. Ibid. See also John Funston, "Thailand and the Indochina Conflict", *Dyason House Papers* 6, no. 1 (1979).

25. John Funston, "Indochina Refugees: The Malaysian and Thai Response", in *Asian Thought and Survey*, vol. 14, September 1980.

26. See, for example, Zainal Abidin, "Malaysian Threat Perceptions and Regional Security", in *Threats to Security in East-Asia and Pacific*, edited by Charles Morrison (Honolulu: Pacific Forum Book, 1983), pp. 103–11.

27. Van Tao, "Vietnam–Indonesia Relations in Historical Perspectives", *Indonesian Quarterly* XII, no. 2 (1984): 245–57.

28. For discussion on Indonesia's threat perception, see Jusuf Wanandi and M. Hadi Soesastro, "Indonesia's Security and Threat Perceptions", in *Threats to Security*, pp. 83–101.

29. See Gareth Porter, "Why Vietnam Invaded Cambodia", *The Nation*, 9 June 1979.

30. See Pham Binh, "Prospects for Solutions to the Problems Related to Peace and Stability in Southeast Asia", *Indonesian Quarterly* XII, no. 2 (1984): 205–33, and Pao-Min Chang, "Beijing Versus Hanoi: The Diplomacy Over Kampuchea", *ASIAN Survey* XXIV, no. 5 (1983). For a more comprehensive discussion, see Nayan Chanda, *Brother Enemy: The War After the War* (San Diego: Hardcourt Brace Javanovich, 1986).

31. Justus van der Kroef, "Hanoi and ASEAN: Is Co-Existence Possible?", *Contemporary Southeast Asia* 16, no. 2 (1983): 164–78. See also *Nhan Dan* Review of Sino-Vietnamese Relations in the Past 30 Years, Summary of World Broadcast (hereinafter referred to SWB), FE/6332/A3/1, 30 January 1980.

32. Ibid. See also Pham Binh, "Prospects for Solutions", pp. 205–33.

33. Weatherbee, "ASEAN and Indochina", p. 10.

34. See Karl D. Jackson, "Indochina in Early 1984: Doves of Peace or Dogs of War, in Weatherbee, ed., *Southeast Asia Divided*, pp. 34–37. See also "An Olive Branch" in *The Nation*, 3 June 1983; "Back to Square One", *The Nation*, 2 July 1983 and "ASEAN Appeal on Kampuchea: A Tactical Manoeuvre?", *The Nation*, 24 September 1983.

35. See "ASEAN to meet Vietnam Halfway", *The Nation*, 25 February 1984; "Indonesian Military Think Tank Proposes", *The Nation*, 27 February 1984.

36. "Divergent Views on Kampuchea", *The Nation*, 3 March 1984. See also Susumo Awanohara, "The Pace Quickens", *Far Eastern Economic Review* (hereinafter referred to as FEER), 15 March 1984.

37. Ibid.

38. "ASEAN Concerto: Squawking off the bear", *The Nation*, 10 February 1985.

39. "ASEAN to highlight 'proximity talks' ", *The Nation*, 5 July 1985.

40. *Asiaweek*, 26 July 1985, p. 8.

41. *FBIS*, 2 May 1986, A3.

42. *FBIS*, 18 August 1987, AA1.

43. *FEER*, 27 August 1987.

44. Ibid.

45. "Khmer Rivals Talk Peace", *Straits Times*, 27 July 1988.

46. *FEER*, 4 August 1988.

47. *Straits Times*, 16 February 1989.

48. See "Consensus Statement of the Chairman of the Jakarta Informal Meeting", *Contemporary Southeast Asia* 11, no. 1 (1989): 108.

49. "Sihanouk unveils 5-point peace plan", *Straits Times*, 28 July 1988.

50. See *ASEAN Information Paper on the International Conference in Paris*, 1989.

51. See *Straits Times* of 28, 29 and 30 August 1989.
52. *Straits Times*, 8 September 1989.
53. *FEER*, 3 November 1988.
54. Amitav Acharya, "Cambodia, the United Nations and the Problems of Peace", *Pacific Review* 7, no. 3 (1994): 297–308.
55. Quotation from a Thai Foreign Ministry Official (unnamed) in the Thai Talk column by Suthichai Yoon, *The Nation*, 5 October 1981, as mentioned in John Funston, *Thai and ASEAN Policy on Cambodia*. (Brunei: University Brunei Darussalam, undated).

# 4

## : ASEAN REGIONAL FORUM
## : Extending the ASEAN Way in
## : Managing Regional Order

### INTRODUCTION

The previous chapter discussed ASEAN's first major attempt at resolving an extramural dispute involving countries, which at that time were not yet members of this association. As discussed, ASEAN's involvement in the conflict was also problematic right from the start. As far as Vietnam was concerned, the Cambodian dispute was an internal dispute that no external party had any *locus standi* to intervene. But for ASEAN, the Vietnamese occupation posed varying threats to regional security and was a blatant violation of the international, and in particular, ASEAN's norms on non-use of force and non-interference in domestic affairs. ASEAN, therefore, was deeply involved in finding a political settlement for the Cambodian conflict.

Among the many salient points that can be learnt from ASEAN's experience in Cambodia are the kinds of limitations that regional organizations face in managing extra-regional disputes. Firstly, notwithstanding its lack of capacity to intervene in the conflict, ASEAN was severely handicapped by the very nature of the conflict. Not only were there differences in position as to whether the Cambodian conflict was an internal matter, the parties involved in the conflict had not also given their consent to the mediating role that ASEAN took on. This made ASEAN's mandate in the resolution of the conflict controversial. Secondly, the conflict became less manageable and more intractable when major powers were involved and their co-operation was not forthcoming. One notes that ASEAN's efforts in the pushing ahead with the "Cocktail" talks were hampered when the United States refused to recognize the Coalition Government of Democratic Kampuchea (CGDK) forces and when China became less hostile to Vietnam. The conflict, therefore, became much more complex when ASEAN found itself having to accommodate the positions of the major powers vis-à-vis the positions of the warring Cambodian factions. Thirdly, ASEAN members themselves have had conflicting interests throughout the duration of the conflict and were exacerbated by divergences in threat perceptions. Hence, their resolve to pursue a settlement of the conflict was affected. This emerged clearly when Thailand decided to switch tack and adopted a new policy on Cambodia which was totally different from the corporate approach taken by ASEAN.

Nevertheless, as argued in Chapter 3, ASEAN was still able to play a significant role in the settlement of the Cambodian imbroglio. More significantly, and for the purpose of this study, ASEAN's experience in the Cambodian conflict reflected a certain pattern of managing conflict in the region. This can be seen in the types of conflict management mechanisms that ASEAN consistently used throughout the duration of the conflict. Predictably, these types of mechanisms were largely informal in nature. And if one were to tease them out again, these were the mechanisms that revolved around dialogue and consensus, on accommodation of various interests, and on norm-building and community-building in Southeast Asia.

This particular experience of ASEAN in managing regional conflict, coupled with several developments that were taking place in and outside the region, provided a meaningful background to the establishment of a new form of conflict management mechanism that reflected the type of mechanisms that ASEAN developed over time. This new mechanism was the establishment of the ASEAN Regional Forum (ARF).[1] This chapter is divided into three parts and begins with a brief background to the events that led to the creation of the ARF. The rest of the chapter proceeds to examine the nature of this mechanism and assesses its impact in managing regional security.

## I. RATIONALE FOR THE ARF

### Shifts in Major Power Relations and Its Impact on ASEAN

There had been several developments in the international arena that occurred around the same time when the Cambodian problem was nearing its resolution. One of these was the series of events that took place in Eastern Europe, particularly the changing political landscape in the former Soviet Union as a consequence of the former Soviet President Michael Gorbachev's policies on *glasnost* (openness) and *perestroika* (economic restructuring). These policies that began in the mid-1980s signalled the slow demise of communism in the Soviet Union, and at the same time a rethinking of Soviet's foreign policy in Asia. In July 1986, Michael Gorbachev announced in Vladivostok the new Soviet foreign policy in the Asia-Pacific. The main thrusts of its policy were to project a new image of the Soviet Union to the outside world, and especially to the Asia-Pacific countries, to show that the new Soviet Union was interested in reducing international tensions and in resolving outstanding conflicts with its neighbours. The policy wanted to impress upon the countries in the region that the Soviet Union was interested in preserving peace and security in the Asia-Pacific through regional co-operation. This policy was articulated again by Gorbachev in Krasnoyarsk in September 1988.

The Vladivostok/Krasnoyarsk initiatives were well received in the Asia-Pacific countries and were interpreted as an important breakthrough in the traditional Soviet political thinking and as an invitation to a meaningful dialogue with Moscow. The Vladivostok/Krasnoyarsk initiatives also paved the way of the disengagement of the Soviet military involvement in Indochina. This meant that Soviet's patronage of Vietnam under the COMECON framework was coming to an end. This was to cost Vietnam its yearly support from the USSR of US$3 billion. It should also be recalled that during this period, Vietnam had formally announced that it was withdrawing all its troops from Cambodia from 1989. This announcement was taken as a sign that without Soviet's support, the toll of war on Vietnam would begin to show. As a consequence, Vietnam was forced to improve relations with her ASEAN neighbours and seek to develop greater economic and political co-operation with them. This also meant that Vietnam could no longer afford to be difficult with regard to the Cambodian problem.

The former USSR's overtures to the region were especially welcomed by ASEAN. By 1989, the Soviet Union's status at the annual ASEAN's Ministerial Meeting was upgraded from being an observer to become a consultative partner of the grouping. Two years later, after the dissolution of the Soviet Union that was precipitated by the coup attempt in August 1991, the Union of the Soviet Sovereign Republics (USSR) was replaced by the Commonwealth of Independent States, comprised of fifteen sovereign states. Three states (Latvia, Estonia, and Lithuania) opted for complete independence while the rest decided to stay together in a very loose commonwealth. For ASEAN, Russia became the principal heir to the USSR and has been its main dialogue partner since 1996.

In the meanwhile, China's relations with the ASEAN countries began to improve. Indonesia and Singapore established formal diplomatic relations with China in 1990. Up until then, countries in Southeast Asia particularly Indonesia and Malaysia had harboured strong suspicions regarding China's political ambitions in Southeast Asia. China's support of the communist parties in Indonesia, Malaysia, Thailand, and even the Philippines in the 1960s convinced these countries that China was bent on expanding its influence in Southeast Asia. Indonesia in particular had severed diplomatic ties with China following the abortive coup staged by the Indonesia Communist Party (PKI) in 1965. On the other hand, Singapore after its independence in 1965, was conscious of its status as being a predominantly Chinese state in the region. Thus, to partly allay the fears of its Malay neighbours (that is, Indonesia and Malaysia) about its ethnic identity and motivations, and to partly defer to Indonesia who had severed diplomatic ties with China, Singapore did not establish diplomatic relations with China at the time of her independence.

The reservations towards China intensified at the height of the Cambodian crisis. China's support of the Khmer Rouge and Thailand's predisposition towards China as a consequence of the Cambodian conflict had caused serious concern among ASEAN countries. These concerns were, however, alleviated when China decided to disengage itself from the Indochinese conflict and when it was forthcoming in its support of ASEAN's efforts to resolve the conflict. China's withdrawal of its support of the Khmer Rouge[2] and, in particular, China's backing of ASEAN's various initiatives towards a comprehensive political settlement of the crisis like the Jakarta Informal Meetings (JIM) I and II went a long way to boost its standing with the ASEAN states.

The equation was different for the United States, however. Against the significant global and regional developments, particularly with the dissolution of the Soviet Union, the United States began to rethink its role in the region. The reduced role of the United States in Asia became a cause for concern among the countries in the region, and these concerns were heightened with the planned closure of the U.S. military bases in the Philippines in 1992. In 1991, the Philippine Senate rejected the renewal of the bases treaty with the United States, thus forcing the closure of the American naval and air bases in the country. However, prior to this closure, there had already been announcements from Washington that the United States was going to reduce its number of forces in the Asia-Pacific region. It was envisaged that the United States was going to cut its forces in Asia by 12 per cent from 135,000 troops to 120,000 by the end of 1992 under the East Asia Security Initiative (EASI).[3]

With the demise of the Soviet Union and the end of the Cold War, global tensions appeared to have been significantly reduced. Thus while the American announcement of U.S. forces reduction, coupled with the announcement by the former Soviet Union that it was going to remove practically all of its naval and air units stationed in Vietnam's Cam Ranh Bay, should have been welcomed by ASEAN, these developments had instead triggered a different effect.

Seen against the thawing of the relations between U.S.–USSR and U.S.–China, the reduction of U.S. forces in the region brought to the fore strategic uncertainties for states that saw the United States as a regional balancing power. There was widespread concern among ASEAN countries that the emerging developments at the end of the Cold War would force the United States to turn inward and lose interest in the region. Furthermore with the withdrawal of Soviet troops from Vietnam, ASEAN also lost a useful counterweight to any possible designs by China for supremacy in Southeast Asia. The anxieties by regional states during this period was best articulated by Singapore's Prime Minister Goh Chok Tong when he said:

> If the rapprochement between the superpowers comes through ... the US presence in this part of the world would diminish ... If this happens, who will be the regional leader then? It will be left to China, India and Japan to contest for the leadership of the region.[4]

There was therefore this shared realization among the countries in the region that until this question of the power vacuum was addressed, the region would be more vulnerable than it had ever been, in spite of the end of the Cold War. Due to the uncertainties posed by this question of power vacuum, many scholars and analysts had described the regional situation during that period as extremely fluid and in a state of flux. This was despite the fact that the region was also experiencing a period of unprecedented peace and economic growth.[5] Thus, it was during this uncertain, yet ironically prosperous period, when many ASEAN leaders had argued for the need to initiate an Asia-Pacific Security Dialogue.[6]

## Economic Integration and Rising Regionalism

As indicated above, the other factor that added impetus to the establishment of a "new" mechanism to address regional uncertainties and/or security challenges was the unprecedented economic growth that was happening in the Asia-Pacific region in which many ASEAN countries were major star performers. From the late 1980s to early 1990s, the vibrant economic growth in the region was remarkable, with many ASEAN countries registering gross domestic product (GDP) growth averaging between 5 and 6 per cent.[7]

Many have explained the rapid economic growth in ASEAN as part and parcel of the emerging trade patterns that was happening across the wider Asia-Pacific region. Highly industrialized economies like Japan had begun to shift their industries to the less developed economies, taking note of comparative advantages that these economies had to offer. ASEAN countries at that time complemented this pattern of economic development by embarking on export-related activities and adopting export-oriented policies to take full advantage of the emerging shifts in the pattern of industrial production in the region.[8] This pattern of trade and industrialization in the region had been commonly described as the "flying geese" model of economic development. This model saw latecomers (like ASEAN) having successfully adopted a strategy of entering into manufacturing sectors where they could capitalize on their comparative advantage in terms of low labour cost and in importing "old" technology from an already mature economy whose competitive advantage in that particular industry was on the decline. These mature economies, like Japan, would later on invest in new industrial products using new technologies for which they have the innovative edge.[9]

However, what was interesting to note during this period was the growing importance of the Newly Industrializing Economies (NIEs). Whereas in the mid-1970s and early 1980s, the NIEs — South Korea, Taiwan, Hong Kong, and Singapore — and ASEAN have had to depend on the United States and the European Community (EC) to sustain their export drive, this had changed from the mid-1980s onwards. Japan became the major importer of the manufactured exports of the NIEs and ASEAN. The impressive high performance of the Asia-Pacific economies was, therefore, being mutually reinforced by the increasing structural inter-dependency along the Japan–NIEs–ASEAN economic axis.[10]

This emerging pattern of regional economic interdependence was well illustrated by the entry of foreign direct investments (FDIs) into

ASEAN. The large number of FDIs coming from East Asia that came into ASEAN were driven largely by the so-called three low phenomena: namely, low effective currency exchange rates, low cost of raw material imports; and low interest rates. Against the rapid appreciation of the yen and the currencies of the other Asian NIEs, the ASEAN economies became major recipients of FDIs from Japan, Taiwan, Hong Kong and South Korea.[11] ASEAN's industrialization, facilitated by the massive inflow of FDIs from Japan and other Asian NIEs enhanced regional economic relations and led to some concern from countries outside the region that East Asia was turning to be a formidable economic bloc.

For some time during those high growth period, there were concerns that the Asia-Pacific region was being divided into subregional economic blocs with the increasing economic activities taking place within these subregions: the Asian-NIEs, ASEAN, and the South Asian Association for Regional Co-operation (SAARC) as well as between the South Pacific Forum, Australia, and New Zealand, and even China which was opening up its economy. While these groups comprised countries that were at different stages of economic development and could arguably be regarded as complementary rather than competitive units, they were more or less perceived as economic blocs emerging from different subregions in the Asia-Pacific. Thus, with this kind of economic regionalism taking place, there were concerns that these would lead to protectionism, closed regionalism, and possibilities of intra-regional conflicts. Against these new concerns, the idea of creating the Asia-Pacific Economic Co-operation (APEC) to encourage open regionalism emerged and was proposed by Australia in 1989.[12]

The introduction of APEC basically underscored the need for the Asia-Pacific region to have a forum where economic issues brought about by the rapid changes in the international and regional economic environment could be discussed and where co-ordinated responses could be achieved. Its objectives as set out in the 1991 Seoul APEC Declaration were:

- to sustain the growth and development of the region for the common good of its peoples and, in this way, to contribute to the growth and development of the world economy;
- to enhance the positive gains, both for the region and the world economy, resulting from increasing economic interdependence, to include encouraging the flow of goods, services, capital, and technology;

- to develop and strengthen the open multilateral trading system in the interest of Asia-Pacific and all other economies; and
- to reduce barriers to trade in goods and services among participants in a manner consistent with GATT principles, where applicable, and without detriment to other economies.[13]

While the formation of APEC was a welcome development in the light of the widening economic interdependence and integration taking place in the region, ASEAN member states however were perceived to be initially cool to the proposal. One of the reasons for ASEAN's reluctance was the concern that in creating a new institution in the region like APEC, the organization (ASEAN) might become redundant.

More significantly, the reservations were also due to the fact that during this period, some ASEAN member countries were coming up with their own ideas on how to effectively manage the kind of economic regionalism that was taking place and how ASEAN countries could best protect their interests. Malaysia, for example, introduced the idea of forming an East Asian Economic Grouping (EAEG).[14] The EAEG was to include the six ASEAN countries, China, Japan, Taiwan, and Hong Kong, but excluding the United States, Canada, Australia, and New Zealand. It was envisaged that the EAEG would provide a framework where member countries could come together and formulate common positions and strategies and to have a stronger voice against other countries which belong to bigger trading blocs like the EC and NAFTA.[15] The EAEG was to have three basic elements:

- Its operation was to be consistent with that of the General Agreement on Tariffs and Trade (GATT). This meant that EAEG was committed to free trade and would adopt the most favoured nation principle and the transparency principle in imposing protective measures.
- It was to run parallel with the scheme for APEC.
- It was to enhance ASEAN.[16]

However, the idea of the EAEG was met with strong opposition from the United States that perceived it as an attempt by East Asian countries to form a bloc.[17] That the word "grouping" aroused suspicion from those excluded led ASEAN (upon the suggestion of Indonesia) to replace it with the word "caucus", thus changing EAEG to EAEC. But the EAEC idea also failed to get the full endorsement from other ASEAN members. And to Malaysia's disappointment, Japan whom it had expected to lead the EAEC did not support it amidst strong objections coming from the United States.

In the meanwhile, some ASEAN countries had also floated similar ideas to enable ASEAN to consolidate its position in the light of new trade blocs in North America and Europe. The Philippines proposed the setting up of the ASEAN Treaty of Economic Co-operation (ATEC) to transform ASEAN to a more cohesive regional group similar to the EC. The proposed ATEC concept called for the creation of "supranational institutions" which were similar to the European Commission and European Council, and the adoption of higher forms of regional economic co-operation.[18] Thailand, on the other hand, has proposed the setting up of an ASEAN Free Trade Area (FTA) within ten to fifteen years. The idea of the FTA was to allow free flow of trade activities among ASEAN countries without affecting trade between ASEAN and the outside world. Singapore suggested the idea of setting up of more growth triangles in the region with the private sector taking the lead and the governments in the region co-ordinating the activities.[19]

From the above, one would therefore note that ASEAN members had been toying with a number of ideas on regional economic co-operation, around the same time when the APEC initiative was introduced. In spite of initial reservations and even misgivings by some ASEAN members about APEC, ASEAN eventually lent its support after having been assured of its core membership status in the organization. More significantly, ASEAN basically agreed with the idea of fostering open regionalism in the Asia-Pacific region and the manner by which this goal was to be achieved, which was through consultation and consensus. The emphases placed on the creation of a sense of community among the countries in the Asia-Pacific with shared interests generally complemented ASEAN's approach in maintaining peace and security in the region. Moreover, in the post-Cold War era, it was felt that the need for the establishment of a broader regional framework for political and economic co-operation had become greater than ever because of the intensive economic interaction that was taking place in the region.

## The China Factor

Many scholars in the region have emphasized the China factor in their analysis of the reasons why ARF was created.[20] With the opening up of China's economy in the mid-1970s and its rapid economic modernization programme, the potential of a powerful, rising China became an area of concern. Whereas in the past, a rising China may had been only a latent worry, the developments resulting from the accelerated economic activities and political developments taking place in the country became too significant for the Southeast Asian states to be complacent about.

Economically, since China embarked on an aggressive economic modernization programme and set up the Special Economic Zones (SEZs), it has attracted massive FDIs especially in the southern coastal provinces of Guangdong, Fujian, and Hainan. These SEZs are close to Southeast Asia. Thus, while China was becoming an important trading partner for the ASEAN states, it was also getting to be a strong competitor for international markets.[21] At least prior to the establishment of the ARF, trade figures of the bilateral trade between China and the ASEAN countries over ten years (from 1980 to 1990) had been small but was on the rise. For example, in 1993 China's combined trade with all six ASEAN countries was only US$9 billion. These figures were considerably lower compared to the total trade between China and Taiwan.[22] Hence, in spite of the prospects of increased trade between ASEAN and the mainland, the competition for markets and FDIs has made China a formidable rival. Given the fact that ASEAN states have been mostly trading economies, it was important for them to have a China that was co-operative and that would use its economic might to further enhance economic co-operation in the Asia-Pacific rather than for nationalistic ambitions.

The rapid economic development in the country also saw China embarking on a modernization programme of its military. While this had been a perceptible trend in the region as other ASEAN states were more or less also on the same track of military modernization,[23] a large and modern Chinese military, particularly its navy, could not be ignored. Beijing's efforts to expand its naval power was regarded as particularly worrisome in the light of China's presence in the South China Sea and its claims to the Paracels and the Spratly Islands. The territorial disputes over the Spratlys has involved mainland China, Taiwan, and the Southeast Asian states of Brunei, Malaysia, the Philippines, and Vietnam.

As the Chinese navy modernized and became stronger, there were concerns that the chances of conflict over the Spratlys could become imminent. These fears were heightened in 1988 when China set up a military presence in the Spratlys and sank three Vietnamese naval vessels. Moreover, in February 1992, the Beijing government passed a "law on its territorial waters and their contiguous areas" which claimed the Spratlys, Paracels, and other South China Sea islands, and reserve the right to use military force to defend those claims. In May of the same year, China also signed an agreement with the U.S. firm, Crestone Energy Group to drill near the islands in an area that Vietnam had claimed as part of its continental shelf.[24] These developments served only to heighten latent fears of an aggressive China that many analysts who write about the China threat have argued. For example, one analyst had pointed out that ASEAN states such as Malaysia have "quietly defined" the Chinese navy as their primary threat and as a consequence, adjusted their defence postures accordingly.[25]

During this period, China's domestic situation was also laden with uncertainties with the prospects of transition to a post-Deng Xiaoping era. There had been concern that the political system in China was changing, increasingly becoming less like the Beijing-centred model of decision-making which prevailed in the past. The Communist party was no longer as dominant while the role and significance of other state institutions (particularly the armed forces) have increased. The emergence of these other interests in China that were said to be openly contending for wealth, power, and influence raised concerns about the country's future stability.[26]

Finally, the domestic developments in China coincided with the period when the country was also redefining its relations with most ASEAN states given the new realities that were taking place.[27] Thus, the confluence of these strategic developments with the developments within China itself had become major concerns shared across the region.

In summary, within the context of the rapid changes in the external political, economic, and strategic environment, ASEAN found itself compelled to adjust to the changing realities and redefine its role as a regional actor. To be sure, the role it has taken in trying to manage regional conflict during the height of the Cambodian crisis was no longer sufficient. The changes that had taken place, both in the international and regional environment in four years since 1989, had been extremely significant and these changes portend to the need for ASEAN to adjust its old approaches to a new set of realities. Questions were raised as to the relevance of ASEAN's prevailing security approaches that mostly emphasized improving bilateral relations and focusing on national resilience. Therefore, the crucial questions confronting ASEAN at that time were, how it was going to define its role and calibrate its approaches in an increasingly complex global, political, economic, and security environment.

## II. PRELUDE TO THE ESTABLISHMENT OF THE ARF

Amidst the power shifts and uncertainties of the post-Cold War era, many states in the Asia-Pacific region, particularly ASEAN, saw the need for a new political and security framework that would help them maintain the necessary equilibrium for sustainable peace and prosperity in the region. Moreover, there was this growing realization that regional security arrangements were increasingly relevant given the imperatives to prevention, containment, and termination of regional and intra-state conflicts that were on the rise in a post-Cold War environment.[28] Given its recent experience with Cambodia, ASEAN members were certainly convinced about the necessity to re-examine regional security arrangements.

Nevertheless, major questions pertaining to the modalities of this "arrangement" remained. One of these was whether it was at all possible to bring together the major powers and interested countries in the region into a single framework, and to engage them in a constructive political and security dialogue, with the objective of bringing about a consensual approach to regional political and security issues. The territorial disputes and differences in political orientation among countries spanning the Asia-Pacific region added another challenge to this effort.

Despite these perceived challenges, a number of countries nevertheless came up with their own initiatives. In July 1990, Australia proposed the idea of a Conference on Security and Co-operation in Asia (CSCA) at an ASEAN Post-Ministerial Conference (PMC) in Jakarta, Indonesia. The CSCA proposal, which was announced by former Australian Foreign Minister Gareth Evans, had the hallmarks of the European CSCE model. In his proposal, Evans suggested that countries in the Asia-Pacific should "look ahead to the new institutional processes that might evolve over time as an appropriate framework for the discussion and handling of security issues".[29] To the proponents of the concept, CSCA could also be a means to ensure that the United States and Japan remain engaged more formally into Southeast Asian security arrangements. CSCA was, therefore, envisioned to comprise the five ASEAN states, its dialogue partners, as well as Vietnam, Cambodia, Papua New Guinea, and states in the Indian subcontinent.

At the same ASEAN meeting, a similar proposal was made by Joe Clark, former Canadian Secretary of State for External Affairs. In pushing the idea, Joe Clark declared that:

> There has not been a structure of security cooperation, of traditional military alliances, of regional political institutions (in Asia-Pacific) to

mirror the European experiences. I suggest it is time to consider security or political institutions in the Asia Pacific.[30]

Japan, on the other hand, had also proposed a similar idea of a security framework but specifically suggested that the format could be that of an extended ASEAN PMC in order to "create a sense of mutual reassurance" among the states in the Asia-Pacific. A year later former President of the Soviet Union, Mikhail Gorbachev, endorsed the CSCA proposal during his trip to Japan in April 1991.[31]

ASEAN reacted ambivalently to the proposals, while expressing interest in the idea of an extended, that is, multilateral framework for regional security co-operation. However, as time passed, the idea of a CSCA-type of regional security framework became less attractive to the countries in the region for a number of reasons. Firstly, it was thought that the CSCE-type process was far too elaborate and complex for a newly emerging framework in the Asia-Pacific region. Many states felt that unlike the CSCE idea which originated since the 1950s before it was institutionalized in 1975, they had no previous experience in region-wide political and security co-operation. Secondly, it was deemed difficult, if not impossible, to transpose a ready-made system from one region to another, in spite of some modifications to the model. The unique qualities and characteristics of the Asia-Pacific region would have to be considered in any initiatives geared towards promoting a regional security framework. Thirdly, the CSCE policy of linking human rights to political and security co-operation has also caused uneasiness among some of the Asian countries. Fourthly, while the early 1990s was an important turning point for the CSCE's renewed activism, there was not much that CSCE could be proud of in terms of its achievements. The years 1990 and 1991 were particularly turbulent years for European security as the crisis in Yugoslavia eventually resulted in the disintegration of the Yugoslavian state. While the crisis was unfolding, CSCE's appeals to renounce military force and to respect the rights of the minorities fell on deaf ears of the warring factions. CSCE's offer to mediate and dispatch observers to Yugoslavia was also turned down. In this case, CSCE proved to be ineffective in addressing the security issues in its own backyard. Therefore, it was not difficult to convince the states in the region that the European model was inappropriate for the Asia-Pacific region.[32]

The fact that the proposals initially came from non-Asian states also did not help to gather sufficient support. In fact the more the non-Asian states tried to push their ideas, the more reservations the member states of this region had. It was therefore not surprising that during the early

1990s, many regional leaders made it a point to repeatedly announce their objections to the CSCE model.[33]

Meanwhile, ASEAN also started to explore other possible models that were more suitable to regional conditions. Between 1990 and 1991, several official meetings were held on this subject. These in turn generated specific proposals emanating from academics, think-tanks, and government officials on how Southeast Asia could address the new security challenges. One of these proposals was the recommendation from the ASEAN Institute of Strategic and International Studies (ASEAN-ISIS) in 1991 that ASEAN should use the PMC forum for political and security dialogues with non-ASEAN countries in the region.[34] The role of ASEAN-ISIS in shaping ideas on regional security and mechanisms of conflict management will be discussed further in the next chapter.

The breakthrough finally came during the Fourth ASEAN Summit in Singapore in January 1992. ASEAN leaders decided to use the existing PMC forum, but extended in composition, as the mechanism to promote an expanded political and security dialogue with countries across the Asia-Pacific region. Beyond ASEAN's dialogue partners,[35] the composition of an "extended" PMC was to be broadened to include South Korea as a regular dialogue partner and India as a "sectoral" partner. More importantly, China and Russia were also to be invited as guests at the ASEAN Ministerial Meeting, and Vietnam and Laos as "observers".[36] Following the agreement at the Summit, preparations were then made during the ASEAN-PMC in Manila in July 1992 to plan the modalities that this regional security forum should take. After its successful deliberations in Manila, ASEAN decided to call for a special ASEAN-PMC meeting at the senior officials level (SOM) to discuss regional security issues and add more substance to the "birth" of a regional forum. The meeting was held in May 1993 and it was during this meeting when Singapore, which held the chairmanship of the ASEAN Standing Committee (ASC) proposed the name "ASEAN Regional Forum" (ARF). The acronym "ASEAN" was used rather than the word "Asian" to reflect ASEAN's leading role in the Forum. Finally, at the ASEAN Foreign Ministers Meeting in Singapore in July 1993, the intention to establish the ARF was formally announced. The ARF was to be composed of eighteen states: the ASEAN-5, Australia, Canada, China, the EC, India, Japan, Laos, New Zealand, Papua New Guinea, Russia, South Korea, the United States, and Vietnam.

## III. DEFINING THE SHAPE AND FORM OF THE ARF

The inaugural meeting of the ARF was held in July 1994 in Bangkok, Thailand. Prior to this meeting, several questions were asked pertaining to: (1) the nature of the forum, i.e., Should it be an informal or formal meeting? (2) its membership, i.e., How inclusive should the ARF be? Should it include all the major powers in order to reflect the various security interests in the region, while at the same time enabling ASEAN to remain in the driver's seat? (3) the pace of development, i.e., How far should the ARF develop, and how fast?

The first meeting of the ARF on 25 July 1994 fell short of providing answers to the questions. At most, after a three-hour, closed-door discussion, the eighteen participants of the historic meeting came out expressing their satisfaction, pointing to the fact that it was the first time "many former enemies had gathered together in an armchair meeting".[37] The official statements that came out recognized that the ARF "had enabled the countries in the Asia-Pacific region to foster the habit of constructive dialogue and consultation on political and security issues of common interest and concern".[38] Therefore, the fact that the meeting took place at all was considered by many as a remarkable achievement in itself.

The significance of this historic meeting cannot be ignored. The meeting expressly signalled the turn towards multilateralism in ASEAN's approach to managing regional security. Given the participation and engagement of major powers, this turn towards multilateralism was indeed a huge leap from ASEAN's "old" modalities that emphasized regional autonomy as expressed through the ZOPFAN framework.[39] Going by the remarks of former Indonesian foreign minister, Ali Alatas, who said that Southeast Asia "can't keep the four powers [the US, Japan, China and the Soviet Union] out of the region", there was the recognition among ASEAN states that regional ideologies had to be balanced with political and security considerations. Thus, ASEAN had no choice but to readjust to changing circumstances and modify its mechanisms accordingly. The impact of establishing the ARF on ASEAN's conflict management mechanisms will be elaborated on in the concluding section of this chapter.

Needless to say, the first ARF meeting set the agenda for this forum. It agreed on "the need to develop a more predictable and constructive pattern of relations for the Asia-Pacific region". More specifically, the ministers endorsed the principles of the ASEAN Treaty of Amity and Co-operation (TAC) in Southeast Asia as a code of conduct governing the relations between states and as a unique diplomatic instrument for regional confidence-building, preventive diplomacy, and political and security co-operation.[40]

## Charting the Course

It was not until the forum's second meeting in Bandar Seri Begawan, Brunei Darussalam in August 1995 that the future course of the ARF was clearly mapped out. The meeting agreed that the ARF should take a "gradual evolutionary approach", and would "move at a pace that was comfortable to all participants". The meeting identified the development of the ARF in three stages:

- Stage I:   Promotion of confidence-building measures (CBMs)
- Stage II:  Development of preventive diplomacy mechanisms; and
- Stage III: Development of conflict-resolution mechanisms.[41]

At the Brunei meeting, the ministers agreed that the ARF concentrate on stage I to promote CBMs and to continue to discuss means of implementing specific CBMs. Specific measures were outlined to promote transparency among members, which included: (1) voluntary submission to the ARF or ARF-SOM by ARF members of an annual statement of their defence policies; (2) increase high level contacts and exchanges between military academics, staff colleges, and training; and (3) participation in the UN Conventional Arms Register.[42] The meeting also acknowledged "the importance of non-proliferation of nuclear weapons in promoting regional peace and stability" and noted "with satisfaction the progress made towards Southeast Asia Nuclear Weapons Free Zone".[43]

Another significant development in this meeting was the creation of "inter-sessional groups" which were organized into three track one (official and governmental) "vehicles" where discussions on certain sensitive issues could be thrashed out and specific measures recommended. These three vehicles were:

1. Inter-Sessional group on Confidence Building Measures, to be co-chaired by Japan and Indonesia;
2. Inter-Sessional group on Peacekeeping, to be co-chaired by Malaysia and Canada;
3. Inter-Sessional Group on Search and Rescue Co-ordination, to be co-chaired by the United States and Singapore.

On the organization of the ARF activities, it was agreed that there would be an annual ARF Ministerial Meeting just after the ASEAN Ministerial Meeting and the host country would chair the meeting. The incoming Chairman of the ASEAN Standing Committee would also chair all the inter-sessional activities of the ARF.[44]

It was further agreed that no institutionalization was required for the ARF nor the need to establish a Secretariat. ASEAN shall be the repository of all ARF documents and information and provide the necessary support to sustain ARF activities.[45] Finally, it was agreed that:

> the rules of procedure of ARF meetings *shall be based on prevailing ASEAN norms and practices, (and) decisions should be made by consensus after careful and extensive consultations. No voting will take place. In accordance with prevailing ASEAN practices, the Chairman of the ASEAN Standing Committee shall provide the secretarial support and coordinate ARF activities.*[46]

The third meeting, which was held in Jakarta in July 1996, further outlined concrete activities to promote CBMs and transparency. These included: publication of defence policy papers; continued dialogue on security perceptions, enhanced high-level defence contacts and exchanges; circulation on a voluntary basis the same data on conventional arms to the ARF countries at the same time of its submission to the UN Register of Conventional Arms (UNRCA); and for ARF members to support actively internationally recognized global arms control and disarmament legal agreements, specifically Non-Proliferation Treaty (NPT), Chemical Weapons Convention (CWC), Biological Weapons Convention (BWC), Convention on Certain Conventional Weapons (CCW), and the successful conclusion of the CTBT.

By the time the ARF had its fourth meeting in Malaysia in July 1997, it already had a proliferation of CBM activities.[47] As one security analyst had observed, "the ARF's track-record has been strengthened considerably over the past two years by the full or partial implementation of a raft of CBMs, and the development of an embryonic agenda of preventive diplomacy measures…".[48] As the ARF's CBM agenda continued to expand, so had its membership.[49] Subsequent ARF meetings also saw the growing involvement and participation of defence and military officials in the work and activities of the ARF.[50]

In charting the ARF's course, one would observe that since its formation, ARF had placed a lot of emphasis on promoting dialogue and confidence-building. It had disclaimed notions that it was aimed at being a military alliance, a type of deterrence and an alternative to a balance of power arrangement. Instead, its member states have consistently argued that the ARF has been more about attempts at co-operative security, and fostering habits of dialogue in an inclusive forum comprising both like-minded and non-like-minded states in the Asia-Pacific region.

ASEAN has had a pivotal role in the ARF, especially with regard to advancing the CBM agenda forward. In the implementation of concrete CBMs, it was also ASEAN that took the initiative to prepare two lists of CBMs. The first list (found in Annex A of the ARF Concept Paper) spelt out measures which could be explored and implemented by ARF members in the immediate future, while the second list (found in Annex B) were measures which could be explored over the medium to long term. Both short to medium-long term CBMs were mostly under the declaratory and transparency categories or a combination of both (like the ones found in Annex B). So far, the ARF has yet to outline CBMs falling under the constraint category. The types of CBMs measures adopted are summarized in Table 4.1.

Thus, the ARF's two-track approach in promoting CBMs have been guided by ASEAN's experience of informal trust and confidence-building through norm-building, without having to implement immediately the more explicit CBMs. This meant that an attempt has actually been made to adopt the ASEAN way as the Asia-Pacific way. And, more concretely, non-ASEAN members of the ARF were encouraged to associate themselves with the principles enshrined in ASEAN's TAC.[51] These two types of approaches dovetailed with the nature of ASEAN's existing mechanisms for conflict management and regional security.

## IV. EXAMINING THE ARF

From the time the ARF was launched, the forum has received mixed responses. The reactions ranged from that of elation — given the ingenious attempt to bring disparate countries with hostile past to sit together and discuss regional security issues — to one of cautious optimism. At the far end was one of pessimism at the efforts by a subregional body such as ASEAN to lead a highly ambitious multilateral security forum.

Among the major reservations regarding the prospects of the ARF pertained to: ASEAN's centrality in the ARF and its assumed leadership to ensure that it remains at the "driver's seat"; the slowness of its pace, specifically its progress in moving beyond the stage of CBMs to preventive diplomacy (PD); and its viability in resolving more intractable regional conflicts like the disputes in the South China Sea, the problems in the

## TABLE 4.1

## Types of Confidence-Building Measures (CBMs)

| | |
|---|---|
| Principles/Declaratory measures | • generalized statements of interests, norms and beliefs<br>• statements can be either explicit/formal (e.g., declarations, treaties) and implicit/informal (e.g., communiqués)<br>• common to other approaches to security co-operation, e.g., preventive diplomacy (PD) or conflict resolution (CR) |
| Transparency measures | • defence White Papers publications<br>• calendar of military activities<br>• exchange of military information<br>• military-to-military contacts<br>• arms registry<br>• military personnel/student exchanges<br>• mandatory consultation on unusual/dangerous activities<br>• notification of military manoeuvres/movements<br>• invitation of observers<br>• surveillance and controls zones<br>• open skies<br>• troop separation and monitoring |
| Constraining measures | • prevention of dangerous military activities<br>• incidents of sea agreements<br>• demilitarized zones<br>• disengagement zones<br>• air/maritime keep-out zones<br>• weapons of mass destruction (WMD)-free zones<br>• limits on personnel numbers, categories and deployment zones<br>• limits on equipment deployment (by geographical area or numbers), category and storage<br>• limits on troop and equipment movements/manoeuvres by size and geographical area<br>• limits on readiness<br>• limits on number of military exercises per year<br>• bans on simultaneous exercises/alerts and/or certain force/unit types |

**Source:** Amitav Acharya, *The ASEAN Regional Forum: Confidence-Building* (Ottawa: Department of Foreign Affairs and International Trade, Government of Canada, 1997).

Korean peninsula, and the challenges from major powers such as the United States, Japan, China, and Russia. These shall be dealt in the following sections.

## The Centrality of ASEAN and the Relevance of the ASEAN Way

Critics and observers have questioned the relevance of ASEAN in its determination to be the "primary driving force" of the ARF. The criticisms centred on the viability of applying the ASEAN way of doing things within the ARF and its impact on ARF's ability to influence real security problems. In the early years of the ARF's inception, the late Michael Leifer, a renowned authority on Southeast Asian security, had expressed this kind of reservation when he noted that "the issue of relevance [of the ARF] is reinforced by ASEAN's insistence on retaining the central diplomatic role in the ARF which confuses power and responsibility and generate frustrations among North-east Asian and Pacific participants".[52] Another scholar, Robyn Lim, said that the "the ARF can do little to promote security because ASEAN insists on its primacy in it".[53] Another study assessing ASEAN also observed that "if ASEAN continues to chair the ARF, the dialogue could stagnate".[54]

The above arguments implicitly suggested that the ARF would move forward and function better if ASEAN were to cease to be in the driver's seat and that leadership be transferred to a non-ASEAN member, presumably a big power like the United States. However, before pursuing these arguments further, one would have to go back and ask why ASEAN had been given the prerogative to be at the driver's seat in the first place? The previous sections of this chapter already mentioned the significant circumstances that led to the creation of the ARF and how ASEAN played the pivotal role in it. It is useful to restate here how ASEAN was able to bring the big powers together in the only multilateral security forum unprecedented of its kind in the world. Ten years after its establishment, the ARF has been recognized as the only forum that brings together the major powers (the United States, China, Russia, Japan) together, as well as EU and India, to discuss security issues. This was realized under the initiative of ASEAN. While others would argue that such an opportunity was presented to ASEAN by default and that is was "strategically convenient" to do so, this does not diminish the fact that ASEAN, in the post-Cold War environment had become — in the words of Michael Leifer — as the "acceptable interlocutor" with the major powers.[55] Equally important was and has been the fact that it was ASEAN that seized the opportunity and was successful in its initiative to form the ARF since "the major Asia-Pacific powers have been incapable of forming a concert arrangement among themselves".[56]

It has been argued that had the United States or Japan initiated the idea of a multilateral security forum, this would have aroused suspicions from China. The same would have applied to Russia as well. Therefore, ASEAN's role in initiating the ARF made it easier to bring the major powers of the Asia-Pacific together. Although ASEAN was no doubt a small subregional grouping within the vast Asian region, at least during the early 1990s, it already had achieved enough diplomatic savvy and credibility to command the respect of the international community. Being one of the most successful regional organizations that had brought about order and stability in Southeast Asia was something that ASEAN earned outside the region.

Thus, ASEAN's skills in creating another mechanism in managing regional security must therefore be recognized, and appreciated better, especially if its role is examined within the context of building trust and generating confidence between the major powers and other states in the Asia-Pacific region. As mentioned above, had the initiative to form the ARF come from either the United States or Japan or even Russia, it would not have been possible to bring in China or North Korea. In this regard, ASEAN was the "safe" player, the middleman who could constructively engage China and the United States together with the rest of the other states in the region. Indeed, if the purpose of multilateral security enterprise like the ARF was to get more player involved in the bigger stake of managing the future of regional security in the wider Asia-Pacific region, the participation of these major players was definitely essential. It must be noted that the ARF is a *sui generis* organization. More significantly, it is a multilateral security forum that has as its members all the major powers in the international system — the United States, China, Russia, Japan, India and the European Union — yet none of them dominates the forum. If one peers through the prism of the realist perspective of international politics, it would not have been imaginable that a modest organization comprising small powers could have played such a major role in steering a multilateral security forum of this nature. Yet, ASEAN has. This is something that cannot be understated.

## Setting the Pace: Too Slow?

With regard to the criticisms that the ARF after ten years is more like a "talk shop" rather than a viable multilateral security organization, given the difficulties it has encountered in moving beyond the phase of confidence-building to preventive diplomacy, one would argue that this view is rather premature and even myopic. The ARF's progress has to be examined against the evolving processes that have been taking place within the Forum. As a fledgling security grouping, one would have to take into consideration the difficulties confronting the ARF in pushing for more substantive progress, particularly in moving the PD agenda forward. This is elaborated further below.

When the ARF concept paper was released in 1995, the ministers agreed that the ARF was going to evolve in three distinct stages: first from CBMs, to preventive diplomacy and then to conflict resolution. At the ARF Senior Officials Meeting in 1997, it was agreed that it was time to push the ARF process further from CBM to PD but the officials, however, noted that both stages could overlap. This was reiterated by the ARF Chairman at the end of the Fourth ARF meeting in Kuala Lumpur in 1997, when he declared that the ministers had already agreed that, "where subject matters at Stage I and Stage II overlap, such matters can proceed in tandem with Stage I".[57] It was interesting to note that during the Fourth ARF meeting, some participants had pushed for a simultaneous approach for Stage I and Stage II activities, citing the overlapping relationship between CBMs and preventive diplomacy.[58] As a compromise, the final agreement was that it would be acceptable for the work on the two stages to proceed in tandem as long as the focus remained on the first stage.[59] To move this process forward, track two (a term used to describe the unofficial, non-governmental bodies engaged in policy discourse) were engaged to help push the process by initiating meetings, workshops, and discussions on how this could materialize.

In spite of such pronouncements, members of the forum were divided between those that wanted to see an institutionalized ARF which moves forward at a faster pace (these would be the Western countries and Japan), and those (like China) that were more cautious and preferred a more incremental approach in directing the nature of institutionalization of the ARF. The latter position had also been shared by ASEAN members.[60]

While preventive diplomacy is described as a "natural follow-up to confidence building", moving this process forward has indeed been slow for the ARF. One of the major problems was in defining the meaning of preventive diplomacy. A noted Australian scholar had succinctly captured the problem when he said that the ARF was bogged down by "conceptual refinement [and] or practical proposals" of preventive diplomacy which might be implemented by the ARF countries.[61]

The ARF Concept Paper has already made some suggestion in this regard. Among the measures introduced included:

- Developing a set of guidelines for the peaceful settlement of disputes, taking into account the principles of the UN Charter and the TAC;[62]
- Seeking the endorsement by other countries of the ASEAN Declaration of the South China Sea;
- Exploring ways of preventing conflict, including the appointment of Special Representatives to undertake fact-finding missions, at the request of the parties involved, and offer their good offices; and
- Exploring the idea of establishing a Regional Risk Reduction Centre to serve as a database for the exchange of information.[63]

After the ARF's Concept Paper was released, the ARF sponsored three seminars on preventive diplomacy at both the track one and track two levels between 1995 and 1997 with the view of soliciting further ideas on how this process could proceed.[64] The first one was in Seoul, Korea in May 1995, the second in Paris in November 1995, and then the third in Singapore in September 1997.

The Seoul meeting generated specific proposals on measures of preventive diplomacy and these included, among others: (1) the establishment of Conflict Prevention or Risk Reduction Centre; (2) the establishment by the ARF of a register of experts; (3) official discussion on the principles of peaceful dispute settlement; and (4) the use of Eminent Persons in mediation efforts.[65]

The Paris meeting followed up on the recommendations and narrowed it down to three measures, namely: production of a regular "regional strategic outlook"; identification of a "core list of CSBMs specifically oriented towards preventive diplomacy"; and the expansion of the role of the ARF Chair to include a "good offices" role.[66] These recommendations were further refined and adjusted during the Singapore meeting to consider the recommendations from the Council for Security Co-operation in the Asia-Pacific (CSCAP).[67] The CSCAP's report had noted "the different circumstances and actual conditions in the Asia-Pacific ... call for different approaches from those employed in other parts of the world".[68]

However, in spite of the proliferation of ideas and recommendations from the three meetings, nothing concrete has emerged. This was the mood when another track two meeting was organized in April 1998 to discuss the future of the ARF. Organized by the Institute of Defence and Strategic Studies in Singapore, the meeting brought together more than seventy people from the academic and policy communities of the ARF countries. During the deliberations, the definitional problematique mentioned earlier by Desmond Ball emerged again as one of the greatest stumbling block in moving the process forward from CBMs to preventive diplomacy. Participants from China had emphasized the need for clarity in the definition and scope of preventive diplomacy and stressed that due attention should be taken to ensure that mutual respect for state's sovereignty was maintained.[69] Other sympathetic participants also stressed that a more institutionalized and structured PD agenda may be premature given the stage the ARF was in and the unique security environment in the region. There were others, however, who felt that there had been too much debate on the definitions of preventive diplomacy, losing sight of what the ARF had achieved, raising the comfort level among diverse participants of the region.

None the less the definitional impasse on the PD agenda received a boost at a track two meeting organized by the CSCAP Working Group on CBMs on Preventive Diplomacy in Bangkok on 28 February–2 March 1999. An agreement on a working definition of preventive diplomacy was reached and this was forwarded to the ARF Inter-sessional Support Group (ISG) on CBMs which had its meeting immediately after the track two meeting. Preventive diplomacy is defined as "consensual diplomatic and political action with the aim of:

- Preventing severe disputes and conflicts from arising between States which pose a serious threat to regional peace and stability;
- Preventing such disputes and conflicts from escalating into armed confrontation; and
- Limiting the intensity of violence and humanitarian problems resulting from such conflicts and preventing them from spreading geographically".[70]

Accompanying such definition are the key principles of preventive diplomacy which are as follows:

(i)  It is about *diplomacy*. It relies upon diplomatic and peaceful methods such as persuasion, negotiation, enquiry, mediation, and conciliation.
(ii) It is *voluntary*. Preventive diplomacy practices are to be employed only at the request of the parties or with their consent.

(iii) It is *non-coercive activity*. Acts that require military action or the use of force, or other coercive practices, such as sanction, are outside the scope of preventive diplomacy.

(iv) It rests upon *international law*. Any action should be in accordance with the basic principles of international law.

(v) It is based on respect for *sovereignty and non-interference* in the internal affairs of a state. This includes the principles of sovereign equality and territorial integrity.

(vi) It requires *timeliness*. Action is to be preventive, rather than curative. Preventive diplomacy methods are most effectively employed at an early state of a dispute or crisis.

Since then, the meetings and deliberations on preventive diplomacy continued. Table 4.2 provides a summary of ARF deliberations both at track one and track two.

As Table 4.2 shows, preventive diplomacy remains at the formative stage in the ARF process. To date, the ARF can account for the following developments:

• Adoption of the concepts and principles of preventive diplomacy (including the eight key principles of PD)
• Establishment of the ARF register of experts/Eminent Persons Group
• Enhanced role of the ARF Chair

The foregoing discussion extensively discussed the problems and reasons why ARF cannot move as fast as many would have preferred. It is not only that the ASEAN countries have been cautious but also that once again, the problem of accommodating differing positions had to be navigated skilfully. This was clearly visible during the track two Meeting on Preventive Diplomacy organized by the CSCAP Working Group on CBMS in February 1999. The problem of having to find common ground arose when the scope of a conflict was defined, that is, whether it was either inter-state or intra-state. China was adamant that sovereignty of the state must be upheld and any preventive exercise when applied to an intra-state conflict would be tantamount to interference. Some participants were supportive of the Chinese case although some thought there were cases when preventive diplomacy could and should include intra-state conflict. Nonetheless, participants knew that unless some form of accommodation from both sides were allowed, there could not be any progress in the discussion.[71]

## TABLE 4.2
### Towards Preventive Diplomacy in ARF and CSCAP

| Date | Development |
|------|-------------|
| 1995 | Track two members held an ARF-sponsored PD seminar in Seoul. Participants considered whether the definition of PD by UN Secretary-General Boutros Boutros-Ghali in his 1992 *Agenda for Peace* adequately addressed the needs and concerns of the Asia-Pacific region. They focused on three broad themes: how ARF members could most usefully define the concept of PD that would provide a workable solution to regional problems; whether specific threats to regional peace and stability amenable to PD could be identified; and whether the seminar could identify specific mechanisms, frameworks, and measures which might enable efforts at PD. First, regarding PD definitions, it was expressed that PD is not the same as crisis management, but focuses on early prevention of latent conflicts — a desirable but not always workable goal. Here consensus was important. Second, participants identified potential sources of threats and conflicts (territorial disputes, proliferation of conventional weapons and WMD, inter-state conflicts such as the Korean peninsula, intra-state conflicts such as in Cambodia and Myanmar, drug trafficking, terrorism, environmental degradation, maritime safety and piracy, unregulated population movements, etc.). It was agreed that application of PD in each instance should be based on consideration of the urgency of the issue in question and its amenability to such efforts. |

Third, participants emphasized that focus on PD should be on perceptions, urgency, and feasibility, rather than hardware concerns. Suggested PD measures included the following: establishing CBM working groups as a first step given the view that the ARF should evolve incrementally; rather than direct involvement, the ARF can endorse, enable and/or buttress existing bilateral and multilateral processes (e.g., US-DPRK talks on nuclear issues) in order to broaden support for them beyond the relevant parties; placing emphasis on principles (e.g., codes of conduct), structures (e.g., regional conflict prevention centre), activities (e.g., promoting crisis prevention exercises), and tracks (e.g., vigorous support for track two processes); establishing a register of experts, discussing principles of peaceful dispute settlement, appointing a High Commissioner for Maritime Affairs, establishing permanent or *ad hoc* committees or working groups, etc. Although participants differed on rapid or gradual approaches to structural development of PD, there was broad agreement, however, that such structures are potentially useful. The importance of political will to the success of any PD effort was also noted.

**TABLE 4.2** – *continued*

| Date | Development |
| --- | --- |
| 1996 | A second ARF-sponsored PD seminar, also under track two auspices, was held in Paris. Consistent with the statement by the Chairman of the third ARF meeting (Jakarta), the seminar sought to develop proposals for PD based on principles set out in the UN Charter, the Treaty of Amity and Cooperation in Southeast Asia, the Five Principles of Peaceful Coexistence, and the 1992 Manila Declaration on the South China Sea. Participants used as a starting point UN Secretary-General Boutros Boutros-Ghali's definition of PD, but recognized that various meanings also existed. They agreed on the following: the need for Annual Security Outlooks (ASOs) and collection of relevant information and analyses; possibility of creating in the future a regional research and information centre; possibility of establishing an early warning system; and possibility of the ARF as a repository of information on PD, including monitoring outcomes of specific cases. Track two, particularly CSCAP, was seen as the appropriate venue for considering these things. Participants agreed that a core list of CBMs specifically oriented towards PD be identified, and proposed that these CBMs be considered by the March 1997 ISG-CBMs. Other PD measures that could be available to the ARF, including those mentioned in the ARF Concept Paper's Annex, were discussed: fact-finding, good offices, mediation, moral suasion, and third-party mediation. Further, the meeting agreed to recommend an ARF role in PD through expansion of the good offices of the ARF Chair, guided by the consensus principle among ARF members. As a longer term measure, it was proposed that the Chair consider the idea of an ARF risk reduction centre. The meeting concluded that any consideration of PD efforts by the ARF is to be subject to the strict adherence to consensus among all ARF members. |
| 1997 | A third ARF-sponsored PD seminar was held in Singapore. The meeting accepted that different circumstances and actual conditions in the region called for different approaches from those employed elsewhere. Some participants felt that CBMs, as one element of PD, had the best prospects of success in the immediate future and efforts should be focused on them. The meeting addressed the EU experience in PD, and exchanged views on prospects for further efforts in PD (as well as CBMs) in Southeast Asia, particularly South China Sea and Cambodia. It discussed China's perspective on PD. The meeting agreed to forward the following |

*continued on next page*

**TABLE 4.2** – *continued*

| Date | Development |
|------|-------------|
| | proposals to the next ISG-CBMs and the ARF SOM for their consideration: the codification of principles regulating international behaviour in the region; an enhanced role for the ARF Chair or third parties in providing good offices in certain circumstances; explore the relevance of Sino-Indian and Sino-Russian experiences in CBMs for PD in the Asia Pacific region; multilateral co-operation as a form of PD on transnational issues (e.g., drug trafficking, population movements, nuclear waste storage, shipment and disposal) as related to security; ASOs to be discussed at track one, but produced by track two. The meeting endorsed the idea that co-operation between the ARF and CSCAP be enhanced. It was agreed that the following proposals be forwarded to CSCAP for further consideration: the utility and feasibility of map (simulation) exercises; and freedom of navigation issues. |
| 1998 | In accordance with the fourth ARF meeting mandate, the ISG addressed areas of overlap between CBMs and PD, although maintaining focus on CBMs. Participants generally agreed to give further consideration to the following tabled proposals: enhanced role for the ARF Chair, particularly the idea of a good offices role; development of a register of experts or Eminent Persons among ARF participants; produce ASOs, provide voluntary background briefings on regional security issues, etc. The possibility of the ARF developing a set of "principles" or "concepts" to guide the ARF's consideration of PD was raised. The ISG agreed to recommend to the ARF SOM and Ministers that one of two meetings of the ISG on CBMs scheduled for the next inter-sessional year be set aside to address the overlap between CBMs and PD. It stressed the importance of proceeding in an incremental, step-by-step manner, of decision by consensus, and sensitivity to the interests and comfort level of all ARF participants. |
| 1999 | The ISG-CBMs was briefed on the CSCAP workshop on PD in Bangkok, which produced a broad definition and principles of PD and suggested ways in which the ARF could promote PD in the region. The ISG also exchanged views on existing CBMs/PD arrangements among various ARF members, and noted important lessons to be drawn from a variety of existing regional arrangements: 1976 Treaty of Amity and Cooperation in Southeast Asia, 1992 Joint Declaration on Denuclearisation of the Korean Peninsula between the two Koreas, 1996 Agreement between China and |

**TABLE 4.2** – *continued*

| Date | Development |
|------|-------------|
| | India on CBMs along the "line of actual control" (LAC) in the Sino-Indian border areas, etc. |
| | The sixth ARF meeting in Singapore endorsed the recommendations of the ARF SOM and ISG-CBMs to discuss the concepts and principles of PD, noting the common understandings reached on four tabled proposals regarding the overlap between CBMs and PD (cf. Table 4.1). It requested ISG-CBMs to further explore these concerns, and welcomed ASEAN's offer to prepare a paper on PD concepts and principles for consideration at the next ARF SOM. |
| 2000 | Consistent with the request of the sixth ARF meeting that ISG-CBMs should further explore the overlap between CBMs and PD, ISG participants discussed the enhanced roles for the ARF Chair and the experts/Eminent Persons register. A possible enhanced role included informal liaisons between the ARF Chair and external parties — notably, meetings between current ARF Chair Surin Pitsuwan and the Secretary-Generals of OAS and the UN — with the consent of ARF members. However, there was agreement that further discussion was needed at the next ISG due to the complexities of building consensus in the ARF regarding principles and procedures for the enhanced role of the ARF Chair's good offices, and of co-ordination between ARF meetings. Participants welcomed and discussed Japan's proposal for an ARF Register of Experts/Eminent Persons, noted the complexities concerning modalities for implementing such a Register, and welcomed proposals by Japan, Canada and New Zealand to further research this issue in preparation for the next ISG. Voluntary submission of ASOs at the track one level by individual participants was acknowledged. Further, preliminary views on Singapore's paper on PD ("Concept and Principles of Preventive Diplomacy") were exchanged, in preparation for fuller discussion at the next ISG. The meeting agreed to recommend to the ARF SOM that discussion on PD be continued in the next inter-sessional year and for Singapore to revise its PD paper in the light of views expressed at the ISG. |
| 2001 | In view of the seventh ARF meeting's decision to enhance the role of the ARF Chair, the eighth ARF meeting expressed appreciation to Vietnam, |

*continued on next page*

**TABLE 4.2** – *continued*

| Date | Development |
| --- | --- |
| | as Chair, for continuing and expanding informal contacts with the UN, OAS and Non-Aligned Movement. Following up on work done by the ISG-CBMs, the Ministers welcomed further progress on the available use, on a voluntary basis, of the ARF Register of Experts/Eminent Persons, and agreed to adopt the Paper on Terms of Reference for ARF Experts/ Eminent Persons finalized by the ISG-CBMs. It was agreed that the Paper on the Concept and Principles of PD be adopted as a snapshot of the state on current discussion on PD, and that the ISG-CBMs continue discussing PD. It also welcomed the voluntary submission of ASOs, compiled as the second volume. |
| | At the third CSCAP general meeting in Canberra, the CSCAP Co-Chair, Singapore's Barry Desker, made a number of proposals for the ARF's evolution towards its PD, including enhancing the role of the ARF Chair; forming consultative committees of Eminent Persons and a register of experts; establishing a good offices role for a troika of past, present, and next ARF Chairs; and forming a Friends of the Chair group of distinguished statesmen from the region to push initiatives on behalf of the Chair. |

**Source:** Adapted from *A New Agenda for the ASEAN Regional Forum* by Tan See Seng, et al. IDSS Monograph No. 4 (Singapore: Institute of Defence and Strategic Studies, 2002), pp. 37–42.

A similar example was cited by a senior official from Brunei at the annual Asia-Pacific Roundtable organized by the ASEAN-Institute of Strategic and International Studies in Kuala Lumpur, Malaysia, which was held in June 1999. In a session that discussed the prospects of the ARF, the Chair, Brunei's Permanent Secretary Pehin Dato Lim Jock Seng, shared his views on the difficulties faced by members in trying to calibrate the discussions on the pace and direction of the ARF. Pehin Dato Lim also held the Chairmanship of the ASEAN Standing Committee when it was tasked to prepare the ARF Concept Paper in 1995. He highlighted the fact that since ASEAN was dealing with a diverse group of countries whose relations ranged from close friendships to hostility and suspicion, getting these countries to deliberate on ideas about how the region's security could be guaranteed was by no means an easy task. It was an experiment![72]

## V.  THE LIMITS OF ARF'S MULTILATERALISM AND THE ASEAN WAY

Finally, one of the major criticisms regarding the ARF has been its inability to address more intractable regional conflicts like the disputes in the South China Sea and the problems in the Korean peninsula. As critics have pointed out, the disputes in the South China Sea and the problems in the Korean peninsula are core regional security issues and if these are not addressed by the ARF, then its ability to influence real security problems in Asia is severely limited.

In addressing this issue, we once again revisit Michael Leifer's observations regarding the ARF when he declared that it would be "a categorical mistake to think that the ARF can actually solve problems". He further argued that:

> The fact of the matter is that the ARF ... is an embryonic, one-dimensional approach to regional security among states of considerable cultural and political diversity and thus suffers from the natural shortcomings of such an undertaking. To interpret its role in terms of a new intellectual paradigm would be the height of intellectual naivety. It is more realistic to regard the Forum as a modest contribution to a viable balance or distribution of power within the Asia-Pacific by other traditional means. Those means are limited, however, and the multilateral undertaking faces the same order of difficulty as the biblical Hebrew slaves in Egypt who were obliged to make bricks without straw. A constituency for any alternative form of security cooperation does not exist in Asia-Pacific.[73]

This argument has been supported by other critics who point to the limits of the ASEAN way as a model for ARF's way of doing things. ASEAN's experience in dealing with conflicts, which emphasizes conflict avoidance and management, are deemed insufficient to address the real security problems in the Asia-Pacific region.[74] The ASEAN's preference for non-confrontation and consensus is also seen as severe shortcomings since the ARF has been reluctant to push ahead with sensitive issues like adopting certain PD mechanisms and are instead "sweeping things under the carpet".

Another scholar had pointed to the fact that even the United States has expressed reservations on the prospects of the ARF and had specifically challenged the leadership of ASEAN. Aside from its reservations on ARF's inability to address problems like the Korean Peninsula and even Taiwan, the United States had also decided that "the key multilateral elements of a new regional order should be really organized by the great powers, and that, if there is any lasting proprietary role, it should really be played by the United States".[75]

These views are not really surprising given that the ARF has yet to show any record of having resolved any regional security problem. Belittling the role of ASEAN and its approach to problem-solving is also understandable given the dominant realist perspectives of international relations where in the absence of balance of power, the influence of smaller states and non-material factors are ignored. Consequently, the value attached to norms and processes which the ASEAN way encapsulates are regarded as inconsequential. Hence, from the realist's perspective unless there is a suitable balance of power, the ARF becomes irrelevant. In this regard, the ARF, as argued by Michael Leifer is at best only "a valuable adjunct to the workings of the balance of power" and that "the prerequisite for a successful ARF may well be the prior existence of a stable balance of power".[76]

However, critics of the ARF who take on this view have ignored the fact that the ARF was not created to become an alternative to the balance of power. If one refers to the history of how the ARF came about, one would observe that it had very modest objectives. The objectives cited in the ARF documents and the 1995 Concept Paper had clearly articulated what the ARF is all about a forum for security co-operation. It is for all intents and purposes a tacit norm-building mechanism that promotes the notion of co-operative security. Even ARF supporters would not claim more than that and would acknowledge that it has to work hand in hand with the other mechanisms of enhancing regional security including bilateral military arrangements and alliances. As a noted ASEAN scholar had rightly argued, "the co-operative security aspects of the ARF are not adjuncts to the workings of the balance of power; they moderate and mitigate — through constant dialogue, CBMs, preventive diplomacy, and the norms of ASEAN's Treaty on Amity and Cooperation — the competitive and conflictual by products of power balancing behaviour."[77]

What is interesting, however, is the extent to which some analysts have continued to push the balance of power perspective in assessing the ARF. In the more recent study on the ARF, Ralf Emmers had posited that the establishment of the ARF was influenced by the balance of power (BOP) practices and that the "co-operative regime" that the ARF represented served to constrain power through political means.[78] In pushing the argument to regard the ARF as a function of the balance of power "factor", Emmers stated that:

> beyond its conventional understanding, the balance of power can also be interpreted in political terms ... based on the premise that potential hegemonic dispositions can be restrained through political and institutional means and without the use of war, the traditional instrument of the balance.[79]

When viewed from ASEAN's perspective of developing mechanisms for regional security, this particular reading of the ARF as suggested by Emmers, which is an extended application of balance of power within the co-operative security approach, present a number of puzzling questions. Even if one were to agree that the "restraint resulting from political association has a power balancing relevance", one pressing question arises: Would a major "hegemon" — that is, China, the major power identified as having hegemonic tendencies — agree to be part of an arrangement that was meant to "constrain" or "balance" her? The other question is: who balances whom — the United States, Japan, ASEAN, versus China? Unfortunately, the same balance of power "factor" was applied in the reading of ASEAN's establishment as well. In this case, it was Indonesia that had been identified as the "power" in Southeast Asia with hegemonic tendencies that had to be constrained through the co-operative regime of ASEAN. Once again, we ask why, if this were so, would Indonesia have agreed to join an association whose objective was to constrain her hegemonic tendencies? Moreover, who would constrain Indonesia? An important point to consider in applying or stretching the balance of power approach to both ASEAN and the ARF is the issue of trust and confidence-building. It would have been extremely difficult for the old members of ASEAN to establish ASEAN if there were mutual suspicions that the objective of coming together was to constrain a hegemon. This was why the earlier efforts at instituting ASA and Maphilindo failed (see Chapter 2). One should therefore be able to carefully distinguish the negative constraining processes under the balance of power framework and the positive or regulatory functions of norm-building projects like ASEAN and the ARF.

The point being made here is that the ARF should be assessed for what it is. This is not to ignore the fact that there are undoubtedly tremendous problems for a loose, highly unstructured multilateral security forum which decides on consensus to ever move on. Unlike the practice in the West that stresses rules and structures, the ASEAN process has often been described as characteristically informal. It is also problematic when it has been consistently stressed that the ARF should "move at a pace comfortable to all participants".[80] However, these differences in approaches must be recognized and must be built into any objective assessment.

## VI. SUMMARY AND CONCLUSION

This chapter began by tracing the events and ideas that led to the creation of the ARF, another mechanism of conflict management initiated by ASEAN. Perhaps the more relevant question to ask at this point is: since the ARF has not yet resolved any conflict, how can it be considered as a conflict management mechanism?

Although it is true that up to now, the ARF has yet to be seen to be "managing" any conflict, it is really not too difficult to see why it is a mechanism in itself if one goes back to two essential points mentioned earlier. The first point is the definition of mechanisms of conflict management adopted in this study (mentioned in Chapters 1 and 2). To recapitulate, mechanisms refer to the processes, methods, devices, techniques, and strategies employed to resolve or manage a conflict. The second point involves the various stages of managing a conflict, namely: conflict avoidance, conflict prevention, conflict settlement, and conflict resolution. Against these two points, the creation of the ARF — for all intents and purposes — fits the fact that it is a process deployed at the very least in avoiding and preventing conflict.

In discussing the evolution of the ARF, this chapter also discussed the perceived limitations of this multilateral forum as it adjusts to the regional developments that have occurred since its inception. I have argued that to dismiss the relevance of the ARF is premature at this point since the grouping is still considered a rather young and even inchoate forum. It is useful to reiterate the point in the ARF Concept Paper when it stated that: "The ARF must be accepted as a *sui generis* organisation. It has no established precedents to follow."[81] It is also useful to remind ourselves that this is the only regional forum that brings together all the major powers of the world. Moreover, as once pointed out by an ASEAN Head of State, the "geographical footprint" of the ARF covers the region in the world that has and will continue to be experiencing major power shifts and "if the ARF did not exist, we would have had to invent it quickly to manage these changes".[82]

Given the time-frame in assessing the ARF and in the context of the security environment after the Cold War, the ARF's current emphasis on confidence-building must be assessed for what it has achieved. Most ARF members are satisfied with the progress on confidence-building measures and are happy with the current state of affairs. For example, former Chinese Foreign Minister Qian Qichen at the fourth ARF meeting in Malaysia had stated that the ARF's central task for a considerable time to come should be "to enhance mutual understanding and trust, and remove misgivings and worries".[83] He also said that the ARF had developed a rather unique co-operation approach which featured participating on an equal footing, seeking common ground, while reserving differences, making decisions by consensus and progressing in a gradual manner.[84]

As mentioned in the earlier section of this chapter, one of the primary motivations for forming the ARF was to engage China. ARF so far has been able to do this and has had China's active participation in the forum. A major progress in this aspect was the specific mention which was made in public to the South China Sea disputes during the second ARF meeting held in Brunei in 1995. A year earlier this subject was discussed but not recorded in any official document nor in the official statement of the Chairman to the press.[85] Since then this issue had been referred to in the subsequent ARF Chairman's Statements. In 1997 China Co-Chaired with the Philippines the ARF's Inter-sessional Group on Confidence Building Measures. At the sixth ARF meeting held in Singapore in July 1999, the ARF took note of the regional Code of Conduct in the South China Sea which was being prepared by ASEAN. The Philippines had earlier on pressed for ASEAN's early adoption of the Code during the ASEAN Ministerial Meeting which was held just before the sixth ARF meeting. In 2002, the Declaration of the Code of Conduct on the South China Sea was finally adopted.

One could argue that China's participation in the ARF has certainly enhanced its relations with the ASEAN states. One could also observe the increase in participation of Chinese delegation in both track one and track two meetings. Chinese participants have been more active and forthcoming in their views, both official and unofficial, particularly at the track two meetings. The confidence exuded by the Chinese participants and their candidness cannot be understated as it clearly adds to the understanding, at least to the participants of these various meetings, of the domestic constraints faced by China and the thinking behind the positions they have taken.[86] It is useful to quote here the account of a

Canadian ambassador who wrote about his observations on the perceptible changes among Chinese delegations. He stated that:

> Over time and with enhanced exposure the Chinese delegation spoke more frequently, often without notes in advancing the Chinese position. Both publicly and privately in corridors, what would and would not wash in Beijing was made clear. Other delegations were told that time was needed to work new ideas through the Chinese system for if Washington had many agencies to consult on security issues so did Beijing ... Counsel was given that "what is important is free and frank discussions; how the discussions are recorded is not that important" (this comment was a reflection of Chinese concern not to record discussions — perhaps because if they were read in certain circles in Beijing there would be negative consequences). In a similar vein, the point was made not to be too precise in setting out objectives for "if we know where we are going we will never set out on the path".[87]

In conclusion, whatever gains the ARF may have had so far, it is still a work in progress. As the region found itself having to cope with the devastating impact on the 1997 Asian financial crisis and the series of crises the followed, there have been signs that the ARF momentum may lose some of its steam as some members, badly affected by the crisis, have been preoccupied with domestic concerns. Clearly the challenges ahead are daunting.

Nevertheless, as an evolving mechanism of conflict management in the region, the ARF clearly has much to offer. If one stacks up its achievements against the original objectives of founding the ARF, there are considerable grounds for optimism.

The pivotal role of ASEAN in the evolution of this process of forming a multilateral security forum as a mechanism of conflict management must be emphasized. In fact, in analysing the evolution and the progress of ARF, one takes another glimpse of the kinds of conflict managing mechanisms employed by ASEAN from the time the idea of the ARF started to the continuing processes of moving the ARF forward. We note, for example, that in the period leading to the announcement of the creation of the ARF, the ASEAN states exercised caution in deciding what form the security forum should take. In doing so, it had to take into full consideration the divergent views of the major powers involved plus their own respective reservations. This again is a clear example of the kind of consultative–consensual approach/mechanism used by ASEAN in trying to accommodate the different views not only of its own members but the outside powers as well.

The process involved in deciding the nature of the forum and the composition of its members, which dealt with the question of inclusiveness has been instructive. Deciding on the pace of development which should be incremental — on the shared understanding by member that the ARF "should not move too fast for those who want to go slow and not too slow for those who want to go fast" — illustrate once again the process of adopting the consultative and consensual practice of ASEAN.

Conscious of the fact that the ARF should be seen as a confidence-building exercise where habits of dialogues are being fostered and with the aim of increasing the comfort levels among new members and former enemies, the ARF is indeed in itself a huge conflict management mechanism. More significantly is the fact that the ARF also embodies the other forms of conflict management mechanisms used by ASEAN such as the development of self-inhibiting norms of inter-state conduct, the consensus decision-making style, the informality of doing things and the cultivation of personal ties or networking.

All these elements are part of the process-oriented mechanisms adopted by ASEAN in building a peaceful community of states in the Southeast Asian region.

Finally, the form that the ARF will take would be dependent on how its members decide it to be, based on their understanding and reading of their structural environment and the quality of interaction that takes place among them. Given the pace of the ARF, it is most unlikely to move into the third stage of conflict resolution in the very near future. With the current preference among member countries to bilateral and subregional mechanisms for conflict management, these preferences will continue to be more important than a pax regional construct such as the ARF. Having said that, however, the fact still remains that the ARF has made considerable progress in the last ten years. Security in the Asia-Pacific can benefit from continued commitment by member countries to an incremental but persistent pursuit of developing the ARF as a viable conflict management mechanism.

## Notes

1. The ASEAN Regional Forum which was formed in 1994 now has twenty-three member countries. These are: Australia, Brunei Darussalam, Cambodia, Canada, China, the European Union, India, Indonesia, Japan, Laos, Malaysia, Myanmar, New Zealand, Papua New Guinea, the Philippines, Russia, Singapore, South Korea, Thailand, the United States and Vietnam. Mongolia joined in July 1998 and North Korea in July 2000.

2. On China's evolving policy on the Cambodian conflict towards the end 1980s, see Robert S. Ross, "China and the Cambodian Peace Process: The Value of Coercive Diplomacy", *Asian Survey* XXXI, no. 12 (1991): 1170–86.
3. See Susumu Awanohara, "America's Easy Options", *Far Eastern Economic Review*, 3 September 1992, p. 23.
4. See Amitav Acharya, *A New Regional Order in South-east Asia: ASEAN in the Post-Cold War Era*, Adelphi Paper 279 (London: International Institute for Strategic Studies, 1993), p. 12.
5. For more analyses on the concerns of regional states at that time, see for example Jusuf Wanandi, "ASEAN and an Asia-Pacific Security Dialogue", in *ASEAN in a Changed Regional and International Political Economy*, edited by Hadi Soesastro (Jakarta: Centre for Strategic and International Studies, 1995), pp. 143–58. See also Mochtar Kusumaatmadja, "Some Thoughts on ASEAN Security Co-operation: An Indonesian Perspective", *Contemporary Southeast Asia* 12, no. 3 (1990): 165–66.
6. Ibid.
7. ASEAN countries referred to here are the main five: Indonesia, Malaysia, the Philippines, Singapore, and Thailand, since Vietnam, Laos, Cambodia, and Myanmar joined only in the last three years. Brunei's economic structure, which relies heavily on revenues received from exports of oil and gas, does not necessarily fit into the economic restructuring that occurred in the ASEAN countries during this period.
8. For a concise discussion on ASEAN's economic policy during this period, see Bruce Glassburner, *ASEAN's "Other Four": Economic Policy and Economic Performance since 1970*, ASEAN–Australia Economic Papers No. 10 (Kuala Lumpur: ASEAN–Australia Join Research Project, 1984).
9. There has been a lot of material on this topic of "flying geese" pattern of development. This framework of economic analysis was popularized by the Japanese economist, Kiyoshi Kojima. Kojima was heavily influenced by the economic theory of Akamatsu Kaname who first crystallized this idea into an economic theory. For the history of this theory, see Pekka Korhonen, *Japan and the Pacific Free Trade Area* (London: Routledge, 1994), pp. 51–63. Kojima expounded on this theory and wrote several essays on this to describe the patterns of Japanese direct foreign investments to the rest of Asia. See, for example, Kiyoshi Kojima, *Japan and a New World Economic Order* (Tokyo: Charles E. Tuttle Company, 1977); and Kiyoshi Kojima, *Trade, Investment and Pacific Economic Cooperation: Selected Essays* (Tokyo: Bunshindo, 1996).
10. For more in-depth discussion on this economic interdependence and trends in industrial production in Asia-Pacific in general and ASEAN in particular, see, for example, S.P. Gupta and Somsak Tambulertchai, eds., *The Asia-Pacific Economies* (Kuala Lumpur: Asian Pacific Development Centre, 1992); Fu-Chen Lo and Kamal Salih, eds., *The Challenge of Asia-Pacific Cooperation*

(Kuala Lumpur: Association of Development Research and Training Institutes of Asia and the Pacific, 1988); Mohamed Ariff and Hal Hill, *Export-Oriented Industralization: The ASEAN Experience* (Sydney: Allen and Unwin Australia Pty. Ltd., 1985).

11. Fu Chen-Lo and Yoichi Nakamura, "Uneven Growth, Mega-Trends of Global Change and the Future of Asia Pacific Economies", in *The Asia Pacific Economies*, edited by Gupta and Tambulertchai, pp. 26–80.

12. The idea of creating regional economic forum was informally introduced by former Australian Minister for Foreign Affairs and Trade, Gareth Evans, during the Annual ASEAN Ministerial Meeting held in Brunei Darussalam in July 1989. This proposal was cautiously received by ASEAN. At the Press conference held by the Australian minister just before the meeting, he carefully outlined three main objectives: first, to develop a more co-ordinate regional response to the present multilateral trade negotiations rounds; secondly, to identify areas of sectoral co-operation, identifying complementarities in the regional economies and working together to find ways of advancing common economic interests; and thirdly, to find ways of helping achieve a greater liberalization of trade within the region and solving trade problems (Press Statement of The Australian Minister for Foreign Affairs and Trade at Brunei International Airport, 5 July 1989).

13. See *APEC Handbook* (Singapore: APEC Secretariat, 1997), p. 1.

14. The EAEG proposal was announced during Malaysian Prime Minister Mahathir Mohamad's visit to China in December 1990 where he met former Chinese Premier Li Peng. ASEAN countries though sympathetic to the need to have a regional caucus failed to endorse the EAEG proposal. None the less, Malaysia has been advocating this idea.

15. For a concise discussion on the EAEG, see David Lim, "The East Asian Economic Grouping Proposal", in *Berita IDS* (Sabah: Institute of Developing Studies, 1991).

16. Ibid.

17. For more discussion on responses to the EAEC, see Lim Kian Teck, "Competing Regionalism: APEC and EAEG: 1989–1990", in *Non-Traditional Security Issues in Southeast Asia*, edited by Andrew Tan and J.D. Kenneth Boutin (Singapore: Select Publishing, 2001), pp. 54–86.

18. These proliferation of ideas of how ASEAN should respond to the emerging economic environment were announced during the run-up to the ASEAN Economic Ministers Meeting which was held in Kuala Lumpur in October 1991. See *New Straits Times* (Malaysia), 7 October 1991.

19. Among all the proposals that were floated during that meeting, it was the Thai proposal of an ASEAN Free Trade Area that was eventually adopted, and in January 1992 at the Fourth ASEAN Summit meeting, the framework agreement for the creation of an ASEAN Free Trade Area was signed. This called for the ASEAN countries to reduce tariffs on all manufactured items

over a fifteen-year period. Furthermore, in order to have accelerated tariff reductions, items were brought onto a Common Effective Preferential Tariff (CEPT) scheme and enjoy significant margins of preference over five to eight years.

20. See, for example, Gerald Segal, *China Changes Shape: Regionalism and Foreign Policy*, Adelphi Paper 287 (London: International Institute for Strategic Studies, 1994), pp. 44–45.

21. For more discussion on this issue, see, for example, Fred Herschede, "Trade between China and ASEAN: The Impact of the Pacific Rim Area", in *Pacific Affairs* 62, no. 2 (1991).

22. See Robert Ross, "China and the Stability in East Asia", in *East Asia in Transition: Toward a New Regional Order*, edited by Robert S. Ross (Singapore: Institute of Southeast Asian Studies, 1995), pp. 106–107. See also Segal, *China Changes Shape*, pp. 44–45.

23. For a comprehensive discussion of ASEAN military modernization, see J.N. Mak, *ASEAN Defense Reorientation 1975–1992: The Dynamics of Modernisation and Structural Change*, Canberra Papers on Strategy and Defence No. 103 (Canberra: Strategic and Defense Studies Centre, the Australian National University, 1993). Mak's monograph provides a comprehensive overview of ASEAN defence planning, and explain the rationale for these countries to shift from counter insurgency warfare (CIW) to maritime defence between 1975 to early 1990s.

24. See "China Insists It Owns the Spratlys Islands", *The Star* (Malaysia), 6 July 1992.

25. See Tai Ming Cheng, *Growth of Chinese Naval Power*, Pacific Strategic Papers (Singapore: Institute of Southeast Asian Studies, 1990). This monograph has comprehensively described Chinese's rationalization of its military programme, zeroing on the rising Chinese navy and the regional implications of such programmes.

26. Jonathan Pollack, "Security Dynamics between China and Southeast Asia: Problems and Potential Approaches", in *China and Southeast Asia into the Twenty-First Century*, edited by Richard Grant (Honolulu: Pacific Forum/ CSIA, vol. XV, no. 4), pp. 30–38. See also Segal, *China Changes Shape*.

27. In July 1992 at the ASEAN Post-Ministerial Conference (ASEAN-PMC) in Manila, Chinese Foreign Minister Qian Qichen suggested that Beijing and ASEAN sign an agreement modelled on the treaty between China and the EC to further economic and trade co-operation. Qian also suggested the setting up of two Sino-ASEAN scientific and technological developments, one to be based in Beijing and the other in an ASEAN state. Most significantly, Qian proposed that a "multilevel and multichannel dialogue mechanisms on security" be established to uphold peace and stability in the region. For more discussion on the emerging institutional linkages between ASEAN and China, see Lee Lai To, "Some Thoughts on ASEAN and China: Institutional

Linkages" in *China and Southeast Asia into the Twenty-First Century*, edited by Grant. See also *The Star*, 27 July 1992.

28. This point was eloquently discussed in Muthiah Alagappa, "Regionalism and the Quest for Security: ASEAN and the Cambodian Conflict", *Journal of International Affairs* 46, no. 2 (1995): 439–67.

29. Statement by Senator Gareth Evans, Foreign Minister of Australia, before the ASEAN-PMC in Jakarta, in July 1990.

30. Quoted from Jane Boulden and John Lamp, "Institution-Building in the Pacific", *Pacific Security 2010: Canadian Perspectives on Pacific Security in the 21st Century*, edited by Mary Goldie and Douglas Ross (Ottawa: Canadian Centre for Arms Control and Disarmament, 1991).

31. In fact, Gorbachev himself suggested a similar proposal for a CSCE-type framework in the Asia-Pacific as early as 1986 during his speech in Vladivostok. Specifically, he had called for the establishment of a conference on security and co-operation in Asia (CSCA) which is for all intents and purposes the precursor for the proposals by Australia and Canada.

32. Some scholars would argue though that the failure of the CSCE in the early years of the post-Cold War period was actually the catalyst for efforts to revitalize the regional body and eventually transform it into an institutionalized organization (OSCE) in 1994. See, for example, Hans-Peter Schwarz, "Crisis and Conflict Management from the European Perspective", in *Security and Regional Order in ASEAN and the Role of the External Powers*, Konrad-Adenauer Stiftung and Institute for Strategic and Development Studies, (Manila: Konrad Adenauer Foundation, 1997).

33. At the ASEAN-PMC in Singapore in July 1993, Chinese Deputy Prime Minister and Foreign Minister Qian Qichen stated that "as Asian countries differ from each other in terms of their national conditions, historical and cultural traditions, values and stages of development, they cannot copy the European model for security issues." Malaysia and Indonesia were also among those who insisted that the Asia-Pacific region should look after its own security. This idea was forcefully declared by Indonesian Foreign Minister Ali Alatas at the first ASEAN Regional Forum in Bangkok in July 1994 when he said that " I do share the view that ... Europe's institutional processes may not easily be transposed unto the Asia Pacific region ... The best way to start laying foundations in the Asia Pacific in not by recreating the CSCE process in the region nor by premature initiation of Pan-Asia security schemes."

34. See *ASEAN ISIS Monitor* (Kuala Lumpur: Institute of Strategic and International Studies, 1991).

35. ASEAN's Dialogue Partners during this period were: Australia, Canada, the European Union, Japan, New Zealand, Republic of Korea, and the United States.

36. For more on the development during this period, see Jusuf Wanandi, "Asia-

Pacific Forums: Rationale and Options from the ASEAN Perspective", in *Security Cooperation in the Asia-Pacific Region*, edited by Desmond Ball, Richard Grant and Jusuf Wanandi (Honolulu, Pacific Forum and Centre for Strategic and International Studies, vol. XV, no. 5, 1993).

37. The Thai press quoted foreign ministers and senior officials of countries which attended the first ARF meeting praising it for the fact that many disparate countries with hostile pasts were able to sit together for the first time, see the *Bangkok Post*, 26 July 1994.

38. "Chairman's Statement of the First Meeting of the ASEAN Regional Forum (ARF)", 25 July 1994, Bangkok.

39. For an excellent general discussion on ASEAN norms and specifically, on the perceptible changes within the context of ARF, see Amitav Acharya, *Constructing a Security Community in Southeast Asia* (London and New York: Routledge, 2003), pp. 165–84.

40. Ibid.

41. "The ASEAN Regional Forum: A Concept Paper", Bandar Seri Begawan, 1 August 1995.

42. "Chairman's Statement of the Second ASEAN Regional Forum (ARF)", Bandar Seri Begawan, 1 August 1995.

43. Ibid.

44. "The ASEAN Regional Forum: A Concept Paper".

45. Ibid.

46. Ibid., para. 20 (emphasis added).

47. "Chairman's Statement of the Fourth Meeting of the ASEAN Regional Forum", Subang Jaya, 27 July 1997.

48. Alan Dupont, "The Future of the ARF: An Australian Perspective", in *Future of the ARF*, edited by Khoo How San (Singapore: Institute of Defence and Strategic Studies, 1999), p. 35.

49. By the time the ARF has its eighth meeting in Bangkok, Thailand in July 2000, it had twenty-three members with North Korea admitted as the latest member.

50. "Chairman's Statement of the Fifth Meeting of the ASEAN Regional Forum", Manila, 27 July 1998.

51. See "The ASEAN Regional Forum: A Concept Paper".

52. Michael Leifer, *"The ASEAN Regional Forum: Extending ASEAN's Model of Regional Security"*, Adelphi Paper 301 (London: International Institute for Strategic Studies, 1996), p. 59.

53. Robyn Lim, "The ASEAN Regional Forum: Building on Sand", *Contemporary Southeast Asia* 20, no. 2 (1998): 115.

54. Jeannie Henderson, *Reassessing ASEAN*, Adelphi Paper 323 (London: International Institute for Strategic Studies, 1997), p. 70.

55. Leifer, *"The ASEAN Regional Forum"*, p. 26.

56. Leifer, *"The ASEAN Regional Forum"*, p. 30.

57. "The ASEAN Regional Forum: A Concept Paper". See also para. 13 of "Chairman's Statement of the Fourth Meeting of the ASEAN Regional Forum".
58. Some countries like Australia and Japan felt that after four years, it was time for the ARF to proceed to Stage II. As a compromise, the ARF accepted ASEAN's proposal that the two stages should be allowed to proceed simultaneously as long as the focus remains on Stage I.
59. "Chairman's Statement, The Fourth Meeting of the ASEAN Regional Forum".
60. Author's personal conversation with ASEAN foreign ministry officials during the Track II-CSCAP's Worshop on Preventive Diplomacy, Bangkok, Thailand, March 1999.
61. See, Desmond Ball "Towards Better Understanding of Preventive Diplomacy", in *The Next Stage: Preventive Diplomacy and Security Cooperation in the Asia-Pacific Region*, edited by Desmond Ball and Amitav Acharya, Canberra Papers on Strategy and Defence No. 191 (Canberra: Strategic and Defence Studies Centre, Research School of Pacific and Asian Studies, The Australian National University, 1999).
62. From Annex A, ASEAN Regional Forum Concept Paper, August 1995.
63. From Annex B, ASEAN Regional Forum Concept Paper, August 1995.
64. This summary of events relies heavily on the Desmond Ball's account of the various ARF meeting on Preventive Diplomacy in his chapter cited at Note 61.
65. "Chairman's Summary, ASEAN Regional Forum (ARF) Seminar on Preventive Diplomacy", Seoul, May 1995 reproduced in Ball and Acharya, eds., *The Next Stage*.
66. "Second ARF Seminar on Preventive Diplomacy: Chairman's Statement", November 1999, reproduced in Ball and Acharya, eds., *The Next Stage*.
67. Established in 1993, CSCAP is a non-official, track two body which is organized for "the purpose of providing a structured process for regional confidence-building and security co-operation in the Asia-Pacific region". See "Establishment of CSCAP: Kuala Lumpur Statement", 8 July 1993, Chapter 5 of this book.
68. "Co-Chairman's Report of the Track Two Conference on Preventive Diplomacy", Singapore, 18 April 1998. This is also reproduced in Ball and Acharya, eds., *The Next Stage*.
69. Seminar on The Future of the ASEAN Regional Forum, Singapore, 27–28 April 1998 where the researcher was a participant at this meeting. There were about forty participants from ARF member countries coming from both official and non-official sectors. During the deliberations, some participants raised that the operating principles had to be clearly defined since the general definition of preventive diplomacy made no distinction between inter-state and intra-state conflict. Boutros Boutros-Ghali's definition of preventive diplomacy in his *Agenda for Peace* (1992) had been used as the

reference definition of PD which defined "Preventive Diplomacy as action to prevent disputes from arising between parties, to prevent existing disputes from escalating into conflicts and to limit the spread of the latter when they occur.

70. "Chairman's Summary: CSCAP Working Group on CBMs' Meeting on Preventive Diplomacy", Bangkok, 28 February–2 March 1999.

71. The author was a participant at this Workshop where she witnessed the robust exchange of views among the participants on coming up with an acceptable definition of preventive diplomacy and its accompanying principles.

72. From the "Chairman's notes on the Session on the ARF", 13th Asia Pacific Roundtable, 2–5 June 1999, Kuala Lumpur, Malaysia.

73. Michael Leifer, *The ASEAN Regional Forum: Extending ASEAN's Model of Regional Security*, Adelphi Paper No. 304 (Oxford: University Press/ International Institute of Strategic Studies, 1996), p. 59.

74. See, for example, Robyn Lim, "The ASEAN Regional Forum", pp. 115–36, and John Garofano, "Flexibility or Irrelevance: Ways Forward for the ARF", *Contemporary Southeast Asia* 21, no. 1 (1999).

75. Jurgen Haacke, "The Aseanization of Regional Order in East Asia: A Failed Endeavor?", *Asian Perspectives* 22, no. 3 (1998): 36.

76. Leifer, *The ASEAN Regional Forum*, p. 57.

77. Yuen Foong Khong, "Making Bricks Without Straw in the Asia-Pacific?", *Pacific Review* 10, no. 2 (1997): 298. This article provides a very thoughtful and critical review of Michael Leifer's monograph.

78. Ralf Emmers, *Cooperative Security and the Balance of Power in ASEAN and the ARF* (London and New York: RoutledgeCurzon, 2003), p. 117.

79. Ibid., p. 154.

80. "Chairman's Statement, Second ASEAN Regional Forum" and "The ASEAN Regional Forum: A Concept Paper".

81. "The ASEAN Regional Forum: A Concept Paper", 1 August 1995.

82. Opening Address of S.R. Nathan at the forum on The Future of the ARF, Singapore, 27–28 April 1998, reproduced in *The Future of the ARF*, edited by Khoo How San (Singapore, Institute of Defence and Strategic Studies, 1999). At the time of delivering of the speech, Mr Nathan was a Singapore ambassador. He is currently President of Singapore.

83. *New Straits Times*, 28 July 1997.

84. Ibid.

85. Gary Smith, "Multilateralism and Regional Security in Asia: The ASEAN Regional Forum and APEC's Geopolitical Value", Background Paper delivered in the Seminar on the Future of the ARF, Singapore, 27–28 April 1998.

86. This was particularly evident to the author who participated at the Workshop on Preventive Diplomacy held in Bangkok in February 1999.

87. Smith, "Multilateralism and Regional Security in Asia", pp. 32–33.

# 5

## : ASEAN'S TRACK TWO DIPLOMACY
## : Reconstructing Regional Mechanisms
## : of Conflict Management

### INTRODUCTION

The previous chapter traced the development of the ASEAN Regional Forum (ARF), which has been ASEAN's more recent initiative in adding more substance to its evolving mechanisms of conflict management. Two points from the foregoing discussion are relevant to this chapter's theme on ASEAN's track two diplomacy and to the overall objective of this study in tracing the elements beyond the ASEAN way.

Firstly, while the ARF has often been regarded as an extension of the ASEAN way of diplomacy as well as a mechanism to manage conflict and regional security, one could argue that its establishment had in fact began to set in motion the thrust towards a more inclusive and/or participatory type of mechanism for conflict management. For a start, the ARF was established to be an inclusive forum, bringing together both like-minded and non-like-minded states in the broader Asia-Pacific region. The main objective was to encourage these states to have a stake in managing regional security.

Secondly, and perhaps of more significance to the purpose of this study, is the fact that in developing the modalities of the ARF, particularly in the various processes that have emerged to move its agenda forward, the ARF and especially ASEAN have opened the doors for non-state actors to be part of the process(es) involved in adjusting their modalities beyond the ASEAN way. It is often observed that ASEAN is a highly state-centric organization and, in most of its initiatives in the diverse areas of regional co-operation, has not allowed non-state actors to be part of the processes involved in crafting these initiatives. This chapter will show that there have been perceptible changes in this regard by highlighting the roles played by non-governmental or non-official institutions. As this chapter will show, ASEAN and its interaction with non-state actors portend towards a movement away from the conventional ASEAN way as these non-state actors, through their activism, have been increasingly able to affect policies and helped the nature of inter-state relations.

When viewed against the liberal and constructivist framework of international relations, the influence that these new actors exert reflect the salience of regarding them as independent variables but nonetheless part of the regional processes that define regional approaches. Constructivism, specifically, allows us to identify these non-state actors as the "agents" who bring with them "ideas" that are critical in shaping state policies. Constructivism also alerts us to perceptible changes in attitudes and approaches within and among states that may be taking place as ideas find their way into concrete policies. These ideas add to the dynamics as state actors, and to a certain extent, non-state actors engage in the processes that bring about intersubjective understanding on how inter-state relations should be. Thus, these non-governmental channels become important building blocks in the formation and generation of intra-state and inter-state/regional policies.

Think-tanks, academics, and members of the "unofficial" policy community make up many of these non-state actors. This chapter specially looks at the role of track two actors who work on security issues and have gained considerable attention through their involvement and participation in track two diplomacy. The term *track two* has been used broadly to refer to a network of academics, experts, members of the civil society, and government officials acting in their private capacities.[1] Track two diplomacy, on the other hand, refers to unofficial contact and interaction aimed at resolving conflicts, both internationally and within states.[2] Hence, it is important to recognize that track two actors and track two diplomacy are significant parts of the evolving mechanisms of conflict management in the region.

Following from the above, it is useful to reiterate here the definition of mechanisms of conflict management adopted in this study, as discussed in Chapter 2. Mechanisms of conflict management are defined as "the processes, methods, devices, techniques and the strategies employed to resolve or manage conflict ... *and/or anything employed in the whole, oftentimes complicated process of resolving or managing conflicts.*"[3] Thus, in fitting in the track two's role with the overall discussion on ASEAN's evolving mechanisms of conflict management, this chapter will examine the types of work that these actors have done to contribute to the management of regional security. In Southeast Asia and the broader

Asia-Pacific region, the most studied track two networks are the ASEAN Institutes of Strategic and International Studies (ASEAN-ISIS) and the Council for Security Co-operation in the Asia-Pacific (CSCAP). This chapter is divided into two sections, with each section separately discussing ASEAN-ISIS and CSCAP. It is important to first understand how these track two "channels" fit within the structure of international politics.

## Track Two Diplomacy and Epistemic Communities: Drawing Linkages

The linkages established by track two with track one through the transmission of ideas approximate the work of epistemic communities. Peter Haas described epistemic communities as "a network of professionals with an authoritative claim to policy relevant knowledge within that domain or issue area".[4] While members of the epistemic community comprise professionals from a variety of disciplines and backgrounds, they share the following characteristics, which include: "(1) shared set of normative and principle beliefs; (2) shared causal beliefs; (3) shared notions of validity; and (4) a common policy enterprise".[5]

By their very nature, epistemic communities provide essential elements in the decision-making processes of governments. Their ability to provide information, plus their ability to create and strengthen their transnational networks provide valuable inputs to decision-makers. These transnational networks of experts support and complement each other in their work and mutually enhance their knowledge and expertise. More significantly, these networks of experts provide valuable inputs by helping to clarify the situation of a particular issue. This is done by the extensive manner in which a particular issue is discussed, covering the nature, extent, causality, and its future trends. After intensive deliberations, these experts then provide possible measures to cope with the issue, which includes actual policy recommendations for intergovernmental co-operation. Thus, in times of uncertainty and flux, decision-makers then turn to epistemic communities for advise. As highlighted by Haas, epistemic communities help decision-makers to: (1) develop various courses of action, (2) clarify complex interlinkages between issues and the chain of events that could result from either failing to take action or from instituting a particular policy, (3) help define the self-interests of states or factions within it, and (4) help formulate policies, anticipate conflicts of interests that would emerge and build coalitions to support the policy.[6]

The influence of epistemic communities on states' policies can be seen through the extent that their ideas have been adopted by decision-makers. According to Haas, epistemic communities influence state interests either by "directly identifying them for decision-makers or by illuminating salient dimensions of an issue from which the decision-makers may then deduce their interests".[7]

Hence, the knowledge and ideas of epistemic communities could be regarded as making up the building blocks of "intersubjective structures" generated from the constantly evolving processes of interaction between state and non-state actors. These ideas in turn constitute the ideational factors that help define international politics. Ideas, identities, and intersubjective understanding among actors are the "other stuff" that explain states' actions beyond the conventional realist perspective that only looks at power.[8] As Goldstein and Keohane noted, the ideas (held by individuals) help to explain political outcomes, particularly those related to foreign policy.[9] Thus, the influence of ideas on policies broadens the study of international relations, and this particular study also relates to the constructivist perspective that focuses on identities and norms in defining the complex dynamics of inter-state relations.

As we refer back to the constructivist perspective of international relations, these epistemic communities can be regarded as the "agents" who bring about change and adds to the dynamic process of building "intersubjective structures". Moreover, these agents help shape the ideational factors that explain states' preferences and behaviour. When applied to the analysis as to why certain mechanisms of conflict management are preferred by states, then the role of these agents is indeed instructive.

Having drawn the linkages between epistemic communities and track two diplomacy, and relating it to the evolving mechanisms of conflict management, we shall now examine the nature of track two diplomacy in ASEAN. The rest of this chapter will now discuss separately the contributions of ASEAN-ISIS and CSCAP.

## I. THE ASEAN INSTITUTES OF STRATEGIC AND INTERNATIONAL STUDIES (ASEAN-ISIS)

The ASEAN-ISIS was established as a regional non-governmental organization with the signing of its Charter on 28 June 1988. It was also registered with the ASEAN Secretariat in the same year. Since its establishment, the ASEAN-ISIS has grown from its original five to nine member institutions. The original five members are: The Centre for Strategic and International Studies (CSIS) in Jakarta; the Institute of Strategic and International Studies (ISIS Malaysia) in Kuala Lumpur; the Institute of Strategic and Development Studies (ISDS) in Manila;[10] the Singapore Institute of International Affairs (SIIA) in Singapore; and the Institute for Security and International Studies (ISIS), Bangkok.[11] In 1995 and coinciding with ASEAN's enlargement to include Vietnam, the Institute of International Relations (IIR) in Hanoi joined ASEAN-ISIS, followed by the Cambodian Institute for Co-operation and Peace (CICP) in 1997, the Institute of Foreign Affairs (IFA) in Vientiane in 1999, and the Brunei Darussalam Institute of Policy and Strategic Studies (BDIPS) in Bandar Seri Begawan in 2000. Except for the three "new" members of ASEAN-ISIS which are part of the Ministries of Foreign Affairs in their respective countries, the five original members are relatively independent, non-governmental institutes.

Although ASEAN-ISIS was formalized only in 1988, its activities actually started as early as 1984. Through the initiative of Jusuf Wanandi, Chairman of the Board of CSIS, Jakarta, a number of informal regional meetings were held among the heads, experts, and scholars from these institutes. These meetings were held amidst the realization that the Southeast Asian region was faced with political, security, and economic challenges affecting the member states of ASEAN. Some of these were the Cambodian conflict, domestic developments in some ASEAN states that impact on regional stability, bilateral disputes in ASEAN, changing economic relations with Japan, the United States, and other key trading partners, as well as the perceived destabilizing effects of major power rivalry in Southeast Asia. At that time, it was thought that "initiating policy dialogues with each other, with ASEAN partners and other states in the region through non-official channels, [these dialogues] were important steps towards reducing tensions and building confidence in the region".[12]

In defining its role, ASEAN-ISIS has sought to provide ASEAN with policy inputs on various issues that affected the region for the consideration of the decision-makers in ASEAN. ASEAN-ISIS has been able to carry out this function by submitting critical policy recommendations (for example, Memoranda) to the ASEAN officials and their respective governments. Among these notable recommendations were the establishment of the ARF, the strengthening of the ASEAN Secretariat, the adoption of the idea that saw the realization of the ASEAN Free Trade Area (AFTA), and the establishment of human rights mechanisms.[13] These recommendations will be tracked in the discussions of the activities of ASEAN-ISIS which are examined below. I shall begin by examining the ideas and activities that ASEAN-ISIS has generated over the years. These can be grouped chronologically according to the period when these ideas were launched.

## Providing a Framework for Multilateral Security Dialogue

A hallmark of ASEAN-ISIS activities since its inception has been its organizations of various regional and international conferences. These ASEAN-ISIS organized conferences had become significant venues for security experts and scholars in and outside the ASEAN region to share information, analyse issues of common concerns, and generate policy recommendations. A significant feature of these meetings is the manner by which discussions are conducted, even on highly sensitive issues. This feature is particularly visible during the biggest multilateral track two conference on security which ASEAN-ISIS organizes annually — the Asia-Pacific Roundtable (APR).[14] It is also at the APR meetings that most of the ideas on security co-operation have been tested and launched.

The APR was initiated in 1987 by ISIS Malaysia (who was already part of the core group that comprised ASEAN-ISIS) and began as a small meeting among academics, security analysts, and experts in ASEAN countries, plus a few select scholars from outside the region.[15] Since 1991, the APR came under the aegis of ASEAN-ISIS. From a small meeting of scholars, the APR started to increasingly attract considerable interest outside Asia. So much so that since 1990, the APR has brought together over two hundred participants from all over the Asia-Pacific and beyond. Whether the enlarged participation was indicative of the growing interest and relevance of track two processes in the post-Cold War period or not, the APR nevertheless became a catalyst in providing the opportunity and the fora for non-governmental entities to discuss regional security issues and, to the extent possible, be part of the regional decision-making process by generating policy recommendations which were then forwarded to governments in the region.

The dynamics of being part of the decision-making process can be seen in many ways. Firstly, the meeting is truly multilateral — it comprises a mixed bag of people of different nationalities. When the APR started, the participants were initially mostly academics and experts who work on political and security issues in ASEAN. Nowadays, it is very common to see government officials (Foreign Ministers and of late, defence officials) from various countries who attend in their private capacities. The value of this non-exclusive participation is manifold. Foremost of which is the opportunity for participants to hear various perspectives on a given issue that allow for a better appreciation of the diversity in views and positions of states with respect to certain policy issues.

Secondly, the APR provides the opportunity for developing policies on ideas that are considered sensitive. As one scholar noted, officials themselves float ideas like trial balloons to test their acceptability and if necessary reformulate them after having benefited from the responses from other officials, who responded in their "private capacities", and academics with policy expertise.[16] For example, issues like the South China Sea disputes and proposals for "Joint Development" of the South China Sea were examined by both officials and experts on the subject. Also discussed were prospects for resolution of conflicts in the Korean peninsula, adopting confidence- and security-building measures (CSBMs) in the Asia-Pacific, and establishing a framework for multilateral security co-operation in Asia.[17]

Thirdly, and closely related to the point on developing policies on subject deemed too sensitive, is the way the discourse on crucial security issues have been managed. This can be analysed from the time preparations for the APR are done to the actual holding of the conference itself. At least six months before the holding of the APR, the organizers, particularly ISIS Malaysia, writes to all network members for suggested topics and/or issues which should be tabled in the forthcoming conference. The purpose of the exercise is to give all network members the chance to be involved in the format and content of the APR. Responses received, sometimes numbering to more than a hundred topics, and the names of suggested prospective speakers and resource persons are then collated, according to issues and relevance to the region. Once this is done, the ASEAN-ISIS committee consult each other and then decide on the final format and content of the APR and who to invite as resource persons for the conference.

One cannot underestimate the process that takes place during these preparations.[18] A lot of time is spent on consultations among network members and deciding why certain topics are more relevant and more urgent than others. For example in the 1998 APR, the Asian region found itself still reeling from the devastating effects of the financial crisis, which eventually ballooned into a regional economic crisis. The ASEAN-ISIS felt that the economic problems that were caused by the crisis, such as massive unemployment and its effects on regional migration, political unrest, and the social costs that the crisis has brought about were top on the lists of issues that had to be discussed. This was not to mention the fact that the region had also just suffered from one of its worst environmental disaster — the pollution or haze problem caused by the forest fires in Indonesia's Kalimantan and Sumatran provinces. The haze enveloped a large part of Southeast Asia, affecting the capitals of Brunei, Malaysia, Singapore, and some parts of the Philippines and Thailand. It was thought that these issues had to take precedence over the conventional security issues oftentimes discussed in the past APRs, such as nuclear weapons proliferation, problems in the Korean peninsula, the South China Sea disputes, and the role of major powers in the region.

Therefore, when the 1998 APR was held, it had as its dominant theme "The Regional Economic Crisis and its Effects on Security in the Asia-Pacific Region". The speakers at the conference had interesting backgrounds. These included, among others, security experts, economists, fund managers, and environmental specialists. Some high-ranking government officials from the region were also invited to speak, including a member of Parliament from Singapore, a minister from Cambodia, the Deputy Prime Minister of Malaysia, and the Secretary-General of ASEAN. During the four-day meeting, governmental officials, economic experts, security analysts, academics, and even regional journalists sat down and deliberated on the causes of the economic crisis and how the region could move ahead in the midst of economic and political instability. More significantly, policy recommendations pertaining to economic reforms like prudent financial management and regulation of financial markets, increasing transparencies, setting up appropriate institutions, political management and others were put forward for the regional governments to consider. At the end of any APR, a network members meeting is usually held to evaluate the content of the conference — what topics were missed, what issues needed more discussions, the nature of participation, and so on. The meeting is also held to get feedback on what else needs to be done and to plan for the next APR.

Lastly, this kind of Roundtable offers the opportunity for networking. Due to the kind of participants that this type of conference attracts, many of whom are high-profile government officials, academics, and experts that come together once a year, most of the regular participants would already book this date in their annual diaries and plan their side meetings accordingly. This type of conference has proven to be very useful to many since in a span of three to four days, strong personal contacts are developed while avenues are opened for intellectual and policy exchanges. More significantly, the APR allows for socialization of the idea of regional co-operation through dialogue. Through networking and building personal relations, co-operative habits are learned, paving the way for increased international co-operation. As highlighted by Haas, these types of multilateral dialogues that foster socialization of ideas help promote international co-operation. This in itself is a mechanism of conflict management at work, informal though it may be. To paraphrase, the kind of socialization provided by track two diplomacy is part of ASEAN's mechanisms of conflict management.

The description of the APR process is just part of the many processes that ASEAN-ISIS are directly managing in helping ASEAN think about, define, and craft its political and security policies. It is also instructive to review some of the more important and relevant initiatives of ASEAN-ISIS as they aim to realize their goal as the region's think-tank. This will be dealt with in the next section.

## Instituting a Multilateral Forum for Political and Security Co-operation in the Asia-Pacific

As mentioned in the previous chapter, the structural changes in the international security environment have had a tremendous impact on the thinking of the region on its current and future security challenges. From the late 1980s to early 1990s, at various meetings and fora, members of the ASEAN-ISIS had echoed these concerns. In the Chairman's report produced after an ASEAN-ISIS Meeting in May 1990 in Thailand, an "agenda for action" was being mooted to respond to the politico-security developments in and outside the region. Among the key issues identified in the report to create a "framework for regional order" were:

1. Increasing the general efficacy of the existing formal and informal mechanisms for consultation, confidence-building, and conflict resolution among ASEAN states.
2. Extending, where possible, this framework for consultation, confidence-building and conflict resolution to include Vietnam, Laos, and Cambodia.[19]
3. Considering new inter-governmental mechanisms and measures for region-wide conflict resolution and co-operation, in order to reinforce the existing ones, for example, a mechanism for negotiating and settling the overlapping South China Sea claims and new measures to revitalize the existing mechanisms and schemes for promoting co-operation regarding the Mekong River.

4. Considering new region-wide non-government or semi-official mechanism to increase consultation, mutual confidence, and co-operation among regional states, for example, some kind of "Southeast Asian PECC".[20]

The recommendations took more shape the following year when the ASEAN-ISIS met in Jakarta from 2 to 4 June 1991. This meeting was extremely important for the network as they felt that the timing was right for them to push their initiatives — among these was the proposal for a mechanism for multilateral security co-operation in the region. It is important to recall here the point made earlier in Chapter 4 on how the ARF came into fruition. In tracking the work of ASEAN-ISIS in this regard, we trace the origins of the ARF.

During this period, ASEAN was already preparing for the Fourth ASEAN Ministerial Meeting (AMM) which was scheduled to be held the following year in January 1992 in Singapore. The Jakarta meeting brought together the Heads of the ASEAN-ISIS institutes, namely: Jusuf Wanandi (CSIS, Jakarta), Noordin Sopiee (ISIS Malaysia), Carolina Hernandez (ISDS, Philippines), Lau Teik Soon (SIIA, Singapore), and Sukhumbhand Paribatra and Kusuma Snitwongse (ISIS, Thailand), and other experts in ASEAN. There were two non-ASEAN participants namely, Yukio Satoh, Director for Research of the Japanese Ministry of Foreign Affairs and Paul Evans, Professor at York University, Canada.

The Jakarta meeting produced the ASEAN-ISIS Memorandum No. 1 entitled "A Time for Initiative: Proposals for the Consideration of the Fourth ASEAN Summit".[21] The memorandum contained concrete proposals that fleshed out the four issues outlined earlier in the Chairman's report. While all were important, the proposal that gained the most attention was the idea of a multilateral security dialogue among Asia-Pacific countries to be held within the framework of the ASEAN Post-Ministerial Conference (PMC). The rest of the proposals are dealt with separately in the paper.

The objectives of the dialogue process were:

> to contribute to the process of reducing conflict and resolving contentious problems, to contribute to the enhancement and enrichment of understanding, trust, goodwill and co-operation, and to contribute to the constructive management of the emerging processes in the region, with the view to the establishment of a multilateral framework of co-operative peace.[22]

The proposal of ASEAN-ISIS for a multilateral security dialogue contained two essential points. The first was the emphasis on the role of ASEAN as the leader and driver of the security dialogue. The idea was for ASEAN "[to] play a central role in whatever processes and mechanisms arise ... [to be] a creative initiator as well as an active participant".[23] The second was to argue for the utilization of the existing framework of the ASEAN PMC instead of creating new institutions. ASEAN-ISIS proposed that after each PMC, "an ASEAN-PMC initiated conference be held at a suitable retreat ... for the constructive discussion of the Asia-Pacific stability and peace ... that the agenda and arrangements ... be prepared by a meeting of senior officials of the ASEAN states and the dialogue partners". The rationale being that the "processes that we build for the Asia-Pacific must be established in the context of the specific characteristics of the Asia-Pacific and must respond to the specific needs of the Asia-Pacific".[24]

The Memorandum was submitted by members of the ASEAN-ISIS to their respective governments and was approved in principle during the Fourth ASEAN Summit in January 1992. The idea was announced during the Manila AMM in July 1993, and the ARF has its first meeting in July 1994.

In analysing the role of this network, one could argue that the idea of a multilateral security forum that ASEAN-ISIS had proposed and was eventually carried out by governments in the region was not entirely novel, but reflected the current thinking at the time even among non-ASEAN government officials. For example, in the interim period when the ASEAN-ISIS Memorandum was being submitted to ASEAN officials, Japanese Foreign Minister Tako Nakayama had also articulated the need for a similar dialogue during the Kuala Lumpur AMM in July 1991 (prior to ASEAN's consideration of the ASEAN-ISIS initiative). But according to one account, the Japanese proposal could be interpreted as an endorsement of the ASEAN-ISIS proposal since this idea was brought to Nakayama's attention by the Japanese head of the Policy Planning Office of its Foreign Ministry who was then present at the ASEAN-ISIS meeting in Jakarta. During that meeting, ASEAN-ISIS had actually requested the official to seek the support of Japan for its initiative should this be brought up at the Kuala Lumpur AMM. Hence, the "unintended Japanese pre-emption of the initiative reflects the time lag between the submission of the [ASEAN-ISIS] memorandum to ASEAN in June 1991 and its approval in principle during the Fourth Summit in January 1992".[25] As it turned out, the specifics of this multilateral security forum, ARF, reflected the main points of the ASEAN-ISIS proposal.

Similarly, one would also note that even before the Japanese announcement, similar ideas were also floating around the region like the 1990 proposals coming from Australia and Canada. This point had been already been discussed earlier in Chapter 4. However, what made ASEAN-ISIS proposal distinct and arguably more acceptable was their views for a more indigenous, regionally driven type of multilateral dialogue. The earlier suggestions by Canada and Australia for an Asia-Pacific version of a Conference on Security and Co-operation in "Asia" were not received favourably by ASEAN and its other dialogue partners. Many had regarded the proposals for rapid institutionalization of any multilateral framework that was patterned after the European process as incompatible with the Asian approach. The ASEAN-ISIS idea, therefore, related more to the requirements of the region and was more in tune with regional sensitivities.

The ASEAN-ISIS initiatives paved the way for closer contacts between ASEAN-ISIS and the ASEAN officials.[26] Through the leadership of Jusuf Wanandi of CSIS, Jakarta, ASEAN-ISIS was able to institutionalize its relationship with ASEAN. In April 1993, the Heads of ASEAN-ISIS had their first meeting with the ASEAN Senior Officials Meeting (SOM) in Singapore. A year later, the Heads of ASEAN-ISIS were able to meet the ASEAN SOM just before the ARF SOM in Pattaya, Thailand in April 1994. This was before the first meeting of the ARF was convened in July 1994 in Bangkok. The Pattaya meeting was particularly significant in that ASEAN-ISIS submitted their proposals on some topics to be included in the draft agenda for the first ARF meeting which addressed the future directions of the ARF.[27] More importantly, it was also during this meeting when ASEAN SOM had expressed their desire to meet with ASEAN-ISIS prior to their annual meetings, which precede the ASEAN AMM.[28] These linkages further developed when ASEAN-ISIS started to have formal meetings with the ASEAN Foreign Ministers in 1999.

As noted above, the ASEAN-ISIS Memorandum No. 1 also flagged three other salient issues (aside from the multilateral security forum) that were subsequently considered by ASEAN officials. These were proposals relating to: (1) a new regional order in Southeast Asia, (2) strengthening ASEAN, and (3) enhancing ASEAN economic co-operation. The adoption of these ideas is discussed briefly below.[29]

## Managing a New Regional Order in Southeast Asia

The ASEAN-ISIS Memorandum No. 1 brought attention to the promotion of regional norms enshrined in the Treaty of Amity and Co-operation

(TAC) to maintain peace and stability in the region. The "New Regional Order in Southeast Asia" had proposed the accession of other Southeast Asian states that were not ASEAN members to the TAC. Moreover, the initiative also urged the initiation at an appropriate time of the process of "constructive dialogue" among all the signatories to the TAC. Vietnam, Laos, and later on Cambodia and Myanmar were invited to accede to the TAC and paved the way for the realization of the ASEAN-10.

## Strengthening the ASEAN Secretariat

Enhancing the capacity of the ASEAN Secretariat was already part of the ASEAN-ISIS agenda even in the early 1990s. In Memorandum No. 1, ASEAN-ISIS had proposed among others, (1) the regular holding of the ASEAN Summit every two years, (2) strengthening the ASEAN Secretariat, including the upgrading of the status of the Secretary-General, its organization and operations, and (3) the expansion of the ASEAN process in the political, security, and defence areas without transforming ASEAN into a military or security pact. As noted, these recommendations were adopted at the Fourth ASEAN Summit in Singapore. As a result, the Summit Meetings were consequently held every three years (and since 1995, ASEAN summits have been held annually). The Secretary-General status was upgraded to the rank of minister and was given new responsibilities to initiate, advise, and co-ordinate ASEAN activities.

## Enhancing ASEAN Economic Co-operation

With regard to suggestions on enhancing economic co-operation in ASEAN, the Memorandum had also proposed, among others, the creation of an ASEAN Free Trade Area (AFTA) with a treaty providing its legal framework.[30] Although there were similar ideas on the need for ASEAN to push for deeper economic integration, the ASEAN-ISIS proposal was more than an articulation of the political sentiments in the region for closer integration. Hence, ASEAN's adoption of this idea during the Fourth Summit could also be read as an endorsement of ASEAN-ISIS' proposal.

Since the submission of the first memorandum, ASEAN-ISIS has also submitted five other memoranda to ASEAN. These are: Memorandum No. 2 on "The Environment and Human Rights in International Relations: An Agenda for Policy Approaches and Responses" (June 1992); Memorandum No. 3 on "Enhancing ASEAN Security Co-operation" (June 1993); Memorandum No. 4 on "Beyond UNTAC: ASEAN's Role in

Cambodia" (October 1993); Memorandum No. 5 on "Confidence-Building Measures in Southeast Asia" (December 1993); and Memorandum No. 6 on "The South China Sea Dispute: Renewal of a Commitment for Peace" (May 1995).[31]

Of the five memoranda, only three were "accepted" and found its way in ASEAN policies. These were the ideas that proposed for enhancing the security co-operation in ASEAN, implementing confidence-building measures (CBMs), as well as the proposals on extending technical assistance to Cambodia. As far as improving security co-operation in ASEAN, the ASEAN officials took note of ASEAN-ISIS proposals to have a subsection of the SOM devoted to security co-operation. Since 1993, senior officials from foreign and defence ministries as well as from the armed forces have met regularly to discuss ways for advancing security co-operation in ASEAN. On ASEAN's relations with Cambodia, the organization has noted the proposals of ASEAN-ISIS for technical and other assistance to Cambodia after the end of the UNTAC mandate. Finally, with regard to ASEAN-ISIS' proposals on CBMs, their recommendations on adoption of CBMs, such as the preparation and publication of defence white paper, promotion of military transparency, and establishment of a regional arms register, have been noted by ASEAN.

## Memorandum No. 5 on "Confidence-Building Measures in Southeast Asia"

The ASEAN-ISIS had been very active in developing the CBM measures in the Asia-Pacific region. In fact, confidence-building and conflict reduction have always been the themes of the annual ASEAN-ISIS Asia-Pacific Roundtable since it was organized in 1987. Discussions on this topic eventually led to the generation of more concrete regional CBMs which were later brought to official channels for their consideration. For example, at the Sixth APR, a paper on CSBM agenda was tabled at the conference and drew active discussions from participants.[32] Constant deliberations on this subject finally bore fruit when ASEAN-ISIS submitted its Memorandum No. 5 to the newly formed ARF Senior Officials Meeting in their April 1994 meeting.

The Memorandum, which was prepared in December 1993, spelt out possible confidence-building measures which the ARF could consider, such as the publication of defence White Papers, increase in the exchange of visits among military and defence officials, and the establishment of a regional arms register.[33] The ASEAN-ISIS proposals were clearly modest in comparison with the more wide-ranging CBMs that, for example, the CSCE have instituted which were mainly military in nature. Some of these CSCE-type CBMs were actually proposed by Australian Foreign Minister Gareth Evans at the ASEAN PMC in July 1991. Examples of these included, among others, military-oriented agenda, transparencies through the exchange of data on military budgets and doctrines, and measures to prevent proliferation of nuclear weapons.[34] Since the ASEAN-ISIS proposals were more realistic and modest to start with, this was easily accepted by the ASEAN officials for their consideration. According to Hernandez, it was notable that during the first ARF meeting, ASEAN "submitted [the] ASEAN-ISIS Memorandum on CBMs as its own document in the absence of its own ... submission ... a clear instance where the lack of time to think through policy issues on the part of the senior officials of ASEAN has contributed to the usefulness of ASEAN-ISIS to the policy decision process..."[35]

The influence of ASEAN-ISIS thinking on the pace and direction of the ARF can therefore be seen in the ARF agenda as reflected in the ARF Concept Paper itself. As discussed in Chapter 4, the ARF eventually settled for two types of CBM measures to be implemented, which were classified under immediate CBMs, and medium to longer term CBMs. The more complex measures which include the Regional Arms Register, maritime information databases, and co-operative approaches to sea line of communications were considered by the ARF as issues which "can be explored over the medium and long-term" but interestingly, are "for the immediate consideration by the track two process".[36] Indeed, the track two processes identified in the concept paper are ASEAN-ISIS and CSCAP.[37]

The role of the CSCAP in the ARF will be discussed later in this chapter. Suffice it to say, however, that as far the ASEAN-ISIS influence on the formation of a regional multilateral dialogue, their contribution has been notably visible and has been officially acknowledged by ASEAN officials themselves. This perhaps is not surprising since members of the ASEAN-ISIS communities have proven themselves to be experts in their own fields. More significantly also, some of the senior members of the ASEAN-ISIS have over the years developed strong personal links with government officials, even prime ministers, deputy prime ministers, foreign and defence officials. This has facilitated easier contacts among

ASEAN-ISIS members and the ASEAN officials, at the same time facilitating the delivery of policy recommendations from the former to the latter.

To sum up, this section began by examining the nature of epistemic communities that give advise to decision-makers in governments by providing crucial information, framing complex issues, and helping define the decision-makers' interests. To the extent possible, the foregoing discussion examined how ASEAN-ISIS has played this role in the region through its policy interventions in ASEAN. Based on the three-step approach, we have examined the nature of ASEAN-ISIS' activities, tracked their proposals and assessed the extent to which these have been successfully endorsed by ASEAN officials. In many respects ASEAN-ISIS has met the criteria outlined above on successful diplomacy.

Finally, the ASEAN-ISIS since its inception has established a wide network of research institutions with "like-minded counterparts in Northeast Asia, North America and Europe".[38] ASEAN-ISIS has also been a key player in the creation of another significant track two forum, namely, CSCAP, to which the next section is devoted.

## II. COUNCIL FOR SECURITY CO-OPERATION IN THE ASIA-PACIFIC (CSCAP)

The establishment of CSCAP is the culmination of three years of track two meetings which began in 1991 and participated by strategic research institutes across the Asia-Pacific.[39] As described by a noted scholar and himself an active participant to these meetings, "these type of meetings which actually started since the 1990s, characterized the proliferation of channels of multilateral discussions of regional security issues in overlapping regions", which have been indicative of the growing interests and concerns over the fluidity and uncertainty of post-Cold War security environment.[40] The general purpose of these meetings was to ponder on the idea of establishing a "more cumulative, systematic and institutionalized track two channel" which would promote co-operation on regional security issues.[41]

Within the ASEAN region, there had been calls for such type of multilateral consultative forum as well. As mentioned earlier, the ASEAN-ISIS Chairman's Report of 1990 did argue for "considering new regionwide non-government or 'semi-official' mechanisms to increase consultation, mutual confidence, and co-operation among regional states, for example, some kind of 'Southeast Asian PECC' ".[42]

However, it was not until 1992 at a track two meeting in Seoul, Korea when the concrete proposal for the establishment of CSCAP was articulated. The meeting was actually the third in a series of meetings on "Security Co-operation" in the Asia-Pacific organized jointly by the Pacific Forum/CSIS, the Japan Institute of International Affairs, the Seoul Forum for International Affairs, and the ASEAN-ISIS. The Seoul Meeting came up with the "Seoul Statement on Security Co-operation in the Asia-Pacific" which formally established the Council.[43] The organizing institutes then proceeded with the formalization of the Council's Steering Committee, creation of sub-committees on finance, setting up the Secretariat, membership, and working groups. In June 1993 at the end of the Seventh Asia-Pacific Roundtable, the establishment of CSCAP was formally announced.[44] Finally, in December 1993, the CSCAP Charter was adopted which finalized the whole structure of CSCAP.

According to its Charter, "CSCAP is organized for the purpose of providing a structured process for regional confidence-building and security co-operation in the Asia-Pacific region."[45] Among its stated functions, CSCAP is to "provide an informal mechanism by which political and security issues can be discussed by scholars, officials, and others in their private capacities"; and "to provide policy recommendation to various inter-governmental bodies on political-security issues".[46]

Currently, CSCAP has twenty-one national member committees[47] from Australia, Brunei, Canada, Cambodia, China, European Community consortium,[48] India, Indonesia, Japan, South Korea, North Korea, Malaysia, Mongolia, New Zealand, Papua New Guinea, the Philippines, Russia, Singapore, Thailand, Vietnam, and the United States. The directors of the UN Regional Peace and Disarmament in Asia and Pacific and the UN Department of Political Affairs' East Asia and the Pacific Division enjoyed affiliate/observer status. Taiwan scholars and security specialists participate in CSCAP and working group meetings only in their private capacities.

Each of these member committees designates at least one representative to the Steering Committee which is the highest decision-making body of the Council. The Steering Committee which meets twice a year, is headed by two co-Chairs — one from an ASEAN Member Committee and another from a non-ASEAN member committee. The co-Chairs have a two-year term.

In defining its relationship with the ARF, CSCAP which pre-dated the establishment of the ARF, sees itself as "providing the necessary support activities for the ARF Agenda, and making recommendations which are relevant for policy implementation by the ARF".[49] Work in this regard started immediately after CSCAP's official announcement of its establishment. Three months before the inaugural meeting of the ARF, CSCAP issued its first official statement, "CSCAP Memorandum No. 1: The Security of the Asia-Pacific Region", which urged the ARF to consider a number of security initiatives, including employing confidence building measures as the "effective mechanisms to promote peace and security in the region.[50] Since then, CSCAP's continued support for the ARF can be seen in the activities undertaken by CSCAP's five working groups, which meet at least once a year, and their linkages to ARF activities. The CSCAP working groups have been "given the tasks of undertaking policy-oriented studies on specific regional political-security problems".[51]

The CSCAP Working Groups are:

• Working Group on Confidence- and Security-Building Measures
• Working Group on Comprehensive and Co-operative Security
• Working Group on Maritime Co-operation
• Working Group on North Pacific
• Working Group on Transnational Crime

Each of these working groups is in itself also a network of specialists in their respective areas, and over the years, their activities have already focused on some of the specific topics outlined in the ARF's Concept Paper of 1995. The activities of these working groups and their linkages to the ARF agenda will be analysed below.

## Working Group on Confidence- and Security-Building Measures

The Working Group on Confidence- and Security-Building Measures (CSBMs) was established to address CSBMs in the Asia-Pacific. Its first meeting, held in Washington in 1994, sought to primarily answer the question: "Are CBMs appropriate for Asia and, if so, what types of measures might apply?"[52] The first meeting was significant in that it reviewed some of the CSBMs that had been tried in Asia and elsewhere and arrived at some guidelines which "provided the assumptions which the working group efforts were based".[53] These guidelines were later summed up in a document prepared by the Working Group, entitled "CSCAP Memorandum No. 2 — Asia-Pacific Confidence and Security

Building Measures".[54] Some of these guidelines are outlined below. These are:

- CSBMs cannot work in the absence of a desire on the participants to co-operate.
- CSBMs are most effective if they build upon or are guided by regional and global norms.
- Foreign models do not necessarily apply.
- CSBMs are stepping stones or building blocks, not institutions.
- CSBMs should have realistic, pragmatic and clearly defined objectives.
- Gradual, methodical, incremental approaches work best.
- The process, in many instances, may be as important as (or more important than) the product.

Applying these guidelines in the Asia-Pacific context, the following observations were made. These are:

- The Asia-Pacific is not a homogeneous region.
- There is a preference for informal structures and a tendency to place greater emphasis on personal relationships (than on formal structures).
- Consensus-building is a key prerequisite.
- There is general distrust of outside "solution".
- There is a genuine commitment to the principle of non-interference in the internal affairs of others.[55]

From the above observations, the working group concluded that the best approach in promoting CBMs in the region were:

> start small; take a gradual, incremental, building block approach; recognize that European models are generally not transferable to Asia and that sub-regional differences exists within the Asia-Pacific; apply individual measures only where they fit; do not overformalise the process...in other words, proceed slowly and carefully, but definitely proceed.[56]

Based on the conclusions stated above, the working group has since then:

1. examined the basic principles for regional confidence-building;
2. investigated the utility and applicability of the UN Register of Conventional Arms to the Asia-Pacific region, while also laying the groundwork for possible development of Asian Arms Register;
3. developed a generic outline for defence policy papers (White Papers) to assist those regional states who have decided to produce or refine current versions of this transparency tool; and

4.  started ground-breaking work on the development of multilateral approaches to nuclear safety and non-proliferation in the region, to include the possible formation of an Asian or Pacific Atomic Energy Commission (PACATOM).[57]

The working group on CSBMs is by far the most active working group in CSCAP. It meets twice a year and, as observed by the previous CSCAP Chair, this group has made more use of electronic dissemination of its reports than any other groups.[58] But more importantly, and as alluded to above, its work on confidence-building measures and more recently on preventive diplomacy have found their way into the ARF's deliberation on how to move these two agenda forward.

The CSBM working group started to work on preventive diplomacy at its fifth meeting held in October 1996. Then, in September 1997, it was heavily involved in organizing the "ARF Track Two Conference on Preventive Diplomacy" which was held in Singapore. As summed up by its Chairman, Ralph Cossa, the group's efforts "have provided both a forward-leaning future vision and recommended steps for getting there [preventive diplomacy] from here, thus setting the stage for future governmental deliberations".[59]

The significant breakthrough came when the working group conducted a workshop on preventive diplomacy on 28 February–2 March 1999 in Bangkok. The workshop was conducted just prior to the ARF's Inter-sessional Support Group (ISG) Meeting on Confidence-Building Measures. The workshop which invited the ISG participants came up with a Chairman's statement that contained (1) a working definition on preventive diplomacy, and (2) an outline of general principles of preventive diplomacy.[60] This was then forwarded to the co-Chairs of the ARF ISG on Confidence-Building Measure for their consideration and which was subsequently tabled by the ARF ISG and endorsed in principle.[61] Since then, and as discussed in Chapter 4, this group has worked closely with the ARF on this subject.

Beyond its work on preventive diplomacy, this working group has also initiated a series of seminars and workshops on arms control, undertaken studies on nuclear energy research and reprocessing facilities, including the plans and attitudes of current non-nuclear energy producing states. The Working Group also sponsors a Nuclear Energy Experts' Group which conducts more in-depth analysis on nuclear energy-related issues. Since 1999, it has also continued to develop and refine the CSCAP Asia-Pacific Nuclear Energy Transparency website.[62]

## Working Group on Comprehensive and Co-operative Security

The main thrust of this working group's work has been to address the multi-dimensional concept of security, specifically to examine alternative concepts of security in the Asia-Pacific region. The purpose of which has been to promote multilateral security co-operation in the region.

As the name of the group suggests, two concepts are studied here, that is, "comprehensive security" and "co-operative security". At the working group's first two meetings held in 1995, these two concepts were analysed in terms of their theoretical content, their relevance to the prevailing situation in the Asia-Pacific region, and the prospects for adopting them to facilitate security management in the region.[63]

There was general agreement that for managing security approaches in the region "an over-arching, organizing concept containing elements of comprehensive, co-operative and common security, to be called concept of 'comprehensive security' could be useful...".[64] This over-arching framework for security was later on reflected in the "CSCAP Memorandum No. 3 — The Concepts of Comprehensive Security and Co-operative Security" prepared by the Group.[65] The Memorandum provided a definition of comprehensive security, which also incorporates elements of co-operative security:

> Comprehensive security is the pursuit of sustainable security in all fields (personal, political, economic, social, cultural, military, environmental) in both the domestic and external spheres, essentially through co-operative means.[66]

The distinctive features of this organizing concept are articulated in the following principles which are contained in the Memorandum. These are:

* principle of comprehensiveness;
* principle of mutual interdependence;
* principle of co-operative peace and shared security;
* principle of self-reliance;
* principle of inclusiveness;
* principle of peaceful engagement; and
* principle of good citizenship.[67]

Due to the extensiveness of this concept, the working group has emphasized the importance of putting in institutions and processes which are structured to address and manage security in comprehensive terms at the national, sub-regional and regional levels. The working group further emphasized the putting in place of over-arching guiding principles for relations between regional states, and for relations between the region and states as well as organizations outside the region.[68]

These organizing concepts of security which the working group had prepared has been useful for the ARF. In the Chairman's Report of the First ARF Meeting in June 1994, the participants were urged to study the "comprehensive concept of security". This again provides a good example of how a track two group could offer support and complement the ongoing work of the ARF in promoting multilateral security co-operation in the region.

The work of the working group has also examined the security problems that emerged from the 1997–98 Asian economic crisis that hit the region. At the working group's fifth and sixth meeting held in July 1998 and May 1999, respectively, the group turned its attention to address the question: Has the Asian economic turbulence damaged the security structures that underpins regional peace and security? These meetings were particularly significant in that it was the first CSCAP meeting to address the linkage between regional economic turbulence and security co-operation. The meetings were also different in that it brought together not only security traditionalists but also economic specialists.

The discussions that emerged had pointed to the need for the region to strengthen current institutions to respond to economic crisis.[69] Turning to ASEAN in particular, although the meetings had generally agreed that the basic structure of regional relations remained consistent, none the less ASEAN had to strengthen its institutions and increase economic co-operation if it were to remain relevant and responsive. Among the specific measures considered were:

- the need for ASEAN to promote economic integration and to increase economic co-operation;
- to push for AFTA to be implemented in 2002 to boost intra-regional trade and investment;
- the need to establish an effective mechanism to monitor short-term capital flows; and
- increased regional co-operation in reducing poverty.[70]

In 1999, against the events in the Kosovo conflict and the NATO intervention that followed, the working group organized its seventh meeting to revolve around the subject of the non-intervention principle. The seventh meeting, held in Seoul in December 1999, drew up a list of current challenges to the principle of non-intervention as applied to the Asia-Pacific region and came up with possible parameters for intervention.[71]

The working group's work on expanding the security concept has led to the creation of two sub-groups on globalization and human security. These sub-groups have been examining various types of "new" security threats brought on by globalization, as well as analysing the varying national perspectives on this new concept on human security.

## Working Group on Maritime Co-operation

The importance of maritime issues in the Asia-Pacific region cannot be understated. In the region lies a vast area, the South China Sea, whose islands, reefs, and atolls are disputed by Brunei, Malaysia, the Philippines, Vietnam, Taiwan, and China. The disputed claims in the South China Sea have been recognized as a potential flashpoint in the region and have been of serious concern to the littoral states. The resolution of these disputes has been made difficult "by the strategic location, the number of claimants, the lack of common ground and power imbalances among them, and the increasing level of international interest in the vast resource potentials suspected to exist in that area".[72]

The above problem and the many issues surrounding the oceans and the seas of the region are the foci of the work being done by the CSCAP Working Group on Maritime Co-operation. The objectives of the working group are:

- to foster maritime co-operation and dialogue among the states of the Asia-Pacific and enhance their ability to manage and use the maritime environment without prejudicing the interests of each other;
- to develop an understanding of regional maritime issues and the scope they provide for co-operation and dialogue;
- to contribute to a stable maritime regime in the Asia-Pacific which will reduce the risks of maritime conflict;
- to undertake policy-oriented studies on specific regional maritime security problems;
- to promote particular preventive diplomacy and maritime confidence- and security-building measures (MCSBMs); and
- to promote adherence to the principles of the 1982 UN Convention on the Law of the Seas (UNCLOS).[73]

At the working group's First Meeting held in Kuala Lumpur in June 1995, the group identified key issues concerning maritime security and defence, maritime confidence- and security-building, shipping, marine environment and science.[74] The comprehensive *tour de force* of the main maritime security concerns reflected the comprehensive approach to security that the group has taken in addressing the issues.

For example, in the area of maritime security and defence, some of the key issues discussed were:

- the destabilizing consequences of conflict maritime territorial claims in the Asia-Pacific region — particularly in the South China — and the importance of mechanisms to manage these disputes;
- the Spratly Islands problems, which needs to be considered in the context of regional maritime security;
- the establishment of resource management regimes, which may be easier than the resolution of sovereignty;
- the competing jurisdictional problems in the Asia-Pacific region, which could confound the management of piracy, drug trafficking, marine pollution, as well as refugees.[75]

So far, the working group has generated concrete outputs in its researches on the security of sea lines of communications (SLOCs), exploitation of marine resources, and search and rescue operations. One of it is the call for the establishment of maritime information systems and databases in the Asia-Pacific region.[76]

Of even more relevance as far as this working group's linkage with the ARF is concerned is their recent initiative of coming up with "CSCAP Memorandum No. 4 on Guidelines for Regional Maritime Co-operation". The Guidelines are a set of fundamental, non-binding principles to guide regional maritime co-operation and to ensure a common understanding and approach to maritime issues in the region.[77] They cover the maritime confidence- and security-building and preventive diplomacy measures which were identified by the ARF and are consistent with the provisions of UNCLOS.[78]

The CSCAP Memorandum No. 4 was submitted by CSCAP to the ARF SOM in 1998. A year later, the ARF Inter-Sessional Group on Confidence-Building Measures tabled the Memorandum in their Inter-Sessional Group Meeting in March 1999. Two years after that, the Working Group produced another CSCAP Memorandum, CSCAP Memorandum No. 5 on Co-operation for Law and Order at Sea, which addressed issues involving maritime crime and law and order at sea. As with its previous practice, Memorandum No. 5 was sent to the ARF in February 2001 for consideration.

So far, this working group has been recognized as one of the most important track two activities that work on maritime security matters in the region. It continues to make important contribution to the development of guidelines and principles for the co-operative management of regional oceans and seas to reduce tensions and the risks of conflict at sea. Like the working group of CSBMs, it has held back-to-back meetings with the ARF ISG on Maritime CBMs. Following its success in generating policy recommendations through submissions of memoranda, it has also recently completed CSCAP Memorandum No. 6 on The Practice of the Law of the Sea in the Asia-Pacific.[79] This work had followed closely the work of the ARF Inter-sessional Meeting on Maritime CBMs, which had also invited this working group to address the issue.

## Working Group on the North Pacific

The main work of the North Pacific working group revolves around the security issues of the North Pacific region, notably the Korean peninsula. This working group differs from other CSCAP working groups in that it focuses on the geographic area rather than a specific problem. When it started, its main objective was "to contribute toward dialogue and security co-operation in North Pacific with specific reference to security issues in Northeast Asia".[80]

The contribution of this working group has been significant, given that it was formed when the ARF began to discuss Northeast Asian issues without the participation of the North Koreans. Note that North Korea was only formally admitted to the ARF in July 2000, hence the absence of North Korea in the ARF deliberations was a big handicap. Thus, the work of this working group has been particularly important in that it not only plugged the lacunae at that time but also complemented the inter-governmental activities, specially since this has been the only multilateral forum that had tried to include all the relevant parties with significant interests in the future of the Korean peninsula. In this regard, the working group has tried to promote the "full house" concept which goes beyond the "2 + 4" approach[81] and has instead used the "N principle". The number is variable depending on the topic under discussion.[82]

This "full house" concept was first realized in the second meeting of the working group which was held in Vancouver, Canada in January 1997. The participation of delegates from North Korea, South Korea, China, Taiwan, Japan, Russia, Canada, the United States, and Europe was extremely significant. The co-Chair of the working group aptly described its significance when he wrote:

> the fact that this second meeting is the first "full house" meeting in Northeast Asia and North Pacific, the relevance and importance of multilateral dialogue in the region is reconfirmed and the effectiveness of the basic principles of CSCAP (a track two approach) — habits of dialogue, informality, inclusiveness, incrementality and so forth — is reaffirmed. It is argued that informal multilateral dialogue can be characterized as "shadow" diplomacy as opposed to "daylight" diplomacy and thus can function as a means to forge close networks among the participating nations upon which diplomacy will be conducted.[83]

Among the many issues that this working group have discussed are: the recent developments in Northeast Asia particularly the unprecedented series of high-level bilateral meetings among the major countries and the bilateral summits involving the United States and China, Russia and China, and Russia and Japan in 1997; the establishment of new arrangements for border CBMs in Northeast Asia as initiated bilaterally by China and five of its neighbours — Russia, the three Central Asian Republics of Kazakhstan, Kyrgyzstan, and Tajikistan, and India; and the institutional arrangements for regional economic co-operation (the levels of which pale dramatically when compared with East and Southeast Asia).[84] Of particular interest, too, are the discussions on the role of the ARF in Northeast Asia. Issues raised in this regard pertain to the question on how receptive the Northeast Asian states would be to an ARF role like good offices of the ARF Chair in Northeast Asian disputes.[85]

Moreover, the working group has, through its meetings, been monitoring the important developments in the Four Party Talks, Korean Peninsula Energy Development Organization (KEDO), and the Northeast Asia Economic Co-operation Dialogue (NEACD). Other topics under discussions are the security implications of the Asian economic crisis on the Northeast Asian region, the potential impact of the introduction of new weapons system into the subregion, particularly the Theater Missile Defense (TMD) system and finally, the analysis of the integration of bilateral and multilateral processes among the Northeast Asian and North Pacific actors.

## Working Group on Transnational Crime

This working group was the latest of the working groups formally formed by CSCAP in December 1997. The main objectives are:

- to gain a better understanding of and reach agreement on the major transnational crime trends affecting the region as a whole;
- to consider practical measures which might be adopted to combat transnational crime in the region; and
- to encourage and assist those countries which have recently become engaged in regional security co-operation, and which are concerned about the problem of transnational crime in the region ... to develop laws to assist in regional and international co-operation to counter drug trafficking, money laundering, mutual assistance, extradition and the like.[86]

The formation of this working group has indeed been timely since the complex issues of transnational crimes like drug trafficking, trafficking of illegal weapons, and counterfeiting have emerged as "extremely dangerous and subversive" trends in the regional security agenda in the post-Cold War environment.[87]

One of the working group's valuable contribution in this regard is its identification of a list of "crime types" which affect the region. These included among others: arms trafficking, illegal drug production, international corporate/white collar crime, smuggling of nuclear materials, counterfeiting, illegal immigration, money laundering and technology crime. In drawing up the list, the working group has placed emphases on explaining the impact of transnational crime on regional security and providing guidance on the approaches that might be considered by the regional governments to deal with identified criminal threats.

The work that this working group has so far been doing ties in well with the number of regional initiatives relating to the threats of transnational crime. Among these are:

- The call by the ASEAN Ministers at the Third ARF to consider "the question of drug trafficking and related transnational issues such as economic crime, including money laundering, which could constitute threats to regional security".
- The ASEAN Ministers' Declaration on Transnational Crime in Manila on 20 December 1997.
- The Manila Declaration on the Prevention and Control of Transnational Crime on 25 March 1998.[88]

The working group has managed to get the participation of law enforcement specialists, criminologist, and lawyers at its workshops. By bringing together both practitioners and specialists in the region, CSCAP is also able to provide valuable service not only to the ARF but also to regional political leadership in "contributing towards the development of policy responses and encouraging the harmonization of criminal law amongst the nations of the region".[89]

As noted by Desmond Ball, the test case of the ability of the security analysts in the region is to "seriously consider the new security agenda as involving real threats to security".[90] In this regard, this working group has proven its relevance as it provides that crucial support to governments in the region that are ill-equipped to handle new security issues and are overwhelmed by the complicated nature of transnational crimes facing this region. Its work on matters of law enforcement and regional co-operation has proved to be useful for governments to alert themselves of the need to enhance inter-governmental co-operation in addressing transnational crime. As mentioned by Desmond Ball, the work of this working group has been recognized by several law enforcement agencies and reported in the regional media.[91]

Its most recent initiative is the CSCAP Memorandum No. 7 on The Relationship between Terrorism and Transnational Crime.[92] Among its recommendations are for CSCAP member countries to endorse and implement the UN Conventions and Protocols, and the supporting regional agreements, against terrorism and transnational crime; and to support the activities of the Financial Action Task Force (FATF) and other relevant anti-money laundering institutions and, where necessary, seek relevant technical and legal expertise to ensure that national commitments are translated into effective national programmes and ensure sufficient resources are allocated to anti-money laundering units so that they can function effectively in identifying terrorist financing.[93]

Finally, this working group has also published several reports on transnational crime, including a book entitled *Transnational Crime and Regional Security in the Asia-Pacific*.[94]

## IV. CONCLUSION

The chapter began by discussing the role of track two actors and their work on track two diplomacy in the development of mechanisms of conflict management in the region. In analysing their role in the overall framework of regional mechanisms of conflict management, the origins and the features of these track two actors, ASEAN-ISIS and CSCAP, were traced and described. Moreover, the analyses of their roles were likened to the role played by epistemic communities who provide advice and expertise to governments which have been limited in their capacities to handle increasingly complex and diverse security issues. It was also noted that other than providing advice, the other important contribution of the epistemic communities is that they engender international co-operation as governments, acting on the experts' advice, move to facilitate and strengthen the multilateral approaches to Asia-Pacific security.

The preceding discussion on the role and activities of ASEAN-ISIS and CSCAP, particularly their linkages with the governments of the region, has illustrated the important functions of epistemic communities as described above. It is useful to reiterate here the constructivist view of these epistemic communities as agents in the building blocks of policy formation. However, I would extend this role further to argue that the ASEAN-ISIS and CSCAP have moved beyond mere provision of advice. On their own accord, they have respectively *initiated* policies without having to wait to be consulted by governments. The ASEAN-ISIS initiative on setting up a multilateral security forum is a good case in point. For CSCAP, the various Memoranda that the Council has generated have been excellent examples in this regard. ASEAN-ISIS and CSCAP have become laboratories of ideas for the region as they continue to experiment with various initiatives to foster understanding and promote regional security co-operation.

The above functions could not have been made possible if the atmosphere of comfort and candidness were absent. This is another salient feature of this track two networks. In a region so diverse and different, and which had experienced intra-mural tensions and conflicts, there are several issues that have been too sensitive and too delicate for governments to handle. This difficult handicap has been addressed by track two through their various meetings and conferences, and more importantly, in the kind of work such as the policy recommendations that they have respectively produced.

ASEAN-ISIS and CSCAP have in themselves become venues for discussion of topics that could not be fully covered in the official channels. To recapitulate, these topics include the prospects of the South China Sea disputes, which have been openly discussed at the Asia-Pacific Roundtable almost annually, and the future of the Korean peninsula. As regards the latter topic, the APR has been able to invite North Korean officials and scholars who have not only been articulate but also forthright in their discussions of the problems in the Peninsula. Whereas before there was a tendency for them to come with prepared text and only read that throughout the meeting, at least in the Twelfth and Thirteenth APR, the North Koreans had been openly candid. Even more remarkable has also been the increasingly active participation of the Chinese delegations in these meetings.[95] Thus if one of the distinct features of the conflict management mechanisms in the region is confidence-building, then it can be argued that ASEAN-ISIS and CSCAP have become part of this evolving mechanism. This has certainly altered the conventional regional modalities that had so far been confined to the ASEAN way of sweeping sensitive issues under the carpet. As argued earlier, the examples of track two diplomacy are therefore perceptible trends that suggest a dynamic evolution of regional conflict mechanisms beyond the ASEAN way.

Yet, having said that, much of the trademark of the ASEAN way remains. One observes that the extensive nature and number of activities of both ASEAN-ISIS and CSCAP have provided for socialization of regional co-operation to take place. In turn, the socialization process that takes place during these meetings is part and parcel of the overall process of norm-building which is again a distinct feature of the region's mechanism for managing conflict. In a region which puts a premium on personal relationships, these meetings continue to improve personal contacts and reinforce the informal dynamics where problems are discussed more meaningfully and decisions made more easily outside the confines of official boundaries.

Finally, the significance of the socialization process is deemed most important by no other than the track two actors themselves. These individuals have realized the need to sustain these networks and expand their resources. These would necessitate increasing the circle of its usual participants and improving their expertise and knowledge on various issues. There has been the growing realization among track two networks, particularly the ASEAN-ISIS, that one of its biggest challenges is to continue to develop their social capital if they want to remain not only responsive but also innovative in their approach. That is why within ASEAN-ISIS there is now this conscious attempt to enlarge its network by bringing in young scholars and other non-governmental representatives, to the extent possible, from all sectors in the society. In fact, one of the biggest projects of ASEAN-ISIS to date is the setting up of an ASEAN People's Assembly where multi-sectoral representation in the decision-making process of the region can be realized. This would then take the process of track two further to that of track three where representatives of the civil society, NGOs, students, workers, and other representatives can participate and contribute. This will be discussed in Chapter 7.

In conclusion, the emergence of the ASEAN-ISIS and CSCAP and their involvement in the development of ASEAN's mechanisms for conflict management fits in with the evolving nature of mechanisms that are emerging in the region. No doubt, the nature of this track two diplomacy that promotes networking, socialization, and consultation on various policy initiatives reinforce the norm-building modalities within ASEAN and the broader Asia-Pacific region. These practices are all part of the pattern of ASEAN's mechanisms of conflict management that are characteristically informal in nature.

The work of ASEAN-ISIS and CSCAP do in fact complement each other. Their track two diplomacy has been an intangible asset for the region. Moreover, their work also provides invaluable support to the work of the ARF. The strides these track two groups have achieved in bringing their Chinese and even North Korean counterparts closer into the network have no doubt been extremely important and a boost to the prospects of engendering a more positive security environment.

While the networking activities and various projects of these track two groups promote habits of constructive dialogue and foster mutual understanding, hence reinforcing the ASEAN way, one must also not miss the emerging, palpable dynamics of evolving mechanisms that are slowly diluting the once state-centric, i.e., only state-actor focused, mechanisms. But while it is also true that these evolving processes are still confined at the level of political élites, these are nonetheless non-state actors. Moreover, there has been a perceptible trend to bring these processes down to the level of the civil society. The ASEAN-ISIS project of convening the ASEAN People's Assembly is an indication of that realization among governments and élites that mechanisms to manage regional security has to move beyond the ASEAN way.

## Notes

1. This definition is taken from Pauline Kerr, "The Security Dialogue in the Asia-Pacific", *Pacific Review* 7, no. 4 (1994). See also Paul Evans, "Building Security: The Council for Security Cooperation in the Asia Pacific (CSCAP), *Pacific Review* 7, no. 2 (1994).
2. The term *track two* was first coined in 1981 by Joseph Montville who was a U.S. diplomat. He used the term *track one* diplomacy, which referred to

diplomatic efforts to resolve conflicts through the official channels of government. See James Notter and John McDonald, "Track Two Diplomacy: Non-governmental Strategies for Peace", *USIA Electronic Journal* 1, no. 19 (1996).

3. See C.R. Mitchell, *The Structure of International Conflict* (New York: St. Martin's Press, 1981), parts 1 and 4 (emphasis added).
4. Peter M. Haas, "Introduction: Epistemic Communities and International Policy Co-ordination", *International Organization* 46, no. 1 (1992): 3.
5. Ibid.
6. Ibid., p. 15.
7. Ibid., p. 4.
8. See Alexander Wendt, "Constructing International Politics", *International Security* 20, no. 1 (1995); Ted Hopf, "The Promise of Constructivism in International Relations Theory", *International Security* 23, no. 1 (1998).
9. Judith Goldstein and Robert O. Keohane, "Ideas and Foreign Policy: An Analytical Framework", in *Ideas and Foreign Policy: Beliefs, Institutions, and Political Change*, edited by Judith Goldstein and Robert Keohane (Ithaca: Cornell University Press, 1993).
10. ISDS was only formally established in 1991, hence the Philippine involvement in ASEAN-ISIS started with a group of experts spearheaded by Carolina Hernandez, Professor of Political Science at the University of the Philippines. She is the current President of ISDS.
11. For an excellent first-hand account and documentation of ASEAN-ISIS, see the following articles by Carolina G. Hernandez: (1) "The Role of ASEAN-ISIS", *ASEAN-ISIS Monitor*, Issue No. 6, April 1994, pp. 1–3; (2) *Complex Interdependence and Track-Two Diplomacy in the Asia-Pacific in the Post-Cold War Era* (Quezon City: Center for Integrative and Development Studies and the University of the Philippines Press, 1994), pp. 1–38; "Governments and NGOs in the Search for Peace: The ASEAN-ISIS and the CSCAP Experience", Paper presented at the Conference on Alternative Security System in the Asia-Pacific, Bangkok, 27–30 March 1997, accessed from < http://www. focusweb.org/focus/pd/sec/hernandez.html > (Paper cited with permission from the author).
12. Hernandez, "The Role of ASEAN-ISIS".
13. Ibid.
14. Apart from the APR which has been its mainstay activity, ASEAN-ISIS had also held regular track two meetings. Until quite recently, these included: the Southeast Asian Forum, the Southeast Asian Roundtable on Economic Development, ASEAN Young Leaders Forum, and the Colloquium on Human Rights. See, for example, Malaya C. Ronas, "ASEAN-ISIS as a Forum on Regional Policy Issues: A Philippines Perspective", in *Dynamo and Dynamite? Cambodia's Future in Asean*, edited by Kao Kim Hourn and Jeffrey Kaplan (London: ASEAN Academic Press Ltd, 1999), pp. 207–17.

15. The idea of organizing a regional multilateral forum started two years earlier in Seoul and in Manila when a group of scholars from ASEAN together with their counterparts in North American, Japanese, and Korean research institutes met to consider a more structured track two meeting on political security issues to parallel the economic fora that were organized earlier. These were the Pacific Forum for Trade and Development (PAFTAD), Pacific Business and Economic Conference (PBEC), and Pacific Economic Cooperation Council (PECC). See Hernandez, "Governments and NGOs in the Search for Peace", p. 2.
16. Pauline Kerr, "The Security Dialogue in Asia Pacific", p. 400.
17. In the early years of the APR, the idea of instituting a framework for multilateral security co-operation post-Cold War era was already being mooted. This gained more clarity and coherence as this idea was frequently discussed in subsequent APR meetings even until the ARF was finally established in 1994. The subsequent discussions on the ARF focused on the kind of pace that it should have, given the three-stage agenda and the desire to move the agenda from CBM to preventive diplomacy.
18. As part of the organizing team of the APR since 1998, the author had been involved in this consultation process among network members and in the collation and distillation of ideas and issues which become the themes and topics of the APRs.
19. At the time this report was prepared, Vietnam, Laos, and Cambodia were not yet members of ASEAN.
20. "Superpower Military Presence and the Security of Southeast Asia: Problems, Prospects and Policy Recommendations", Chairman's Report of ASEAN-ISIS Meeting, Bangkok, 1990, reproduced in *ASEAN-ISIS Monitor*, July 1991. Emphasis added.
21. See ASEAN Institutes for Strategic and International Studies, *A Time for Initiative: Proposals for the Consideration of the Fourth ASEAN Summit* (Kuala Lumpur: Institute of Strategic and International Studies, 1991).
22. Ibid.
23. Ibid.
24. Ibid.
25. See Hernandez, "Governments and NGOs in the Search for Peace". For a similar account of the ASEAN-ISIS initiative being somewhat ahead of the official Japanese position, see Kerr, "The Security Dialogue in the Asia-Pacific", p. 403.
26. Even within their domestic settings, the members of the ASEAN-ISIS were known to have close linkages with their respective governments with some acting as consultants and advisers to ministers.
27. Jusuf Wanandi, "ARF: Objectives, Processes and Programmes", *ASEAN ISIS Monitor* (June 1995), p. 17.
28. Hernandez, *Complex Interdependence and Track Two Diplomacy*.

29. The observations of official endorsement of ASEAN-ISIS proposals draws extensively from Hernandez's detailed documentation of the work of ASEAN-ISIS, see ibid.

30. Ibid. One would note that prior to the ASEAN Economic Meeting in October 1991, ideas proliferated on how ASEAN should respond to the emerging economic environment from various circles, both official and non-official.

31. In 1998, the *ASEAN-ISIS Summary of Report of the Sixth Southeast Asian Forum* was submitted to the ASEAN SOM in July 1998. The Report outlined policy recommendations on the challenges facing ASEAN, namely: the Asian financial crisis, ASEAN enlargement, the Cambodian problem, the haze problem, and the social crisis in ASEAN. *ASEAN-ISIS Summary Report* (Kuala Lumpur: Institute of Strategic and International Studies, July 1998).

32. See Paul Dibb, " The CSBM Agenda in the Asia-Pacific Region: Some Aspects of Defence Confidence Building, in *Confidence Building and Conflict Reduction in the Pacific, Proceedings of the Sixth Asia-Pacific Roundtable*, edited by Rohana Mahmood and Rustam A. Sani (Kuala Lumpur: Institute of Strategic and International Studies, 1993), pp. 167–76.

33. "ASEAN-ISIS Memorandum No. 5: Confidence Building Measures in Southeast Asia", December 1993.

34. Statement by Senator Gareth Evans at the ASEAN Post Ministerial Conference, Kuala Lumpur, 22 July 1991.

35. Hernandez, "Governments and NGOs in the Search for Peace", p. 7.

36. Ibid., para. 10.

37. Ibid., para. 11.

38. See *ASEAN ISIS at the Turn of the Century: A Mission Statement* (Kuala Lumpur: Institute of Strategic and International Studies, 1992), para. 5.

39. There have been several articles that traced the evolution of CSCAP written by the pioneers of CSCAP themselves. See, for example, Evans, "Building Security"; Desmond Ball, "CSCAP: Its Future Place in the Regional Security Architecture", in *Managing Security and Peace in the Asia-Pacific*, edited by Bunn Negara and Cheah Siew Ean (Kuala Lumpur: Institute of Strategic and International Studies, 1996), pp. 289–325.

40. Evans, "Building Security", p. 125.

41. Ibid., p. 129.

42. Chairman's Report of the ASEAN-ISIS Meeting.

43. "Seoul Statement on Security Cooperation in the Asia Pacific", 3 November 1992.

44. See "Establishment of CSCAP: Kuala Lumpur Statement".

45. "The Charter of the Council for Security Cooperation in the Asia-Pacific (CSCAP)", (revised and adopted by the Steering Committee at the Tenth Steering Committee Meeting, Manila, December 1998).

46. Ibid. Article II, para 2(a) and 2(d).

47. These national member committees are set up by the following institutes: Strategic and Defence Studies Centre, Australian National University; Brunei

Darussalam Institute for Policy and Strategic Studies; Cambodian Institute for Cooperation and Peace (CICP); Institute of International Relations, University of British Columbia, Canada; China Institute of International Studies (CIIS); Institut Francais des Relations Internationals (IFRI), Europe; Institute for Defence Studies and Analyses (IDSA), India; Centre for Strategic and International Studies (CSIS), Indonesia; Institute of Strategic and International Studies (ISIS), Malaysia; Institute of Security and International Studies (ISIS), Thailand; Institute for Strategic and Development Studies (ISDS), Philippines; Institute of Defence and Strategic Studies (IDSS), Singapore; Japan Institute of International Affairs (JIIA); Graduate School of International Studies, Yonsei University, South Korea; Institute of Disarmament and Peace, North Korea; Institute for Strategic Studies, Mongolia; Centre for Strategic Studies, New Zealand; The National Research Institute, Papua New Guinea; Ministry of Foreign Affairs, Russia; Institute for International Relations, Vietnam; and the Pacific Forum/CSIS, U.S.

48. The CSCAP-Europe was officially admitted as full member in December 1998. Prior to this it was an associate member.

49. "The Security of the Asia Pacific Forum, CSCAP Pro-Tem Committee, Memorandum No. 1", April 1994, p. 6.

50. "CSCAP Memorandum No. 1", April 1994.

51. "Establishment of the Council for Security Cooperation in the Asia Pacific (CSCAP)", Kuala Lumpur Statement, 8 June 1993.

52. This section relies heavily on the articles and reports prepared by the Co-Chair of the Working Group on CSBMs, Mr Ralph Cossa. These reports are mostly limited in circulation. However, a published version of this report on the first meeting can be found in Ralph Cossa, "Asia Pacific Confidence and Security Building Measures", in *Asia Pacific Confidence and Security Building Measures*, edited by Ralph Cossa (Washington: Center for Strategic and International Studies, 1995), Chapter 1, pp. 1–17.

53. Ralph Cossa, "CSCAP and Preventive Diplomacy: Helping to Define the ARF's Future Role", Remarks given at the Opening Session of the ARF Track II Conference on Preventive Diplomacy, 9–11 September 1997, Singapore.

54. See "CSCAP Memorandum No. 2 — Asia Pacific Confidence Security Building Measures".

55. Cossa, "CSCAP and Preventive Diplomacy".

56. Ibid.

57. Ibid. An updated version of this report is also found in Ralph Cossa, "CSCAP and Preventive Diplomacy: Helping Define the ARF's Future Role", Remarks presented at the annual Asia-Pacific Roundtable, 31 May–2 June 1999, Kuala Lumpur, p. 4.

58. See Desmond Ball, *The Council for Security Cooperation in the Asia-Pacific: Its Record and Its Prospects*, Canberra Papers on Strategy and Defence No. 139 (Canberra: Strategic and Defence Studies Centre, Research School of Pacific and Asian Studies), p. 15.

59. Cossa, "CSCAP and Preventive Diplomacy", p. 4.
60. "Preventive Diplomacy: Definition and Principles, Prepared by the Council for Security Cooperation in the Asia Pacific (CSCAP) International Working Group on Confidence and Security Building Measures", 1 March 1999, Bangkok. See also "Chairmen's Summary of the CSCAP Workshop on Preventive Diplomacy", Bangkok, 28 February–2 March 1999.
61. "Working Group Report of the CSCAP Working Group on Confidence and Security Building Measures", presented at the Eleventh CSCAP Steering Committee Meeting, Kuala Lumpur, 30 May 1999.
62. See Ball, *CSCAP: Its Records and Its Prospects*, pp. 16–17. See also the CSCAP website at < http://www.cscap.org >.
63. "Working Group Report on Comprehensive and Cooperative Security", published in *CSCAP Newsletter*, No. 4, February 1996, pp. 2–3.
64. Ibid.
65. "CSCAP Memorandum No.3: The Concepts of Comprehensive and Cooperative Security".
66. Ibid.
67. Ibid.
68. "Working Group Report on Comprehensive and Cooperative Security".
69. "Report of the Fifth Meeting of the Working Group on Comprehensive and Cooperative Security", Wellington, 14–15 July 1998 and "Report of the Sixth Meeting of the Working Group on Comprehensive and Cooperative Security", Beijing, 24–25 May 1999.
70. "Report of the Sixth Meeting of the Working Group on Comprehensive and Cooperative Security".
71. See David Dickens and Guy Wilson-Roberts, eds., *Non-Intervention and State Sovereignty in the Asia Pacific* (Wellington: Centre for Strategic Studies, Victoria University, 2000).
72. "ASEAN-ISIS Memorandum No. 6 — The South China Sea Dispute — Renewal of a Commitment for Peace", May 1995, para. 1.
73. See Sam Bateman and Stephen Bates, "Introduction" in their edited volume *Calming the Waters: Initiatives for Asia Pacific Maritime Cooperation*, Canberra Papers on Strategy and Defence No. 114 (Canberra: Strategic and Defence Studies Centre, Australian National University, 1996), p. 1.
74. "First Report of the Maritime Security Cooperation Working Group", in *CSCAP Newsletter*, No. 3, August 1995, pp. 6–7.
75. Ibid.
76. See Sam Bateman, "Maritime Information and Data Exchange", in *The Seas Unite: Maritime Cooperation in the Asia Pacific Region*, edited by Sam Bateman and Stephen Bates (Canberra: Strategic and Defence Studies Centre, Australian National University, 1996), pp. 175–93.
77. "CSCAP Memorandum No. 4: Guidelines for Regional Maritime Cooperation", CSCAP, December 1997.

78. Ibid.
79. See "CSCAP Memorandum No. 6: The Practice of the Law of the Sea in the Asia Pacific", CSCAP, December 2002.
80. "First Report of the North Pacific Working Group", *CSCAP Newsletter*, No. 3, August 1995, p. 4.
81. Some of the other dialogue activities in the region have tended to involve only the major powers or a precise number of participants. In this case the 2 + 4 formula or the four party talks have focused on replacing the armistice on the Korean peninsula.
82. "North Pacific Working Group Report", *CSCAP Newsletter*, No. 6, June 1997, p. 8.
83. "A Report from the Second Meeting of the North Pacific Working Group", 31 January–2 February 1997, Vancouver (see particularly the Chairmen's Summary, p. I).
84. "A Report of the Third Meeting of the North Pacific Working Group (NPWG)", Makuhari, Japan, 14–16 December 1997 (see Chairmen's Summary, p. iii).
85. Ibid.
86. See CSCAP Working Group on Transnational Crime, at < http://www. cscap.org/crime.htn >.
87. As mentioned in the Keynote Address of the Secretary of the Philippine Department of the Interior and Local Government and Chairman of the National Police Commission, Hon. Epimaco Velasco during the Third Meeting of the CSCAP Working Group Meeting in Manila, 23 May 1998. See *CSCAP Philippines Newsletter*, No. 1, July–December 1998, p. 1.
88. See the *AUS-CSCAP Newsletter*, No. 7, October 1998, pp. 12–13.
89. Ibid., p. 13.
90. See Ball, *CSCAP: Its Records and Its Prospects*, p. 21.
91. Ibid., p. 23.
92. See "CSCAP Memorandum No. 7: The Relationship Between Terrorism and Transnational Crime", CSCAP, July 2003.
93. Ibid. See also Working Group on Transnational Crime, at < http://www. cscap.org.htm >.
94. Ibid.
95. The author has been a participant of the Twelfth and Thirteenth APR and has also been involved in the organization of these conferences. When contacts and enquiries are done with the North Korean Embassy in Kuala Lumpur with regard to their participation in these meetings, the responses have also been quite positive and prompt.

# 6

## THE ASIAN ECONOMIC CRISIS AND OTHER CHALLENGES
## Turning Points beyond the Comfort Zone?

ASEAN rose out of the ashes of Konfrontasi...
— *Ghazali Shafie, Malaysia (1981)*

It will be immensely difficult for ASEAN to manoeuvre itself through an era which will see many treacherous cross currents. With new crew on board, it will become even more difficult to navigate. It will take time for our new members to adjust and be moulded into a part of the ASEAN team. This is a real challenge.
— *Kishore Mahbubani, Singapore (1997)*

We need mechanisms and processes which enable bridges to be formed, make accommodation possible, and achieve compromises. We must certainly avoid "burning bridges" because it leads to standoff, disputes and the use of force — the route to disaster.
— *Prince Ranarridh, Kingdom of Cambodia (1997)*

Increasingly, ASEAN will have to summon regional, cooperative solutions for problems that are, more and more, regional in scope. Indeed, the way in which ASEAN is dealing and has to deal with its most outstanding problems today sheds light on the way in which ASEAN will and must handle its problems in the new millennium; that is, is a co-ordinated, cooperative way.
— *Rodolfo Severino, ASEAN Secretary-General (1998)*

## INTRODUCTION

In 1997, ASEAN was gearing up to celebrate its thirtieth anniversary with a toast. In the run up to its Commemorative Summit in Kuala

Lumpur that was scheduled in December 1997, year-long preparations were set in place aimed at highlighting the achievements of ASEAN as a successful regional organization. More significantly, the Summit was also supposed to showcase the fulfillment of the vision of ASEAN's founding fathers of bringing together all the states in Southeast Asia. Laos, Myanmar, and Cambodia were to be admitted as ASEAN's new members. However, the events that followed turned what would have been a joyous regional event into a more subdued affair. It was in 1997 when a series of crises hit the region, casting a pall on the celebrated success of ASEAN. This period and the years that followed became a watershed in ASEAN's history.

The crises that unfolded not only raised doubts about the ability of ASEAN to manage the difficult challenges that emerged. More importantly, the questions about the viability of ASEAN also undermined the confidence that it had earned. In analysing these issues, two major points about ASEAN had been raised by several observers that would have a bearing on the ability and viability of the organization. The first was the lack or even absence of institutions in ASEAN that could effectively respond to the kinds of problems that emerged. The second was the very norms that ASEAN had internalized which, to many observers, had become obstacles to effective regional responses.

As an essential part of our narrative about ASEAN's mechanisms of conflict management, this chapter will now examine the crises and the challenges to the ASEAN way, as well as the responses that ASEAN took to address these crises. The objective is to analyse the implications of these responses on ASEAN's mechanisms. In doing so, this chapter speaks to the questions about the lack or absence of regional institutions and the problem of norms. To illustrate the implications of ASEAN's responses to the 1997 crises on its prevailing mechanisms, we begin this chapter with the necessary "digression" by taking stock of where ASEAN stood at that point in history when it found itself besieged by several crises. The purpose of which is to strike a clearer comparison of ASEAN's responses to regional challenges before and after 1997. With this approach, we will be able to draw the linkage between the issues raised in the previous chapters about the mechanisms of ASEAN and get our "compass" right, before we proceed to examine the extent to which its mechanisms may have unravelled and/or changed as it grappled with the multi-faceted impacts of the regional crises. The ultimate objective of this exercise is to gauge the extent to which ASEAN has moved beyond the ASEAN way.

This chapter will therefore be organized as follows. Section I provides a consolidated summary of ASEAN's mechanisms and a brief assessment of its performance in crisis management before the 1997 economic crisis. Section II examines ASEAN's responses in the aftermath of the crises. Section III extends our analysis of ASEAN's responses to a new set of problems that shook the region after 11 September 2001 or the 9/11 terrorist attacks in the United States. Section IV examines the status of ASEAN's mechanism post-1997 and 9/11 crises by addressing the issues of institutionalization and norms, and finally Section V concludes by responding to the question of change in the ASEAN way.

## I. ASEAN'S MECHANISMS OF CONFLICT MANAGEMENT: THE THIRTY-YEAR SCORECARD

As discussed in Chapter 1, ASEAN was like many other regional organizations that were formed at the height of the Cold War to set about managing regional order and maintaining peace. Present ASEAN, the member states in Southeast Asia, provided themselves with a regional framework for managing inter-state relationship to prevent future conflicts. Michael Leifer had described ASEAN succinctly as "an institutional product of regional conflict resolution".[1]

Over the past thirty years (1967–97), the successful management of inter-state relations was undergird by the members' assiduous cultivation of certain mechanisms, arguably distinct to ASEAN. Since the nature of these mechanisms, as discussed in Chapter 2, fall outside the conventional types of formal and institutionalized structures, this study adopted the constructivist approach to locate ASEAN's experience against the broader field of conflict management and to identify what these mechanisms are, how they have been shaped and the extent to which these mechanisms have worked.

I had argued in Chapter 2 that the constructivist approach has been useful in the analysis of ASEAN's mechanisms because of its emphases on the non-material factors that help us explain the behaviour of states. The constructivist's premise that the fundamental structures of international politics are "social *rather than strictly* material" have been instructive in delving into the practices of ASEAN member states and the nature of regional social structures which have been made up of shared knowledge. These structures — whether formal or informal — have also been products of the nature of social relationships among states in Southeast Asia. Moreover, the emphases placed on agents and ideas have been particularly useful in understanding the nuances and inflections that have emerged in the kinds of mechanisms that ASEAN has developed over the years. To be sure, constructivism helps in understanding why ASEAN has preferred to manage conflicts the ASEAN way instead of dealing with them in ways normally defined and prescribed in the literature on managing conflict. Through this framework, several observations have been raised in this study about ASEAN, its mechanisms, and how it has coped with regional challenges. These are recapitulated below, as follows:

- ASEAN's mechanisms of conflict management are multi-faceted, embodying both formal and informal processes.

The types of mechanisms for conflict management found in ASEAN come in many forms but have been essentially geared towards preventing and managing conflicts. ASEAN's mechanisms therefore are multi-faceted. In the literature of conflict management, mechanisms are defined as processes, methods, devices, techniques and strategies employed to resolve or manage conflict.[2] And as far as regional institutions are concerned, we noted that they could employ a number of mechanisms to prevent and manage conflicts. These can either be formal mechanisms such as third-party mediation, and arbitration, or informal mechanisms like assurance building and norm-setting. The choice of which mechanisms to use would usually depend on the nature of the conflict, i.e., domestic, inter-state, or involving external actors. Moreover, the choice of mechanisms would also be predicated largely on the capabilities and resources available to these regional institutions.[3]

In our study of ASEAN's mechanisms of conflict management, we had identified two types of interlocking mechanisms: (1) the formal agreements and treaties that encourage co-operation in several areas, and (2) the informal processes that emphasize the need and desirability for co-operation. Between the two, it is the latter that has often caught the attention of most analysts and had been widely studied — often overlooking the formal agreements that have defined the nature of intra-ASEAN co-operation. The point being stressed here is the need to see ASEAN as a framework that embodies both formal and informal processes.

In ASEAN's history, particularly during its formative years, its mechanisms were mostly concentrated on building and institutionalizing certain norms and principles of inter-state relations. These norms, reflected in the ASEAN Concord, had emphasized peaceful means in the settlement of intra-regional disputes; and strengthening political solidarity by promoting the harmonization of views, co-ordinating position and, where possible and desirable, taking common actions. For extra-regional relations, ASEAN adopted the Zone of Peace, Freedom and Neutrality (ZOPFAN) and the Treaty of Amity and Co-operation (TAC). The TAC, in particular, has essentially embodied ASEAN's constitutive norms and defined its basic approach in managing inter-state conflict in the region. The norms and principles of mutual respect, non-interference and effective co-operation have represented the informal mechanisms of ASEAN and have found their expression in the so-called ASEAN Way of managing conflict.

- In its practice of managing conflict, ASEAN appeared to have consistently relied more on its informal mechanisms.

The emphasis on informal mechanisms has prevailed over the past three decades of ASEAN's evolution as a regional organization. As discussed in Chapters 2 and 3, ASEAN members had observed, to the extent possible, the norms of respect, non-interference, and inter-state co-operation. This is in spite of the fact that there had been a number of outstanding territorial disputes that remain unresolved between some ASEAN members. These included the dispute by Malaysia and the Philippines over the territory of Sabah, dispute between Malaysia and Singapore over Pedra Branca, and the dispute between Indonesia and Malaysia over the islands of Sipadan and Ligitan.[4] In spite of these territorial problems and bilateral disputes, none of the member states has tried to invade any state. Moreover, these territorial problems have not got in the way of members co-operating with each other, and strengthening their economic linkages by embarking on regional joint development programmes such as the formation of subregional growth triangles. The SIJORI Growth Triangle, bringing together Singapore, Malaysia, and Indonesia, was the first of such ventures; followed by Indonesia, Malaysia and Thailand (IMT) Growth Triangle, and the Indonesia, Malaysia, Singapore (IMS) Growth Triangle and most recently, the Brunei-Indonesia-Malaysia-Philippines East ASEAN Growth Area (BIMP-EAGA).

The preference for these types of mechanisms has been articulated *ad nauseum* by ASEAN leaders and officials in the many public and even private forums. However, as pointed out by several scholars and observers, the observance of these norms has not really resolved the serious territorial disputes mentioned above. As mentioned in Chapter 2, ASEAN, as a corporate body, does not resolve conflicts. Bilateral issues, including border and territorial disputes, are resolved bilaterally. What ASEAN does therefore is merely to provide the framework where members can work their issues amicably. ASEAN has been the arena that allows member states to manage problems. Caveat notwithstanding, it has also been recognized that these informal processes without concrete institutional support to settle disputes had been a major limitation of ASEAN. However, many ASEAN officials and some observers have argued that the lacunae of institutions in ASEAN to settle dispute has been a function of its evolution as a regional organization in Southeast Asia. For a long period, member states were still getting to know one another and were coming out of an environment characterized by intra-mural tension, mutual suspicion, and distrust. Thus, the improvement of inter-state relations and building of confidence were the paramount tasks at hand. Plunging immediately into highly contested issues would have only severed what, at that time, was a tenuous relationship among not-so-friendly neighbours. This meant that ASEAN's *raison d'etre* was and has still been regional reconciliation.

- Informal approaches to conflict management have been closely linked to regional approaches to security.

One can discern close linkages between ASEAN's mechanisms of conflict management and its approaches to regional security. The ASEAN Concord, ZOPFAN, and TAC have stressed that regional peace was possible only if member states do not fight one another. Hence, building military alliances were eschewed. Instead, a web of overlapping bilateral co-operation on defence and security issues was created. One would also note that during the Cold War period, the pioneer members of ASEAN (Indonesia, Malaysia, the Philippines, Singapore, and Thailand) had opted to foster amity with its neighbours (Vietnam, Laos, and Cambodia), which had politically and ideologically opposite orientations. More importantly, ASEAN had also emphasized the need for each member state to be domestically resilient by concentrating on their respective task of nation-building, addressing their domestic problems, and building their economies. At that time, ASEAN's comprehensive concept of security drew attention to non-military threats that had to be addressed to achieve national security. The regional "ideology" then was to build regional resilience through national resilience in order to protect states and weather the vicissitudes of major power competitions.[5]

As noted in Chapter 1, ASEAN's approach to security have been characterized by:[6]

- *Comprehensiveness*: Security encompasses both military and non-military threats including political, economic, social, and environmental.
- *Emphasis on national and regional resilience*: Based on comprehensive security, the ASEAN states had to aim for national resilience in order to build regional resilience. Hence, internal threats to security must be resolved as these are far more important than external threats. This approach engendered a relatively stable and peaceful environment that, in turn, facilitated closer political and economic relations among member states.
- *Emphasis on confidence-building measures*: In tandem with fostering closer political co-operation, ASEAN encouraged building trust and confidence among members, as well as external states through cultivating the habit of dialogue. The informal confidence-building measures translated through informal meetings have been encouraged to facilitate the exchanges of views, consultation, and dialogue on matters of common concern. These meetings had led to the formation of a close network of regional "friends" whose familiarity and camaraderie have also been reinforced through a myriad of meetings which, to date, total about 300 annually.

Hence, drawing the close linkage between ASEAN's approach to regional security and the emphases on norms enables us to understand why the informal approaches were the preferred mechanisms of ASEAN in managing conflict. It is from this perspective as informed by the constructivist's approach that we can appreciate the nexus between ASEAN's security approach and mechanism of conflict management.

- Decision-making is incremental and done through consultation and consensus, coupled with quiet diplomacy.

While norm-setting is a dominant feature of ASEAN's informal mechanism of conflict management, the other important feature is the slow and incremental manner by which decisions are arrived at. The practice of *musyawarah* (consultation) and *muafakat* (consensus) in decision-making has been maintained, together with quiet diplomacy, to allow for problems to be discussed behind closed door. Confrontation is avoided and solutions are arrived at incrementally. This practice of quiet diplomacy has been strictly adhered to, at least in the past, particularly with regard to political decisions that had led to joint positions on issues like Cambodia, the problems in the South China Sea, and other "sensitive" topics.

Chapter 3 on Cambodia illustrated how the practice of *musyawarah* and *muafakat* were exhausted in trying to come up with joint positions despite the divergence in threat perceptions among member states and their differences in policy approaches in the search for a political settlement to the crisis. One would note that intra-ASEAN disputes and problems on arriving at policy initiatives from the Kuantan Declaration to the Jakarta Informal Meeting (JIM) I and II talks were never aired publicly. Instead, differences were dealt with quietly and gaps in communication among members were overcome through the practice of "shuttle diplomacy" undertaken by certain ASEAN members like Thailand and Malaysia, and also through the appointment of a member-state interlocutor like Indonesia that ensured that decisions and policies would be passed without causing undue friction among members.

The same practice of quiet diplomacy was also observed to the extent possible in inter-state conflicts sparked by bilateral tensions on issues like the Philippine–Singapore spat over the hanging of the Filipina maid, and the Singapore–Malaysia dispute over agreements on water-pricing, among others.[7]

• Emphasis on process rather than outcome.

The development of "new" mechanisms of conflict management has consistently placed considerable emphasis on process over outcome. This approach was well captured in ASEAN's initiative and stewardship of the ASEAN Regional Forum (ARF). As noted in Chapter 4, the decision to establish a multilateral security forum in the region was made only after long discussions among ASEAN's Foreign Ministers and Heads of Government. These discussions allowed for a meeting of minds on the nature of the multilateral security co-operation that was to be embarked on with external powers. The accent on process-oriented co-operative security became even more pronounced as ASEAN and other countries decided on the pace and the direction that ARF was taking. Many outsiders have criticized the slowness of the ASEAN-led ARF in moving beyond stage I on confidence-building measures to stage II on preventive diplomacy.[8] But for many, if not most of the ARF members, agreeing to move only at a pace that was comfortable with other members and stressing the importance of the process of dialogue rather than insisting on tangible outcome was the only way to go if the ARF was to stay intact.

- Processes are reinforced by "agents" represented by ASEAN's epistemic communities.

As discussed in Chapter 5, track two networks represented by the ASEAN-ISIS and CSCAP have played a significant role in helping to reinforce the processes of maintaining ASEAN's mechanisms of conflict management by adopting similar modalities in the way they have conducted track two diplomacy. Their contribution to the establishment of the ARF was discussed at length in Chapter 5. Track two diplomacy has helped to develop closer dialogue and intense consultation not only among track two networks and but also between tracks one and two. Such practice has abided by the ASEAN way of doing things. The experiences of the various working groups within ASEAN-ISIS and CSCAP reflect the reality that unless these practices were observed, co-operation and progress were going to be hampered.

As previously mentioned, the nature and the extent of the networking activities undertaken by these track two organizations have also fostered the process of community-building in ASEAN and the wider Asia-Pacific region. Ambitious as the goal may have been, given that memberships of these track two bodies extend beyond the ASEAN region, these ongoing community-building processes nonetheless buttress the sustained efforts towards creating a collective identity of shared interest in the region.

- Mechanisms are dynamic rather than static.

Finally, while ASEAN's mechanisms of conflict management have been fundamentally informal in nature, this feature has not necessarily been immutable. The events leading to the establishment of the ARF indicate that ASEAN had, in fact, began to adjust it modalities in keeping with the changes in the international environment. As argued in Chapter 5, the turn to multilateralism through the establishment of the ARF had set in motion the thrust towards a more inclusive type of conflict management mechanism where both like-minded and non-like-minded states were brought together and enjoined to have a stake in managing regional security.

One could also argue that multilateralism prior to the ARF was not really a novel approach in the region. If multilateralism were defined as a security approach involving more than two parties in the management of security, then ASEAN, at the very least, has been a regional multilateral endeavour, albeit in its simpler form. But if multilateralism were viewed as necessitating the involvement of major powers, as well as other states in adopting a co-operative approach to security, then the ARF is a "new" extended, co-operative approach — a mechanism that ASEAN has initiated in managing regional security.

Thus, to conclude this section on the thirty-year scorecard of ASEAN's mechanisms, one could fairly arrive at a positive assessment of the way conflict has been managed in the region. One could in fact also push the argument that because ASEAN had been successful in managing security, it has been heading towards becoming a security community, although in a form that is slightly different from the more rigid Deutschian framework which was informed by the experience of integration of countries in North Atlantic.[9] Regardless of what alternative framework one would prefer to use, such as framework suggested by Adler and Barnett who had postulated three variations of security communities, namely "nascent", "ascendant", and "mature",[10] suffice it to say that after thirty years of successful conflict management, ASEAN could reasonably be depicted as evolving into a latent security community. ASEAN was able to do this by developing over a period of time regional practices that shaped its collective identity.[11]

These examples dovetail with the constructivist assumptions that the inter-subjective understanding of states — the ideational elements — do play a significant role in explaining state or in this case, regional behaviour. As one scholar has aptly framed it:

> The ASEAN case reinforces ... observations that "common conceptions absent interactions are not likely to be sustained, and dense interactions are likely to produce a perception of common destiny or regionness".[12]

## II. CHALLENGES TO THE THIRTY-YEAR SCORECARD: MOVING AWAY FROM THE COMFORT ZONE?

ASEAN's thirty-year scorecard in managing conflict became a subject of intense scrunity as the region went through an unexpected period of crises and systemic shocks brought on by a number of grave security challenges. This section will highlight these security issues, assess their impact, and examine ASEAN's responses.

## The 1997 Regional Economic Crisis

The speed with which the financial crisis spread in the region caught many states by surprise. By most accounts, the first symptoms of the crisis started with the attack of foreign currency speculators on Thailand's currency, the baht. The inability of the Thai Government to defend the baht led to its rapid decline in value. This phenomenon, described as the so-called *tomyam* effect, triggered similar currency devaluations in other ASEAN states. Initially, Thailand and Indonesia took the beating with the values of their currencies falling and causing their stock markets to crash. Soon, Malaysia and the Philippines followed. Although the severity of the impact was comparably lesser for these two latter countries, the effects on their respective economies were nevertheless significant. In a span of twelve months, the range of depreciation of regional currencies against the U.S. dollar ranged from between 39 per cent, as in the case of the Malaysian ringgit, to 84 per cent for the Indonesian rupiah. With the onslaught of the crisis, a host of problems ensued within a short period of time. These included massive private sector debt, a credit crunch, decline in economic production, decline in consumption, falling investments, high unemployment, inflation, labour migration, rising social problems, and political unrest. As these countries geared up for economic recession, it soon became clear that they were up against not merely a financial crisis, but, particularly for badly hit countries like Indonesia and Thailand, a social and political crisis as well.

The Indonesian story mirrored the gravity of the economic crisis and its attendant problems. Hyper-inflation saw prices of basic commodities such as food more than doubled. Unemployment rates ballooned from the pre-crisis level of 10 per cent to 24 per cent of the working population, meaning that at the height of the crisis about 15 million people in Indonesia were unemployed. Poverty rates increased and the International Labour Organization estimated that in mid-1998, about 37 per cent of the population, or 75 million people, were expected to be living below the poverty line (defined as US$1 per person per day).[13] It should be noted that up until 1997, Indonesia was cited by the World Bank as the only country in the world that had remarkably improved its Human Development Index (HDI), having started from a very low base in 1975. In effect, the crisis reduced the country's economy into shambles.

The Indonesian Government's economic restructuring policies, led by the International Monetary Fund (IMF), that included the foreclosure of sixteen banks and the steep price hike, such as the 71 per cent increase in petrol prices, triggered political unrest. A number of student protests and demonstrations occurred in several cities. In May 1998, after a ten-day student demonstration at Trisakti Univeristy in Jakarta, four students were killed, sparking a wave of violent riots that raged through the country's capital. Angry mobs looted and burnt buildings indiscriminately. Hundreds of deaths were reported, and people who could, fled the country as the capital came to a standstill.[14] The violence that shocked the country led to mounting calls for President Soeharto to resign, until the fateful day on 21 May 1998 when Soeharto finally stepped down after thirty-three years in power.

The impact of the economic and political events in Indonesia reverberated across the region. The events dashed hopes for early economic recovery for the other economies in ASEAN. It also exacerbated the loss of confidence in the region by foreign investors and other financial institutions. More importantly, the events brought a number of uncertainties to regional security. These included the tensions that arouse among member states as a result of the crisis. One of the issues that led to bilateral frictions was the deportation of illegal foreign workers in Malaysia and Thailand.[15]

At the height of the Asian crisis, ASEAN was roundly criticized for its inability to respond urgently and cohesively to address the devastating consequences of the crisis that threatened the economies of many member countries. In spite of the fact that several measures were instituted to contain the damage, including rescue packages that saw Singapore and Malaysia extending financial support to crisis-stricken members like Indonesia and Thailand, ASEAN's responses were widely regarded as generally inadequate in responding to what at that time was a spiralling economic crisis.[16]

To analyse ASEAN's mechanisms to manage the economic crisis, let us review some of the measures it adopted. Firstly, months before the fall of the Thai baht that triggered the currency crisis, the ASEAN Finance Ministers met to discuss, among others, the urgent need to exchange views on macroeconomic policies and improve transparency of financial policies and regulations. The meeting was organized amid growing concerns at that time over the volatility of regional currencies. Meanwhile, ASEAN central banks were said to have already been working at increasing financial co-operation to strengthen the region's capacity to combat currency volatility. It is also important to note that the ASEAN banks had in fact provided large-scale support for the Thai baht in May

1997, when it was being attacked aggressively by currency speculators. However, against the massive capacity of currency speculators, the ASEAN central banks found themselves defenceless.[17] ASEAN also convened several meetings at three levels (Heads of State/Government, Economic and Finance Ministers, and representatives from the private sectors) to work out an ASEAN response. The meetings came up with several measures to address the crisis. The key elements of these included:

- Joint call for international support to address problems in international currency trading and international finance.
- Joint appeal to the large economies such as the United States, Japan, and the European Union to help resolve the crisis.
- The promotion of trade within Southeast Asia and East Asia using local currencies.
- The establishment of a regional surveillance mechanism which was essentially aimed at promoting a more effective surveillance over the economic policies and practices of ASEAN members, facilitated by fuller disclosure of relevant economic data.[18]

The introduction of the ASEAN Surveillance mechanism was particularly significant given that member countries would have to effectively allow for "peer review" of its economic and financial policies, including the possibility of fuller disclosure of relevant data. This idea was later on expanded within the ASEAN + 3 framework in the establishment of the ASEAN + 3 early warning systems (EWS). A regional EWS prototype was being developed with the help of the Asian Development Bank, which comprised four components:

> (1) a set of macroprudential indicators, broadly defined as indicators of health and stability of financial systems; (2) a non-parametric EWS model designed to assess the probability of a currency crisis within 24-month horizon based on the signaling approach; (3) a parametric EWS designed to assess the probability of a currency crisis with a 24-month time horizon based on probit analysis; and (4) a set of leading indicators of business cycles.[19]

During the crisis some ASEAN countries with more resources also contributed generously to the rescue packages for Thailand and Indonesia. Malaysia, for example, pledged US$1 billion to Jakarta, while Singapore invested considerable effort to provide guarantee letters of credit for Indonesian banks for exporting companies.[20] Moreover, as a response to huge capital flights from these countries and the rising inflation that followed that were bleeding the regional economies, the Bilateral Swap Arrangements (also known as the Chiang Mai Initiative) was introduced in 1998. The mechanism allowed for stand-by emergency funds to assist economies badly affected by the crisis, aside from the financial assistance provided by multilateral financial institutions (for example, the IMF). This was introduced within the ASEAN + 3 Framework.

Lastly, the crisis did not deter ASEAN from pushing ahead with its commitment to the ASEAN Free Trade Areas (AFTA). In October 1998, ASEAN Economic Ministers agreed to accelerate tariff reduction by three years. In December 1998, ASEAN leaders declared that:

> We reaffirm our commitment to the greater integration of our economies as a primary expression of our cooperation and solidarity ... ASEAN reaffirms its commitment to trade and investment liberalization and facilitation, at the multilateral and regional levels and will continue to undertake concrete measures towards these objectives.[21]

## Controversy over Myanmar and Cambodia's Membership

ASEAN was also mired in controversy over the admission of new members. Just as ASEAN was preparing for the ASEAN Ministerial Summit in July 1997 and its thirtieth anniversary celebrations, Cambodia was caught in a power struggle. Cambodia's second prime minister, Hun Sen, staged a coup to oust Prince Ranariddh as first prime minister. As a consequence, ASEAN decided to delay Cambodia's admission into ASEAN. ASEAN's decision was to drive home the point that no leadership or form of government by violent means was ever to be encouraged.

The deferment of Cambodia's membership juxtaposed against the admission of Myanmar earned ASEAN a lot of flak for its inconsistency and double standard. ASEAN's position was that while Myanmar's political conditions were regarded as internal matters of the state, Cambodia's case was viewed differently. The latter was regarded as one that had serious implications for ASEAN since Cambodia broke the regional norm of the non-use of force. As a consequence, ASEAN insisted that Cambodia met certain conditions before its admission, which included among others, the holding of free and fair elections and the establishment of the Cambodian Senate. ASEAN also formed the ASEAN Troika to deal with efforts at restoring political stability in Cambodia.[22] However, ASEAN's drawing of a distinction between the cases of Myanmar and Cambodia based on the norms of non-interference and non-use of force was not lost on its critics. (The criticism on

ASEAN's non-interference principle will be discussed in more detail in the later section of this chapter.)

Controversy notwithstanding, the Cambodian episode eventually led to the formal establishment of the ASEAN Troika in 1999. As defined by its experience in Cambodia, the ASEAN Troika was to be an *ad hoc* body comprising the ASEAN Foreign Ministers of the present, past, and future chairs of the ASEAN Standing Committee (ASC). The positions would rotate in accordance with the ASC's chairmanship. The purpose of the Troika was to enable ASEAN to address urgent and important political and security issues in a timely manner. However, the mandate of the Troika as stipulated in the Troika paper had to be compatible with the principles enshrined in the TAC, particularly the core principles of consensus and non-interference in domestic affairs of states.[23]

## The Regional Haze Problem

The regional challenges brought on by the financial crisis were exacerbated by the onset of the haze problem that enveloped most of Southeast Asia between 1997 and 1998. The environmental damage brought on by the haze problem became a test case of ASEAN's ability to deal co-operatively with problems in one country that had severely affected its neighbours. Although the environmental disaster happened in Indonesia, it inflicted considerable damage to neighbouring countries like Singapore, Malaysia, and Brunei. At the height of the problem, it was estimated that Malaysia and Singapore suffered about $1 billion losses in economic activity, such as tourism, air travel, and immediate health cost.[24] Against the flak that the Indonesian Government received from the international community, former Indonesian President Soeharto appeared on television to apologize for the country's inability to avert the regional disaster.

As part of the regional efforts to mitigate the impact of the environmental problem,[25] ASEAN instituted the Regional Haze Action Plan (RHAP) which the ASEAN Ministers of the Environment endorsed in 1997. The RHAP called for each ASEAN member to develop a National Haze Action Plan that would require each of them to report its plans to combat fires and haze in their respective environment. ASEAN also put into place a joint regional technical assistance project with the Asian Development Bank to assist member countries requiring technical support in fire-fighting procedures. In spite of the regional agreement and co-operation that have been instituted, the recurrences of fires and the attendant haze problem continued to affect several states in the region. Some of the factors cited that cause the ineffectiveness of the RHAP has been the lack of sufficient institutional support to prioritize environmental law and policy-making in ASEAN, plus the omissions of the Indonesian national system.[26]

The serious challenges that confronted ASEAN brought on by the crippling effect of the financial crisis, the crisis in Indonesia, the problems in Cambodia, plus the haze problem, among others, brought to the core the inadequacy of the organization to respond to new security challenges. But while the crisis in its many forms was a painful reality check for the region, most of the criticisms about the growing irrelevance of ASEAN pointed more to the obstructive nature of its norms rather than the problem of institutional capacity.[27] To many critics, the lack of institutions in ASEAN was a function of its strict adherence to the principle of non-intervention. As events unfolded, the call to rethink this mechanism was no longer confined to outsiders but became an issue within ASEAN itself.

## Intramural Challenges to ASEAN's Norm of Non-Interference

Whatever intramural differences that may have occurred during the period of crises appeared to have heightened when one of ASEAN's members openly challenged the principle of non-interference. Before the annual ASEAN Ministerial Meeting was held in Manila in July 1998, reports about Thailand's proposal of the "constructive intervention" policy emerged. Regional newspapers carried stories about the Thai Foreign Minister's spokesman, Kobsak Chutikul, explaining Thailand's initiative. Chutikul was reported to have quoted Thai Foreign Minister Dr Surin Pitsuwan who remarked that "it was time to modify the principle of non-intervention in ASEAN, or at least to reach a new understanding on the principle which is too strict."[28] The timing of the Thai pronouncement which came a year after former Malaysian Deputy Prime Minister Anwar Ibrahim mooted the idea of "constructive involvement" in 1997, indicated the calls for change within the organization. Anwar's proposal was in response to the events in Cambodia that year.[29] We recall that during that period, Cambodia's formal entry into ASEAN was delayed due to the domestic conflict brought about by the power struggle between Cambodia's first and second prime ministers.

While the two proposals, which came sequentially, spoke on the issue of non-interference, a comparison of these two proposals actually reveals important differences in the nature of intervention suggested. Anwar Ibrahim's "constructive intervention" proposal called for a proactive policy of involvement and assistance to Southeast Asia's weaker nations in order to prevent their internal collapse. Anwar outlined the specifics of this policy in an essay carried by *Newsweek* magazine in July 1997. These were:

- direct assistance to firm up electoral processes;
- an increased commitment to legal and administrative reforms;
- the development of human capital; and
- the general strengthening of civil society and the rule of law.

Note, however, that other than the specific proposal of strengthening civil society, the rest of the proposals seemed no different from the existing ASEAN practice of helping and supporting its members. ASEAN's role in Cambodia was a good example.[30]

On the other hand, Surin's proposal of "constructive intervention" which was renamed, "flexible engagement" a month later seemed to suggest a marked difference in the way ASEAN should practice the non-interference principle. His proposal, contained in the Thai Non-Paper on the Flexible Engagement Approach stated that,

> Many domestic affairs have obvious external or transnational dimensions, adversely affecting neighbours, the region and the region's relations with others. In such cases, the affected countries should be able to express their opinions and concerns in an open, frank and constructive manner, which is not, and should not be considered interference in fellow-members' domestic affairs ... ASEAN countries should have sufficient self-confidence in one another, both to discus all issues once considered 'taboos' with one another with candour and sincerity and to speak out on such issues in good faith when necessary and appropriate.[31]

Essentially, the paper reflected two fundamental differences in ASEAN's current practice of inter-state relations. Firstly, the manner by which communication and diplomacy was to be conducted. While the ASEAN way advocated quiet diplomacy, characterized by private discussions and use of oblique language, Surin's proposal called for open and frank discussion. Secondly, the proposal seemed to set out a broad set of domestic issues where "interference" was justified especially when they impact on bilateral, regional, and extra-regional relations. However, Surin's proposal did not spell out the parameters between domestic affairs and the issues that justified "open" discussion by members. While there was obvious concern for the environmental problems that have affected the major capitals in the region brought about the forest fires of Indonesia's Kalimantan and Sumatra provinces, and for the increasing fears of the effects of cross-border migration by receiving countries like Malaysia, Singapore and Thailand which were exacerbated by the region's financial crisis, the other areas and issues with cross-border effects have not really been defined by Surin (not to mention the fact that within ASEAN there was a lack of consensus on this matter).

Among the ASEAN members, it was only the Philippines that openly supported the Thai proposal. Whatever official debate that transpired on the proposal for flexible engagement effectively stopped at the ASEAN Ministerial Meeting in Manila in July 1998 when ASEAN ministers declared that ASEAN, in the light of new security challenges, would be practising "enhanced interaction". This new lexicon apparently meant that ASEAN could have more open exchanges on issues which have cross-border effects like the haze problem while respecting the principle of non-interference. The former Indonesian Foreign Minister Ali Alatas summed up ASEAN's position when he said:

> If the proposition is to replace the principle of non-intervention or in any way to tinker with it, then Indonesia won't accept. However, if the proposition is that ASEAN ... taking into account all the changes in the world, should be more active in dealing with one another on problems that may originate in one country but may have an impact on the other ASEAN countries, then by all means let us talk about it.[32]

Given the ASEAN history on dealing with issues, it was therefore not surprising that the initial proposal of "constructive intervention" was shot down and that the ASEAN members settled for an accommodated position of "enhanced interaction". On reflection, one could surmise that whatever controversy that may have arose over Surin's proposal was the fact that crucial issues of regional concern were not going to be discussed. The problem was that the proposal suggested a change in the way problems were to be discussed. Essentially, the Surin proposal called for open and frank discussion — a departure from the ASEAN way of quiet diplomacy. Moreover, while the proposal had also argued for ASEAN to be more actively involved, it actually did not sanction members to freely interfere in each other's internal affairs. Herein lies the ambiguity of this norm.

## Negotiating the Norm of Non-Interference

Against the intramural challenge on the norm of non-interference, it is noteworthy to explore what the ASEAN members actually meant by the practice of non-interference. If ASEAN's policy of non-interference essentially meant that member states "refrain from open criticisms of others and provide no support to a neighbouring country's opposition movement",[33] then it appeared that this policy has not been strictly observed since there had been several cases in the past which contradicted this norm. For example, amid the protests and confusion in the Philippines during the "people power" revolution in February 1986 to bring down former President Ferdinand Marcos, ASEAN jointly called on "all parties [in the country] to restore national unity ... and to act with restraint and join efforts to pave the way for a peaceful resolution to the crisis".[34] Some of the more recent examples in this regard include the spats between Malaysia and Singapore where political leaders in the past had openly and unreservedly commented on each other's affairs.[35] The comments coming from both sides had touched on domestic and sensitive bilateral issues. At the height of the financial crisis, for instance, Singapore openly complained about Malaysia's forced closure of the Central Limit Order Book (CLOB), a facility where Malaysian shares were traded in Singapore. Around the same time, Malaysia criticized Singapore for being "unfriendly" when Singaporean banks offered high interest rates for Malaysian ringgit deposits which encouraged Malaysian capital to leave the country and hurt the Malaysian economy.[36]

Perhaps in what may be considered as even bolder criticisms were the comments by former Indonesian President Habibie and Philippine President Estrada who openly expressed their respective concern over the treatment of former Malaysian Deputy Prime Minister Anwar Ibrahim after he was summarily dismissed by then Prime Minister Mahathir in September 1998. These intrusive comments happened to have been expressed during their bilateral meetings at the sidelines of the APEC Summit in Kuala Lumpur on 13 October 1998. The comments elicited a diplomatic protest from Kuala Lumpur.[37] Similarly, in February 1999, Singapore Prime Minister Goh Chok Tong called on Indonesia to hold elections that would be accepted as fair and legitimate by the Indonesian people.[38] In fact, a year prior to the ousting of former Indonesian President Soeharto, Singapore Senior Minister Lee Kuan Yew suggested that the international business community might raise questions about the suitability of then Vice-President Habibie to take over Indonesia's presidency.

There are many more examples of this nature in ASEAN's experience where contradictions have existed in official declarations of ASEAN and in the actual practice in their inter-state relations. But while these were indeed exceptions to the rule, ASEAN has essentially observed this principle as one of its core mechanisms in managing conflict. This also meant that despite these periodic episodes of bilateral tensions and public spat, the mechanism of restraint has essentially prevailed; and while leaders might have agreed to disagree on certain matters, bilateral frictions were not allowed to get in the way of ASEAN moving forward in political and economic co-operation. This approach was reaffirmed by Singapore's Goh Chok Tong at a joint press conference with his Malaysian counterpart when he stated that:

> Although differences between (the two) countries might arise from time to time, it was important to narrow the gap and work towards maximizing common areas. And where we could agree, we will agree and where we disagree on certain things, we agree to come back tomorrow.[39]

Therefore, Thailand's much talked about proposal on flexible engagement did not have any significant impact on the ASEAN way of non-interference since one could argue that the practice of this principle has after all been negotiated. The events that suggested a departure from this principle did not stir serious confrontation leading to escalation of crisis. Instead the practice of quiet diplomacy eventually prevailed. Nevertheless, the challenge to the norm remained and continued to resurface as ASEAN faced up to new challenges.

## The East Timor Crisis

Following the economic crisis, the most difficult challenge to ASEAN's modalities was the tragic events in East Timor in 1999. ASEAN, and even the ARF, came under severe criticisms for their inability to stem the violence and gross violations of human rights that followed. As noted in many accounts, ASEAN could not initiate any form of conflict preventive action to stop the atrocities that occurred in many parts of the country soon after the East Timorese voted for independence from Indonesia. It was not until the United Nations organized a peacekeeping mission under the framework of the International Force for East Timor (INTERFET) that violence was controlled and large-scale humanitarian relief operations could be carried out.[40] The events leading up to crisis and ASEAN's response are briefly discussed below.

Violence started to erupt through large parts in East Timor after Indonesia's decision on 30 August 1999 to allow the then province to have a referendum on its future status — either to become an autonomous province or independent state. During this period, the UN Mission in East Timor (UNAMET) was established to help prepare East Timor for the referendum. UNAMET comprised 241 international staff, 420 UN volunteers, up to 280 civilian police, and some 4,000 local staff. Within ASEAN, the Philippines contributed to UNAMET by sending civilian police, staff members, and electoral volunteers.

In spite of the presence of UNAMET, violence escalated and spread throughout East Timor leading to the declaration of martial law on 7 September. By then, East Timor lost human lives, suffered massive property destruction, while thousands of terrified people were also forcibly displaced to West Timor. The International Commission of Inquiry on East Timor, released by the UN Office of the High Commissioner for Human Rights and the Indonesian Government's report on the Inquiry into Human Rights Abuses drew similar conclusions that the atrocities were committed by the local militia, and the Indonesian Armed Forces (TNI) were in complicity.[41]

Many governments, either individually or collectively through the UN, urged Indonesia to enforce law and order in East Timor. While there were indeed expressions of concerns coming from ASEAN countries, it took the Australian initiative to offer its troops for a UN peacekeeping force before any international action could begin to stop the violence in East Timor. Even then, it was not until Indonesia consented to an international peacekeeping force in East Timor that ASEAN officials began to discuss their countries' possible participation in the UN peacekeeping force. Incidentally, discussions took place at the sidelines of the APEC Summit in Auckland and prior to that, no *ad hoc* ASEAN meeting was convened to address what was at that time a spiralling humanitarian crisis in the region.

On 15 September 1999, the UN Security Council adopted Resolution 1264 creating the International Force for East Timor (INTERFET) under Chapter VII of the UN Charter. Australia headed the multinational force and within ASEAN, the Philippines, Singapore, Malaysia, and Thailand contributed forces. Most of the ASEAN team volunteers were composed of support personnel, medical, engineering, and security task forces. The intervention of INTERFET allowed the UN to begin large-scale humanitarian relief operations in the country. Apart from providing basic relief goods, INTERFET repaired damaged infrastructure, ran medical clinics and, most importantly, established security to a war-torn territory.

By 25 October, the Security Council passed Resolution 1272 to authorize Secretary General Kofi Annan to set up the UN Transitional Authority in East Timor (UNTAET) in order to "exercise all legislative and executive authority including the administration of justice" in East Timor until formal independence. UNTAET's mandate was: to provide security and maintain law and order throughout the territory of East Timor; to establish an effective administration; to assist in the development of civil and social services; to ensure the co-ordination and delivery of humanitarian, rehabilitation, and development assistance; to support capacity-building for self-government; and to assist in the establishment of conditions for sustainable development. UNTAET formally replaced INTERFET in February 2000 and a Filipino officer, Lt. Gen. Jaime de los Santos became the head of the UN peacekeeping force, replacing the former head Major-General Peter Cosgrove from Australia.

The East Timor crisis was viewed by many as a humanitarian disaster waiting to happen and which ASEAN, conscious of its policy of non-intervention, did not do anything to prevent. Although some ASEAN members participated in the INTERFET, its contributions were lost in the barrage of criticisms against the extent to which ASEAN went to "intervene" in what was considered by the organization as an intra-state conflict. Criticisms were even more strident of the ARF which was silent throughout the crisis. Once again, ASEAN's inability to respond to the crisis in East Timor was seen as a litmus test of its inadequacy as a regional institution to act in times of crisis or to prevent crisis from happening.

ASEAN's perceived lack of leadership in East Timor was in sharp contrast to the proactive role it had assumed in the search for a comprehensive political settlement of the Cambodian conflict. One would recall that throughout the crisis, whatever ASEAN lacked in terms of political authority to influence the behaviour of the warring factions was made up for through its intense lobbying in the UN and facilitating dialogues between the warring Cambodian parties which culminated in the famous Jakarta Informal Meetings (JIM I and JIM II). While it could be argued that ASEAN's swift reaction was predicated on its protest against Vietnam's occupation of Cambodia which violated the international norms of respect for a country's sovereignty and the right of self-determination (principles also found in ASEAN's own TAC), as against the internal dimension of the East Timor conflict, the latter none the less presented a strong case of gross violation of international norms.

ASEAN officials have responded to the criticisms by declaring that only the UN had the legitimacy and the capabilities to undertake any peacekeeping operation and mobilize the massive resources necessary to respond to the East Timor crisis. What ASEAN had done instead was to "undertake consultations, arrived at consensus and let the individual members decide on what specific contributions to make to the UN effort".[42] Although these were consistent with its processes and mechanisms of conflict management, ASEAN's actions against expectations reflected the stark reality that the nature of regional mechanisms were largely indicative of the availability of resources or lack thereof of regional organizations. It should be noted too that the East Timor crisis happened at the time when most ASEAN states were still recovering from the devastating effects of the Asian financial crisis. Thus most countries were preoccupied with national concerns and could offer no more than limited contribution.

Moreover, the East Timor crisis highlighted ASEAN's sensitivity to the issue of national sovereignty when it came to setting up an international inquiry into the atrocities in East Timor. ASEAN member states demonstrated their strict adherence to the principle of non-interference by opposing such a resolution that was sponsored by the European Union. This reservation was suggestive of the fear of some ASEAN countries that a similar kind of international response could be directed against them if and when the international community considers it justifiable to undertake humanitarian intervention.[43]

## III. POST-1997 AND THE AFTERMATH OF SEPTEMBER 11: NEW CHALLENGES TO THE ASEAN WAY

Just when the region appeared to have recovered from the repercussions of the economic crisis, the impact of the September 11 terrorist attacks in the United States raised new security concerns and brought new dimensions to the security agenda of ASEAN. The event and its aftermath saw the region embarking on its "own war" against terrorism amid prevailing fears and concern that Al-Qaeda or Al-Qaeda-linked terrorist networks could be operating in the region. This threat became starker with the bombing incidents in Bali, Indonesia, which occurred in

October 2002. Some of the Southeast Asian groups that were reported to have alleged links with the Al-Qaeda network were the Jemaah Islamiyah (JI) group which is said to have cells in Singapore and Indonesia, Kumpulan Mujahiddeen based in Malaysia, Laskar Jihad in Indonesia, and the Moro Islamic Liberation Front (MILF) and the Abu Sayaff Group in the Philippines.

The impact of the terrorist attacks in the United States and the threats posed by terrorist networks around the globe prompted ASEAN to adopt an ASEAN Declaration on Joint Action to Counter Terrorism during the seventh ASEAN Summit in November 2001. The statement outlined several measures to fight terrorism, which include, among others:

- Reviewing and strengthening national mechanisms to combat terrorism;
- Deepening co-operation among front-line law enforcement agencies in combating terrorism and sharing "best practices";
- Enhancing information/intelligence exchange to facilitate the flow of information, in particular, on terrorists and terrorist organizations, their movement and funding, and any other information needed to protect lives, property, and the security of all modes of travel;
- Strengthening existing co-operation and co-ordination between the ASEAN Ministerial Meeting on Transnational Crime (AMMTC) and other relevant ASEAN bodies in countering, preventing, and suppressing all forms of terrorists acts. Particular attention would be paid to finding ways to combat terrorist activities, support infrastructure and funding, and bringing the perpetrators to justice;
- Strengthening co-operation at bilateral, regional, and international levels in combating terrorism in a comprehensive manner and affirm that at the international level the UN should play a major role in this regard.[44]

Under the ASEAN framework, ASEAN states also signed the Agreement on Information Exchange and Establishment of Communication Procedures on 7 May 2002 to promote co-operation in combating transnational crime, including terrorism. The areas of co-operation included combined training, hotlines and border controls. Malaysia, Philippines, and Indonesia were the initial signatories to the Agreement, joined later by Cambodia and Thailand. Furthermore, ASEAN and the United States issued a Joint Declaration for Co-operation to Combat International Terrorism on 1 August 2002, which committed the

United States and all ten ASEAN members to improve intelligence-gathering efforts, strengthen capacity-building measures and enhance mutual co-operation.

There have also been several activities undertaken under the auspices of the ARF. After the September 11 attacks, two workshops were held under the ARF Inter-Sessional Group (ISG) on Confidence Building Measures. The first was organized by Malaysia–U.S. Workshop on Financial Measures Against Terrorism held in Honolulu on 24–25 March 2002 and the Thailand–Australia Workshop on Prevention of Terrorism held in Bangkok on 17–19 April 2002. The recommendations of both meetings were adopted in the statement of the Ninth ARF Meeting in July 2002.

As ASEAN countries grappled with the intractable problems of terrorism being unravelled in the region, the threats threw another dimension to the challenges confronting the existing regional mechanisms in dealing with this problem. Although ASEAN countries presented a united front as revealed in the initiatives undertaken by the organization, regional efforts and co-ordination have been hampered by the domestic politics of member states.[45] Countries like Indonesia and Malaysia that have large Muslim populations have had to tread carefully in handling this problem given the domestic sensitivities involved in apprehending Muslim militant groups. Initially, Indonesia was perceived to be in a denial mode. The government was slow in responding to calls for the arrest of certain individuals who were reported to be involved directly in the terrorist acts perpetuated by terrorist groups. It was not until the Bali incident that the Indonesian Government was finally seen to have acted more decisively with the arrests and trials of suspected terrorists like Abu Bakar Bashir, alleged leader of JI, and Amrozi.[46]

The "war on terrorism" and the role of the United States had also appeared to be a divisive issue in ASEAN. Indonesia and Malaysia did not endorse the U.S.-led attack on Afghanistan, while the Philippines and Thailand tacitly supported it by allowing U.S. overflights over their territories. In contrast, Brunei and Singapore endorsed the war by pointing to the UN resolution. There has also been disquiet about the U.S. military presence in the region given the close co-operation between the United States and the Philippines in the country's battles against the MILF and Abu Sayaff. But as noted above, the differences have not been allowed to hamper bilateral and regional co-operation in fighting terrorism.

## SARS and the Health Crisis

As the threats of terrorism continued to loom ahead, the unexpected onset of the infectious diseases, Severe Acute Respiratory Syndrome (SARS), triggered another crisis in the region. SARS was a rude awakening to ASEAN whose already expanding list of non-traditional security issues did not include health and human security.

The first known outbreak of SARS started in late February 2003. Within just two months after its reported outbreak, SARS had infected close to 6,000 people and killed 200 in at least twenty-six countries. By the time the World Health Organization (WHO) declared that the disease had peaked, the total number of infection came up to 8,402 with 772 deaths in twenty-nine countries.[47] With no known cure in sight, SARS saw medical teams around the globe working feverishly to contain the problem while the death toll was rising. The rapidity of the spread of SARS across borders, not to mention the attendant disruption in business and travel, caught many governments by surprise to the extent that containing the spread of SARS became the immediate task at hand.

The Asian region was the most heavily affected region in the world, with China, Hong Kong, Taiwan, Singapore, and Vietnam making it to the list of SARS-hit countries. To avert a possible global epidemic, travel alerts were issued by WHO against SARS-affected countries, namely China and its various provinces, Hong Kong, Vietnam, Singapore, and Canada. As the disease spread, the list was expanded to include Taiwan and the Philippines.

The extent of the SARS crisis had been clearly reflected in the sudden disruption of economic activity in several economies in Asia. With travel advisories issued against SARS-affected countries, there was a drastic fall in tourism and travel, making these two sectors the most badly hit sectors in most economies. However, there was also the fear of a possible domino effect. Starting with the fall in consumer confidence, drop in domestic demands and poor business sentiments, many businesses were threatening to be on the brink of collapse as the cost of SARS started to rise. Economic growth prospects began to be reassessed as forecasts for GDP growth in Asia were reduced to fall between 0.5 and 1 per cent. The WHO put the cost of SARS to Asia at US$30 billion, while a health expert of BioEnterprise Asia projected that the cost stood at US$50 billion for the region and up to US$150 billion globally. In Hong Kong, for example, which recorded the second highest number of

SARS cases, government estimates placed the cost of SARS to about US$1.7 billion, while in Singapore, the government forecast indicated that SARS could shave as much as a half to one percentage point off its GDP growth forecast.[48]

Within three months of the outbreak, in the period between mid-March to mid-May 2003, the tourism and travel sectors hit an unprecedented low as people began to shy away from travelling to SARS-affected countries like China, Hong Kong, Singapore, and Vietnam. Tourist data from Hong Kong indicated that inbound tourists fell by 70 to 80 per cent while outbound tourists were down by 20 per cent. Since early April, passenger traffic on Cathay Pacific (Hong Kong's flag carrier) decreased by around 75 per cent.[49] In Singapore, tourist arrivals fell to 70 per cent.[50] In the first few week of April, Singapore Airlines' passenger traffic also went down by 25 per cent.[51] Added to this was the impact of reduced travel to the hotel industry, with many countries reporting hotel occupancy rates of below 10–30 per cent.[52] Topping all these was the huge slump in the retail industry which had seen a 20–50 per cent drop in business for many countries.[53]

ASEAN acted promptly to put in place several mechanisms to address the health crisis. Two months after the outbreak, ASEAN convened an emergency meeting among its health ministers and its leaders. A special ASEAN + 3 meeting was also held back-to-back with the ASEAN meetings.[54] These meetings had outlined several measures to address the SARS epidemic. These included immediate measures such as:

- exchange of information, best practices in containing infectious diseases, and even legislation (quarantine laws);
- strengthening co-operation among front-line enforcement agencies such as health, immigration, customs, transport, and law enforcement;
- harmonization of travel procedures to ensure proper health screening at the points of origin and arrival; and
- protection of foreign nationals who may be suspect or actual SARS cases:

ASEAN have been also looking at measures geared towards enhancing co-operation between ASEAN and WHO; developing an ASEAN Centre for Disease Control; and developing a regional surveillance system to complement the WHO-inspired Global Outbreak Alert and Response Network.[55]

## IV. REASSESSING THE THIRTY-YEAR SCORECARD

The foregoing discussion on "new" regional challenges and ASEAN's responses present a mixed picture of the capacities of ASEAN in crisis and/or conflict management. Sections II and III had highlighted the nature of these myriad challenges to underscore the fact that ASEAN has had to confront new types of problems that were beyond what its mechanisms had set out to do. The argument presented in this chapter is that unless we have assessed what ASEAN's mechanisms were meant to address, it would be difficult to objectively evaluate what ASEAN has failed to do. More often than not, the benchmark used to gauge the abilities of ASEAN had failed to recognize that the association and its mechanisms were created for specific purpose at a certain time. Hence, before we proceed to examine the effects of the crises on ASEAN's mechanisms of managing crisis, we need to refer back to the ASEAN "compass" as described in Section I. In doing so, we come up with the following observations.

Firstly, it has been argued that ASEAN and by extension, the ARF, had been mostly an "enterprise" for regional reconciliation. As such, the institutional development of ASEAN was parsimonious, and whatever institutions it has had were geared mainly for engendering an environment for trust and confidence-building among members who during the establishment of ASEAN were not exactly the best of friends. Over the past four decades, ASEAN chose to take a very conservative path to ensure a stable transition and, to the extent possible, a smoother calibration of relationships among its members. As a consequence, when crisis occurred that needed specialized expertise to respond to financial meltdowns, environmental disasters, peacekeeping operations, and highly infectious epidemics, ASEAN was more often unprepared. The kinds of crises and challenges that confront the region today require much more than what a loosely structured organization could provide.

Secondly, against the lack of institutional capacity and/or expertise, ASEAN's responses to crises have, at best, been *ad hoc*. These types of responses were most visible during the 1997–78 period when the region was beset by a series of crisis. To recapitulate, these *ad hoc* responses included:

1.  The establishment of the ASEAN Troika to help Cambodia in restoring the country's political stability. Since then, not much has been heard about the status of the ASEAN Troika;

2.  The institutionalization of the Bilateral Swap Arrangement as a mechanism to help member countries that were badly affected by the 1997-98 financial crisis, as well as the introduction of the regional surveillance mechanism as a form of an early-warning system to avert potential financial crisis in the future.
3.  The adoption of the Regional Haze Action Plan (RHAP) to fight regular forest fires and manage the resulting haze/environmental problems.
4.  The signing of the Agreement on Information Exchange and Establishment of Communication Procedures to promote co-operation in combating transnational crimes, including terrorism.
5.  The adoption of several measures to jointly contain infectious diseases, including the development of an ASEAN Centre for Disease Control.

Thirdly, while the above responses may have been *ad hoc*, one must note that ASEAN had nevertheless attempted to address the crises. Moreover, while these responses may have been widely regarded as quite inadequate, this does not detract us from the fact that ASEAN members had managed to work together to face the crises. Under the given circumstances, ASEAN was the framework that allowed states to co-operate within their capabilities to do so. Yet, clearly there were certain crises which were beyond the limited capacities of ASEAN and its member states.

Nevertheless, the big issue of the effectiveness of these regional *ad hoc* responses remains. In this regard, one would agree that without a strong Secretariat, the effectiveness of initiatives taken by ASEAN, which require close co-ordination and constant monitoring among member states, would be severely handicapped. Unlike the EU, which has huge reservoir of human resources to support its activities, the ASEAN Secretariat has a limited number of staff that attends to its burgeoning activities. This also means that many of ASEAN initiatives languish through a lack of resources, both financial and human capital.

Given the above factors, the nature of regional capacities and responses indicates one crucial fact, that is, ASEAN could only be as strong and as effective as how member states want it to be. Whether or not member states agree to push the limits of their organization and move towards adopting new institutions and adopt new mechanisms would also depend on their respective domestic capacities to cope with their own domestic challenges.

Against these observable trends, it is not surprising that one comes up with a rather ambivalent assessment of ASEAN's capacity to respond to new challenges. As pointed out earlier, ASEAN has been created for a specific purpose during a particular milieu. Four decades later, the international and regional landscape had dramatically changed. At the very least, one could argue that ASEAN has attempted to respond to changing circumstances. The previous discussion has attempted to highlight some of the new attempts and/or regional mechanisms that have evolved over the years since ASEAN was established. However, these attempts have yet to prove themselves sufficiently adequate to respond to emerging and more complex challenges.

## V. CONCLUSION: WHITHER THE COMFORT ZONE?

It is often said that crisis also presents opportunities. The 1997 series of crises, as well as the post-September 11 security challenges, have forced ASEAN to act proactively and rethink the fundamentals of what it is all about. Given the altered international environment, has ASEAN changed, and how?

The answer to this question would depend on what we mean by change and how that change is defined. If change refers to reforming ASEAN's organizational structure and provide it with the capabilities to deal with regional crisis, then the emergence of new mechanisms reflected in the number of agreements found in the economic and political-security area indicate that ASEAN has indeed been moving in that direction, albeit at a slow pace.

One of the important observations that can be made from ASEAN's experience during the times of crises is the fact that these difficulties only deepened the nature of its co-operation — be it in the political, economic, and security-related areas. While the problems of co-ordination and implementation are plenty, this trend towards closer co-operation has debunked the expectations that regional crises and domestic crises would preoccupy most member states, make them inward-looking and would consequently make them disinterested in regional initiatives. Against the prediction that ASEAN was going to be irrelevant and stood the risk of being rendered obsolete,[56] it had instead moved into areas that consolidate its position as regional organization. A solid case in this instance is the realization of and the progress that AFTA has achieved. AFTA has been a showcase of how "bold" ASEAN has gone to change the modalities of ASEAN from informal agreements to more rules-based, institutional arrangements to promote regional economic co-operation. The regional project on regional surveillance mechanisms for financial co-operation and the plans to develop a regional surveillance system for infectious diseases are other examples to demonstrate this trend towards more institutionalization. Moreover, the enhanced intelligence sharing to fight terrorism leading to harmonization of certain national laws and procedures are indicative of the new tools that ASEAN has crafted to address new security issues.

At this point in ASEAN's history, one could repeat the observation cited in Section I that the ASEAN way has not been static. In fact, the new mechanisms that have evolved signal a nascent trend towards greater institutionalization for ASEAN. Furthermore, from the foregoing discussions in the previous chapters that tracked the periods of ASEAN's development and the evolution of its mechanisms in responding and managing conflict, one would argue for a more comprehensive understanding of what ASEAN has been and what it had become. In other words, understanding the nature of ASEAN — specifically its mechanisms to respond to crisis — has to go beyond examining the normative features of the ASEAN way. Yet, more often than not, presenting ASEAN as a co-operative regional enterprise is often harder to capture than by explaining its norms and other mechanisms. This explains why the discourse on ASEAN's norm of non-interference usually becomes the focus of many analyses, instead of delving deeper into the types of regional co-operative activities that have been taking place in the political, economic, and security area.

However, if reform implies a far more institutionalized and organized ASEAN, with supra-national institutions that can develop norms that both guide and restrain the action of states and in effect, make these inter-state institutions as actors in their own right with the ability to both influence and be influenced by states, then this prospect does not appear to be forthcoming, at least in the immediate to short-term future. After all, ASEAN has been, for all intents and purposes, a political decision by states to remain a co-operative enterprise of separate, sovereign states. Unless member states muster the political will to drastically reverse that decision, much of that old ASEAN way will still remain. Nevertheless, this does not diminish the fact that the ASEAN way is not immutable. The challenge therefore is to identify and capture these nuances as one follows the ASEAN story.

So far, what we have seen of ASEAN is that in coping with trying times, its emerging modalities have stuck very closely to the "comfort zone", that the extent to which ASEAN members are still able to remain reassured that things will not drastically change, in spite of the dramatic developments around the region. Thus most of the new modalities have not necessarily been bold enough but rather incremental in nature. New modalities have also been tailored to be flexible and non-threatening to regime security of ASEAN states. Going by the ASEAN experience, the decision for incremental changes have been due to several reasons, among these are the perils of expansion and domestic capacity for change.

## The Perils of Expansion

Considering that ASEAN is comprised of ten states, four which are relatively new members (known as the CLMV countries) with political and economic attributes that are very much different from the "old" members; instituting new and bold changes to ASEAN modalities would not be easy. The differential nature of new members has consequently widened the diversity of political identities and interest within the group. Moreover, diversity has also been linked to political controversy (such as what is happening in Myanmar today) with the effect of exposing internal divisions within ASEAN. As argued by the late Michael Leifer, regardless of the benefits ASEAN has had with institutional enlargement so as to enhance diplomatic weight, "the key to the efficacy of any regional institution is its ability to display consensus with credibility".[57] To be sure, the political impasse in Myanmar is a big dilemma for ASEAN and unless progress is made, the issue of ASEAN's credibility becomes more acute when Myanmar takes over the Chairmanship of ASEAN in 2006.

ASEAN's expansion is, therefore, a major drawback in pushing for drastic reform in ASEAN modalities. The fact is that the comfort level among members in the old ASEAN is no longer the same with an expanded association; although it can also be argued that with the changes in leadership among the old members the feature of like-minded leaders may have already changed the quality of interaction among ASEAN élites. However, the issue here is not about stretching the comfort level among ASEAN leaders but to the extent possible, maintaining or keeping it as close as possible to the previous levels to maintain cohesion within the organization.

## Domestic Capacity for Change

Another significant factor in determining prospects for reform is the domestic capacity of ASEAN member states to cope with their own internal challenges. One need not go into details about the complex fault lines that beset each and every member of ASEAN. The Indonesian story is more than sufficient to demonstrate how crucial it is for members to build their capacity to manage their own domestic issues to make it easier for them to join and commit to regional endeavours. Hence, what happens in these countries, like in Indonesia which has been the epicentre of ASEAN, is of great consequence to other members and to the nature of the group itself.

Similarly, the capacities of CLMV countries that are comparatively handicapped in more ways than one to cope with emerging challenges — both locally and regionally — would also have implication for other ASEAN members. The development gap between the richer and poorer member states in ASEAN is considerable with Singapore having the highest per capita income of more than US$20,000, followed by Brunei with US$15,174, Malaysia and Thailand with about US$2,000–4,000, and the Philippines and Indonesia under US$1,000. In sharp contrast, Cambodia, Laos, Myanmar, and Vietnam have an average of less than US$300 per year! To bridge this economic divide, ASEAN leaders launched the Initiative for ASEAN Integration (IAI) in November 2002. The aim of the IAI was to assist the CLMV countries in their economic integration process within ASEAN and also to avoid the emergence of a two-tier ASEAN. Therefore, pushing for drastic changes in the *modus operandi* of ASEAN, particularly in certain issue areas would not be realistic given some of the limitations cited above.

To conclude, the major challenges to all these responses and mechanisms remain. These are the extent to which they have been sufficiently adequate and effective in addressing the myriad issues, whether the agreed modalities have been implemented at various levels, and finally whether these initiatives are in fact sustainable. Once again, ASEAN is at a crossroad and the question as to whether ASEAN can reinvent itself continues to resonate.[58] Increasingly, among the many actors that have echoed this call for change are the civil society organizations which have hardly featured in ASEAN's history. The next chapter will now turn to these actors and analyse whether they could become another mechanism for ASEAN in managing conflict and maintaining regional security.

## Notes

1.  Michael Leifer, *ASEAN and the Security of Southeast Asia* (New York: Routledge, 1989), p. 17.

2. C.R. Mitchell, *The Structure of International Conflict* (New York: St. Martin's Press, 1981), Parts 1 and 4. For further discussions on the approaches to conflict resolution, see Edward E. Azar and John W. Burton, eds., *International Conflict Resolution: Theory and Practice* (Boulder, CO: Lynne Rienner, 1986).

3. We refer back to the various types of conflict management mechanisms outlined by Muthiah Alagappa, in "Regional Institutions, The UN and International Security", *Third World Quarterly* 18, no. 3 (1997): 421–41.

4. There have also remained unresolved boundary problems between ASEAN member states like the border dispute between Thailand and Malaysia, between Indonesia and Vietnam on their demarcation like on the continental shelf in the South China Sea under Natuna Islands, boundary disputes between Malaysia and Vietnam on their offshore demarcation line, boundary disputes between Indonesia and the Philippines in the Celebes Sea, border disputes between Malaysia and Brunei over the unmarked 247-kilometre land border between Brunei and Malaysia. This excludes the disputes over the Spratly Islands which have been considered as a potential flashpoint in the region.

 At the time of writing, the Sipadan-Ligatan dispute between Malaysia and Indonesia, which were referred to the International Court of Justice (ICJ), has been resolved. On 17 December 2002, ICJ ruled that the resource-rich islands which are located in the Sulawesi Sea belong to Malaysia. See reports from Radio Singapore International, on <http://www.rsi.com.sg/english/indonesiawatch/view/20030103151226/1/.html>, accessed on 10 February 2004.

5. See Dewi Fortuna Anwar, *Indonesia in ASEAN: Foreign Policy and Regional* (Singapore: Institute of Southeast Asian Studies, 1994).

6. See Mely C. Anthony, "Challenges to Southeast Asian Security Cooperation", in *An Asia-Pacific Security Crisis? New Challenges to Regional Stability*, edited by Guy Wilson-Roberts (Wellington: Centre for Strategic Studies, 1999), pp. 51–65. See also Jusuf Wanandi, *ASEAN Political and Security Cooperation* (Jakarta: Centre for Strategic and International Studies, 1993); Dewi Fortuna Anwar, "Twenty-Five Years of ASEAN Political Cooperation", in *ASEAN in a Changed Regional and International Political Economy*, edited by Soesastro, Hadi (Jakarta: Centre for Strategic and International Studies, 1995), pp. 108–28.

7. For more on the ongoing disputes over bilateral agreements on water, see *Water Talks? If Only It Could* (Singapore: Ministry of Information, Communication and the Arts, 2003).

8. Robyn Lim, "The ASEAN Regional Forum: Building on Sand", *Contemporary Southeast Asia* 20, no. 20 (1998): 115–36. See also Tobias Ingo Nischalke, "Insights from ASEAN's Foreign Policy Cooperation: The ASEAN Way, A Real Spirit or Phantom?", *Contemporary Southeast Asia* 22, no. 1 (2000): 89–112.

9. Karl Deutsch's definition of security community refers to " a group that has

become integrated, where integration is defined as the attainment of a sense of community, accompanied by formal or informal institutions or practices, sufficiently strong and widespread *to assure peaceful change among members of a group with reasonable certainty over a long period of time."* See Karl Deutsch, "Security Communities", in *International Politics and Foreign Policy*, edited by James Rosenau (New York: Free Press, 1961), p. 98. Emphasis added.

10. Emanuel Adler and Michael Barnett, "A Framework for the Study of Security Communities", in *Security Communities*, edited by Emanuel Adler and Michael Barnett (Cambridge: Cambridge University Press, 1998), pp. 29–65.

11. According to Amitav Acharya, there are four elements that have been important in the process of building a security community in ASEAN. These are: multilateralism, norms, symbols (here he includes the ASEAN way of consensus-seeking and informal decision-making procedures), and a shared quest for regional autonomy. This study has discussed most, if not all, of the elements which Acharya has mentioned. See Amitav Acharya, "Collective Identity and Conflict Management in Southeast Asia", in *Security Communities*, pp. 198–227, and Amitav Acharya, *Constructing a Security Community in Southeast Asia* (London and New York: Routledge, 2001).

12. Khong Yueng Foong, "ASEAN and the Southeast Asian Security", in *Regional Order: Building Security in a New World*, edited by David A. Lake and Patrick A. Morgan (Pennsylvania: The Pennsylvania State University Press, 1997), p. 322.

13. See *The Asian Crisis and Human Security* (Tokyo: Japan Centre for International Exchange, 1999), pp. 56–57, and *The Quest for Human Security*, edited by Pranee Thiparat (Bangkok: Institute of Strategic and International Studies, 2001).

14. See "Ten days that shook Indonesia", from Indahnesiah.com at < http://www.indahnesia.com/DB/Story/Item.php >, accessed 10 February 2004.

15. As recession began to bite in Thailand and Malaysia, both countries began deporting hundreds of foreign workers, most of them illegal, back to Myanmar and Indonesia respectively. Some quarters in Indonesia had expressed disquiet over the timing of the repatriation of these workers given the volatile labour situation in the country. See, for example, Caballero-Anthony, "Challenges to Southeast Asian Security Cooperation", and Rizal Sukma, "Security Implications of the Economic Crisis in Southeast Asia", in *An Asia-Pacific Security Crisis? New Challenges to Regional Stability*, edited by Guy Wilson-Roberts (Wellington: Centre for Strategic Studies), pp. 39–65.

16. See "Has ASEAN Lost its Voice on Asian Security Issues", *Japan Times*, 1 August 1999; Michael Wesley, "The Asian Crisis and the Adequacy of Regional Institutions", *Contemporary Southeast Asia* 21, no. 1 (1999): 54–73.

17. There have been numerous accounts on ASEAN's concerted response to the currency crisis. See, for example, Hadi Soesastro, "ASEAN during the Crisis",

*ASEAN Economic Bulletin* 15, no. 3 (1998) and John Funston, "ASEAN: Out of its Depths", *Contemporary Southeast Asia* 20, no. 3 (1998).

18. This idea was later on expanded within the ASEAN Plus Three (APT) framework in the establishment of the APT early warning systems. See *Asian Economic Monitor*, July 2002, p. 24.

19. See ibid.

20. See Funston, "ASEAN: Out of Its Depth", p. 34.

21. Quoted in Rodolfo C. Severino, *ASEAN Today and Tomorrow* (Jakarta: ASEAN Secretariat, 2002), p. 95.

22. For a detailed account of ASEAN's initiatives in getting Cambodia to agree to its terms to restore political stability in the country, see Juanito Jarasa, "The ASEAN Troika on Cambodia: A Philippine Perspective", in *The Next Stage: Preventive Diplomacy and Security Cooperation in the Asia-Pacific*, edited by Desmond Ball and Amitav Acharya (Canberra: Strategic and Defence Studies Centre, Australian National University, 1999), pp. 209–14.

23. See "The ASEAN Troika", < http://www.aseansec.org/11841.htm >.

24. Simon Tay, "The Environment and Security in Southeast Asia", in *Beyond the Crisis: Challenges and Opportunities*, edited by Mely C. Anthony and Mohamed Jawhar Hassan (Malaysia: Institute of Strategic and International Studies, 2001), p. 154.

25. During the haze crisis, fire-fighters from Malaysia and Singapore came together to help battle the forest fires in Indonesia's Sumatra and Kalimantan provinces.

26. Ibid.

27. See, for example, Jeannie Henderson, *Reassessing ASEAN*, Adelphi Paper 323 (London: International Institute for Strategic Studies, 1997).

28. "Thailand to Pursue 'Constructive Intervention Policy' ", *New Straits Times*, 8 June 1998.

29. The Malaysian Government had, however, said that this initiative was only from Anwar Ibrahim and did not reflect the position of the government. Although not explicitly denied by the government in the local newspaper, officials from the Foreign Ministry quite willingly clarified the government's position. This was also revealed to the author by a Malaysian diplomat in one of track two meetings held where the author was a participant.

30. The author had argued this point in her earlier paper. See Mely C. Anthony, "ASEAN: How to Engage or Cooperate". Paper delivered at the ASEAN-ISIS Conference on ASEAN 2020: Vision, Crises and Change, Singapore, 21–22 July 1999. See also Funston, "ASEAN: Out of Its Depth".

31. See Thailand's "Non-Paper on the Flexible Engagement Approach", Press Release 743/2541, Thai Ministry of Foreign Affairs, 27 July 1998, at < http://www.thaiembdc.org >.

32. "ASEAN Ministers Converge in Manila for Yearly Meeting", *Asian Wall Street Journal*, 27 July 1998.

33. Amitav Acharya, "Sovereignty, Non-Intervention and Regionalism", paper presented for the International Conference on "Constructive Engagement in Asia: Political and Economic Dimensions", Bangkok, 20–23 August 1997. See also Funston, "ASEAN: Out of its Depth", and Anthony, "ASEAN: How to Engage and Cooperate".

34. "ASEAN Joint Statement on the Situation in the Philippines", Jakarta, 23 February 1986, accessed from < http://www.aseansec.org/2477.htm >.

35. See "Kuan Yew's Book Draws Flak from Malaysia", New Straits Times, 15 September 1998.

36. See, for example, "Government to Pursue CLOB Issues with KL: BG Lee", Business Times, 26 May 1999; "Singapore Exploits Neighbours' Weaknesses, says PM", New Straits Times, 15 September 1998.

37. New Straits Times, 15 October 1998.

38. Goh Chok Tong's speech to the Asian Society, Sydney, 2 March 1999.

39. "Malaysia and Singapore Agree to Set Aside Differences", New Straits Times, 6 November 1998.

40. For more detailed discussion on the East Timor crisis, see Ian Martin, Self-Determination in East Timor, International Peace Academy Occasional Paper Series (Boulder, CO: Lynne Rienner Publishers, Inc., 2001). See also Leonard S. Sebastian and Anthony L. Smith, "The East Timor Crisis: A Test Case for Humanitarian Intervention", Southeast Asian Affairs 2000 (Singapore: Institute of Southeast Asian Studies, 2000).

41. Martin, Self Determination in East Timor.

42. See "Sovereignty, Intervention and the ASEAN Way", Address by Secretary General Rodolfo Severino at the ASEAN Scholars' Roundtable, Singapore, 3 July 2000.

43. Carolina G. Hernandez, "The East Timor Crisis: Regional Mechanisms on Trial and Implications for Regional Political and Security Cooperation". Paper delivered at ARF Professional Development Programme, Bandar Seri Begawan, 23–28 April 2000.

44. See "Joint Communique of the Special ASEAN Ministerial Meeting on Terrorism", Kuala Lumpur, 20–21 May 2002. See also "2001 ASEAN Declaration on Joint Action to Counter Terrorism", Bandar Seri Begawan, 5 November 2001.

45. Barry Desker, Islam and Society in Southeast Asia After September 11, IDSS Working Paper No. 3 (Singapore: Institute of Defence and Strategic Studies, 2002).

46. Tatik S. Hafidz, The War on Terror and the Future of Indonesian Democracy, IDSS Working Paper No. 46 (Singapore: Institute of Defence and Strategic Studies, 2002).

47. The World Health Organization Update on SARS, at < http://www.who.int.com >, accessed on 5 July 2003.

48. "The Cost of SARS: US$11 Billion and Rising", *Far Eastern Economic Review*, 24 April 2003.
49. Sourced from GIC Daily Bulletin, 26 May 2003, p. 4.
50. Nizam Idris, "The Impact of SARS on Singapore's Economy", IDEAglobal Ltd.
51. *GIC Daily Bulletin*, 26 May 2003, p. 4.
52. "The Cost of SARS", *FEER*.
53. Ibid.
54. "Joint Statement of the Special ASEAN+3 Health Ministers Meeting on Severe Acute Respiratory Syndrome (SARS)", Siem Reap, Cambodia, 10–11 June 2003, accessed from < http://www.aseansec.org/14824.htm >.
55. Ibid.
56. See Shaun Narine, *Explaining ASEAN: Regionalism in Southeast Asia* (Boulder, CO: Lynne Rienner, 2002), pp. 193–209.
57. Michael Leifer, "Regionalism Compared: The Perils and Benefits of Expansion", in *The Asia Pacific in the New Millennium*, edited by Mely C. Anthony and Jawhar Hassan (Kuala Lumpur: Institute of Strategic and International Studies, 2001), p. 504.
58. For more discussion on reinventing ASEAN, see *Reinventing ASEAN*, edited by Simon Tay, Jesus P. Estanislao and Hadi Soesastro (Singapore: Institute of Southeast Asian Studies, 2003).

# 7

## : ASEAN AND CIVIL SOCIETY
## : Enhancing Regional Mechanisms
## : for Managing Security

> The shaping of a future of peace, friendship and co-operation is far too important to be left to governments and government officials. The need is for ever-expanding involvement and participation of the people.... As someone who has shared in the privilege of giving life to ASEAN, I may be permitted to observe that while ASEAN has indeed made impressive progress in many fields of co-operative endeavour, much more needs to be done, especially in the non-governmental sphere.
>
> — *Adam Malik, circa 1980*
> *(Former Foreign Minister of Indonesia)*[1]

### INTRODUCTION

As noted in the previous chapter, the economic crisis of 1997 became a watershed for ASEAN, particularly in the way it had to respond to regional problems brought on by the crisis. There is however a paradox to the crisis. While the attendant challenges stemming from the crisis should have resulted in a less cohesive association, as members were expected to turn inward to attend to domestic problems, the crisis however became a rallying point for ASEAN to become more responsive and bolder in instituting mechanisms to handle regional problems. We noted that it was in December 1997, just a few months after the onset of the financial crisis, when ASEAN leaders unveiled the ASEAN Vision 2020 at the ASEAN Second Informal Summit in Kuala Lumpur. The ASEAN Vision 2020 articulated the leaders' vision of an "ASEAN as a concert of Southeast Asian nations, outward looking, living in peace, stability and prosperity, bonded together in partnership in dynamic development and in a community of caring societies".[2]

A closer look at the preamble of the ASEAN Vision 2020 would reveal that the Vision had essentially set out the three-part agenda of

ASEAN in the new millennium. These were: political and security co-operation, economic co-operation, and building a community of caring society. This agenda was reaffirmed and rearticulated at the Ninth ASEAN Summit in October 2003 when the ASEAN leaders adopted the ASEAN Concord II (also referred to as Bali Concord II) that declared the establishment of an ASEAN Community comprising three pillars, which are essentially the same as three areas of co-operation identified in the Vision 2020. Thus, the Vision 2020 and the Bali Concord II are indicative of a qualitative response from ASEAN to address new security dynamics found within its respective members and in the region. As highlighted in Chapter 6, these qualitative responses are translated into new and bolder mechanisms to address problems regionally. To recapitulate, these mechanisms included: the decision to pursue with AFTA and bring forward the agreement on tariff reductions under the FTA scheme from 2003 to 2002, as well as putting in place the dispute settlement mechanisms under the Protocol on Dispute Settlement; the adoption of the regional haze action plan and the transboundary pollution agreement; and the institution of the ASEAN surveillance mechanism and the ASEAN Troika. All these developments point to the trend towards more institutionalized mechanisms within ASEAN, albeit *ad hoc* in the way these were adopted. This has led one observer to describe this trend of evolving mechanisms as "patchwork" institutionalization.[3]

In spite of this perceptible trend towards institutionalization in ASEAN, the nature of new security challenges had only served to increase expectations on getting ASEAN to be even more proactive. Given the rising uncertainties in the regional and global environment manifested in a growing list of security problems, the perceived inadequacies of regional institutions — particularly ASEAN — became more pronounced than ever. In this regard, it is interesting to recall that one of the buzzwords that resonated during these crises periods was "getting fundamentals right". Certainly not confined only to economic matters, fundamentals in this context referred to the challenge for states to get their security fundamental rights. Indeed, given the historical context within which ASEAN was formed, it became increasingly clear that the regional ideology of "national/regional resilience", which had defined the region's security approaches was proving to be inadequate, despite the fact that the region's conceptualization of security was already deemed to be quite comprehensive.

In July 1998, ASEAN-ISIS — the track two network mentioned in Chapter 5 — submitted the "Report of the Eighth Southeast Asian

Forum" to the ASEAN Senior Officials Meeting (SOM).[4] The Report
reflected the summary of discussions and recommendations on regional
challenges deliberated at the said Forum (which was also organized by
ASEAN-ISIS and which brought together a motley group of scholars,
policy-makers, and representatives of civil society in the region). One
key recommendation highlighted in the Report was the critical need for
more decisive policies to address the emerging socio-economic problems
brought on by the effects of globalization and the economic crisis.
Among the issues identified that had both domestic and regional
repercussions were the problems of illegal migration, HIV/AIDS pandemic,
illegal trafficking of women and children, and environmental degradation.
The Report clearly noted that ASEAN had not been structurally equipped
to respond to these new security issues. This was in sharp contrast to the
growing activism of non-governmental organizations (NGOs) and civil
society organizations in the region that were working with different
sectors in the regional community in addressing many of their political,
socio-economic, and security problems. Since the nature of ASEAN's
interaction in fostering regional co-operation had been limited to a
rather exclusive club of ASEAN bureaucrats and elites in the region, the
Report henceforth urged ASEAN to address the crucial issue of opening
up its mechanisms to include the participation of civil society. This
specific recommendation, therefore, raised an important challenge for
ASEAN to democratize its core function of setting the regional agenda
and to engage with the civil society organizations in the region.

   The main objective of this chapter is to analyse ASEAN's response to
that challenge by examining the genesis and progress of the ASEAN
People's Assembly (APA) — a track three organization under the auspices
of ASEAN-ISIS. More importantly, this chapter examines the implications
of this new configuration of tracks two and three processes on the
evolving regional mechanisms for managing security. A major question
that will be addressed here is the extent to which APA's engagement of
ASEAN and vice versa can be another example of the emerging trends
that point us beyond the ASEAN way in managing regional security. This
chapter will be divided into three sections. Section I will provide a brief
overview of the nature of civil society organizations (CSOs) in Southeast
Asia and locate the role these CSOs play in our overall study of regional
mechanisms for managing conflict. The second section will trace the
genesis of APA and track its work in relation to the mechanisms that are
evolving in the region. Finally, Section III concludes with some
observations on the prospects of APA becoming a "new" mechanism in

ASEAN and how this portends to emerging transformations of regional mechanisms beyond the ASEAN way.

## I. CIVIL SOCIETY ORGANIZATIONS IN SOUTHEAST ASIA

There has been a rapid proliferation of CSOs in Southeast Asia. This trend was particularly notable in the late 1980s and early 1990s when the region was in the throes of rapid structural and societal transformations. For the purpose of this chapter, I shall adopt a very broad definition of civil society to refer to NGOs,[5] advocacy groups, and a variety of social movements that have in one way or another expressed their views on various issues such as rights of ethnic groups, the environment, and economic displacement. This broad definition, however, include the specific characteristic of CSOs being non-profit and voluntary and would have also been "transformative and innovative" with emphasis on their alternative views to development, governance, and security. Against these parameters, business groups, which are organized for the sole purpose of profit, and political parties would not be included.

To get a picture of the development of CSOs in Southeast Asia, the following statistics of a recent study on NGOs/CSOs in the region are instructive. There are 19,878 registered NGOs in Thailand, 14,000 in Malaysia, and 70,200 in the Philippines. The number in Indonesia showed a massive increase from 10,000 in 1996 to 70,000 in 2000, while in Singapore CSOs represented by registered charities and social organizations is placed at 4,562.[6] Another study which included socialist states like China, and Vietnam reported that there are more than 200,000 registered NGOs in China and about 600 at the provincial level and several thousands at district and community level in Vietnam.[7] While mindful of the fact that there are dependent variables that influence the disparities in number of CSOs in certain countries, such as its proportion to the country's population and the nature of and changes in political systems that either stymie or encourage the formation of CSOs, the trend towards increasing prominence and activism of CSOs is "here to stay".

Most of these CSOs share common concerns essentially rooted in helping and assisting local communities, alleviating the miserable living conditions of the poor, the underprivileged, and looking into the plight of abused women and children, among others. CSOs also share in the common objectives of empowering these groups to fight for social justice, human rights, improved environmental conditions, and a better quality of life. More often, CSOs reflect the wide array of challenges faced by individuals and communities in areas related to poverty, economic, and social injustice, women's and children's rights, minority rights, and the environment and its resources, both on land and water, that neither the government nor the market could adequately address. In less democratic societies, civil societies essentially come in two different forms; those that concentrate in activities geared towards community development to promote the idea of people-centred development; and those that focus on organizing specifically defined constituencies to generate social movements.[8]

While it is beyond the scope of this study to provide a comprehensive picture of the various types of civil societies found in Southeast Asia, a few NGOs are described below to characterize the different features of CSOs found in the region. Some are locally (national) based while the others are organized regionally.

In Thailand, the Assembly of the Poor is one of the more active and significant CSOs that have been fighting for the interests of poor farmers in the country. This is in spite of the fact that it is a loosely structured CSO and lacks legal status. One of its recent achievements was to force the Thai Government to negotiate with Thai farmers who were displaced due to land appropriation project for building of dams and industrial estates. It did this by mobilizing thousands of poor farmers countrywide to participate in a "sit-in" protest in front of the Government House to demand for fair compensation. The Assembly of the Poor is an example of CSOs in the region that are fighting for distributive justice and good governance.[9]

There are also the pro-democracy groups — PollWatch and the Confederation for Democracy — that played a significant part in the democratization and political reform of Thailand since 1992. PollWatch was created in March 1992 to serve as an election monitoring mechanism. The activities of PollWatch raised the level of public concern over the proliferation of vote buying and money politics in election campaigns, which contributed to popular demand for political reforms. Similarly, the Confederation for Democracy was a loosely organized group that fought against military rule in 1991 and 1992. It became the key organizer of the urban middle-class uprising in May 1992 which eventually brought an end to military rule in Thailand.[10]

The work and experience of PollWatch and the Confederation for Democracy has its own equivalent in the Philippines. The National Citizens' Movement for Free Election (NAMFREL) along with several CSOs in the Philippines had been noted for their contribution in the process of democratization in the country during the Martial Law period under the Marcos regime. NAMFREL was founded in 1983 by concerned individuals and activists to restore faith in the country's electoral process that was reintroduced after its suspension in 1972. NAMFREL mobilized more than half a million volunteers in poll-watching activities during the 1986 elections. It became a powerful symbol of the power of civil society force when thousands of its volunteers staged a dramatic walk-out — captured live on Philippine television — when the counting of votes were reportedly rigged. This was one of the events that precipitated the People Power Movement in 1986 that brought down the Marcos dictatorship regime.

Many of the CSOs in the Philippines have also established coalitions and networks within the country to strengthen their work and improve their engagement strategies with the government. Some of these include the Caucus of Development NGO Network (CODE-NGO), the Philippine Partnership for the Development of Human Resources in Rural Areas (PhilDHARRA), and the NGO Co-ordinating Committee for Rural Development (NGO-CORD). The consolidation of NGOs in the country is part of the growing trend to improve their strategies for more recognition and access to state authorities in their advocacy work. The consolidation is done in an *ad hoc*, issue-defined manner.[11] The other examples of national coalitions in other countries include the NGO-CORD in Thailand, the Environmental Protection Society of Malaysia, and the Wahana Lingkungan Hidup (WALHI), a network of concerned environmental NGOs in Indonesia.[12]

Southeast Asia is also home to many regional CSOs. These regional NGOs share many of the characteristics of the national NGOs and are also mostly issue-based. The prominent NGOs in this region are usually those that are identified in their work towards democratization, promotion of human rights, and advocacy against globalization. The Asian Forum for Human Rights and Development (FORUM-ASIA) based in Bangkok, has been at the forefront in the campaign against human rights abuses in the region. There is also the Asian Cultural Forum for Development (ACFOD), also based in Bangkok, that works on human rights and social issues.

Among the high-profile NGOs that have been continually campaigning against the negative impact of globalization include Focus on the Global South which is based in Chulalongkorn University in Thailand and has been prominent in its research and publication, networking, and advocacy work. There is also the Asian Regional Exchange for New Alternatives

(ARENA), a network of Asian scholar-activists that aims to foster exchange among scholars and formulate alternative development perspectives to counter corporate-led globalization. Similar NGOs also include The Third World Network, which was first established in Penang, Malaysia and has now become an international NGO with offices globally.[13]

Labour-based regional NGOs include the Asian Migrant Center (AMC), which focuses particularly on the plight of migrant workers, and the Asia Monitor Resource Center (AMRC), which initially started as a monitoring group for transnational corporations (TNCs). The ISIS International, with headquarters in Manila, deals with gender and women's issues, as well as the Committee for Asian Women (CAW), which regularly undertakes studies and conducts seminars on gender issues.[14]

The current developments and activism of CSOs in Southeast Asia are, therefore, significant, given the fact that in the early 1980s many states in the region were characterized as semi-authoritarian states that stifled the development of CSOs. This was the period when the notions of state power and legitimacy were very much predicated on a country's rapid economic growth and development — a legitimation criteria otherwise known as "performance legitimacy". Hence, the rapid regional economic growth and development largely made up for the absence of effervescent CSOs in many states in the region. There were of course exceptions like in the case of the Philippines that went through a difficult transition from martial law to democracy, aggravated by poor economic growth.

Thus, it was only during the 1997–98 economic crisis that the number of CSOs rose dramatically and their visibility increased. While there were already national and regional CSOs that had rallied against the social consequences of the neo-liberal model of economic development, it was with the onset of the 1997–98 regional economic crisis that their views and influence became more popular and widely disseminated.[15] With "performance legitimacy" losing its credence in some states in the region and the dissatisfaction with prevailing neo-liberal policies, many CSOs in Southeast Asia joined the "Battle of Seattle" demonstration in 1999 which provided them a platform to voice their protests against the policies of the WTO, World Bank, IMF, and even the Asian Development Bank (ADB).

Moreover, as CSOs began to form coalitions and networks nationally, regionally and globally, their strategies of engagement also became more sophisticated aided by the advances in information and communications technology. While the latter made many prominent NGOs media-savvy, the influence gained by their building of coalitions and networks across national boundaries has led to the trend of "transnationalization" of CSOs which became a significant factor in their growing activism. As noted by Wilkin,

> The emergence of transnational network of civil society groups has brought together a wider range of NGO work in the fields of peace, security and development across national boundaries against both the interests and exploitation of the global forces of production and finance. These transnational NGO networks begin to ensure meaningful participation of civil society association in international decision-making. In addition to advancing resistance to the current orthodoxy of neo-liberalism, these emerging transnational networks of voluntary organizations are actively involved in creating alternative routes for development.[16]

While once excluded in the exclusive domain of state actors, the emerging transnationalization of CSOs has not only increased their visibility but has also made them significant actors that have entered the arena of decision-making. Because of their increasing numbers and their spread and reach across the globe, CSOs have now been described as powerful countervailing forces against states and markets as they contest for political space and voice.

Nonetheless, despite the increased visibility of CSOs in many parts of the world, questions still remain with regard to their actual influence in policy-making and governance. In Southeast Asia, the achievements of CSOs beyond the processes of engagement with state actors to policy inputs are anecdotal at best and marginal at worst. Since the time when CSOs have made their presence felt in this region, many of the challenges CSOs face in engaging the centres of power — not least having to cope with hostile and strictly regulated environment — still exist. A constant dilemma for CSOs, therefore, has to do with finding appropriate mechanisms to remain actively engaged in the arena of contestation among power centres (state and market) while continuing with the enterprise of coalition building and networking.

Hence, as we track models of constructive engagement — i.e. *modus vivendi* between CSOs and state/market — that are aimed at improving governance and attaining security, the emergence of the ASEAN Peoples' Assembly (APA) provides us with an interesting case. This will be discussed in the next section of this chapter.

## II. THE ASEAN PEOPLE'S ASSEMBLY: CRAFTING ANOTHER MECHANISM FOR REGIONAL GOVERNANCE AND SECURITY

### The Genesis of APA

The idea of ASEAN engaging with civil society is not new. The quoted excerpt cited at the beginning of this chapter from a 1980 speech of Adam Malik, former Indonesian Foreign Minister and one of ASEAN's founding fathers, indicates that as far back as in the 1980s, ASEAN officials already thought it apropos to engage with the peoples in this region. But while this idea was floated around for many years, how this was going to be realized and how this mechanism was going to take shape became a regular subject of discussion in the track one and track two meetings in the region in the years that followed.

With the growing involvement of track two in the ASEAN process, this agenda received an extra push since there were many in the regional track two circles who felt that while track two meetings and interactions with the ASEAN governments have increased and intensified, very rarely have they (track two) had the opportunity to interact with the NGOs. The opportunity was even more rare with track one (official) actors. More importantly, there was growing recognition that the NGOs have been excluded in the agenda setting and decision-making in ASEAN.

Furthermore, there had always been impression that NGOs had been excluded in the regional decision-making processes. Even before the onset of the Asian financial crisis, ASEAN had always been regarded as a "club of élites", disconnected from the people in the region. A good indication of this state of affairs was the very fact that while ASEAN was well its into its thirtieth year when it had its commemorative celebrations in July 1997 and had expanded its membership to all ten Southeast Asian states, it remained an unknown entity for most of the peoples of the region.[17] For that matter too, beyond the discourses at the official level, track two, and the academe, discussions about ASEAN did not feature in many of the meetings of NGOs in the region.

Against this background, the ASEAN-ISIS took it upon itself, as one of its missions, to continuously push for the idea of a people's assembly in its interactions with track one officials in ASEAN and in the various track two fora, particularly at its annual Asia Pacific Roundtable meetings in Kuala Lumpur. The opportunity finally presented itself at the ASEAN Ministerial Meeting in Brunei in 1995 when the Foreign Minister of Thailand, called for the establishment of a "congress of ASEAN peoples". The Thai Foreign Ministry through ISIS Thailand assigned ASEAN-ISIS to conceptualize the modalities and procedures for such an assembly. To the ASEAN officials, the original idea of a people's group was for it to be a kind of a regional inter-parliamentary union.

However, the ASEAN-ISIS came up with a different version and shaped its own concept paper of "an assembly of the peoples of ASEAN". According to the principal author of the concept paper, given the fact that NGOs in the region had already organized activities parallel to and often opposed to those held by governments, it was critical to come up with a regional mechanism that could develop common responses to common challenges.[18] The ASEAN-ISIS concept paper had argued that setting up a group similar to an inter-parliamentary union would not be appropriate since its own idea of a multi-sectoral representation of a people's assembly would include: "national and local government officials in their private capacity; academe; business; culture and the arts; relevant rural-based groups; village leaders and community leaders; media; labour; sectors concerned with women and children; other professionals; undergraduate and graduate students; religious organizations; and other sectors as are relevant to individual ASEAN member states." Moreover, it was envisaged that the assembly was to be expanded on a step-by-step basis to eventually include "all sectors of ASEAN societies".[19]

The ASEAN-ISIS concept paper outlined the objectives of APA to include: (a) promoting greater awareness of an ASEAN community; (b) promoting mutual understanding and tolerance for the diversity of culture, religion, ethnicity, social values, political cultures and processes, and other elements of ASEAN diversity; (c) obtaining insights and inputs on how to deal with socio-economic problems affecting ASEAN societies; (d) facilitating the bridging of gaps between ASEAN societies through confidence-building measures; and (e) assisting in the building of an ASEAN community of caring societies as sought by the ASEAN Vision 2020.[20]

For the ASEAN-ISIS, the APA was to be this regional mechanism, which was "meant to create a regular people's gathering where they would meet on a regular basis, discuss issues they consider timely, important and relevant; seek solutions for them and make recommendations to government on these matters". The ASEAN-ISIS would serve as the "convenor of APA, its fund-raiser, its facilitator, its spokesperson, its driving force in the initial years, until it takes a life of its own".[21]

The ASEAN-ISIS envisaged that this track two and track three collaborative process would benefit ASEAN Heads of State/Government since APA "is meant to be more sensitive to the practical realities of ASEAN and is intended to be held very year to coincide with the regular and informal summits of ASEAN". The timing of the holding of APA is therefore crucial to enable APA "to provide inputs to ASEAN leaders on issues that are of concern to the people of the region and how they think these can be addressed."[22]

## The Launching of APA

The ambitious APA project took about four years to be realized and during this period, it encountered several setbacks which almost jeopardized the launching of the project. Firstly, was the problem of funding. Although ASEAN officials endorsed in principle the idea of an APA, the ASEAN Foundation that was the donor agency that was approached by ASEAN-ISIS for funding support, turned down its application twice (1999–2000). Usually it was the ASEAN Senior Officials that decided on funding grants for the ASEAN Foundation based on the practice of consensus. Hence, the fact that the application was denied twice was indicative of the reservations that some ASEAN governments had about the launching of APA. The attitude of certain governments in ASEAN, therefore, became its second and most difficult obstacle. Ironically, the ASEAN Foundation was set up to promote the ASEAN 2020 project that had as its critical component "building a community of caring societies".[23] Moreover, when ASEAN Foundation held its round of consultations about the priority projects, there was apparently a consensus that the APA project would be one of these.[24] It was, therefore, interesting that the implementation of this "consensus" turned out to be problematic.

Thirdly, the failure of ASEAN-ISIS to get funding from the ASEAN Foundation also revealed the lack of success and influence that some members of this track two network had with their own governments in pushing for this idea. This setback however did not deter some members within the ASEAN-ISIS network to press ahead and seek for alternative funding. Encouraged by the fact that APA project had the support of the ASEAN Secretary-General and Japanese Foreign Ministry, ASEAN-ISIS began to look for partners outside the region.[25] By mobilizing its own networks, some key players within the ASEAN-ISIS lobbied hard and sought funding from outside sources. Among those that were supportive of the project include: the Canadian International Development Agency (CIDA)-funded Southeast Asia Co-operation Project, Japan Official Development Assistance, the Open Society, Batam Industrial Authority, and the Asia Foundation. Eventually, ASEAN-ISIS successfully persuaded these agencies in spite of the lack of official blessing of ASEAN governments.[26] Their success indicated that these donor agencies saw the potential of APA as a people-empowering mechanism.

Finally, without much fanfare, the first APA was held in Batam, Indonesia on 24–25 November 2000. The choice of the date and the place to hold APA was indeed symbolic. The launching of APA was set to coincide with the Fourth ASEAN Summit Meeting which was held in neighbouring Singapore on 22–25 November 2000. Batam is less than an hour ferry-ride from Singapore and while it would have been more convenient to hold the meeting in Singapore, it was learnt that it was not possible to hold the first regional people's assembly there due to political reasons.[27]

In spite of its initial setbacks, the APA 2000 managed to bring together about 300 representatives of NGOs, grassroots leaders and activists, think-tanks, and businesses. ASEAN-ISIS also managed to persuade some of the prominent regional NGOs like Forum Asia and Focus on the Global South to attend its inaugural meeting, as well as a few government officials who came in their private capacity.[28] These were then Indonesian President Abdurrahman Wahid, Ali Alatas, former Indonesian Foreign Minister, and Jose Almonte, former National Security Adviser of the Philippines. The serving ASEAN-Secretary General Rodolfo Severino also attended.

The issues that were tabled for discussions at the first APA covered a wide range of social, political, and economic challenges that were of critical relevance to ASEAN. These included:

- the impact of globalization;
- efforts to address poverty;
- the limits and opportunities of environmental management;
- events in Myanmar and East Timor;
- the possibility of a regional human rights mechanism; and
- the power of women and their empowerment.

In addressing these plethora of issues, the role of the people in setting ASEAN's agenda was highlighted as a compelling reason for ASEAN — the organization — to engage with civil society, the media, and all sectors that had a stake in building a regional community in Southeast Asia.

The launching of the first APA was an exhilarating experience for the members of ASEAN-ISIS who had worked hard to realize their project. Of great interest too was the dynamics that emerged when a diverse set of CSOs in Southeast Asia were brought together for the first time. This dynamic was best depicted in a piece written by a Malaysian participant of APA 2000, who described the Assembly as:

> ... packed with 70 speakers into an intense couple of 14-hour days ... audiences nonetheless attentive; floor speakers often outshone panelists ... it was at times an incoherent babble of voices... The fact of it having been successfully convened at all was, for the moment, enough encouragement for the "people-to-people" connection now seen as a critical element of ASEAN's interrelationships.[29]

Inspired by its first success, ASEAN-ISIS decided to convene the second APA two years later on 30 August–1 September 2002 in Bali, Indonesia. Following its first theme of "An ASEAN of the People, By the People and For the People", APA-II adopted "We the ASEAN Peoples and Our Challenges" as its second theme. The momentum gained in organizing both APA I and II led to the convening of the third APA in Manila on 25–27 September 2003. In response to the newly launched Bali Concord II, APA III took up as its theme the third pillar of the ASEAN Community, which was "Towards an ASEAN Community of Caring Societies".

## III. APA'S PROSPECTS AS A REGIONAL MECHANISM FOR GOVERNANCE AND SECURITY

In tracking the progress of APA and the developments of this track three diplomacy, it is important at this juncture to examine the implications of this embryonic mechanism on the overall evolution of ASEAN's mechanism in managing security. After all, our ultimate objective is to find out how ASEAN's mechanisms have gone beyond the ASEAN way. But before we address this question, a few observations regarding the birth of APA are noteworthy if only to bring into perspective the context within which this mechanism emerged. I shall highlight some of these below.

Firstly, in examining the dynamics of bringing different actors together, APA is significant in that it showed that it is possible for a track two initiative to get the endorsement of track three actors. Its salience becomes more palpable given the fact that ASEAN-ISIS has also been perceived in certain circles as being too close to the government, an exclusive "elite" club, and "sometimes a gatekeeper for expanded popular participation in ASEAN concerns". As noted by Carolina Hernandez, head of the ASEAN-ISIS counterpart in the Philippines, who herself has been a key player of the APA process:

> APA must have been seen as a window of opportunity to get the people's views heard beyond their usual circles, never mind if through ASEAN ISIS. It must also be a sign of the times — one characterised by an increasing willingness by actors in the second and third tracks to engage including the unlike-minded for the achievement of the goals they cannot obtain in isolation from or in hostile opposition to each other. It can also be a sign of the level of trust earned by these actors within each track for those in the other track. Or it might have been a case of simply giving the APA initiative a chance.[30]

Secondly, the very fact that an Assembly took place with the participation of a wide range of NGOs and other CSOs had been a remarkable feat. But even more remarkable has been the fact that in spite of the "babble of incoherent voices and the cacophony", a multi-sectoral regional mechanism can be seen to be emerging, comprising different actors who are finding their relevant niches in and contribution to regional security. The different ideas that they bring with them in so far as how they conceptualize regional security further leads to the creation of yet again additional ideational linkages that are geared towards enriching the discourses that are found in the region.

Thirdly, the dynamics between these two tracks (two and three) reflect their appreciation of the fact that while there are many different and specialized CSO networks in the region, there is still the need for horizontal dialogue among networks, across different sectors in society. Equally important is the cognisance of the need to get these CSOs involved in the work of ASEAN in order to make ASEAN more known and more accountable to its people — hence, highlighting the importance of a vertical dialogue among state and non-state actors.

With the foregoing observations, we can now tease out the linkages between the developments we see in APA with the developments of ASEAN's mechanisms in managing security. Against the background of APA, we can draw the following observations.

First, is the fact that the launching of APA was by no means accidental. As described in the discussions thus far, there had been a sustained effort by many actors at all three levels to realize this vision of an ASEAN for the people and with the people. If ASEAN, according to its founding fathers, were indeed to be the means to building a community in Southeast Asia, sharing a shared destiny and sense of identity, it was therefore inevitable for ASEAN — the organization — to have to engage with the peoples in the region. Community-building, however, requires sustained effort of cultivating trust and confidence among the people of divergent backgrounds in the region, and more importantly, between the people and ASEAN. As mentioned earlier, the processes towards community-building in the region had been confined to the political élites in ASEAN.

Second, promoting awareness among relevant actors and sectors in ASEAN within and outside the government contributes to the acceptability of the idea that the people must participate in ASEAN's agenda setting. It is in this area where one must pay close attention to and APA's work provides interesting insights on the dynamics of bringing in state and non-state actors together. Since its inception, APA has set in place an ambitious APA Action Plan that highlights the human security issues of the people in this region. The Action Plan identifies seven areas that deserve greater attention, more in-depth examination and follow-up action by civil society groups.[31] These are:

1. developing a human rights scorecard;
2. identifying threats to democracy by developing "democracy promoting indicators and/or democracy eroding indicators" — co-ordinated by CSIS Indonesia;
3. developing a framework to evaluate the progress of gender mainstreaming;
4. developing a Code of Ethics for (governance in) NGOs;
5. promoting co-operation in tackling HIV/AIDS;
6. promoting co-operation among media groups; and
7. developing the Southeast Asian Human Development Report.

Of the seven areas identified, APA's works on human rights, democracy, and human development have significant bearing on ASEAN, particularly its mechanisms. As far as human rights and democracy are concerned, it is interesting to note that APA in conjunction with other CSOs in the region has been drawing up a human rights and democracy scorecard. The main objectives of developing the scorecards are to find indicators to assess the state of democracy and human rights in Southeast Asia, while bearing in mind the peculiarities that each country would have; as well as to use these scorecards for advocacy on issues pertaining to democracy and human rights. On the other hand, with regard to APA's work on human development, it is also currently working on producing a regional Human Development Report (SEA-HDR). The implications of these APA projects on ASEAN's mechanism are discussed separately below.

## An ASEAN Human Rights Scorecard

The idea of an ASEAN human rights scorecard has been percolating in the region for some time, particularly within the track two circles. But even prior to this, one notes that a regional, albeit informal, Working Group on Human Rights was established soon after the twenty-sixth ASEAN Ministerial Meeting in Singapore in 1993, when the foreign ministers agreed that ASEAN should also consider the establishment of an appropriate regional mechanism on human rights.[32] The primary objective of the working group, formally known as the Regional Working Group for an ASEAN Human Rights Mechanism (WG on AHRM), is the establishment of an inter-governmental human rights mechanism in Southeast Asia. Over the years, the working group grew to become an informal coalition of individuals and groups within the region who are working with government institutions and NGOs that are involved in the promotion and protection of human rights. The breakthrough for this working group came in 1996 when they were to have regular meetings and consultations with the ASEAN senior officials. This consequently institutionalized consultation between track two and track three. Their engagement in the ASEAN process and their inputs have been reflected in the Joint Communiques of the ASEAN foreign ministers since 1998, leading to the Draft Agreement on the establishment of an ASEAN Human Rights Commission in July 2000. This draft agreement has been the subject of the Annual Workshops for a Regional Mechanisms on Human Rights in ASEAN, held annually since 2001 that brings together government officials, NGOs, academe, and members of national human rights commission in some ASEAN countries (i.e. Indonesia, Malaysia, the Philippines, and Thailand).[33]

The ASEAN-ISIS which also organizes its own Annual Colloquium on Human Rights (AICOHR) since 1993 has lent its support to this working group by joining them in their meetings, seminars, and their annual interface with the ASEAN SOM. Through AICOHR, the informal working group also gets to disseminate information regarding the progress of its work on the establishment of the ASEAN Regional Human Rights Commission.

At the second APA in 2002, ISDS-Philippines, which has been the home to the ASEAN-ISIS AICOHR, broached the idea of developing an

ASEAN human rights scorecard. Specifically, the scorecard was initially developed to document the international human rights instruments to which each of the ASEAN members had acceded to. At the third APA in 2003, the scorecard was further developed to include monitoring national legislations, orders, decrees, rules, and regulations that have been adopted by each of the ASEAN member states which would reflect their commitment to the international human rights instruments which they have ratified. These will cover the wide spectrum of human rights protection to include civil and political rights, social, economic and cultural rights, and the right to development. It is envisioned that data and other relevant information for this scorecard will be collected with the help of CSOs, local academics, donor agencies, and other relevant actors. While still under construction, the scorecard is primarily meant to be a useful tool to determine how far human rights promotion and protection has gone in the region. It could also be used by human rights advocates as a neutral instrument in their work on the promotion of human rights.[34]

The positive response to the idea of a scorecard eventually led to the establishment of an APA Working Group on the ASEAN Human Rights Scorecard. The APA working group brings together representatives from regional CSOs like Forum Asia, members of the ASEAN-ISIS network, as well as members of the informal Regional WG on AHRC. In sum, APA's work on developing an ASEAN Human Rights Scorecard dovetails well with ASEAN-ISIS AICOHR activities as well as that of the Informal Regional WG on AHRC. This development is indicative of the increasing constituency of both human rights advocates in the region that are now actively engaging officials at national and regional levels in the promotion and protection of human rights.

At the very least, the developments on APA's work on human rights, the networks it has linked itself into, plus the ongoing engagement of tracks two and three at the ASEAN level (albeit, indirectly through its linkages with the informal WG on AHRC) has increased pressure on ASEAN to finally establish a regional mechanism on human rights. Moreover, given that the roadmap has already been set as to how an appropriate regional mechanism can be established in ASEAN, it would therefore be very interesting to see if this goal could eventually be attained. Needless to say, these developments and their implications on ASEAN's norm on non-interference can only be taken to mean that at best at the official discourse, ASEAN can be seen moving away from that compelling practice of the ASEAN way. One could argue that the fact that over the past ten years, ASEAN officials have been consistently engaging with the relevant non-state actors on matters pertaining to human rights issues could imply that the norm on non-interference is a nuanced norm in practice and, therefore, the picture of a rigid ASEAN way have to be altered.

## Rethinking Human Development and Regional Security

One of main rationale in getting the people involved in the agenda-setting is to put the people at the heart of development efforts. To APA, human development is not predicated only by per capita income and living standards but embraces a wider range of issues that impinge on the well-being and security of individuals and societies. At the sessions on human development held at both APA II and APA III, what came out as common human development issues among ASEAN countries went beyond poverty to health, protection of women and children, personal security, as well as political and religious freedom. What clearly emerged from these deliberations were the intricate linkages between human development and human security.

Since its second meeting in 2002, APA has embarked on an initiative to produce a regional Human Development Report (SEA-HDR). Given the fact that there is yet to be an HDR for Southeast Asia in comparison to the other six regions in the world that have their own, APA's work in this regard is significant.[35] The SEA-HDR, which is patterned after the global Human Development Report, aims to develop a regional annual report by working on a set of measurable indicators to assess selected goals of the ASEAN's Vision 2020 that speaks to the issues of human development and human security.[36] This initiative has already caught the interest and support of the Philippine Office of the United Nations Development Programme (UNDP)[37] and at the time of writing, a working group within APA has already started to work on this project.

The objectives of this project are twofold: one is to develop a group of CSOs that will be engaged in monitoring the performance of ASEAN's developmental goals, both at the country and regional levels; and the other is to eventually use the SEA-HDR as a major vehicle for influencing official policies in ASEAN through the discussion and dissemination of the report to all concerned.[38] Once again, APA hopes that data generation in the preparation of this work would not only be dependent on official sources but from civil society groups that are willing to provide relevant information on the multi-dimensional components of human development.

To be sure, APA's work on developing the SEA-HDR is more than just bringing in the people's perspective on development. The identification of certain indicators to development that are closely linked to the idea of human security signals the attempts of civil society to be part of the ongoing processes that are geared towards the reconceptualization of security. As discussed in the previous chapters, despite the fact that ASEAN's concept of security is quite comprehensive and goes beyond the traditional notions of state and military security, proponents of human security in ASEAN have argued that there is a need not only to broaden the subjects of security but also its object. Hence, security should respond to the questions: security for whom and whose security? The call for human security therefore focuses attention on the security of individuals and communities, not just the state.

Since the devastating impact of the Asian financial crisis in 1997, track two discourses have started to promote the idea of human security, which shifts the discourse from a state-centric framework of security to focus on the security of individuals and communities. ASEAN-ISIS, as well as CSCAP, has been actively propagating this new security thinking in various fora. In their attempt to bring this concept closer to ASEAN officials, ASEAN-ISIS through ISIS-Thailand organized a regional workshop on human security in Bangkok to coincide with the thirty-third ASEAN Ministerial Meeting in July 2000. Former Thai Foreign Minister Surin Pitsuwan was invited to speak. As with usual practice, the heads of ASEAN-ISIS also met up the ASEAN Foreign Ministers. In his keynote address, Dr Pitsuwan articulated the urgency for both track two groups and officials in ASEAN to come up with a human security agenda for the region. Drawing lessons from the 1997 financial crisis, he argued for ASEAN member states to adopt human-centred development projects and make the ASEAN Vision 2020 that called for the creation of "a community of peaceful, socially cohesive and prosperous Southeast Asia" a reality.[39]

One could therefore argue that the evolving work of APA on human development on one hand and the reconceptualization of security are not mutually exclusive. These two ongoing dynamics are essentially interlinked by the common need to broaden both the subjects and the objects of security. These complementing trajectories reflect a salient point that both development and security — which can be two sides of the same coin — could only be meaningfully attained if it is defined by several actors of society, apart from the state. In this context, the role of civil society, that is, APA, is all the more important since its inclusion in the "ideal" multi-actor/multi-level approach in the attainment of security provides an alternative voice and creates added political space for different sectors of the ASEAN community to be included in the processes of redefining security. These initiatives on the reconceptualizing of security have significant implications on the region's prevailing security practices and the sustained campaign from CSOs could potentially create tension if these trajectories continue to diverge.

## IV. CONCLUSION

The establishment of APA reflects the broad agreement among CSOs in the region on the need to engage with ASEAN. Its work so far is also indicative of the broad strategies that APA has employed to work with the regional centres of power. In its plan of action, one notes that APA's preferred approaches encourage peaceful participation and constructive dialogue with ASEAN officials while shunning extremism and violence. Arguably, these approaches are in keeping with the ASEAN way of peaceful engagement and non-confrontation.

However, as this chapter has discussed, the consequences of providing political space for CSOs in the region and their linkages with track two diplomacy will inevitably impact on the norms and modalities of ASEAN. To be sure, ASEAN has found itself having to engage now with CSO groups. At the APA III held in Manila, ASEAN's Secretary-General had expressed the desire of ASEAN to learn from the APA initiative.[40] Whereas ASEAN's interaction has mostly been confined to the region's political élites, its linkages with track two networks, as discussed in Chapter 5, and now with track three have and would continue to redefine the nature of that interaction that is perceptibly different from the "old" ASEAN way.

APA is for all intents and purposes, a platform for CSOs in the region to come up with common agenda for human development and security. APA can therefore be considered as an embryonic regional mechanism for regional security. At this inchoate stage, any realistic assessment of the prospect of APA therefore would have to be cautious rather than definitive. Indeed, much remains to be seen as to the way the APA process will unfold. Likewise, many other issues will arise with regard to the effectiveness and sustainability of this emerging mechanism. There is also concern that while the APA concept is a novel mechanism for regional governance and security, the voices of the ASEAN peoples may yet fall on deaf ears.

Thus, more questions will be raised about APA and its novel approach to regional security. But one could argue that what is more important at this stage is to be aware that a mechanism has emerged in ASEAN which has brought together different interest groups in this region. More significantly, ASEAN has also been seen now to be engaging with APA. If the capacity to manage security requires, among others, being able to accommodate "pluralities and incoherence", as well as allowing the horizontal and vertical co-ordination of public policies in ways that "are more sensitive to the societal environment than the traditional mode of governing",[41] then APA can yet become that mechanism that could contribute to the human development and human security in Southeast Asia. The analyses of APA therefore offer interesting insights on the myriad initiatives that this region has seen over the years, and it is important to capture this particular development as we continue to track and examine how ASEAN's mechanisms in managing regional security have evolved.

## Notes

1. Excerpt from Adam Malik's acceptance speech upon receiving the Tun Abdul Razak Award for Peace and International Understanding, cited in Ali Alatas, "ASEAN: An Association in Search of People or the People's Search for an Association?", *Report of the First ASEAN People's Assembly* (Jakarta: Centre for Strategic and International Studies, 2001), p. 109.
2. See "ASEAN Vision 2020", available at < http://www/aseansec.org/summit/vision97.htm >.
3. See Simon Tay, "Institutions and Process: Dilemmas and Possibilities", in *Reinventing ASEAN*, edited by Simon Tay, Jesus P. Estanislao and Hadi Soesastro (Singapore: Institute of Southeast Asian Studies, 2001), p. 255.
4. See *Report of the Eighth Southeast Asian Forum* (Kuala Lumpur: Institute of Strategic and International Studies, 1998).
5. It appears that by default, civil society has become always synonymous with NGOs. See, for example, Niraya Gopal, "Civil Society in India", in *Governance and Civil Society in a Global Age*, edited by Tadashi Yamamoto (Japan: Japan Center for International Exchange, 2001), pp. 116–53.
6. See Bob Hadiwinata, *The Politics of NGOS in Indonesia* (London and New York: Routledge Curzon, 2003), p. 1.
7. See Tadashi Yamamoto, "The Future of Civil Society in Asia", in *Beyond the Crisis: Challenges and Opportunities*, edited by Mely C. Anthony and Jawhar Hassan (Kuala Lumpur: Institute of Strategic and International Studies, 2000), p. 43.

8. Hadiwinata, *Politics of NGOs in Indonesia*, p. 25.

9. Suchit Bunbongkarn, "Civil Society in Thailand", in *Governance and Civil Society in the Global Age*, edited by Yamamoto, pp. 66–88. See also Prudhisan Jumbala, "Civil Society and Democratisation in Thailand", in *Beyond the Crisis: Challenges and Opportunities*, edited by Anthony and Jawhar Hassan.

10. Ibid.

11. Malaya Ronas, "Civil Society in the Asia-Pacific: Development, Challenges and Prospects", in *Beyond the Crisis: Challenges and Opportunities*, edited by Anthony and Jawhar Hassan, pp. 49–60.

12. Yamamoto, "The Future of Civil Society in Asia".

13. Teresa S. Tadem and Eduardo C. Tadem, "Anti-Globalisation Movements in Southeast Asia", in *Mondialisation des Resistance*, edited by Samir Amin and Francois Houtart (Paris: L'Harmattan, 2002).

14. Ibid.

15. Ibid.

16. Peter Wilkin, "New Myths for the South: Globalisation and the Conflict between Private Power and Freedom" in *Globalisation and the South*, edited by Wilkin and Thomas (Great Britain: Macmillan Press, Ltd), p. 57, cited in Tadem and Tadem, "Anti-Globalisation Movements".

17. Carolina Hernandez, "A People's Assembly: A Novel Mechanism for Bridging the North-South Divide in ASEAN" (unpublished manuscript).

18. Ibid.

19. Ibid.

20. See *Report of the First ASEAN People's Assembly* (Jakarta: Centre for Strategic and International Studies, 2001).

21. Ibid.

22. Ibid.

23. For the text of the "ASEAN Vision 2020", see the ASEAN Secretariat website at < www.aseansec.org/summit/vision97.htm >.

24. Ibid.

25. The Japanese Foreign Ministry wanted to use half of the Japanese Government's contribution to the ASEAN Foundation Fund for the APA project but could not do so due to bureaucratic procedures. (Author's interview with Carolina Hernandez, President of the Institute of Development and Strategic Studies (ISDS), the Philippine counterpart of ASEAN-ISIS, 3 September 2003).

26. The lack of ASEAN official endorsement did not however stop then Thai Foreign Minister Surin Pitsuwan and the Deputy Foreign Minister Sukhumbhand Paribatra from openly endorsing APA (Author's interview with Carolina Hernandez, see note 25).

27. Ibid.

28. For a full documentation of APA 2000, see *Report of the First ASEAN People's Assembly*.

29. Rehman Rashid, "Agenda Malaysia: The ASEAN People's Assembly", in *Report of the First ASEAN People's Assembly*, pp. 237–40.
30. Hernandez, "A People's Assembly".
31. See *APA 2002 Report: Challenges Facing the ASEAN People* (Jakarta: Centre for Strategic and International Studies, 2003), pp. 5–7.
32. See the Joint Communique of the Twenty-Sixth ASEAN Ministerial Meeting, Singapore, 23–24 July 1993.
33. Wigberto Tanada, "Towards A Regional Human Rights Mechanism in Southeast Asia: A Road Map", Speech delivered at the 11th ASEAN ISIS Colloquium on Human Rights, Manila, 13 February 2004.
34. Carolina G. Hernandez, "Towards An ASEAN Human Rights Scorecard: A Concept Paper and Proposal", March 2003, cited in Herman Kraft, "Assessing Human Rights in Southeast Asia: The need for an instrument", presented at the 11th ASEAN-ISIS Colloquium on Human Rights, 12–13 February 2004 (cited with permission from author).
35. See *APA 2002 Report*, p. 7.
36. See *ASEAN Vision 2020* (Jakarta: ASEAN Secretariat, 1998).
37. Hernandez, "A People's Assembly". ISDS Philippines, along with its partner institutions, is currently developing the modalities of SEA-HDR.
38. Ibid.
39. Surin Pitsuwan, "ASEAN Vision 2020: Strengthening Human Security in the Aftermath of the Economic Crisis", Keynote Address delivered at the ASEAN 2020 Conference on Human Security in the 21st Century, organized by ISIS Thailand and ASEAN-ISIS, 21–22 July 2000.
40. Welcome Speech of Mr Ong Keng Yong, Secretary-General of ASEAN at the Third ASEAN People's Assembly, 24 September 2003, Manila. The speech was read by Deputy Secretary-General of ASEAN, Dr. Wilfrido Villacorta.
41. Ali Kazancigil, "Governance and Science: Market-like Modes of Managing Society and Producing Knowledge", quoted in Niraya Gopal Jayal, "Civil Society in India", p. 127.

# 8

## CONCLUSION
## Beyond the ASEAN Way

This study began with a narrative of how ASEAN has evolved in its management of regional security since its establishment in 1967. In following ASEAN's journey, we went through the different phases of ASEAN's development as a regional organization, starting from its periods of consolidation, expansions and what could be described as its current phase of reconsolidation. In doing so, we examined ASEAN's responses to periods of crises and the various challenges that had emerged. The purpose was to study ASEAN's mechanisms in the way it had managed challenges and threats to regional security. As we tracked these periods, we also explored the changes that have occurred in these mechanisms and went on to identify the relevant actors, beyond the member states of ASEAN, that had been instrumental in the way these mechanisms have evolved further in the nearly four decades that this association has been in existence. Finally, we took note of the more recent regional developments and examined how these could have significant implications on ASEAN's mechanisms.

Having gone through the panoramic and colourful history of ASEAN's journey and having examined its various attempts to respond and remain relevant despite crises and challenges, we now revisit the question stated in the introduction of this book: Is there something beyond the ASEAN way?

This book has argued that the ASEAN way has not been impervious to change. As ASEAN finds its way through periods of crises and continues to confront the many challenges ahead, ASEAN and its mechanisms — which we have defined as the processes, methods, and strategies employed to resolve or manage conflicts — have already been transformed beyond the narrow confines of the modalities associated with the ASEAN way. As we track in tandem the changes in the political and security landscape of the region, revealing the democratic transitions taking place in some member states, we are now witnessing a much more dynamic set of regional processes that are taking place in Southeast Asia. These dynamics are reflected in the changing nature of state-society relations in some states and the perceptible changes in the nature of regional socialization taking place between states and non-state actors; and the emergence of new regional institutions and the trends towards reconceptualization of security and rethinking of regional security practices. These developments have had an impact on ASEAN. Thus, it has been the ultimate objective of this study of ASEAN's mechanisms to capture these dynamics that had evolved over time and to show, through a narrative of ASEAN in different phases, the extent to which the association has indeed gone beyond the ASEAN way.

What the study does not argue is the withering away of the ASEAN way, despite the perceptible transformations. Indeed, as the association faces up to the difficulties of maintaining cohesion in an expanded ASEAN, and as it tries to accommodate competing national interests and reconciles conflicts and differences, much of the ASEAN way remains. As presented in the preceding chapters of this book, the features of the ASEAN way — portrayed through the observance of norms and principles in inter-state conduct, the consensual and consultative modalities in decision-making, as well as the preference for informal structures and the attitudes towards accommodation and non-confrontation — have continued to be defining facets of ASEAN. Nonetheless, the study argues that the characteristic features of the ASEAN way are being calibrated to slowly adjust to the new realities that have unfolded in the region. Calibrating the ASEAN way also meant that some of its features would have had to be fitted in with the new mechanisms that have been instituted in order for the association to adequately manage regional security.

It has been said repeatedly that in the new millennium, ASEAN is at a crossroad. This has been a regional cliché. But as this study argues, what is of importance to ASEAN scholars and analysts at this point in time is not just to draw up a list of regional challenges and harp on ASEAN's inadequacy, as has often been the case. Given the fact that the ASEAN "playing field" has been opened to non-state actors, we should now also pay closer attention to the changing dynamics and processes that are unfolding as these actors engage ASEAN. What this study is arguing then is to look beyond the state-centric modalities and look out for these emerging processes and examine the extent to which they affect the prevailing modalities beyond the ASEAN way, and their implications on the future of ASEAN's mechanisms and regional security.

This concluding chapter is divided into two sections. The first section will summarize some of the key points made in the first half of this book regarding the nature of ASEAN's mechanisms on managing conflict and regional security. The second section will address the issues raised regarding the implications of the new developments on ASEAN.

## I. WHAT MATTERED IN ASEAN

The first half of this study revisited ASEAN's *raison d'être* and the agenda of regional security. Chapters 1 and 4 took us through a sweeping view of ASEAN's evolution as a regional organization concerned with managing conflicts in Southeast Asia. There are essentially three points that we need to reiterate here before we proceed to look at the implications of the dynamic changes in regional processes on ASEAN's mechanism.

• ASEAN and its mechanisms for managing conflict matter for regional security.

In Chapter 1, it was argued that regional organizations have an important role to play in managing regional security, in spite of the chequered experiences of regional organizations around the world. ASEAN and its story of regional reconciliation has been a good case in point. Over the years, many scholars and analysts have praised ASEAN for its qualified success in managing inter-state disputes and managing regional security. However, for a regional organization that had been under-institutionalized and obviously lacking in capacity, we wanted to find a better way of explaining what accounted for this relative success. We proposed that one of the ways to assess its role, as a conflict manager in Southeast Asia, is to examine the nature of its mechanisms in managing conflicts.

Bearing in mind that mechanisms in this context refers to a broad range of processes, methods, devices, techniques, and strategies employed to resolve or manage conflict, we adopted the constructivist approach in identifying what these mechanisms are in the context of Southeast Asia. Constructivism proved to be a useful framework in explaining the lack or absence of concrete, formal mechanisms in ASEAN since the approach goes beyond the consideration of power and material interest and sensitizes us to the salience of ideational factors, to actors and agents that shape these ideas beyond the state and the intersubjective understanding that take place. These ideational elements are, therefore, instructive in understanding the nature of ASEAN's mechanisms of conflict management and how they have worked, as well as in explaining why some mechanisms have been preferred over others. Constructivism places a lot of emphasis on the nature of socialization among actors, an important facet in explaining why certain mechanisms and/or approaches have endured for some time and why these could also *change* over time. Constructivism, therefore, allows us to meaningfully study ASEAN and the changes in its mechanisms since these changes (in regional institutions) are products of man-made understandings over certain ideas, over time.

In identifying these mechanisms, as discussed in Chapter 2, we noted that unlike the types of mechanisms that other regional organizations have that are commonly identified in the literature on conflict, what we have in ASEAN are mostly informal in nature and do not speak to the broader literature on conflict resolution. ASEAN's mechanisms had been more inclined towards norm-building and community-building through socialization and networking, assurance rather than deterrence, and informal third-party mediations rather than formal dispute settlement mechanisms. We also noted that the major considerations for the preference of informal mechanisms over the legalistic, albeit extremely limited alternatives, were not only due to the lack of institutional capacity within ASEAN. The reason for this was primarily due to the overriding objectives of instilling trust and building confidence among members that were getting to know each other during the formative years of ASEAN. Hence, the informal types of mechanisms for managing conflict and security had become the more distinctive types of mechanisms that defined the association. We also noted and included in our list of mechanisms the other types of more institutionalized agreements that ASEAN had developed that were geared towards increasing socio-economic and political co-operation among member states. The rationale for considering them into our list of mechanisms is that these co-operative agreements in various areas significantly contribute to ASEAN's overall aim of engendering an atmosphere for peace and security.

•   Despite the challenges, regional norms and practices matter.

In our examination of ASEAN's mechanisms, we highlighted the importance of regional norms in defining the nature the various mechanisms that have evolved. However, these norms and practices, encapsulated in the ASEAN way, were met with a number of challenges starting from the conflict in Cambodia. ASEAN's diplomacy in the Cambodian conflict, as discussed in Chapter 3, severely tested the limits of the ASEAN way. It not only challenged the norms of non-use of force and non-intervention that ASEAN had been promoting through the 1976 TAC and ZOPFAN. The conflict also exposed ASEAN's inadequacy in dealing with "extra-regional" conflicts, bearing in mind that Cambodia at that time was not a member of ASEAN and the nature of conflict was also perceived as a proxy war that involved the interests of major powers. Nevertheless, through its sustained efforts in promoting conciliation among the warring Khmer factions, and between the Khmers and the Vietnamese, ASEAN proved to be a skilful mediator and conflict manager at least until the time when the resolution of the conflict necessitated the involvement of major powers and the UN Security Council.

What was instructive, however, about ASEAN's experience in managing the Cambodian conflict had been the fact that its role was not only about conflict management. As discussed in Chapter 3, the Cambodian experience significantly proved to be an exercise of identity and community-building in ASEAN. Through the unceasing efforts placed on consultations and consensus in responding to the conflict, the Cambodian experience had jelled the old ASEAN members together, and found them having to define and redefine their interests and identity as a corporate body that was working for regional peace through the observance of certain norms and principles. Throughout the duration of the conflict, one observed how the policies of ASEAN member states pertaining to Cambodia had to be recalibrated ever so often, to accommodate the interests of those that became most vulnerable to the crisis, while assuring the security of its front-line state, Thailand. The Cambodian experience had therefore instilled the idea among the old members in ASEAN that for the association to succeed and in the interest of regional security, its mechanisms must be geared towards engendering a sense of community through shared norms and identity — regardless of incremental nature of its results. Even at that time, the importance of process-oriented approaches to regional security was underscored.

- The ASEAN way could be extended and transformed into a wider regional process of promoting co-operative security practices, albeit at its most basic, to maintain regional stability.

As noted in Chapter 4, the establishment of the ASEAN Regional Forum (ARF), which saw the pivotal role of ASEAN, had been seen as an extension of the ASEAN way. When viewed as a wider Asia-Pacific enterprise on confidence-building measures where habits of dialogues are being fostered, and comfort levels are increased among new members and former enemies, the ARF has been and still is a huge conflict management mechanism. More significantly, the ARF's development also embodies most of ASEAN's distinctive mechanisms such as norm-building, consensual and consultative style in decision-making, the informality of doing things, and the preference of soft institutionalization against institutionalized structures.

Nonetheless, as discussed in Chapter 5, the ARF and its soft institutions have yet to be tested. As the next half of the study had revealed, there had been several conflicts in the region, such as the East Timor crisis, which to many observers could have been the litmus test of ARF's capacity to respond but these expectations later turned out to be unrealistic. As argued in the study, the ARF, like its core group ASEAN, was geared mainly for conflict prevention and was not equipped to deal with outbreaks of conflicts. In spite of this limitation, things have been evolving, particularly in ASEAN.

## II. WHAT MATTERS CAN ALSO CHANGE

The first half of this book essentially went back to the basics of ASEAN — that is, a framework for regional reconciliation and whose mechanisms that were geared for preventing conflict had been largely depicted in the ASEAN way. To this extent, it is understandable that most assessments of ASEAN were done through the prism of the ASEAN way. But, over time and through several periods of crises, not to mention the changes in the international strategic landscape, it would have been rather unrealistic and ineffectual to still be guided by the ASEAN way in appraising ASEAN's performance as a regional conflict manager. The consequences that came with the structural transformations in the strategic and security environment brought on by the end of the Cold War; its reverberations in other parts of the globe; the emergence of other players in the international arena besides state actors; and lastly the impact of globalization would have alerted us to the rapid and overwhelming changes which the Southeast Asian region was not immune.

Hence, against the background of the experience of Cambodia and the events that led to the establishment of the ARF as discussed in

Chapter 4, we can already tease out some of the palpable shifts in ASEAN's mechanisms or specifically, the ASEAN way. These trends can be grouped under the themes described below.

## Rationalization of Norms and State Practices

The ARF signalled the turn to multilateralism in Southeast Asia. This meant that certain adjustments to ASEAN's principles, like the ZOPFAN, and the practice of its independent regional security policy had to be made. I do not argue that ZOPFAN had been rigidly applied in this region before the ARF. As discussed in Chapter 1, ASEAN had allowed for flexibility in the adoption of ZOPFAN, bearing in mind the bilateral security arrangements that some of its member states (the Philippines and Thailand) had with the United States, and the presence of U.S. military bases in the Philippines at least until 1992. The approach taken then by ASEAN, particularly Indonesia and Malaysia, was to encourage a more independent regional policy that did not align ASEAN to any major power, especially at the height of the Cold War. But ASEAN's experience in Cambodia and its decision to be proactive in the establishment of the ARF were already indicative of the change in thinking at that time.

After the end of the Cold War, the perceived power vacuum pushed many states to review the region's security approaches and to recognize the need for a new political and security framework that would maintain the necessary equilibrium for sustainable peace and prosperity in the region.[1] Nevertheless, while the main concern was to engage the major powers and other interested countries into a single framework, the objective of having a new regional security framework was not to balance one major power against another. Hence, deciding the modality of this type of arrangement became of utmost importance so that ASEAN could convince the major powers and the other regional states to be part of this "project". This had been extensively discussed in Chapter 4. The result that emerged was a regional mechanism, that is, a security forum that is *sui generis*. The ARF is the only security forum in the world that has as its members all the major powers in the international system — the United States, China, Russia, Japan, India, and the European Union. As can be gleaned from its concept paper and the subsequent documents of the forum, the ARF was never intended to be a military alliance, nor aimed at deterrence, nor created to replace or become an alternative to the balance of power. Instead the ARF was meant to promote constructive political and security dialogue, and encourage a more consensual approach to regional security.[2]

In sum, the history of ARF's inception is a telling example of how ASEAN could rationalize its norms and principles to adjust to the realities of a rapidly changed strategic environment. In this regard, the ASEAN way has been craftily adjusted while maintaining the centrepiece of its normative terrain.[3]

## Transformative Impact of Ideas and Agents

In analysing the ARF and the other mechanisms that have evolved in ASEAN, one would also note how ideas and actors/agents had contributed to the development of certain mechanisms. These factors offer salient points about the changing modalities in ASEAN which have to be carefully analysed. As discussed in Chapter 5, track two networks like the ASEAN-ISIS and by extension, CSCAP, had been largely instrumental in the establishment of the ARF and on the nature of this forum. Scholars have described the ASEAN-ISIS as the agents who essentially shaped ASEAN's vision of a multilateral security co-operation. Moreover, by being part of CSCAP, it has also contributed significantly to the work and policy inputs for the ARF. What this indicate is the movement beyond state-centric approaches to managing security to one of pluralism, as reflected in the kinds of interaction that state and non-state actors have in crafting emerging mechanisms.

Aside from the ARF initiative, the ASEAN-ISIS that essentially formed an integral part of track two diplomacy in Southeast Asia, had also been actively participating in the processes of conflict management in ASEAN by providing timely policy inputs to ASEAN officials and their respective governments on various issues that affected the region. Their recommendations, submitted either through Memoranda sent to ASEAN and through their regular meetings with ASEAN SOMs, have been quite effective. As described in Chapter 5, the ASEAN- ISIS have been persuasive in their recommendations on the establishment of the ARF, their recommendations on the strengthening of the ASEAN Secretariat, and on the realization of the ASEAN Free Trade Area (AFTA); including their support for establishing a regional human rights mechanism and their initiative in forming the ASEAN People's Assembly, discussed in Chapter 7, to realize ASEAN Vision 2020's plan to create a community of caring societies. Thus, the nature of track two diplomacy had indeed been quite significant in the study of ASEAN's mechanisms in three major areas.

One of these is their influence in starting the trend towards more open discourses at all levels — from track one to track three that challenge some of the elements of the ASEAN way. The discourses that challenged the norm of non-interference that resonated loudly at the height of the 1997 financial crisis had been a good example. Some members of the ASEAN-ISIS had openly called for a rethinking of the practice of this principle and were openly supportive of Thailand's proposal on "flexible engagement".[4] Although this principle, as argued in Chapter 6, had and still appears to be often violated by ASEAN officials and among leaders themselves in their comments and uninvited remarks about the internal affairs of their ASEAN neighbours, ASEAN-ISIS through their workshops, reports, and regular interactions with ASEAN officials have, however, brought these discourses into the public domain and indirectly compelling ASEAN officials to talk openly about it and/or defend this norm.

The ASEAN-ISIS advocacy on the establishment of a regional human rights commission as well as its successful initiation of the ASEAN People's Assembly (APA), as described in Chapter 7, have also been highly significant. Their work is not only suggestive of the dynamic developments taking place in the region, but also indicative of the trends towards the institutionalization of civil society engagement with ASEAN. Although the APA experiment is at its inchoate stage and bears inconclusive results, its emergence as an embryonic mechanism of governance and regional security must be regarded as a perceptible departure from the state-centric and state-driven mechanisms encapsulated in the ASEAN way. The working groups in APA that work on the development of a human rights and democracy scorecards, as well as the working group that is developing a Southeast Asian Human Development Report would inevitably impinge on the issue of non-interference as these groups push for the realization of these projects. Since ASEAN has officially engaged with track two and track three networks, these types of engagement that revolve around regional concerns are already indicative of a qualitatively altered socialization processes that are taking place in the region. Compared with the kind of socialization characterized in the ASEAN way that limited socialization mostly among state officials, this "new" socialization — though inchoate in nature — can have a transformative effect on the kind of regionalism that has prevailed in Southeast Asia. In this regard, it would be of great interest to examine the extent to which these types of vertical engagement could be constitutive of new norms and practices in the region.

The other area that is illustrative of the impact that non-state have on the development of ASEAN mechanisms, either at track two or track three, have been the inevitable consequences of forcing the association to make itself relevant to the people in the region. If the general impressions of ASEAN were: (1) a "club of élites" set apart from the majority of the citizens in ASEAN countries, and (2) whose work/policies have not effectively addressed the needs of people in the region; then one could suggest that, at best, the devastating impact of the 1997 financial crisis and the several other crises that followed provided the impetus for ASEAN to revisit the issue of instituting concrete regional mechanisms that can address regional problems beyond the informal mechanisms that was part of the ASEAN way. While it would be presumptuous to claim that these actors outside the official ASEAN track were the main drivers in the adoption of the "new" regional institutions post-1997, needless to say, the urgency of having to respond to regional concerns combined with the criticisms hurled at ASEAN for its inability and lack of capacity to address problems would have had pushed ASEAN to finally confront the issue of institutionalization.

Hence, the clearest indicators of ASEAN's mechanisms having evolved beyond the confines of ASEAN way would be the number of new mechanisms and new types of institutionalized arrangements that have surfaced post-1997. As discussed in Chapter 6, these new mechanisms that address both political-security issues and socio-economic issues include:

- The establishment of the ASEAN Troika to help Cambodia in restoring the country's political stability. Since 2000, the ASEAN Troika has been formally institutionalized.
- The adoption of the Regional Haze Action Plan (RHAP) to fight regular forest fires and manage the resulting haze/environmental problems. Related to this is the development of an ASEAN Legal Framework on Transboundary Haze Pollution.
- The signing of the Agreement on Information Exchange and Establishment of Communication Procedures to promote co-operation in combating transnational crimes, including terrorism.
- The institutionalization of the Bilateral Swap Arrangement as a mechanism to help member countries that were badly affected by

the 1997–98 financial crisis, as well as the introduction of a regional surveillance mechanism as a form of an early-warning system to avert potential financial crisis in the future.

- The adoption of several measures to jointly contain infectious diseases, including the development of an ASEAN Centre for Disease Control.

These new mechanisms do not include the earlier decision by ASEAN to pursue with AFTA and bring forward the agreement on tariff reductions under the Common Effective Preferential Tariff (CEPT) scheme from 2003 to 2002 for the ASEAN-6, as well as putting in place the dispute settlement mechanisms under the Protocol on Dispute Settlement. The developments on AFTA is the best indication of how far ASEAN has departed from the ASEAN way and has been a showcase of how "bold" ASEAN has gone to change its modalities from informal agreements to more rules-based, institutional arrangements to deepen regional economic co-operation.

The implications of these "new" mechanisms are demonstrative of the extent to which ASEAN members have obviously worked around the problem of intrusiveness and protection of national sovereignty. Most of the new mechanisms that have been created required states to subject themselves to a measure of "interference" as they work together to address regional problems. At least post-1997, ASEAN is moving towards more institutionalization and, as Miles Kahler had noted in the case of AFTA, more legalization.[5] These developments therefore debunk the earlier prognosis of ASEAN that it is unable to move beyond the ASEAN way. An example of this type of prognosis is the observation by Shaun Narine who wrote:

> Despite the apparent need to reform ASEAN to make it more relevant and effective in the modern world, it is highly unlikely that such reform is possible. A strongly institutionalized and binding ASEAN with the ability to intervene in, or even comment upon, the domestic politics and policies of its member states is diametrically opposed to everything that ASEAN has represented. ASEAN's principle of non-intervention has been the single greatest factor accounting for the association's durability ... Reforming ASEAN to make it more intrusive will undermine the foundations of the organization's durability and abrogate the principles on which it was built.[6]

Such premature yet definitive analyses of ASEAN would understandably lead one to postulate that ASEAN was at risk of fading into irrelevance.[7] However, had Narine examined how members of an association could actually "pool sovereignty" — a type of approach that works around competing interests, a *modus vivendi* — when they agreed to be part of regional arrangements that impinge on national sovereignty; and had Narine studied patterns of co-operation among these members through their joint regional endeavours in addressing regional problems like fighting the haze and forest fires in Indonesia, restoring stability in Cambodia, and participating in the East Timor peacekeeping operations under the UN framework, then a more nuanced and qualified assessment of ASEAN would have resulted. This is not to argue that these joint endeavours have been without problems. As discussed in Chapter 6, difficulties do remain. But a closer examination of these difficulties are not so much because countries hide behind the cloak of national sovereignty but in many instances, it had been largely due to domestic inadequacies brought on by lack of national capacity.

## Shifting Patterns of Regionalism

Lastly, in these changing trends beyond the ASEAN way pertains to the ongoing project of constructing a regional identity in Southeast Asia. The ASEAN way, according to Amitav Acharya, has contributed to the sense of common identity, "we feeling", in ASEAN. He argued that the ASEAN way has resulted in the development of an institutional culture that also "fostered a common feeling of regional belonging and led to claims about institutional exceptionalism underpinning such constructs as the ASEAN way".[8]

Few would disagree with Acharya's observations about the ASEAN way and its effects on building a sense of regional identity. The discussions in the first half of this book reinforce Acharya's remarks that ASEAN — at least before its membership expansion and the series of crises that hit the region — had instilled an institutional culture that had helped manage conflicts among member states, hence leading several scholars to regard the association as a nascent security community where members would no longer consider the use of force to settle disputes.

However, as Acharya himself conceded, this sense of regional identity had been confined to ASEAN's foreign policy élites and over the last three decades has not really filtered through the societies of ASEAN states. In this sense, the kind of regional identity and community that has developed through the ASEAN way do not speak to and are not shared by the wider regional community in Southeast Asia. Even within the circles of the policy élites, the changes in leadership in several states in Southeast Asia have already changed the quality of interaction between leaders, and between leaders and their societies. As mentioned at the start of this book, the elections in 2004 in Indonesia, Malaysia, and the Philippines, and Thailand in 2005, as well as the change of guards in Singapore, will bring new faces in to the ASEAN "family" that had been around for some time. This is only within the context of the old ASEAN-6. In fact, one would note that the comfort level among members in the ASEAN-6 is no longer the same. However, with an expanded association, the issue here is not only about stretching that comfort level among ASEAN leaders but to the extent possible, maintaining or keeping it as close as possible to the previous levels in order to maintain cohesion within the organization.

This study adds that the picture of a close community may be qualitatively changing with the expansion of ASEAN activities and the widening of political space through a myriad of processes that are taking place in the region. While one could argue that the participation of track two and track three actors in ASEAN processes as discussed in Chapters 5 and 7 are contributing to the building of constituency of a Southeast Asian community and regionalism, the issue however is in the nature of that evolving community which may no longer be anchored on the ASEAN way, or in the institutional culture that the ASEAN elites had assiduously cultivated throughout the association's history. Hence, of great interest here would be the kind of regionalism that would evolve in Southeast Asia that could move beyond the normative framework and soft institutionalization that had become the enduring features of ASEAN.

In offering possible scenarios as to how the ASEAN way could evolve, Jurgen Haacke noted that ASEAN's diplomatic and security culture "may not *noticeably* evolve because ASEAN leaders are reluctant to endorse shifts in collective understanding that to them might amount to opening a Pandora's box".[9] The point here is not to discount the possibility that it is evolving but more on how this will evolve. The initiatives undertaken jointly and separately by the track two networks in ASEAN and the APA, which comprises a motley group of transnational civil society organizations, are directed at engaging ASEAN, specifically in their desire to be part of setting the agenda in the region. This might just open that Pandora's box.

As acknowledged by Haacke, the issues that track two and track three networks are now working have gone beyond the conventional security discourse to move into directions of human rights and human security, democracy, and good governance. This has been reinforced in the discussions on the work of APA and ASEAN-ISIS in Chapter 7. Therefore, while one would be understandably cautious about offering scenarios regarding the changes beyond the ASEAN way, to be sure indications of change will now come not so from governments but more importantly from the non-state actors who will persist to push the limits of the ASEAN way.

Indeed, these reflections on changing the ASEAN way become highly relevant as we now probe further into the implications of ASEAN's new initiatives under the Bali Concord II.

## III. TOWARDS AN ASEAN COMMUNITY

### "Bonding Together in Partnership in Dynamic Development"

While several scholars have already referred to ASEAN as a *community* and while ASEAN's declarations like the ASEAN Vision 2020 has talked about a "community of caring societies", the Bali Concord II adopted by ASEAN leaders in October 2003 is certainly the most definitive indication of how far this association is officially willing to go to build that ASEAN community. Of the three pillars identified, the plans for setting up the twin pillars of an ASEAN Economic Community (AEC) and ASEAN Security Community (ASC) in so far as they provide some insights on the directions beyond the ASEAN way have been most interesting.

We have discussed that ASEAN's progress on AFTA and its current work on plotting the road ahead for the AEC are most suggestive of how far institutionalized ASEAN has become. Building on from the ASEAN Vision 2020, the AEC has envisioned ASEAN by the year 2020 to be a single market and production base with free flow of goods, services, investments, capital and skilled labour.[10] In realizing this vision, the ASEAN High Level Task Force (HLTF) on Economic Integration has unveiled a set of bold and ambitious economic initiatives with clear deadlines, many by 2005, to expedite the process of economic integration that has been started. These initiatives include:

- fast-tracking the integration of eleven priority sectors;
- introducing faster customs clearance and simplified customs procedures;
- eliminating barriers to trade;

- accelerating the implementation of the Mutual Recognition Arrangements (MRAs) for key sectors, for example, electrical and electronic equipment and telecommunications equipment; and
- harmonizing standards and technical regulations.[11]

In the area of trade in goods, improvements in the Common Effective Preferential Tariffs (CEPT) Scheme Rules of Origin (ROO) will be finalized by end 2004. This would require more transparency, predictability, and standardization of procedures among ASEAN countries in this area. To ensure transparency on Non-Tariff Measures (NTMs) and eliminate those that are barriers to trade, certain measures are being introduced, which include, establishing a set of clear and definitive work programme for the removal of such barriers (by 2005) and adopting the WTO agreements on Technical Barriers to Trade; Sanitary and Phyto-Sanitary and Import Licensing Procedures and develop implementation guidelines appropriate for ASEAN (by 2005).[12]

One of the most important recommendations by the HLTF was the creation of a more effective dispute settlement mechanism (DSM) with powers to make legally binding decisions in resolving trade disputes among member states. Since it is expected that the number of trade disputes will likely rise as the region moves towards a higher level of economic integration, a credible DSM would be extremely critical for the AEC to succeed. In this regard, the ASEAN Secretariat will be strengthened to improve its capacity to undertake some of the necessary functions in this area. By end 2004, for example, a legal unit within the ASEAN Secretariat will be set up to provide legal advice on trade disputes. Plans are also underway to establish a unit on ASEAN Consultation to Solve Trade and Investment Issues in order to provide quick resolution to operations problems (this would be similar to the EU mechanism), as well as the establishment of ASEAN Compliance Body.[13]

More significantly, in a stark departure from the ASEAN modality of decision-making by consensus, ASEAN may also use the "2 + X" formula besides the "ASEAN-X" formula that had already been adopted in economic matters. The "2 + X" approach allows two member countries that are ready to integrate certain sectors to go ahead while the others could follow later. This arrangement would enable countries like Thailand and Singapore to lead the way in realizing the AEC before 2020.

As with the current practice of engaging non-state actors in ASEAN processes, the track two networks like the ASEAN-ISIS and the Institute of Southeast Asian Studies (ISEAS) have contributed respective concept papers on realizing the AEC. The ASEAN HLTF had acknowledged their contribution and their ideas, which have been subsequently reflected in the annexed recommendations on the AEC that came out from HLTF. To be sure, all these processes and initiatives indicate that ASEAN is committed in getting the AEC project started. More significantly, these processes and emerging mechanisms reinforce the trends beyond the ASEAN way.

## "Living in Peace, Stability and Prosperity"

The roadmap of the ASC provides even more interesting insights of the kinds of mechanisms that ASEAN have in mind with regard to enhancing its capacity to manage security. A careful reading of the Bali Concord II reveals four important elements that the ASC has identified to realize the idea of a security community. These are: norms-setting, conflict prevention, approaches to conflict resolution and post-conflict peace-building.[14] Other than norms-setting which is already an integral part of the ASEAN way, the three other elements are novel initiatives that have found their way in official discourses and are now being taken up at the official level. The question is how these three other elements are going to be translated into concrete mechanisms.

It is interesting to note that Indonesia has been behind the idea of the ASC after it took over as chair of the ASEAN Standing Committee beginning in June 2003.[15] While there has not been much information on the modalities of the ASC in the Bali Concord II as of this writing, nevertheless press reports and briefings given by Indonesian officials, as well as interviews from representatives of the ASEAN-ISIS[16] have revealed some information about the kinds of mechanisms that are being deliberated at the official level.

The ideas currently being floated to push the agenda for conflict prevention include a range of measures to further enhance ASEAN confidence-building measures and preventive diplomacy. These include: convening regular ASEAN Defence Ministers Meetings, more military exchanges between defence officials, military academies, in addition to enhanced bilateral military exchanges, and production of ASEAN Annual Security Outlook. These measures are strikingly similar with those being adopted by the ARF.

To respond to rising concerns regarding maritime security, the establishment of an ASEAN Maritime Safety and Surveillance Unit has been proposed with the aim of standardizing procedures and classification of criminal acts at sea such as armed robbery at sea, piracy, maritime terrorism, and illegal, unregulated, and unreported (IUU) fishing. On the regional fight against terrorism, there have also been discussions with regard to the possibility of forming an ASEAN police task force, besides enhancing the co-operation and intelligence sharing that is already taking place among ASEAN Police (ASEANPOL). Malaysia had already indicated support for this idea.[17]

As regards conflict prevention, ideas on instituting an ASEAN Dispute Settlement Mechanism on political and security areas are also being deliberated on. In contrast to the AEC where officials are already working on the possibility of establishing a high-level judicial body that will be staffed by judges from every ASEAN member country to enforce the Protocol on DSM, this has been a contentious issue when dealing with political disputes. So far, the only formal mechanism that ASEAN has had that was meant to resolve political disputes was the High Council of the Treaty of Amity and Co-operation, which had never been instituted. In this regard, there have been suggestions to make the High Council become more like a judicial body rather than a political entity. This would be in line with the AEC's move to take out dispute settlement mechanism on economic issues out of the political realm and be brought into the legal realm.[18] Aside from the proposal on DSM, the possibility of establishing an Eminent Persons Group and an expert advisory committee to provide advice and extend assistance to conflict parties are also being discussed.

To be sure, these proposals will take some time to materialize. Nonetheless, one could interpret these proposals, specifically on effective dispute settlement mechanism for conflict resolution, as indicative of the willingness by member states to now consider a regional institution that can resolve rather than manage conflicts. This is in stark contrast to the ASEAN way that had preferred to defer issues, "sweep them under the carpet", and if possible resort to informal third-party mediation (refer to Chapter 2). Given the practice of bilateral negotiations already taking place in cases of non-territorial disputes and the precedent set by members to seek international arbitration on territorial matters to the International Court of Justice (ICJ) as in the case with Malaysia and Singapore over Pedra Branca, and Malaysia and Indonesia over Sipadan and Ligitan, the possibility of establishing a judicial body of some kind may no longer seem impossible. Moreover, ASEAN's experience with AFTA has shown that slowly, the reticence towards supra-national jurisdiction among member states for the attainment of a regional good is being overcome.

Another "bold" proposal is the idea of establishing an ASEAN peacekeeping force. In explaining the rationale for this proposal, a spokesperson for the Indonesia Government remarked, "ASEAN countries should know one another better than anyone else and therefore [we] should have the option ... to take advantage of an ASEAN peacekeeping force to be deployed if they so wish."[19] The Indonesian hand behind the proposal is indeed interesting in that if there was any country in the region that had the propensity for intra-state conflicts, it is Indonesia. Its recent experience with East Timor has had a demonstrative impact on some of its restive provinces like Aceh and West Papua that had been clamouring for either more autonomy or self-rule. It was also Indonesia after the change of regime in 1998 that witnessed the painful consequences of ethnic and religious conflicts.

Moreover, against ASEAN's experience and the participation of some countries in the peacekeeping and peace-building efforts in East Timor, the proposal for a regional peacekeeping force indicates a radical shift from the regional norms constituted in the ASEAN way. Thus, the implications for this initiative are tremendous, yet bring to light an emerging new thinking on how some ASEAN member states regard the issues of sovereignty and non-intervention. Given that the Philippines had allowed a Malaysian team to observe the peace talks in Southern Philippines between the Philippine Government and the Moro Islamic Liberation Front (MILF) and the fact that Indonesia had allowed Thai and Filipino military monitors to observe the ceasefire between the Indonesian Government and the rebel forces in Aceh province, these are emerging examples of how member states in ASEAN are adopting the "pooling of sovereignty" approach beyond that of "protecting sovereignty" that is characteristic of the ASEAN way.

If the peacekeeping idea is not bold enough, the other ideas being proposed by Indonesia under the ASC plan of action also include the possibility of an ASEAN-wide extradition treaty and a non-aggression treaty.[20] Finally, under the rubric of post-conflict peace-building, Indonesia had been pushing for the inclusion of the establishment of a Regional Human Rights Commission — a regional agenda that has been stalled for some time.[21] What is indeed novel in all these developments is the fact that these ideas are already part of the official discourses, which not too long ago were once considered imponderable.

## IV. CONCLUSION

The declaration of creating an ASEAN Community and the proliferation of new ideas floating around have been keeping ASEAN officials and non-state actors preoccupied as they collectively put these ideas into shapes and forms. These ongoing events as well as the number of contemporary changes occurring in ASEAN that were presented in the other chapters in this book are reflections of the kinds of challenges that the association has had to confront to remain relevant under the present circumstances. These challenges and particularly the kinds of responses that have been identified in our narrative of the ASEAN story can only indicate that ASEAN does matter for the member states and societies in this region.

If indeed crises also spell opportunities, one would then look at how ASEAN's mechanism in managing regional conflicts, crises, and security had evolved over time to determine if there is anything significant beyond the ASEAN way. ASEAN, as explained to us by many officials and scholars, was not purposefully built to deal with any real conflicts. Notwithstanding its inherent limitations, we also saw how ASEAN had responded with a growing list of activities, changing agendas, and establishing a number of institutional mechanisms. Hence, the processes involved in the generation of all these initiatives should already tell us that there is more that is happening out there beyond the ASEAN way.

Many of these changes may never be adopted in practice, while some of them have to be skilfully negotiated into a form that is, at the very least, acceptable to all members. In the months and years to come, there are bound to be increasing tensions, more propensities for caution and conservatism, and many more diversions that could torpedo the bolder mechanisms that are being proposed. Nevertheless, it is important that we capture the changes that are taking place as the processes of contestation and accommodation continue.

As we follow the ASEAN story beyond the ASEAN way, we will continue to see dynamic processes taking place almost at the same time, either driven by states or by different agents in both domestic and regional settings. The picture that emerges from all these dynamic changes could be one of chaos and incoherence, leaving one overwhelmed at the rapidly changing regional environment. To be sure, the processes of change that one hopes to capture in this study would defy attempts to compose it into one simple picture. Hence, the picture that we have of

ASEAN beyond the ASEAN way is not neat and clear. But what we have, however, is a regional collage. And the interpretation of that collage would also depend very much on how one reads the dynamic processes and the forces captured in it. Whether we choose to view this ASEAN collage from a perspective of a glass half full or a glass half empty, we are nevertheless directed to the dynamism of change that this region is and will continue to grapple with in the years to come.

In Southeast Asia, we saw post-1997 as the greatest period of change yet in ASEAN. This period has brought us to that vantage point where we can assess how ASEAN has evolved from the time it had adopted the Bali Concord I in 1976 up to its declaration of an ASEAN Community in Bali Concord II. If one views the ASEAN collage from a glass half full, the Bali Concord II therefore can be regarded as coming full circle to the dream of the founding fathers that the regional project of reconciliation will be finally realized into a vision of an ASEAN community. Only this time, that "we feeling" that had been faithfully constructed by a selected few would no longer remain in the abstraction. As member states are now compelled to work out regional issues together and address regional challenges through regional mechanisms, that sense of regional identity, perhaps even beyond the ASEAN way, could eventually be shared by states and societies in the region.

## Notes

1. Muthiah Alagappa, "Regionalism and the Quest for Security: ASEAN and the Cambodian Conflict", *Journal of International Affairs* 46, no. 2 (1995): 439–67.
2. See "The ASEAN Regional Forum: Concept Paper", Bandar Seri Begawan, Brunei, 1 August 1995.
3. See Jurgen Haacke, *ASEAN's Diplomatic and Security Culture: Origins, Development and Prospects* (RoutledgeCurzon: London and New York, 2003), p. 214.
4. See, for example, Carolina Hernandez, "Towards Re-examining the Non-Intervention Principle in ASEAN Political Cooperation", *Indonesian Quarterly* 26, no. 3 (1998): 164–70, and Jusuf Wanandi, "The Strategic Implications of the Economic Crisis in East Asia", *Indonesian Quarterly* 26, no. 1 (1998): 2–6.
5. See Miles Kahler, "Legalization as Strategy: The Asia-Pacific Case", *International Organization* 54, no. 3 (2000): 549–71.
6. Shaun Narine, *Explaining ASEAN: Regionalism in Southeast Asia* (Boulder, CO: Lynne Rienner Publishers, Inc.), p. 204.

7. Ibid., p. 208.
8. Amitav Acharya, *Constructing a Security Community in Southeast Asia: ASEAN and the Problem of Regional Order* (London and New York: Routledge, 2001), p. 202.
9. Haacke, *ASEAN's Diplomatic and Security Culture* (emphasis added).
10. The ASEAN Vision 2020 envisaged "a stable, prosperous and highly competitive ASEAN Economic Region in which there is a free flow of goods, services and investments, a freer flow of capital, equitable economic development and reduced poverty and socio-economic disparities".
11. See Recommendations of the High-Level Task Force on ASEAN Economic Integration at < http://www.aseansec.org >.
12. Denis Hew and Hadi Soesastro, "Realizing the ASEAN Economic Community by 2020: ISEAS and ASEAN-ISIS Approaches", in *ASEAN Economic Bulletin* 20, no. 3 (2003): 292–96.
13. Ibid.
14. See "Declaration of Bali Concord II", specifically subsection on the ASEAN Security Community, at < http://www.aseansec.org/15160.htm >.
15. See "Indonesia Proposing ASEAN Security Community Concept", *Jakarta Post*, 16 June 2003, and "ASEAN Plans Security Forum", *The Nation*, 17 June 2003.
16. The ASEAN SOM had requested the ASEAN-ISIS to deliberate on the ASC's Plan of Action prepared by the senior officials of ASEAN and to provide their inputs and recommendations. Interview with Dr Rizal Sukma, 21 February 2004.
17. "KL and Jakarta want to form ASEAN Police Taskforce", in *The Star Online*, 21 January 2003, accessed from < http://www.thestar.com.my/services/2003/1/21/nation/ljmge.asp >.
18. See Hadi Soesastro, "ASEAN Economic Community: Ideas, Significance and Feasibility", Paper delivered at the 17th Asia Pacific Roundtable, Kuala Lumpur, 7–9 August 2003.
19. "Indonesia Proposes Southeast Asian Peacekeeping Force", 21 February 2004, accessed from < http://www.aseansec.org/afp/20p.htm >.
20. Ibid. See also "Indonesia Proposes ASEAN Peacekeeping Force", 21 February 2004, *Borneo Bulletin Online*, accessed from < http://www.brunei-online.com/bb/mon/feb23w4.htm >.
21. Presentation by Umar Hadi, Senior Officer, Indonesian Foreign Ministry at the third ASEAN People's Assembly, 26 September 2003, Manila.

# Appendix I

## : DECLARATION OF ASEAN CONCORD II
## : (BALI CONCORD II)

The Sultan of Brunei Darussalam, the Prime Minister of the Kingdom of Cambodia, the President of the Republic of Indonesia, the Prime Minister of the Lao People's Democratic Republic, the Prime Minister of Malaysia, the Prime Minister of the Union of Myanmar, the President of the Republic of the Philippines, the Prime Minister of the Republic of Singapore, the Prime Minister of the Kingdom of Thailand and the Prime Minister of the Socialist Republic of Viet Nam;

**RECALLING** the Declaration of ASEAN Concord adopted in this historic place of Bali, Indonesia in 1976, the Leaders of the Association of Southeast Asian Nations (ASEAN) expressed satisfaction with the overall progress made in the region;

**NOTING** in particular the expansion of ASEAN to ten countries in Southeast Asia, the deepening of regional economic integration and the impending accession to the Treaty of Amity and Cooperation (TAC) by States outside Southeast Asia;

**CONSCIOUS** of the need to further consolidate and enhance the achievements of ASEAN as a dynamic, resilient, and cohesive regional association for the well being of its member states and people as well as the need to further strengthen the Association's guidelines in achieving a more coherent and clearer path for cooperation between and among them;

**REAFFIRMING** their commitment to the principles enshrined in the ASEAN Declaration (Bangkok, 1967), the Declaration on Zone of Peace, Freedom, and Neutrality (Kuala Lumpur, 1971), the Treaty of Amity and Cooperation in Southeast Asia (Bali, 1976), the Declaration of ASEAN Concord (Bali, 1976), and the Treaty on the Southeast Asia Nuclear Weapons Free Zone (Bangkok, 1995);

**COGNIZANT** that the future of ASEAN cooperation is guided by the ASEAN Vision 2020, the Hanoi Plan of Action (1999–2004), and its succeeding Plans of Action, the Initiative for ASEAN Integration (IAI), and the Roadmap for the Integration of ASEAN (RIA);

**CONFIRMING** further that ASEAN Member Countries share primary responsibility for strengthening the economic and social stability in the region and ensuring their peaceful and progressive national development, and that they are determined to ensure their stability and security from external interference in any form or manner in order to preserve their national interest in accordance with the ideals and aspirations of their peoples;

**REAFFIRMING** the fundamental importance of adhering to the principle of non-interference and consensus in ASEAN cooperation;

**REITERATING** that the Treaty of Amity and Cooperation in Southeast Asia (TAC) is an effective code of conduct for relations among governments and peoples;

**RECOGNIZING** that sustainable economic development requires a secure political environment based on a strong foundation of mutual interests generated by economic cooperation and political solidarity;

**COGNIZANT** of the interdependence of the ASEAN economies and the need for ASEAN member countries to adopt "Prosper Thy Neighbour" policies in order to ensure the long-term vibrancy and prosperity of the ASEAN region;

**REITERATING** the importance of rules-based multilateral trading system that is equitable and that contributes towards the pursuit of development;

**REAFFIRMING** that ASEAN is a concert of Southeast Asian nations, bonded together in partnership in dynamic development and in a community of caring societies, committed to upholding cultural diversity and social harmony;

**DO HEREBY DECLARE THAT:**

1.   An ASEAN Community shall be established comprising three pillars, namely political and security cooperation, economic cooperation, and socio-cultural cooperation that are closely intertwined and mutually reinforcing for the purpose of ensuring durable peace, stability and shared prosperity in the region;

2.   ASEAN shall continue its efforts to ensure closer and mutually beneficial integration among its member states and among their peoples, and to promote regional peace and stability, security, development and prosperity with a view to realizing an ASEAN Community that is open, dynamic and resilient;

3.   ASEAN shall respond to the new dynamics within the respective ASEAN Member Countries and shall urgently and effectively address the challenge of

translating ASEAN cultural diversities and different economic levels into equitable development opportunity and prosperity, in an environment of solidarity, regional resilience and harmony;

4.    ASEAN shall nurture common values, such as habit of consultation to discuss political issues and the willingness to share information on matters of common concern, such as environmental degradation, maritime security cooperation, the enhancement of defense cooperation among ASEAN countries, develop a set of socio-political values and principles, and resolve to settle long-standing disputes through peaceful means;

5.    The Treaty of Amity and Cooperation in Southeast Asia (TAC) is the key code of conduct governing relations between states and a diplomatic instrument for the promotion of peace and stability in the region;

6.    The ASEAN Regional Forum (ARF) shall remain the primary forum in enhancing political and security cooperation in the Asia Pacific region, as well as the pivot in building peace and stability in the region. ASEAN shall enhance its role in further advancing the stages of cooperation within the ARF to ensure the security of the Asia Pacific region;

7.    ASEAN is committed to deepening and broadening its internal economic integration and linkages with the world economy to realize an ASEAN Economic Community through a bold, pragmatic and unified strategy;

8.    ASEAN shall further build on the momentum already gained in the ASEAN + 3 process so as to further draw synergies through broader and deeper cooperation in various areas;

9.    ASEAN shall build upon opportunities for mutually beneficial regional integration arising from its existing initiatives and those with partners, through enhanced trade and investment links as well as through IAI process and the RIA;

10.    ASEAN shall continue to foster a community of caring societies and promote a common regional identity;

**DO HEREBY ADOPT:**

The framework to achieve a dynamic, cohesive, resilient and integrated ASEAN Community:

## A. ASEAN SECURITY COMMUNITY (ASC)

1.    The ASEAN Security Community is envisaged to bring ASEAN's political and security cooperation to a higher plane to ensure that countries in the region

live at peace with one another and with the world at large in a just, democratic and harmonious environment. The ASEAN Security Community members shall rely exclusively on peaceful processes in the settlement of intra-regional differences and regard their security as fundamentally linked to one another and bound by geographic location, common vision and objectives.

2. The ASEAN Security Community, recognizing the sovereign right of the member countries to pursue their individual foreign policies and defense arrangements and taking into account the strong interconnections among political, economic and social realities, subscribes to the principle of comprehensive security as having broad political, economic, social and cultural aspects in consonance with the ASEAN Vision 2020 rather than to a defense pact, military alliance or a joint foreign policy.

3. ASEAN shall continue to promote regional solidarity and cooperation. Member Countries shall exercise their rights to lead their national existence free from outside interference in their internal affairs.

4. The ASEAN Security Community shall abide by the UN Charter and other principles of international law and uphold ASEAN's principles of non-interference, consensus-based decision-making, national and regional resilience, respect for national sovereignty, the renunciation of the threat or the use of force, and peaceful settlement of differences and disputes.

5. Maritime issues and concerns are transboundary in nature, and therefore shall be addressed regionally in holistic, integrated and comprehensive manner. Maritime cooperation between and among ASEAN member countries shall contribute to the evolution of the ASEAN Security Community.

6. Existing ASEAN political instruments such as the Declaration on ZOPFAN, the TAC, and the SEANWFZ Treaty shall continue to play a pivotal role in the area of confidence building measures, preventive diplomacy and the approaches to conflict resolution.

7. The High Council of the TAC shall be the important component in the ASEAN Security Community since it reflects ASEAN's commitment to resolve all differences, disputes and conflicts peacefully.

8. The ASEAN Security Community shall contribute to further promoting peace and security in the wider Asia Pacific region and reflect ASEAN's determination to move forward at a pace comfortable to all. In this regard, the ARF shall remain the main forum for regional security dialogue, with ASEAN as the primary driving force.

9.   The ASEAN Security Community is open and outward looking in respect of actively engaging ASEAN's friends and Dialogue Partners to promote peace and stability in the region, and shall build on the ARF to facilitate consultation and cooperation between ASEAN and its friends and Partners on regional security matters.

10.   The ASEAN Security Community shall fully utilize the existing institutions and mechanisms within ASEAN with a view to strengthening national and regional capacities to counter terrorism, drug trafficking, trafficking in persons and other transnational crimes; and shall work to ensure that the Southeast Asian Region remains free of all weapons of mass destruction. It shall enable ASEAN to demonstrate a greater capacity and responsibility of being the primary driving force of the ARF.

11.   The ASEAN Security Community shall explore enhanced cooperation with the United Nations as well as other international and regional bodies for the maintenance of international peace and security.

12.   ASEAN shall explore innovative ways to increase its security and establish modalities for the ASEAN Security Community, which include, inter alia, the following elements: norms-setting, conflict prevention, approaches to conflict resolution, and post-conflict peace building.

## B. ASEAN ECONOMIC COMMUNITY (AEC)

1.   The ASEAN Economic Community is the realisation of the end-goal of economic integration as outlined in the ASEAN Vision 2020, to create a stable, prosperous and highly competitive ASEAN economic region in which there is a free flow of goods, services, investment and a freer flow of capital, equitable economic development and reduced poverty and socio-economic disparities in year 2020.

2.   The ASEAN Economic Community is based on a convergence of interests among ASEAN members to deepen and broaden economic integration efforts through existing and new initiatives with clear timelines.

3.   The ASEAN Economic Community shall establish ASEAN as a single market and production base, turning the diversity that characterises the region into opportunities for business complementation making the ASEAN a more dynamic and stronger segment of the global supply chain. ASEAN's strategy shall consist of the integration of ASEAN and enhancing ASEAN's economic competitiveness. In moving towards the ASEAN Economic Community, ASEAN shall, *inter alia,* institute new mechanisms and measures to strengthen the implementation of its

existing economic initiatives including the ASEAN Free Trade Area (AFTA), ASEAN Framework Agreement on Services (AFAS) and ASEAN Investment Area (AIA); accelerate regional integration in the priority sectors; facilitate movement of business persons, skilled labour and talents; and strengthen the institutional mechanisms of ASEAN, including the improvement of the existing ASEAN Dispute Settlement Mechanism to ensure expeditious and legally binding resolution of any economic disputes. As a first step towards the realization of the ASEAN Economic Community, ASEAN shall implement the recommendations of the **High Level Task Force on ASEAN Economic Integration as annexed**.

4.    The ASEAN Economic Community shall ensure that deepening and broadening integration of ASEAN shall be accompanied by technical and development cooperation in order to address the development divide and accelerate the economic integration of Cambodia, Lao PDR, Myanmar and Viet Nam through IAI and RIA so that the benefits of ASEAN integration are shared and enable all ASEAN Member Countries to move forward in a unified manner.

5.    The realization of a fully integrated economic community requires implementation of both liberalization and cooperation measures. There is a need to enhance cooperation and integration activities in other areas. These will involve, among others, human resources development and capacity building; recognition of educational qualifications; closer consultation on macroeconomic and financial policies; trade financing measures; enhanced infrastructure and communications connectivity; development of electronic transactions through e-ASEAN; integrating industries across the region to promote regional sourcing; and enhancing private sector involvement.

## C. ASEAN SOCIO-CULTURAL COMMUNITY (ASCC)

1.    The ASEAN Socio-cultural Community, in consonance with the goal set by ASEAN Vision 2020, envisages a Southeast Asia bonded together in partnership as a community of caring societies.

2.    In line with the programme of action set by the 1976 Declaration of ASEAN Concord, the Community shall foster cooperation in social development aimed at raising the standard of living of disadvantaged groups and the rural population, and shall seek the active involvement of all sectors of society, in particular women, youth, and local communities.

3.    ASEAN shall ensure that its work force shall be prepared for, and benefit from, economic integration by investing more resources for basic and higher education, training, science and technology development, job creation, and social protection. The development and enhancement of human resources is a

key strategy for employment generation, alleviating poverty and socio-economic disparities, and ensuring economic growth with equity. ASEAN shall continue existing efforts to promote regional mobility and mutual recognition of professional credentials, talents, and skills development.

4.    ASEAN shall further intensify cooperation in the area of public health, including in the prevention and control of infectious diseases, such as HIV/AIDS and SARS, and support joint regional actions to increase access to affordable medicines. The security of the Community is enhanced when poverty and diseases are held in check, and the peoples of ASEAN are assured of adequate health care.

5.    The Community shall nurture talent and promote interaction among ASEAN scholars, writers, artists and media practitioners to help preserve and promote ASEAN's diverse cultural heritage while fostering regional identity as well as cultivating people's awareness of ASEAN.

6.    The Community shall intensify cooperation in addressing problems associated with population growth, unemployment, environmental degradation and transboundary pollution as well as disaster management in the region to enable individual members to fully realize their development potentials and to enhance the mutual ASEAN spirit.

We hereby pledge to our peoples our resolve and commitment to bring the ASEAN Community into reality and, for this purpose, task the concerned Ministers to implement this Declaration.

Done in Bali, Indonesia, on the Seventh Day of October in the Year Two Thousand and Three.

For Brunei Darussalam

HAJI HASSANAL BOLKIAH
Sultan of Brunei Darussalam


For the Republic of Indonesia

MEGAWATI SOEKARNOPUTRI
President


For Malaysia

DR. MAHATHIR BIN MOHAMAD
Prime Minister


For the Republic of the Philippines

GLORIA MACAPAGAL-ARROYO
President


For the Kingdom of Thailand

DR. THAKSIN SHINAWATRA
Prime Minister

For the Kingdom of Cambodia

SAMDECH HUN SEN
Prime Minister


For the Lao People's Democratic
Republic

BOUNNHANG VORACHITH
Prime Minister


For the Union of Myanmar

GENERAL KHIN NYUNT
Prime Minister


For the Republic of Singapore

GOH CHOK TONG
Prime Minister


For the Socialist Republic of Viet Nam

PHAN VAN KHAI
Prime Minister

# Appendix II

## INTRODUCTION

1.  The realization of a fully integrated economic community requires implementation of both liberalization and cooperation measures. The Task Force while focusing its recommendations relating to liberalization and facilitation measures in the area of trade in good, services and investment, acknowledges on the need to enhance cooperation and integration activities in other areas. These will involve among others, human resource development and capacity building; recognition of educational qualifications; closer consultations on macroeconomic and financial policies; trade financing measures; enhanced infrastructure and communications connectivity; development of electronic transactions through e-ASEAN; integrating industries across the region to promote regional sourcing; and enhancing private sector involvement.

## ASEAN ECONOMIC COMMUNITY

2.  As a step towards the realization of ASEAN Economic Community for trade in goods, services and investment, the HLTF took into account the experience of other Regional Trading Arrangements (RTAs), ASEAN's own experience, the development perspective in ASEAN and also the views contained in the following documents:

    (i)   ASEAN Vision 2020, the Hanoi Plan of Action (HPA), and RIA;
    (ii)  ASEAN Competitiveness Study;
    (iii) ASEAN Economic Community: Concept Paper by ISEAS; and
    (iv) ASEAN ISIS: Towards an ASEAN Economic Community.

3.  The HLTF is of the view that the elements of the AEC in the area of goods, services and investment have been elaborated in ASEAN Vision 2020, HPA and RIA, and recommends that the AEC should be:

(i)   The end-goal of economic integration as outlined in the ASEAN Vision 2020;
(ii)  Characterized as a single market and production base, with free flow of goods, services, investment and skilled labour, and freer flow of capital by 2020; and
(iii) Approached on a progressive basis with clear timelines by strengthening existing initiatives and building new initiatives to enhance economic integration.

## RECOMMENDATIONS

4.   Recognizing that not all ASEAN member countries can meet the recommended deadlines, the HLTF recommends that flexibility be allowed in its implementation to enable those member countries that are ready to proceed first.

## I. CURRENT ECONOMIC COOPERATION INITIATIVES

5.   The HLTF recommends that cooperation under the current economic initiatives be further strengthened in the following areas:

## A. Trade in Goods

(i)   By end-2004, finalize the improvement to the CEPT Scheme Rules of Origin (ROO) by:

   • Making it more transparent, predictable and standardized and taking into account the best practices of other RTAs including the WTO ROO; and
   • Adopting substantial transformation as alternative criteria for conferring origin status.

(ii)  Ensure transparency on Non-Tariff Measures (NTMs) and eliminate those that are barriers to trade:

   • Establish ASEAN Database of NTMs by mid-2004;
   • Set clear criteria to identify measures that are classified as barriers to trade by mid-2005;
   • Set a clear and definitive work programme for the removal of the barriers by 2005; and
   • Adopt the WTO agreements on Technical Barriers to Trade; Sanitary and Phyto-Sanitary and Import Licensing Procedures and develop implementation guidelines appropriate for ASEAN by end-2004.

## Customs

(i)   Ensure full implementation of the Green Lane system for CEPT products at entry points of all Member Countries by 2004;

(ii)  Adopt WTO agreement on Customs Valuation and develop implementation guidelines appropriate for ASEAN by end-2004;

(iii) Adopt service commitment (client charter) by ASEAN customs authorities; and

(iv)  Adopt the Single Window approach including the electronic processing of trade documents at national and regional level.

## Standards

(i)   Accelerate the completion and implementation of the Mutual Recognition Arrangements (MRAs) for the five identified priority sectors (electrical and electronic equipment, cosmetics, pharmaceuticals, telecommunications equipment and prepared foodstuff) within 2004/2005; and other sectors with significant potential for trade;

(ii)  Set specific targets for the harmonization of standards and technical regulations to trade focusing on sectors with significant trade value and those with potential for trade in the future; and

(iii) Develop ASEAN technical regulations, where possible, for national applications.

# B. Trade in Services

(i)   Set clear targets and schedules of services liberalization for each sector and each round towards achieving free flow of trade in services; and AEM to provide specific mandate in every round of services negotiations. The end date to achieve free flow of trade in services earlier than 2020;

(ii)  Accelerate services liberalization in specific sectors earlier than end-date by countries which are ready, through the application of the ASEAN-X formula;

(iii) Complete MRAs for qualifications in major professional services by 2008 to facilitate free movement of professional/skilled labor/talents in ASEAN;

(iv)  Promote the use of ASEAN professional services through the establishment of a "Professional Exchange" by 2008;

(v)   Recognise the AEM as the coordinator for services liberalization across all sectors; and

(vi)  Each country to be represented by senior officials who are authorized to negotiate on behalf of the government.

## C. Investment

(i)   Speed up the opening of sectors currently in the sensitive list to TEL, using the ASEAN-X formula, beginning 2004;

(ii)  Encourage and promote companies to relocate within ASEAN and where appropriate, special incentives should be given;

(iii) Institute a mechanism to monitor the specific activities and timelines undertaken by each country vis-à-vis their submitted planned actions/activities on annual basis;

(iv)  Establish a network of ASEAN free trade zones (FTZs) so that companies could structure their manufacturing processes across different ASEAN countries to take advantage of their comparative strengths; and in the process increase intra-ASEAN trade and investment. Special marketing efforts should be undertaken for ASEAN-based companies; and

(v)   Undertake more effective joint ASEAN facilitation and promotion measures and develop new sources of inward FDI, particularly from potential countries such as China, India and ROK.

## D. Intellectual Property Rights (IPRs)

6.   ASEAN IPR cooperation beyond trademarks and patents by including cooperation in copyrights information exchange and enforcement by 2004.

## E. Capital Mobility

7.   To facilitate trade and investment flows, expedite the implementation of the Roadmap for Integration of ASEAN in Finance.

## II. NEW INITIATIVES AND MEASURES

*Priority Integration Sectors*

8.   The Special Informal AEM agreed to accelerate 11 priority sectors for integration to be coordinated by the following countries.

(i)    Indonesia: Wood-Based Products and Automotives;

(ii)   Malaysia: Rubber-Based Products; Textiles and Apparels;

(iii)  Myanmar: Agro-Based Products and Fisheries;

(iv)   Philippines: Electronics;

(v)    Singapore: e-ASEAN and Healthcare; and

(vi)   Thailand: Air Travel and Tourism

9. The approach recommended for the integration of these priority sectors be premised on:

(i) Combine the economic strengths of ASEAN Member Countries for regional advantage;

(ii) Facilitate and promote intra-ASEAN investments;

(iii) Improve the condition to attract and retain manufacturing and other economic activities within the region;

(iv) Promote out-sourcing programme within ASEAN; and

(v) Promote the development of "Made in ASEAN" products and services.

10. Roadmap should be developed for each of the priority sectors and be implemented with the active involvement of the private sector, beginning 2004.

11. Possible measures proposed for the goods sector:

(i) Zero internal tariffs;

(ii) Immediate removal of barriers to trade;

(iii) Faster customs clearance and simplified customs procedures; and

(iv) Accelerated development of MRAs and harmonization of products standards and technical regulations.

12. Integration of services sectors be implemented through:

(i) Accelerated liberalization of these priority sectors by 2010;

(ii) Accelerated development of MRAs; and

(iii) Promote joint ventures and cooperation, including in third country markets.

13. Facilitate mobility of business people and tourists through:

(i) Visa exemption for intra-ASEAN travel by ASEAN nationals by 2005;

(ii) Harmonizing the procedures for issuing visas to international travelers in ASEAN by 2004; and

(iii) Developing ASEAN agreement to facilitate movement of business persons and skilled labour and talents by 2005.

## III. INSTITUTIONAL STRENGTHENING

14. To streamline the decision-making process and ensure effective implementation of all ASEAN economic initiatives, the following measures are recommended:

(i)   Re-affirm the AEM as the coordinator of all ASEAN economic integration and cooperation issues;

(ii)  Issues of policy in nature to be resolved by AEM/AFTA Council/AIA Council;

(iii) Technical/operational issues to be resolved by SEOM and the various committees/working groups;

(iv)  Decision-making process by economic bodies to be made by consensus, and where there is no consensus, ASEAN to consider other options with the objective of expediting the decision-making process.

(v)   By end-2004, establish an effective system to ensure proper implementation of all economic agreements and expeditious resolution of any disputes. The new system should provide for advisory, consultative, and adjudicatory mechanisms as follows:

- Establish a legal unit within the ASEAN Secretariat;
  *(Advisory — the legal unit will provide legal advice on trade disputes)*
- Establish the ASEAN Consultation to Solve Trade and Investment Issues (ACT);
  *(Consultative — the ACT is the ASEAN equivalent of the EU SOLVIT mechanism to provide quick resolution to operational problems)*
- Establish the ASEAN Compliance Body (ACB); and
  *(Adjudication — modeled after the WTO Textile Monitoring Body and make use of peer pressure)*
- Enhanced ASEAN DSM to make it more practical.
  *(Adjudication — amend the ASEAN DSM to ensure expeditious and legally binding decision in resolving trade disputes)*

The proposed concept, elements and flow chart of the new system appear as **ANNEX 1**.

(vi)  Enhance the capability of the ASEAN Secretariat to conduct research and analytical studies related to trade, investment and finance.

## IV. OUTREACH

15. To promote better appreciation and understanding of ASEAN economic issues among business/investor community and public sector agencies, the HLTF recommends the following:

(i)   Conduct out-reach programmes annually at both national and regional level; and

(ii)  Consult regularly with private sector representatives at national and regional level to address issues of concern/interest relating to the implementation of ASEAN economic initiatives.

## V. DEVELOPMENT AND TECHNICAL COOPERATION

16. The recommendations to address the development divide and accelerate economic integration of CLMV:

(i)   Expand the coverage of the AISP products; and
(ii)  Implement IAI projects through mobilization of resources from within ASEAN.

## CONCLUSION

17. The HLTF recommends that a review be made after one year of its implementation and the Secretary General of ASEAN to submit an annual progress report of its implementation to the AEM.

ANNEX 1

# MECHANISM OF THE DISPUTE SETTLEMENT SYSTEM

## ADVISORY MECHANISM

## ASEAN Consultation to Solve Trade and Investment Issues (ACT)

(i) The ACT is adapted from the EU SOLVIT mechanism. It is a network of government agencies (one from each country) to allow the private sector to cut through red tape and achieve speedy resolution of operational problems encountered, thus helping to create a pro business environment in ASEAN.

(ii) Private individuals and businesses faced with operational problems related to countries' ASEAN commitments, either at home or in other ASEAN countries, can highlight these problems to the ACT in their country (Host ACT). For problems encountered within the home country, the Host ACT will direct the problem to the appropriate government agencies, and ensure that a proposed solution is sent to the individuals/businesses within 30 calendar days.

(iii) For problems encountered in other ASEAN countries, the Host ACT will forward the problem to the other countries' ACT (Lead ACT). The Lead ACT will be responsible for directing the problem to the appropriate government agencies in its country, and ensuring that a proposed solution is sent to the individuals/businesses via the Host ACT within 30 calendar days. To minimise delays, communication between Host and Lead ACTs should be via electronic means, for instance an online database accessible to all member countries.

(iv) If the proposed solution does not resolve the problem highlighted, the private individuals/businesses can request that their government raise this issue to the other dispute settlement mechanisms described below.

## ASEAN Legal Unit

(i) The ASEAN Legal Unit will be staffed by qualified lawyers specialising in trade laws employed by the ASEAN Secretariat. The unit will offer legal interpretation/ advice on potential trade dispute issues upon request from countries. The advice is purely advisory and non-binding in nature.

(ii)  The ASEAN Legal Unit would play a useful role in screening out issues that are operational/technical in nature which could be resolved through bilateral consultations, rather than being surfaced to the ASEAN Compliance Monitoring Body or the Enhanced ASEAN Dispute Settlement Mechanism. The ASEAN Legal Unit will also be responsible for providing legal advice and secretariat support to the ASEAN Compliance Monitoring Body and enhanced ASEAN Dispute Settlement Mechanism.

## CONSULTATIVE MECHANISM

## ASEAN Compliance Monitoring Body (ACMB)

(i)  The ACMB is modelled after the Textile Monitoring Body of the WTO, and makes use of peer adjudication, which is less legalistic and offers a speedier channel, to help countries resolve their disputes.

(ii)  In cases of non-compliance by one or more ASEAN Member Country/ Countries in any ASEAN economic integration agreement, ACMB members from countries not involved in the dispute will upon request, review and issue findings on the case within a stipulated timeframe. The case findings of the ACB are not legally-binding. However, any opinion pointing to non-compliance should lead to the offending ASEAN Member Country/Countries to seriously consider measures to rectify the non-compliance. Moreover the ACMB's findings would be tabled as inputs to the DSM should the case be raised to the DSM.

(iii)  Subject to agreement by both Parties, Member Countries who do not wish to avail of the ACMB after going through the ACT can go directly to the ASEAN DSM panel.

(iv)  AEM had earlier directed SEOM to work out a Terms of Reference for this monitoring body.

## Conciliation and Mediation Processes

(i)  Upon mutual voluntary agreement, member countries can at any time, engage in conciliation and mediation procedures to resolve their dispute before it is surfaced for adjudication at the enhanced ASEAN Dispute Settlement Mechanism.

(ii)  Proceedings under these conciliation and mediation procedures, including respective positions taken by parties to the dispute during the proceedings, shall be confidential.

(iii) The ASEAN Secretary General may, acting in an ex officio capacity, offer good offices, conciliation and mediation procedures.

## ENFORCEMENT MECHANISM

### Enhanced ASEAN Dispute Settlement Mechanism (DSM)

(i)   To ensure that binding decisions can be made based solely on legal considerations, changes should be made to the procedures of the existing ASEAN DSM to depoliticise the entire process.

(ii)   The enhanced ASEAN DSM would be modeled after the WTO DSM, which have already established a proven track record in resolving trade disputes. It would include the following key features: (i) having panels of three independent professionals from countries not involved in the disputes (including non-ASEAN countries) to rule on the disputes and administer the appellate process. To ensure de-politicisation of the processes, ASEAN should replace the AEM with an appellate body comprising of well-qualified, independent and experienced professionals as the appeal body for the panels' decisions, and adopt the existing WTO DSM panel selection procedures, including the listing of qualified individuals who can serve as panelists and members of the appellate body (maintained by the WTO Secretariat); (ii) strict and detailed procedures and timeline governing each stage of the dispute settlement process (adopted from the WTO DSM procedure) to ensure speedy progress towards a fair outcome, and (iii) effective mechanisms, including the possibility of imposing sanctions on non-compliant countries, to ensure full implementation of the DSM rulings.

# Appendix III

## ⠂ ASEAN VISION 2020

We, the Heads of State/Government of the Association of Southeast Asian Nations, gather today in Kuala Lumpur to reaffirm our commitment to the aims and purposes of the Association as set forth in the Bangkok Declaration of 8 August 1967, in particular to promote regional cooperation in Southeast Asia in the spirit of equality and partnership and thereby contribute towards peace, progress and prosperity in the region.

We in ASEAN have created a community of Southeast Asian nations at peace with one another and at peace with the world, rapidly achieving prosperity for our peoples and steadily improving their lives. Our rich diversity has provided the strength and inspiration to us to help one another foster a strong sense of community.

We are now a market of around 500 million people with a combined gross domestic product of US$600 billion. We have achieved considerable results in the economic field, such as high economic growth, stability and significant poverty alleviation over the past few years. Members have enjoyed substantial trade and investment flows from significant liberalisation measures.

We resolve to build upon these achievements.

Now, as we approach the 21st century, thirty years after the birth of ASEAN, we gather to chart a vision for ASEAN on the basis of today's realities and prospects in the decades leading to the Year 2020.

That vision is of ASEAN as a concert of Southeast Asian nations, outward looking, living in peace, stability and prosperity, bonded together in partnership in dynamic development and in a community of caring societies.

### A CONCERT OF SOUTHEAST ASIAN NATIONS

We envision the ASEAN region to be, in 2020, in full reality, a Zone of Peace, Freedom and Neutrality, as envisaged in the Kuala Lumpur Declaration of 1971.

ASEAN shall have, by the year 2020, established a peaceful and stable Southeast Asia where each nation is at peace with itself and where the causes for conflict have been eliminated, through abiding respect for justice and the rule of law and through the strengthening of national and regional resilience.

We envision a Southeast Asia where territorial and other disputes are resolved by peaceful means.

We envision the Treaty of Amity and Cooperation in Southeast Asia functioning fully as a binding code of conduct for our governments and peoples, to which other states with interests in the region adhere.

We envision a Southeast Asia free from nuclear weapons, with all the Nuclear Weapon States committed to the purposes of the Southeast Asia Nuclear Weapons Free Zone Treaty through their adherence to its Protocol. We also envision our region free from all other weapons of mass destruction.

We envision our rich human and natural resources contributing to our development and shared prosperity.

We envision the ASEAN Regional Forum as an established means for confidence-building and preventive diplomacy and for promoting conflict-resolution.

We envision a Southeast Asia where our mountains, rivers and seas no longer divide us but link us together in friendship, cooperation and commerce.

We see ASEAN as an effective force for peace, justice and moderation in the Asia-Pacific and in the world.

## A PARTNERSHIP IN DYNAMIC DEVELOPMENT

We resolve to chart a new direction towards the year 2020 called, ASEAN 2020: Partnership in Dynamic Development which will forge closer economic integration within ASEAN.

We reiterate our resolve to enhance ASEAN economic cooperation through economic development strategies, which are in line with the aspiration of our respective peoples, which put emphasis on sustainable and equitable growth, and enhance national as well as regional resilience.

We pledge to sustain ASEAN's high economic performance by building upon the foundation of our existing cooperation efforts, consolidating our achievements, expanding our collective efforts and enhancing mutual assistance.

We commit ourselves to moving towards closer cohesion and economic integration, narrowing the gap in the level of development among Member Countries, ensuring that the multilateral trading system remains fair and open, and achieving global competitiveness.

We will create a stable, prosperous and highly competitive ASEAN Economic Region in which there is a free flow of goods, services and investments, a freer flow of capital, equitable economic development and reduced poverty and socio-economic disparities.

We resolve, *inter-alia*, to undertake the following:

- maintain regional macroeconomic and financial stability by promoting closer consultations in macroeconomic and financial policies.
- advance economic integration and cooperation by undertaking the following general strategies: fully implement the ASEAN Free Trade Area and accelerate liberalization of trade in services, realise the ASEAN Investment Area by 2010 and free flow of investments by 2020; intensify and expand sub-regional cooperation in existing and new sub-regional growth areas; further consolidate and expand extra-ASEAN regional linkages for mutual benefit cooperate to strengthen the multilateral trading system, and reinforce the role of the business sector as the engine of growth.
- promote a modern and competitive small and medium enterprises (SME) sector in ASEAN which will contribute to the industrial development and efficiency of the region.
- accelerate the free flow of professional and other services in the region.
- promote financial sector liberalisation and closer cooperation in money and capital market, tax, insurance and customs matters as well as closer consultations in macroeconomic and financial policies.
- accelerate the development of science and technology including information technology by establishing a regional information technology network and centers of excellence for dissemination of and easy access to data and information.
- establish interconnecting arrangements in the field of energy and utilities for electricity, natural gas and water within ASEAN through the ASEAN Power Grid and a Trans-ASEAN Gas Pipeline and Water Pipeline, and promote cooperation in energy efficiency and conservation, as well as the development of new and renewable energy resources.
- enhance food security and international competitiveness of food, agricultural and forest products, to make ASEAN a leading producer of these products, and promote the forestry sector as a model in forest management, conservation and sustainable development.
- meet the ever increasing demand for improved infrastructure and communications by developing an integrated and harmonized trans-

ASEAN transportation network and harnessing technology advances in telecommunication and information technology, especially in linking the planned information highways/multimedia corridors in ASEAN, promoting open sky policy, developing multi-modal transport, facilitating goods in transit and integrating telecommunications networks through greater interconnectivity, coordination of frequencies and mutual recognition of equipment-type approval procedures.

- enhance human resource development in all sectors of the economy through quality education, upgrading of skills and capabilities and training.
- work towards a world class standards and conformance system that will provide a harmonised system to facilitate the free flow of ASEAN trade while meeting health, safety and environmental needs.
- use the ASEAN Foundation as one of the instruments to address issues of unequal economic development, poverty and socioeconomic disparities.
- promote an ASEAN customs partnership for world class standards and excellence in efficiency, professionalism and service, and uniformity through harmonised procedures, to promote trade and investment and to protect the health and well-being of the ASEAN community,
- enhance intra-ASEAN trade and investment in the mineral sector and to contribute towards a technologically competent ASEAN through closer networking and sharing of information on mineral and geosciences as well as to enhance cooperation and partnership with dialogue partners to facilitate the development and transfer of technology in the mineral sector, particularly in the downstream research and the geosciences and to develop appropriate mechanism for these.

## A COMMUNITY OF CARING SOCIETIES

We envision the entire Southeast Asia to be, by 2020, an ASEAN community conscious of its ties of history, aware of its cultural heritage and bound by a common regional identity.

We see vibrant and open ASEAN societies consistent with their respective national identities, where all people enjoy equitable access to opportunities for total human development regardless of gender, race, religion, language, or social and cultural background.

We envision a socially cohesive and caring ASEAN where hunger, malnutrition, deprivation and poverty are no longer basic problems, where strong families as the basic units of society tend to their members particularly the children, youth, women and elderly; and where the civil society is empowered and gives special attention to the disadvantaged, disabled and marginalized and where social justice and the rule of law reign.

We see well before 2020 a Southeast Asia free of illicit drugs, free of their production, processing, trafficking and use.

We envision a technologically competitive ASEAN competent in strategic and enabling technologies, with an adequate pool of technologically qualified and trained manpower, and strong networks of scientific and technological institutions and centers of excellence.

We envision a clean and green ASEAN with fully established mechanisms for sustainable development to ensure the protection of the region's environment, the sustainability of its natural resources, and the high quality of life of its peoples.

We envision the evolution in Southeast Asia of agreed rules of behaviour and cooperative measures to deal with problems that can be met only on a regional scale, including environmental pollution and degradation, drug trafficking, trafficking in women and children, and other transnational crimes.

We envision our nations being governed with the consent and greater participation of the people with its focus on the welfare and dignity of the human person and the good of the community.

We resolve to develop and strengthen ASEAN's institutions and mechanisms to enable ASEAN to realize the vision and respond to the challenges of the coming century. We also see the need for a strengthened ASEAN Secretariat with an enhanced role to support the realization of our vision.

## AN OUTWARD-LOOKING ASEAN

We see an outward-looking ASEAN playing a pivotal role in the international fora, and advancing ASEAN's common interests. We envision ASEAN having an intensified relationship with its Dialogue Partners and other regional organisations based on equal partnership and mutual respect.

## CONCLUSION

We pledge to our peoples our determination and commitment to bringing this ASEAN Vision for the Year 2020 into reality.

Kuala Lumpur
15 December 1997

# Appendix IV

## DECLARATION OF ASEAN CONCORD
## INDONESIA, 24 FEBRUARY 1976

The President of the Republic of Indonesia, the Prime Minister of Malaysia, the President of the Republic of the Philippines, the Prime Minister of the Republic of Singapore and the Prime Minister of the Kingdom of Thailand:

**REAFFIRM** their commitment to the Declarations of Bandung, Bangkok and Kuala Lumpur, and the Charter of the United Nations;

**ENDEAVOUR** to promote peace, progress, prosperity and the welfare of the peoples of member states;

**UNDERTAKE** to consolidate the achievements of ASEAN and expand ASEAN cooperation in the economic, social, cultural and political fields;

**DO HEREBY DECLARE:**

ASEAN cooperation shall take into account, among others, the following objectives and principles in the pursuit of political stability:

1.   The stability of each member state and of the ASEAN region is an essential contribution to international peace and security. Each member state resolves to eliminate threats posed by subversion to its stability, thus strengthening national and ASEAN resilience.

2.   Member states, individually and collectively, shall take active steps for the early establishment of the Zone of Peace, Freedom and Neutrality.

3.   The elimination of poverty, hunger, disease and illiteracy is a primary concern of member states. They shall therefore intensify cooperation in economic and social development, with particular emphasis on the promotion of social justice and on the improvement of the living standards of their peoples.

4.   Natural disasters and other major calamities can retard the pace of development of member states. They shall extend, within their capabilities, assistance for relief of member states in distress.

5.   Member states shall take cooperative action in their national and regional development programmes, utilizing as far as possible the resources available in the ASEAN region to broaden the complementarity of their respective economies.

6.   Member states, in the spirit of ASEAN solidarity, shall rely exclusively on peaceful processes in the settlement of intra-regional differences.

7.   Member states shall strive, individually and collectively, to create conditions conducive to the promotion of peaceful cooperation among the nations of Southeast Asia on the basis of mutual respect and mutual benefit.

8.   Member states shall vigorously develop an awareness of regional identity and exert all efforts to create a strong ASEAN community, respected by all and respecting all nations on the basis of mutually advantageous relationships, and in accordance with the principles of selfdetermination, sovereign equality and non-interference in the internal affairs of nations.

**AND DO HEREBY ADOPT**

The following programme of action as a framework for ASEAN cooperation.

## A. POLITICAL

1.   Meeting of the Heads of Government of the member states as and when necessary.

2.   Signing of the Treaty of Amity and Cooperation in Southeast Asia.

3.   Settlement of intra-regional disputes by peaceful means as soon as possible.

4.   Immediate consideration of initial steps towards recognition of and respect for the Zone of Peace, Freedom and Neutrality wherever possible.

5.   Improvement of ASEAN machinery to strengthen political cooperation.

6.   Study on how to develop judicial cooperation including the possibility of an ASEAN Extradition Treaty.

7. Strengthening of political solidarity by promoting the harmonization of views, coordinating position and, where possible and desirable, taking common actions.

## B. ECONOMIC

1. Cooperation on Basic Commodities, particularly Food and Energy

    i)   Member states shall assist each other by according priority to the supply of the individual country's needs in critical circumstances, and priority to the acquisition of exports from member states, in respect of basic commodities, particularly food and energy.

    ii)  Member states shall also intensify cooperation in the production of basic commodities particularly food and energy in the individual member states of the region.

2. Industrial Cooperation

    i)   Member states shall cooperate to establish large-scale ASEAN industrial plants particularly to meet regional requirements of essential commodities.

    ii)  Priority shall be given to projects which utilize the available materials in the member states, contribute to the increase of food production, increase foreign exchange earnings or save foreign exchange and create employment.

3. Cooperation in Trade

    i)   Member states shall cooperate in the fields of trade in order to promote development and growth of new production and trade and to improve the trade structures of individual states and among countries of ASEAN conducive to further development and to safeguard and increase their foreign exchange earnings and reserves.

    ii)  Member states shall progress towards the establishment of preferential trading arrangements as a long term objective on a basis deemed to be at any particular time appropriate through rounds of negotiations subject to the unanimous agreement of member states.

    iii) The expansion of trade among member states shall be facilitated through cooperation on basic commodities, particularly in food and energy and through cooperation in ASEAN industrial projects.

    iv)  Member states shall accelerate joint efforts to improve access to markets outside ASEAN for their raw material and finished products by seeking the elimination of all trade barriers in those markets, developing new usage for these products and in adopting common approaches and actions in dealing with regional groupings and individual economic powers.

v)   Such efforts shall also lead to cooperation in the field of technology and production methods in order to increase the production and to improve the quality of export products, as well as to develop new export products with a view to diversifying exports.

4.   Joint Approach to International Commodity Problems and Other World Economic Problems

i)   The principle of ASEAN cooperation on trade shall also be reflected on a priority basis in joint approaches to international commodity problems and other world economic problems such as the reform of international trading system, the reform on international monetary system and transfer of real resources, in the United Nations and other relevant multilateral fora, with a view to contributing to the establishment of the New International Economic Order.

ii)  Member states shall give priority to the stabilisation and increase of export earnings of those commodities produced and exported by them through commodity agreements including bufferstock schemes and other means.

5.   Machinery for Economic Cooperation

Ministerial meetings on economic matters shall be held regularly or as deemed necessary in order to:

i)    formulate recommendations for the consideration of Governments of member states for the strengthening of ASEAN economic cooperation;

ii)   review the coordination and implementation of agreed ASEAN programmes and projects on economic cooperation;

iii)  exchange views and consult on national development plans and policies as a step towards harmonizing regional development; and

iv)   perform such other relevant functions as agreed upon by the member Governments.

## C. SOCIAL

1.   Cooperation in the field of social development, with emphasis on the well being of the low-income group and of the rural population, through the expansion of opportunities for productive employment with fair remuneration.

2.   Support for the active involvement of all sectors and levels of the ASEAN communities, particularly the women and youth, in development efforts.

3.   Intensification and expansion of existing cooperation in meeting the problems of population growth in the ASEAN region, and where possible, formulation of new strategies in collaboration with appropriate international agencies.

4.   Intensification of cooperation among members states as well as with the relevant international bodies in the prevention and eradication of the abuse of narcotics and the illegal trafficking of drugs.

## D. CULTURAL AND INFORMATION

1.   Introduction of the study of ASEAN, its member states and their national languages as part of the curricula of schools and other institutions of learning in the member states.

2.   Support of ASEAN scholars, writers, artists and mass media representatives to enable them to play an active role in fostering a sense of regional identity and fellowship.

3.   Promotion of Southeast Asian studies through closer collaboration among national institutes.

## E. SECURITY

Continuation of cooperation on a non-ASEAN basis between the member states in security matters in accordance with their mutual needs and interests.

## F. IMPROVEMENT OF ASEAN MACHINERY

1.   Signing of the Agreement on the Establishment of the ASEAN Secretariat.

2.   Regular review of the ASEAN organizational structure with a view to improving its effectiveness.

3.   Study of the desirability of a new constitutional framework for ASEAN.

DONE, at Denpasar, Bali, this Twenty-Fourth Day of February in the year One Thousand Nine Hundred and Seventy-Six.

For the Republic
of Indonesia:

SOEHARTO
President

For Malaysia:

DATUK HUSEIN ONN
Prime Minister

For the Republic
of the Philippines:

FERDINAND E. MARCOS

For the Republic
of Singapore:

LEE KUAN YEW
Prime Minister

For the Kingdom
of Thailand:

KUKRIT PRAMOJ
Prime Minister

# SELECTED REFERENCES
# AND FURTHER READINGS

## BOOKS AND ARTICLES

Acharya, Amitav. "The Association of Southeast Asian Nations: 'Security Community or Defence Community'?". *Pacific Affairs* 64, no. 2 (1991): 159–78.
_____. *A New Regional Order in South-east Asia: ASEAN in the Post-Cold War Era.* Adelphi Paper 279. London: International Institute for Strategic Studies, 1993.
_____. "Regional Approaches to Security in the Third World: Lessons and Prospects". In *The South at the End of the Twentieth Century*, edited by Larry A. Swatuk and Timothy M. Shaw, pp. 79–94. London: Macmillan, 1994.
_____. "Collective Identity and Conflict Management in Southeast Asia". In *Security Communities*, edited by Emanuel Adler and Michael Barnett, pp. 198–227. Cambridge: Cambridge University Press, 1998.
_____. *Constructing a Security Community in Southeast Asia: ASEAN and the Problem of Regional Order.* London and New York: Routledge, 2001.
Adler, Emanuel and Michael Barnett, eds. 1998. *Security Communities.* Cambridge: Cambridge University Press, 1998.
Alagappa, Muthiah (1993). "Regionalism and the Quest for Security: ASEAN and the Cambodian Conflict". *Journal of International Affairs* 46, no. 2 (Winter 1993): 439–68.
_____. "Regionalism and Conflict Management: A Framework of Analysis". *Review of International Studies* 21 (1995): 359–97.
_____. "Regional Institutions, The UN and International Security". *Third World Quarterly* 18, no. 3 (1997): 421–41.
_____, ed. *Asian Security Practice: Material and Ideational Influences.* Stanford, CA: Stanford University Press, 1998.
Anand, R.P. and Purificacion Quisumbing, eds. *ASEAN Identity, Development and Culture.* Quezon City: University of the Philippines Law Center and East-West Center Culture Learning Institute, 1981.
Antolik, Michael. *ASEAN and the Diplomacy of Accommodation.* Armonk, NY: M.E. Sharpe, 1990.
Ashley, Richard K. "Foreign Policy as Political Performance". *International Studies Notes* (1988).
Asia Pacific Economic Co-operation. *APEC Handbook.* Singapore: APEC Secretariat, 1997.

Azar, Edward E. and John W. Burton, eds. *International Conflict Resolution: Theory and Practice*. Boulder, CO: Lynne Rienner Publishers, 1986.

Ball, Desmond. "CSCAP: Its Future Place in the Regional Security Architecture". In *Managing Security and Peace in the Asia-Pacific*, edited by Bunn Negara and Cheah Siew Ean, pp. 289–325. Kuala Lumpur: Institute of Strategic and International Studies, 1996.

———. *The Council for Security Cooperation in the Asia-Pacific: Its Record and Its Prospects*. Canberra Papers on Strategy and Defence No. 139. Canberra: Strategic and Defence Studies Centre, Research School of Pacific and Asian Studies, 2001.

——— and Amitav Acharya, eds. *The Next Stage: Preventive Diplomacy and Security Cooperation in the Asia-Pacific Region*. Canberra Papers on Strategy and Defence No. 191. Canberra: Strategic and Defence Studies Centre, Research School of Pacific and Asian Studies, 1999.

Barnett, Michael. "Partners in Peace? The UN, Regional Organisations and Peacekeeping". *Review of International Studies* 21 (1995): 411–33.

Bateman, Sam and Stephen Bates, eds. *Calming the Waters: Initiatives for Asia Pacific Maritime Cooperation*. Canberra Papers on Strategy and Defence No. 114. Canberra: Strategic and Defence Studies Centre, Research School of Pacific and Asian Studies, 1996.

———. *The Seas Unite: Maritime Cooperation in the Asia Pacific Region*. Canberra: Strategic and Defence Studies Centre, 1996.

Boutros-Ghali, Boutros. *An Agenda for Peace: Preventive Diplomacy, Peacemaking and Peacekeeping*. New York: United Nations Press, 1992.

Broinowski, Alison, ed. *Understanding ASEAN*. London: Macmillan Press, 1982.

Bunbongkarn, Suchit. "Civil Society in Thailand". *Governance and Civil Society in the Global Age*, edited by Tadashi Yamamoto, pp. 66–90. Japan: Japan Center for International Exchange, 2001.

Bunn Negara and Cheah Siew Ean, eds. *Managing Security and Peace in the Asia-Pacific*. Kuala Lumpur: Institute of Strategic and International Studies, 1996.

Busse, Nikolas. "Constructivism and the Southeast Asian Security". *Pacific Review* 12, no. 1 (1999): 39–60.

Buszynski, Leszek. "Southeast Asia in the Post-Cold War Era: Regionalism and Security". *Asian Survey* XXXII, no. 9 (1992): 830–47.

Buzan, Barry, Ole Waever, and Jaap de Wilde. *Security: A New Framework of Analysis*. Boulder, CO: Lynne Rienner Publishers, 1998.

Caballero-Anthony, Mely. "Mechanisms of Dispute Settlement: The ASEAN Experience". *Contemporary Southeast Asia* 20, no. 1 (1998): 38–66.

———. "Challenges to Southeast Asian Security Cooperation". In *An Asia-Pacific Security Crisis? New Challenges to Regional Stability*, edited by Guy Wilson-Roberts, pp. 51–65. Wellington: Centre for Strategic Studies, 1999.

——— and Mohamed Jawhar Hassan, eds. *Beyond the Crisis: Challenges and Opportunities*. Kuala Lumpur: Institute of Strategic and International Studies, 2000.

_____, eds. *The Asia Pacific in the New Millennium*. Kuala Lumpur: Institute of Strategic and International Studies, 2001.

Cady, John. *Southeast Asia: Its Historical Development*. New York: McGraw-Hill, 1964.

Capie, David and Paul Evans. *Asia-Pacific Security Lexicon*. Singapore: Institute of Southeast Asian Studies, 2002.

Chanda, Nayan. *Brother Enemy: The War After the War*. New York: Harcourt Brace, Jovanovich, 1986.

Chandler, David. "Strategies for Survival in Kampuchea". *Current History* (April 1985), pp. 141–53.

_____. "Cambodia in 1984: Historical Patterns Re-asserted". *Southeast Asian Affairs 1985*, pp. 177–86. Singapore: Institute of Southeast Asian Studies, 1985.

Chin Kin Wah. *The Defense of Malaysia and Singapore: The Transformation of a Security System, 1957–1971*. Cambridge: Cambridge University Press, 1983.

_____. "ASEAN: Consolidation and Institutional Change". *Pacific Review* 8, no. 3 (1995): 424–39.

Commission on Human Security. *Human Security Now: Protection and Empowering People*. New York: Commission on Human Security, 2003.

Cossa, Ralph, ed. *Asia Pacific Confidence and Security Building Measures*. Washington: Center for Strategic and International Studies, 1995.

Desker, Barry. *Islam and Society in Southeast Asia After September 11*. IDSS Working Paper No. 3. Singapore: Institute of Defence and Strategic Studies, 2002.

Deutsch, Karl. "Security Communities". In *International Politics and Foreign Policy*, edited by James Rosenau. New York: Free Press, 1961.

_____. *Political Community in the North Atlantic Area: International Organization in the Light of Historical Experience*. New York: Greenwood Press Publishers, 1969.

Dewi Fortuna Anwar. *Indonesia in ASEAN: Foreign Policy and Regional*. Singapore: Institute of Southeast Asian Studies, 1994.

Dickens, David and Guy Wilson-Roberts, eds. *Non-Intervention and State Sovereignty in the Asia Pacific*. Wellington: Centre for Strategic Studies, Victoria University, 1999.

Draguhn, Warner. "The Indochina Conflict and the Positions of the Countries Involved". *Contemporary Southeast Asia* 5, no. 1 (1983): 93–116.

Duffy, Charles and Werner J. Feld. "Wither Regional Integration Theory". In *Comparative Regional Systems*, edited by Gavin Boyd and Werner Feld. New York: Pergamon Press, 1980.

Dupont, Alan. "The Future of the ARF: An Australian Perspective". In *The Future of the ARF*, edited by Khoo How San, pp. 31–48. Singapore: Institute of Defence and Strategic Studies, 1999.

Emmers, Ralf. *Cooperative Security and the Balance of Power in ASEAN and the ARF*. London and New York: RoutledgeCurzon, 2003.

Evans, Paul. "Building Security: The Council for Security Cooperation in the Asia Pacific (CSCAP)". *Pacific Review* 7, no. 2 (1994).

Fifeld, Russell H. "ASEAN: The Perils of Viability". *Contemporary Southeast Asia* 2, no. 3 (1980): 199–212.

Finnemore, Martha and Kathryn Sikkink. "International Norm Dynamics and Political Change". *International Organisation* 52, no. 4 (Autumn 1998): 887–918.

Flores, Jamil Maidan. *ASEAN: How it Works*. Jakarta: ASEAN Secretariat, 2000.

Frost, Frank. "The Origins and Evolution of ASEAN". *World Review* 19, no. 3 (1980).

———. "Introduction: ASEAN Since 1967 — Origins, Evolution and Recent Developments". In *ASEAN into the 1990s*, edited by Alison Broinowski, pp. 1–31. London: Macmillan, 1990.

Fu Chen Lo and Kamal Salih, eds. *The Challenge of Asia-Pacific Cooperation*. Kuala Lumpur: Association of Development Research and Training Institutes of Asia and the Pacific, 1988.

Funston, John. "Thailand and the Indochina Conflict". *Dyason House Papers* 6, no. 1 (1979).

———. "Indochina Refugees: The Malaysian and Thai Response". *Asian Thought and Survey* 14 (September 1980).

———. "Thai and ASEAN Policy on Cambodia". Unpublished manuscript. University Brunei Darussalam, 1989.

———. "ASEAN: Out of its Depths". *Contemporary Southeast Asia* 20, no. 3 (1998): 22–37.

———. "Challenges Facing ASEAN in a More Complex Age". *Contemporary Southeast Asia* 21, no. 2 (1999): 205–19.

Garofano, John. "Flexibility or Irrelevance: Ways Forward for the ARF". *Contemporary Southeast Asia* 21, no. 1 (1999): 74–94.

Goldstein, Judith and Robert O. Keohane, eds. *Ideas and Foreign Policy: Beliefs, Institutions and Political Change*. Ithaca: Cornell University Press, 1993.

Gopal, Niraya. "Civil Society in India". In *Governance and Civil Society in a Global Age*, edited by Tadashi Yamamoto. Japan: Japan Center for International Exchange, 2001.

Gou Yan and Dong Nan. "The Kampuchean Issues: Its Origins and Major Aspects". *Beijing Review*, No. 37, September 1983, pp. 3–27.

Gupta, S.P. and Somsak Tambulertchai, eds. *The Asia-Pacific Economies*. Kuala Lumpur: Asian Pacific Development Centre, 1992.

Haacke, Jurgen. *ASEAN's Diplomatic and Security Culture: Origins, Development and Prospects*. London and New York: RoutledgeCurzon, 2003.

———. *Flexible Engagement: The Significance, Origins and Prospects of Spurned Policy Proposal*. Singapore: Institute of Southeast Asian Studies, 1999.

———. "The Aseanization of Regional Order in East Asia: A Failed Endeavor?". *Asian Perspectives* 22, no. 3 (1998).

Haas, Ernst B. *Beyond the Nation-State*. Stanford: Stanford University Press, 1964.
_____. *The Obsolescence of Regional Integration Theory*. Berkeley: University of California Press, 1975.
Haas, Michael. *The Asian Way to Peace: A Story of Regional Co-operation*. New York: Praeger Publishers, 1989.
Haas, Peter. "Knowledge, Power and International Policy Coordination". *International Organization* 46, no. 1 (Winter 1992): 1–35.
Hadiwinata, Bob. *The Politics of NGOs in Indonesia*. London and New York: Routledge Curzon, 2003.
Hall, D.G.E. *A History of Southeast Asia*. Hong Kong: Macmillan Educational Limited, 1982.
Hanggi, Heinner. *ASEAN and the ZOPFAN Concept*. Singapore: Institute of Southeast Asian Studies, 1991.
Henderson, Jeannie. *Reassessing ASEAN*. Adelphi Paper 323. London: Oxford University Press for International Institute for Strategic Studies, 1999.
Hernandez, Carolina. "The Role of ASEAN-ISIS". *ASEAN-ISIS Monitor*, Issue No. 6, April 1994, pp. 1–3.
_____. *Complex Interdependence and Track-Two Diplomacy in the Asia-Pacific in the Post-Cold War Era*. Quezon City: Center for Integrative and Development Studies and the University of the Philippines Press, 1994.
_____. "Governments and NGOs in the Search for Peace: The ASEAN-ISIS and the CSCAP Experience". Paper presented at the Conference on Alternative Security System in the Asia-Pacific, Bangkok, 27–30 March 1997. Accessed from < http://www.focusweb.org/focus/pd/sec/hernandez.html >.
_____. "Towards Re-Examining the Non-Intervention Principle in ASEAN Political Co-operation". *Indonesian Quarterly* 26, no. 3 (1998): 164–70.
_____. "A People's Assembly: A Novel Mechanism for Bridging the North-South Divide in ASEAN". Unpublished manuscript, 2002.
Hew, Denis and Hadi Soesastro. "Realizing the ASEAN Economic Community by 2020: ISEAS and ASEAN-ISIS Approaches". *ASEAN Economic Bulletin* 20, no. 3 (2003).
Higgott, Richard. "Ideas, Identity and Policy Coordination in the Asia-Pacific". *Pacific Review* 7, no. 4 (1994): 367–78.
Hoang Anh Tuan. "ASEAN Dispute Management: Implications for Vietnam and an Expanded Vietnam". *Contemporary Southeast Asia* 18, no. 1 (1996): 61–80.
Hopf, Ted. "The Promise of Constructivism in International Relations Theory". *International Security* 23, no. 1 (1998): 171–200.
Indorf, Hans H. *ASEAN: Problems and Prospects*. Occasional Paper no. 38. Singapore: Institute of Southeast Asian Studies, 1975.
Jacob, Philip E. and James V. Toscano, eds. *The Integration of Political Communities*. Philadelphia: Lippencott, 1964.
Jepperson, Ronald, Alexander Wendt, and Peter Katzenstein. "Norms, Identities and Culture in National Security". In *The Culture of National Security: Norms*

*and Identity in World Politics,* edited by Peter Katzenstein, pp. 33–75. New York: Columbia University Press, 1996.

Job, Brian. "Matters of Multilateralism: Implications for Regional Conflict Management". In *Regional Orders: Building Security in a New World,* edited by David A. Lake and Patrick M. Morgan. Pennsylvania: Pennsylvania State University Press, 1997.

Jorgensen-Dahl, Arnfinn. *Regional Organisation and Order in Southeast Asia.* New York: St. Martin's Press, 1982.

Jumbala, Prudhisan. "Civil Society and Democratisation in Thailand". In *Beyond the Crisis: Challenges and Opportunities,* edited by Mely C. Anthony and Jawhar Hassan. Kuala Lumpur: Institute of Strategic and International Studies, 2000.

Kahler, Miles. "Legalization as Strategy: The Asia-Pacific Case". *International Organization* 54, no. 3 (2000): 549–71.

Kamarulzaman Askandar. "ASEAN as a Process of Conflict Management: ASEAN and Regional Security in Southeast Asia: 1967–1994". Ph.D. thesis, Department of Peace Studies, University of Bradford, 1996.

———, Jacob Bercovitch, and Mikio Ioishi. "The ASEAN Way of Conflict Management: Old Patterns and New Trends". *Asian Journal of Political Science* 10, no. 2 (December 2002): 21–42.

Katzenstein, Peter et al. "International Organization and the Study of World Politics". *International Organization* 52, no. 4 (Autumn 1998): 645–85.

Keohane, Robert. "International Institutions: Can Interdependence Work?". *Foreign Policy* (Spring 1998).

——— and Joseph S. Nye. *Power and Interdependence.* 2nd ed. Glenville, IL: Scott Foresman, 1989.

Kerr, Pauline. "The Security Dialogue in the Asia-Pacific". *Pacific Review* 7, no. 4 (1994): 397–409.

Khong, Yuen Foong. "Making bricks without straw in the Asia Pacific?". *Pacific Review* 10, no. 2 (1997): 289–300.

———. "ASEAN and the Southeast Asian Security Complex". In *Regional Orders: Building Security in a New World,* edited by David Lake and Patrick Morgan, pp. 319–39. University Park: Pennsylvania State University Press, 1997.

Khoo How San, ed. *The Future of the ARF.* Singapore: Institute of Defence and Strategic Studies, 1999.

Klintworth, Gary. *Vietnam's Intervention in Cambodia International Law.* Canberra: Australian Government Publishing Service, 1989.

Koh, Tommy. *The Quest for World Order.* Singapore: Times Academic Press, 1998.

Kojima, Kiyoshi. *Japan and a New World Economic Order.* Tokyo: Charles E. Tuttle Company, 1977.

———. *Trade, Investment and Pacific Economic Cooperation: Selected Essays.* Tokyo: Bunshindo, 1996.

Koslowski, Ray and Friedrich V. Kratochwil. "Understanding Change in International Politics: The Soviet Empire's Demise and the International System". *International Organization* 48, no. 2 (Spring 1994): 215–47.

Kraft, Herman. "Assessing Human Rights in Southeast Asia: The Need for an Instrument". Paper delivered at the 11th ASEAN-ISIS Colloquium on Human Rights, 12–13 February 2004.

Lao Mong Hay. "Kampuchea: A Stalemate?". *Southeast Asian Affairs 1984*, pp. 153–61. Singapore: Institute of Southeast Asian Studies, 1984.

Lau Teik Soon. *Conflict Resolution in ASEAN: The Sabah Issue*. Occasional Paper No. 5. Singapore: Department of Political Science, National University of Singapore, 1974.

Leifer, Michael. *ASEAN and the Security of Southeast Asia*. London and New York: Routledge, 1989.

_____. *The ASEAN Regional Forum: Extending ASEAN's Model of Regional Security*. Adelphi Paper 302. London: International Institute for Strategic Studies, 1996.

_____. "The ASEAN Peace Process: A Category Mistake". *Pacific Review* 12, no. 1 (1999): 25–28.

_____. "Regionalism Compared: The Perils and Benefits of Expansion". In *The Asia Pacific in the New Millennium*, edited by Mely C. Anthony and Jawhar Hassan. Kuala Lumpur: Institute of Strategic and International Studies, 2001.

Lim Kian Teck. "Competing Regionalism: APEC and EAEG: 1989–1990". In *Non-Traditional Security Issues in Southeast Asia*, edited by Andrew Tan and J.D. Kenneth Boutin, pp. 54–86. Singapore: Select Publishing, 2001.

Lim, Robyn. (1998). "The ASEAN Regional Forum: Building on Sand". *Contemporary Southeast Asia* 20, no. 2 (1998): 115–36.

Lindberg, Leon and Stuart A. Scheingold, eds. *Regional Integration: Theory and Research*. Cambridge, MA: Harvard University Press, 1971.

Lizee, Pierre. "Civil Society and Regional Security: Tensions and Potentials in Post-Crisis Southeast Asia". *Contemporary Southeast Asia* 22, no. 3 (2000): 550–69.

MacFarlane, Neil S. and Thomas G. Weiss. "Regional Organizations and Regional Security". *Security Studies* 2 (Autumn 1992): 6–37.

Mackie, J.A.C. *Konfrontasi: The Indonesian-Malaysian Dispute 1963–1966*. Kuala Lumpur: Oxford University Press, 1974.

MacIntyre, Andrew. "Interpreting Indonesian Foreign Policy: The Case of Kampuchea, 1979–1986". *Asian Survey* XXVII, no. 5 (1987): 515–34.

Mak Joon Nam. *ASEAN Defense Reorientation 1975–1992: The Dynamics of Modernisation and Structural Change*. Canberra Papers on Strategy and Defence No. 103. Canberra: Strategic and Defense Studies Centre, Research School of Pacific Studies, 1993.

Martin, Ian. *Self-Determination in East Timor*. International Peace Academy Occasional Paper Series. Boulder, CO: Lynne Rienner Publishers, 2001.

Matthews, Jessica T. "Redefining Security". *Foreign Affairs* LXVIII, no. 3 (1989): 162–77.

Mearsheimer, John. "The False Promise of International Relations". *International Security* 19, no. 3 (Winter 1994/1995): 5–49.

Miller, Lynn. "The Subordinate System: Types of Regional Organizations". In *The International Politics of Regions: A Comparative Approach*, edited by Louis J. Cantori and Steven L. Spiegel. Englewood Cliffs, NJ: Prentice Hall, 1970.

Mochtar Kusumaatmadja. "Some Thoughts on ASEAN Security Co-operation: An Indonesian Perspective". *Contemporary Southeast Asia* 12, no. 3 (1990): 161–71.

Mohamed Jawhar Hassan. "Managing Security in Southeast Asia: Existing Mechanisms and Processes to Address Regional Conflicts". *Australian Journal of International Affairs* 47 (1993): 210–20.

———. "Towards A Pacific Concord". In *Bringing Peace to the Pacific*, edited by Mohamed Jawhar Hassan and Sheikh Ahmad Rafie, pp. 37–45. Kuala Lumpur: Institute of Strategic and International Studies, 1996.

Mohamed Ariff and Hal Hill. *Export-Oriented Industrialization: The Asean Experience*. Sydney: Allen and Unwin Australia, 1985.

Morrison, Charles, ed. *Asia Pacific Security Outlook*. Tokyo: Japan Center for International Exchange, 2000.

———. *Asia Pacific Security Outlook*. Tokyo: Japan Center for International Exchange, 1999.

———, ed. *Threats to Security in East-Asia and Pacific*. Honolulu: Pacific Forum Book, 1983.

Muhammad Ghazali Shafie. "Problems in Southeast Asia: Hopes and Fears". In *Malaysia: International Relations, Selected Speeches*, by Muhammad Ghazali Shafie, pp. 331–21. Kuala Lumpur: Creative Enterprise Sendirian Berhad, 1982.

Narine, Shaun. *Explaining ASEAN: Regionalism in Southeast Asia*. Boulder, CO: Lynne Rienner Publishers, 2002.

Nischalke, Tobias Ingo. "Insights from ASEAN's Foreign Policy Cooperation: The ASEAN Way, A Real Spirit or Phantom?". *Contemporary Southeast Asia* 22, no. 1 (2000): 89–112.

Noble, Lela Garner. "The National Interest and the National Image: Philippine Policy in Asia". *Asian Survey* 13, no. 6 (1973): pp. 567–69.

Notter, James and John McDonald. "Track Two Diplomacy: Non-governmental Strategies for Peace". *USIA Electronic Journal* 1, no. 19 (1996).

Nye, Joseph. *Peace in Parts: Integration and Conflict in Regional Organization*. Boston: Little, Brown and Company, 1971.

Osler, Fen and Brian Mandell. "Managing Regional Conflict: Security Cooperation and Third Party Mediators". *International Journal* XLV (Spring 1990): 191–201.

Pao-Min Chang. "Beijing Versus Hanoi: The Diplomacy Over Kampuchea". *Asian Survey* XXIV, no. 5 (May 1983).

Paribatra, Sukhumbhand. "Preparing ASEAN for the Twenty-First Century" < http://www.mfa.go.ht/Policy/fm03.htm > (accessed on 31 July 1998).

Paridah Abdul Samad and Mokhtar Mohammad. "ASEAN's Role and Development as a Security Community". *Indonesian Quarterly* 23, no. 1 (1995): 41–68.

Pekka Korhonen. *Japan and the Pacific Free Trade Area*. London and New York: Routledge, 1994.

Pham Binh. "Prospects for Solutions to the Problems Related to Peace and Stability in Southeast Asia". *Indonesian Quarterly* XII, no. 2 (1984): 205–33.

Pitsuwan, Surin. "ASEAN Vision 2020: Strengthening Human Security in the Aftermath of the Economic Crisis". Keynote Address delivered at the ASEAN 2020 Conference on Human Security in the 21st Century, organized by ISIS Thailand and ASEAN-ISIS, 21–22 July 2000.

Pollack, Jonathan. "Security Dynamics between China and Southeast Asia: Problems and Potential Approaches". In *China and Southeast Asia into the Twenty-First Century*, edited by Richard Grant. *Pacific Forum* XV, No. 4 (1993): 30–38.

Porter, Gareth. "ASEAN and Kampuchea: Shadow and Substance". *Indochina Issues* 14 (February 1981).

Rajaretnam, M. "Principles in Crisis: The Need for New Directions". In *ASEAN's Non-Interference Policy: Principles Under Pressure*, edited by Kao Kim Hourn, pp. 37–49. London: ASEAN Academic Press, 2000.

Rashid, Rehman. "Agenda Malaysia: The ASEAN People's Assembly". *Report of the First ASEAN People's Assembly*. Jakarta: Centre for Strategic and International Studies, 2001.

Raymond, Gregory A. "Problems and Prospects in the Study of International Norms". *International Studies Review*, No. 1 (1997): 205–45.

Risse-Kappen, Thomas. "Ideas do not float freely: Transnational coalitions, domestic structures, and the end of the Cold War". *International Organizations* 48, no. 2 (Spring 1994): 185–214.

Rittberger, Volker. "International Regimes and Peaceful Conflict Regulation". In *Peace Research: Achievements and Challenges*, edited by Peter Wallersteen, pp. 144–65 (1988).

Rivlin, Benjamin. "Regional Arrangements and the UN System for Collective Security and Conflict Resolution: A New Road Ahead?". *International Relations* XI, no. 2 (1992): 95–110.

Rosenau, James, ed. *International Politics and Foreign Policy*. New York: Free Press, 1961.

Ross, Robert S. "China and the Cambodian Peace Process: The Value of Coercive Diplomacy". *Asian Survey* XXXI, no. 12 (December 1991): 1170–86.

———. "China and the Stability in East Asia". In *East Asia in Transition: Toward a New Regional Order*, edited by Robert S. Ross, pp. 106–107. Singapore: Institute of Southeast Asian Studies, 1995.

Rothman, Stanley. "Multilateral Approaches to Security". Speech at the Henry L. Stimson Center, 21 July 1998. Accessed from < http://www.stimson.org/cbs/asls/roth/htm >.

Ruggie, John Gerard. "What Makes the World Hang Together? Neo-utilitarianism and the Social Constructivist Challenge". *International Organization* 52, no. 4 (Autumn 1998): 855–85.

Ruland, Jurgen. "ASEAN and the Asian Crisis: Theoretical Implications and Practical Consequences for Southeast Asian Regionalism". *Pacific Review* 13, no. 3 (2000): 421–51.

Sandhu, K.S. et al. *The ASEAN Reader*. Singapore: Institute of Southeast Asian Studies, 1992

Scalapino, Robert, Seizaburo Sato, Jusuf Wanandi, and Sung-joo Han, eds. *Regional Dynamics: Security, Political and Economic Issues in the Asia-Pacific Region*. Jakarta: Centre for Strategic and International Studies, 1990.

Schwarz, Hans-Peter. "Crisis and Conflict Management from the European Perspective". In *Security and Regional Order in ASEAN and the Role of the External Powers*. Manila: Konrad Adenauer Stiftung and Institute for Strategic and Development Studies, 1997.

Sebastian, Leonard and Anthony L. Smith. "The East Timor Crisis: A Test Case for Humanitarian Intervention". *Southeast Asian Affairs 2000*, pp. 64–83. Singapore: Institute of Southeast Asian Studies, 2000.

Segal, Gerald. *China Changes Shape: Regionalism and Foreign Policy*. Adelphi Paper 287. London: Institute of Strategic and International Studies, 1994.

Simon, Sheldon W. *The Future of Asia-Pacific Security Collaboration*. Lexington, MA: Lexington Books, 1988.

_____. "Realisms and Neoliberalism: International Relations Theory and Southeast Asian Security". *Pacific Review* 18, no. 1 (1995): 5–24.

_____. *The Economic Crisis and ASEAN States' Security*. Carlisle, PA: Strategic Studies Institute, 1998.

Soesastro, Hadi, ed. *ASEAN in a Changed Regional and International Political Economy*. Jakarta: Centre for Strategic and International Studies, 1995.

_____, ed. *One Southeast Asia in a New Regional and International Setting*. Jakarta: Centre for Strategic and International Studies, 1997.

_____. "ASEAN during the Crisis". *ASEAN Economic Bulletin* 15, no. 3 (1998).

_____. "ASEAN Economic Community: Ideas, Significance and Feasibility". Paper delivered at the 17th Asia Pacific Roundtable, Kuala Lumpur, 7–9 August 2003.

Sopiee, Mohamed Noordin. "Towards a Neutral Southeast Asia". In *Asia and the Western Pacific: Towards a New International Order*, edited by Hedley Bull, pp. 132–58. Sydney: Nelson, 1975.

Stein, Janice Gross. "Reassurance in International Conflict Management". *Political Science Quarterly* 106, no. 3 (1991): 431–51.

Suhrke, Astri. "Human Security and the Interest of States". *Security Dialogue* 30, no. 3 (September 1999): 265–75.

Sukma, Rizal. "Recent Developments in Sino-Indonesian Relations: An Indonesia View". *Contemporary Southeast Asia* 16, no. 1 (1994): 35–45.

―――. "Security Implications of the Economic Crisis in Southeast Asia". In *An Asia-Pacific Security Crisis? New Challenges to Regional Stability*, edited by Guy Wilson-Roberts, pp. 39–65. Wellington: Centre for Strategic Studies, 1999.

Tadem, Teresa S. and Eduardo C. Tadem. "Anti-Globalisation Movements in Southeast Asia". *Mondialisation des Resistance,* edited by Samir Amin and Francois Houtart. Paris: L'Harmattan, 2002.

Tai Ming Cheng. *Growth of Chinese Naval Power*. Pacific Strategic Papers. Singapore: Institute of Southeast Asian Studies, 1990.

Tatik S. Hafidz. *The War on Terror and the Future of Indonesian Democracy*. IDSS Working Paper No. 46. Singapore: Institute of Defence and Strategic Studies, 2002.

Tay, Simon and Obood Talib. "The ASEAN Regional Forum: Preparing for Preventive Diplomacy". *Contemporary Southeast Asia* 19, no. 3 (1997): 252–68.

Tay, Simon, Jesus Estanislao, and Hadi Soesastro, eds. *Reinventing ASEAN*. Singapore: Institute of Southeast Asian Studies, 2003.

Taylor, Paul. "Regionalism: The Thought and the Deed". In *Frameworks for International Cooperation*, edited by A.J.R. Groom and Paul Taylor, pp. 151–71. New York: St. Martin's Press, 1990.

*The Asian Crisis and Human Security.* Tokyo: Japan Centre for International Exchange, 1999.

Thai Ministry of Foreign Affairs. "Thailand's Non-Paper on Flexible Engagement". Accessed from < http://222.thaiembdc.org.pressctr/pr/pr743.htm > in 1998.

Theeravit, Khein. "Thai-Kampuchean Relations: Problems and Prospects". *Asian Survey* XXII, no. 6 (1982): 561–76.

Thiparat, Prannee, ed. *The Quest for Human Security.* Bangkok: Institute of Strategic and International Studies, 2001.

Tow, William T. *Subregional Security Cooperation in the Third World.* Boulder, CO: Lynne Rienner Publishers, 1990.

Ullman, Richard. "Redefining Security". *International Security* 8. no. 1 (1983): 129–53.

Van der Kroef, Justus. "Hanoi and ASEAN: Is Co-Existence Possible?". *Contemporary Southeast Asia* 1, no. 2 (1979): 164–78.

―――. "The Kampuchean Problem: Diplomatic Deadlock and Initiative". *Contemporary Southeast Asia* 5, no. 3 (1983): 263–72.

Van der Kroef, Justus. "Cambodia: The Vagaries of 'Cocktail' Diplomacy". *Contemporary Southeast Asia* 9, no. 4 (1987): 300–20.

Van Tao. "Vietnam-Indonesia Relations in Historical Perspectives", *Indonesian Quarterly* XII, no. 2 (1984): 245–57.

Vitit Muntarbhorn. *The Challenge of Law: Legal Cooperation among ASEAN Countries*. Bangkok: Institute of Security and International Studies, 1986.

Wallersteen, Peter, ed. *Peace Research: Achievements and Challenges,* pp. 119–43. Boulder and London: Westview Press, 1988.

Walt, Stephen. *The Origin of Alliances*. Ithaca and London: Cornell University Press, 1987.

Wanandi, Jusuf. *Security Dimensions of the Asia-Pacific in the 1980s*. Jakarta: Centre for Strategic and International Studies, 1979.

———. "An Introduction to China's Role in Regional Problems". In *ASEAN and China: An Evolving Relationship*, edited by Joyce K. Kallgren, Noordin Sopiee, and Soedjati Djiwandono, pp. 177–88. Berkeley, CA: University of California Press), 1988.

———. "Asia-Pacific Forums: Rationale and Options from the ASEAN Perspective". In *Security Cooperation in the Asia-Pacific Region,* edited by Desmond Ball, Richard Grant, and Jusuf Wanandi. *Pacific Forum* XV, No. 5 (1993).

———. *ASEAN Political and Security Cooperation*. Jakarta: Centre for Strategic and International Studies, 1993.

———. "The Strategic Implications of the Economic Crisis in East Asia". *Indonesian Quarterly* 26, no. 1 (1998): 2–6.

Weatherbee, Donald. "The View from ASEAN's Southern Flank". *Strategic Review,* Spring 1983.

———. *Southeast Asia Divided: The ASEAN-Indochina Crisis*. Boulder, CO: Westview Press, 1985. pp. 131–45.

Wendt, Alexander. "Constructing International Politics". *International Security* 20, no. 1 (Summer 1995): 71–81.

———. "Anarchy is What States Make of It: The Social Construction of Power Politics". *International Organization* 46, no. 2 (Spring 1992): 391–425.

———. (1994). "Collective Identity Formation and the International State". *American Political Science Review* 88, no. 2 (June 1994): 384–96.

Wesley, Michael. "The Asian Crisis and the Adequacy of Regional Institutions". *Contemporary Southeast Asia* 21, no. 1 (1999): 54–73.

Wilcox, Francis W. "Regionalism and the United Nations". *International Organization* 19 (Summer 1965): 789–811.

Wilken, Peter. "New Myths for the South: Globalisation and the Conflict between Private Power and Freedom". In *Globalisation and the South,* edited by Peter Wilken and Caroline Thomas, pp. 18–35. Great Britain: Macmillan Press, 1995.

Yamamoto, Tadashi. "The Future of Civil Society in Asia". In *Beyond the Crisis:*

Challenges and Opportunities, edited by Mely C. Anthony and Jawhar Hassan. Kuala Lumpur: Institute of Strategic and International Studies, 2000.
_____, ed. Governance and Civil Society in the Global Age. Japan: Japan Center for International Exchange, 2001.

## ASEAN DOCUMENTS (IN CHRONOLOGICAL ORDER)

"ASEAN Declaration" (Bangkok Declaration) August 8, 1967.
"Kuala Lumpur Document on the Zone of Peace, Freedom and Neutrality", 27 November 1971.
"Treaty of Amity and Cooperation in Southeast Asia", Indonesia, 24 February 1976.
"Joint Statement, Special Meeting of ASEAN Foreign Ministers on the Current Political Development in the Southeast Asian Region", Bangkok, 12 January 1979.
ASEAN Documents. Bangkok: Ministry of Foreign Affairs, 1983.
"Joint Statement by the ASEAN Foreign Ministers on the Kampuchean Problem", Kuala Lumpur, 8 July 1985.
"Joint Statement on the Situation in the Philippines", Jakarta, 23 February 1986, accessed from <http://www.aseansec.org/2477.htm>.
"ASEAN Consensus Statement of the Chairman of the Jakarta Informal Meeting", in Contemporary Southeast Asia 11, no. 1 (June 1989).
"ASEAN Information Paper on the International Conference in Paris", 1989.
"Singapore Declaration", issued at the Fourth ASEAN Summit, 28 January 1992.
"Joint Communique of the Twenty-Sixth ASEAN Ministerial Meeting", Singapore, 23–24 July 1993.
"ASEAN Vision 2020", Kuala Lumpur, 15 December 1997.
"Chairman's Statement of the Fifth Meeting of the ASEAN Regional Forum", Manila, 27 July 1998.
ASEAN Into The Next Millennium: ASEAN Vision 2020, The Hanoi Plan of Action, Jakarta: ASEAN Secretariat, 1999.
"The ASEAN Troika: Concept Paper", Thailand, July 2000.
"Rules and Procedures of the High Council of the Treaty of Amity and Cooperation in Southeast Asia", Hanoi, 23–27 July 2001.
"ASEAN Declaration on Joint Action to Counter Terrorism", Bandar Seri Begawan, 5 November 2001.
"Joint Communique of the Special ASEAN Ministerial Meeting on Terrorism", Kuala Lumpur, Malaysia, 20–21 May 2002.
"Joint Statement of the Special ASEAN + 3 Health Ministers Meeting on Severe Acute Respiratory Syndrome (SARS)", Siem Reap, Cambodia, 10–11 June 2003.

"Declaration of ASEAN Concord II" (Bali Concord II), 7 October 2003.
"Recommendations of the High-Level Task Force on ASEAN Economic Integration", 7 October 2003.


# ARF DOCUMENTS (IN CHRONOLOGICAL ORDER)

"Chairman's Statement of the First Meeting of the ASEAN Regional Forum (ARF)", 25 July 1994, Bangkok.
"The ASEAN Regional Forum: A Concept Paper", Bandar Seri Begawan, 1 August 1995.
"Chairman's Statement of the Second ASEAN Regional Forum (ARF)", Bandar Seri Begawan, 1 August 1995.
"Chairman's Statement of the Fourth Meeting of the ASEAN Regional Forum", Subang Jaya, 27 July 1997.
"Co-Chairs' Consolidated List of Possible New ARF CBMs", annexed to the "Chairman's Statement of the Fifth ASEAN Regional Forum", 27 July 1998.
"Chairman's Statement of the Seventh Meeting of the ASEAN Regional Forum", Bangkok, 27 July 2000.
"Concept and Principles of Preventive Diplomacy", Bangkok, 27 July 2000.


# ASEAN-ISIS DOCUMENTS (IN CHRONOLOGICAL ORDER)

*ASEAN ISIS Monitor*. Kuala Lumpur: Institute of Strategic and International Studies, 1991.
*A Time for Initiative: Proposals for the Consideration of the Fourth ASEAN Summit*. Kuala Lumpur: Institute of Strategic and International Studies, 4 June 1991.
*ASEAN ISIS at the Turn of the Century: A Mission Statement*, Kuala Lumpur: Institute of Strategic and International Studies, 1992.
*ASEAN-ISIS Memorandum No. 5: Confidence Building Measures in Southeast Asia*, December 1993.
*ASEAN-ISIS Memorandum No. 6: The South China Sea Dispute — Renewal of a Commitment for Peace*, May 1995.
*ASEAN-ISIS Summary of Report of the Sixth Southeast Asian Forum*. Kuala Lumpur: Institute of Strategic and International Studies, July 1998.
*Report of the First ASEAN People's Assembly (APA)*. Jakarta: Centre for Strategic and International Studies, 2001.
*Second APA Report: Challenges Facing the ASEAN People*. Jakarta: Centre for Strategic and International Studies, 2003.

## CSCAP DOCUMENTS (IN CHRONOLOGICAL ORDER)

"Seoul Statement on Security Cooperation in the Asia Pacific", 3 November 1992.

"Establishment of CSCAP: Kuala Lumpur Statement" (Kuala Lumpur Statement), 8 June 1993.

"The Security of the Asia Pacific Forum, CSCAP Pro-Tem Committee", CSCAP Memorandum No. 1, Kuala Lumpur, April 1994.

"CSCAP Memorandum No. 2: Asia Pacific Confidence Security Building Measures", 1995.

"CSCAP Memorandum No. 3: The Concepts of Comprehensive and Cooperative Security", 1995.

"CSCAP Memorandum No. 4: Guidelines for Regional Maritime Cooperation", December 1997.

"The Charter of the Council for Security Cooperation in the Asia-Pacific (CSCAP)", Revised at the Tenth Steering Committee Meeting, Manila, December 1998.

"CSCAP Memorandum No. 5: Cooperation for Law and Order at Sea", February 2001.

"CSCAP Memorandum No. 6: The Practice of the Law of the Sea in the Asia Pacific", December 2002.

"CSCAP Memorandum No. 7: The Relationship Between Terrorism and Transnational Crime", July 2003.

"First Report of the Maritime Security Cooperation Working Group", *CSCAP Newsletter*, No. 3, August 1995.

"First Report of the North Pacific Working Group", *CSCAP Newsletter* No. 3, August 1995.

"Working Group Report on Comprehensive and Cooperative Security", *CSCAP Newsletter*, No. 4, February 1996.

"CSCAP Report of the Fifth Meeting of the Working Group on Comprehensive and Cooperative Security", Wellington, New Zealand , 14–15 July 1998.

*AUS-CSCAP Newsletter*, No. 7, October 1998, pp. 12–13.

*CSCAP Philippines Newsletter*, No. 1, July-December 1998.

"CSCAP Report of the Sixth Meeting of the Working Group on Comprehensive and Cooperative Security", Beijing, 24–25 May 1999.

"Preventive Diplomacy: Definition and Principles", Prepared by the Council for Security Cooperation in the Asia Pacific (CSCAP) International Working Group on Confidence and Security Building Measures, Bangkok, 1 March 1999.

"Chairmen's Summary of the CSCAP Workshop on Preventive Diplomacy", Bangkok, 28 February–2 March 1999.

"Working Group Report of the CSCAP Working Group on Confidence and Security Building Measures", presented at the Eleventh CSCAP Steering Committee Meeting, Kuala Lumpur, 30 May 1999.

## NEWS AGENCIES AND NEWSPAPERS

Agency France Press
*Asian Wall Street Journal*
*Bangkok Post*
*Borneo Bulletin Online*
*Jakarta Post*
*The Nation*
*The New Straits Times*
*The Star*
*Straits Times*
*Philippine Star*
*Philippine Daily Inquirer*

# : INDEX

# ABOUT THE AUTHOR

**Mely Caballero-Anthony, Ph.D.**, is Assistant Professor at the Institute of Defence and Strategic Studies (IDSS), Singapore. At IDSS, she teaches a course on Government and Politics in Southeast Asia and is currently project co-ordinator of the IDSS-FORD Project on Non-Traditional Security in Asia. Her research interests include regionalism and regional security in the Asia-Pacific, multilateral security co-operation, politics and international relations in ASEAN, conflict prevention and management, as well as human security. She has been very involved in track two work through her close association with the Council for Security Cooperation in the Asia Pacific (CSCAP) and the ASEAN Institutes of Strategic and International Studies (ASEAN-ISIS) network.

She has published articles on ASEAN, the ARF, Malaysian and Philippines security issues which appeared in journals such as *Asian Survey, Asian Perspective, Contemporary Southeast Asia, Southeast Asian Affairs*, and *Indonesian Quarterly*, and contributed several book chapters on regional security trends and human security. She has also co-edited several books, such as The Asia Pacific in the New Millennium: Political and Security Challenges (Kuala Lumpur: Institute of Strategic and International Studies, 2001) and is currently working on an edited volume on The UN Peace Operation and its Implications on Asia Pacific Security.

Aside from her academic interest, she enjoys music of different genres and is herself an accomplished musician.